Modernization and Marine Fisheries Policy

Modernization and Marine Fisheries Policy

Edited by

John R. Maiolo
Michael K. Orbach

ANN ARBOR SCIENCE
THE BUTTERWORTH GROUP

Library of Congress Catalog Card Number 81-69470
ISBN 0-250-40515-6

Butterworths, Ltd., Borough Green, Sevenoaks
Kent TN15 8PH, England

PREFACE

The foundations of fisheries management and policy have been laid traditionally by biologists, politicians and administrators whose common purpose was, first, the conservation of the biological species, and, second, the distribution of costs and benefits of the fisheries based on the climate of their time. Though the goals of these policymakers were social and economic as well as biological, their policies and management processes were most often formally couched solely in the terms of conservation.

Similarly, the study of fisheries management and policy has been traditionally either the study of conservation in the biological sense or the study of politics. In this collection of works by sociologists and anthropologists, the study of fisheries management and policy takes on a new dimension: that of a complex process of human behavior and interaction characterized as much by the social and cultural values of the participants as by the compelling drive for conservation of marine biological species or the achievement of political purpose.

In the last 100 years most of the world's fisheries have undergone a transition from sail power and a subsistence orientation to technologically sophisticated industries in the midst of social, economic and ecological complexity beyond the imagination of the fisherman or the fishery manager of the last century. In the process, our understanding of the human systems inherent in both the fisheries and the fishery management agencies has often lagged behind our understanding of the biology or the business economics of fishing.

In two sections, one dealing with the assumptions and behaviors of managers and policymakers and the other with the dynamics of fishing communities themselves, *Modernization and Marine Fisheries Policy* uses the lens of modernization on examples from North and South America, Scandinavia, Africa and Oceania. Through this lens, we examine the powerful and evolving interaction between the marine fisheries policy process and the fishermen—their industries, families and communities.

John R. Maiolo
Michael K. Orbach

ACKNOWLEDGMENTS

All but one of the chapters in this volume were written for a symposium held at East Carolina University. The title of the original symposium was *Modernization of Fishing Industries and Communities.* It was jointly sponsored by the Department of Sociology and Anthropology and the Institute for Coastal and Marine Resources at East Carolina University. Encouragement and support were received from the University of North Carolina Sea Grant College Program and the Society for Applied Anthropology. Funding was obtained from Dr. John Howell of the East Carolina University Office of the Vice Chancellor for Academic Affairs, and Dr. William Queen of the Institute for Coastal and Marine Resources. Supplementary funds were obtained from the East Carolina University Alumni Association and Dr. C. Q. Brown of the Office of the Director of Institutional Development.

Peter Fricke and Milton Altschuler served with John Maiolo as Co-Coordinators of the symposium, and provided technical assistance in selecting the authors and topics. Peter Fricke also participated in the editing of two of the papers.

Many others participated in a variety of ways to make the symposium successful. James Sabella, Michael Orbach and Edward Knipe provided critiques, and Orbach later joined the effort as co-editor. Reba Lewis, Betty Lou Lovegrove, Ruth Maiolo, Helen Rountree, Gail Spencer and Cindy Stack were involved in arrangements, typing, xeroxing and all of the other crucial activities that determine the outcome of such an event. A special thanks is due Jo Ann Sutton and Shirley Smith for their patience in typing the manuscript.

John R. Maiolo is Professor and Chairman of the Department of Anthropology and Sociology at East Carolina University, Greenville, North Carolina. He received his PhD from the Pennsylvania State University and has taught at Notre Dame and Indiana Universities. Dr. Maiolo has written 55 papers and several monographs, most of which deal with public policy issues. His current research concerns the social and economic organization of fisheries, fishing communities and coastal zone management at the state, federal and international levels.

Michael K. Orbach is Associate Research Professor and Associate Director of the Center for Coastal Marine Studies at the University of California at Santa Cruz. He received his BA in economics from the University of California at Irvine, and his MA and PhD in anthropology from the University of California at San Diego. Dr. Orbach taught at the University of California and spent three years as Social Anthropologist and Social Science Advisor to the National Oceanic and Atmospheric Administration in Washington, DC. He specializes in applied social research with marine resource issues and has published widely on this subject, including *Hunters, Seamen and Entrepreneurs*, an ethnography of the United States high seas tuna fleet.

To

Joseph and Filomena Maiolo,
who inspired and taught perseverance

and

Richard Schaefer, who kept the U.S. Fishery Management
structure together through the implementation of the
Fishery Conservation and Management Act of 1976

CONTENTS

Section 1
Government Policy and Management Assumptions

Section 2
Social Dynamics and Technoeconomic Adaptations

SECTION 1
GOVERNMENT POLICY AND
MANAGEMENT ASSUMPTIONS

INTRODUCTION

The purpose of this collection of papers is to contribute to our body of knowledge about the process of modernization in fishing communities, and the role of government policy in that process. In editing to meet this objective we have engaged in two general tasks.

The first was to reexamine the term *modernization* itself in the context of fisheries management. This term encompasses more than the adoption of new physical and social technologies, although these technologies are, to be sure, crucial. We use the term in a broader sense to include the process of coming to grips with new political and organizational structures and behaviors. Further, modernization means coming to grips with the effects of decisions made at a distance, out of which emerge guidelines or management schemes which we may call *social policies*. Essential to our definition and use of the term modernization is the notion of an acculturative process to which people react and which itself shapes the nature of the development and implementation of extra-local social policy.

We translated this first task into a specific examination of the role of governments in the modernization process, and the assumptions on which government policies, as management tools, are based. Section 1 is the core of this examination, which involves linking specific day-to-day activity in coastal communities with the emergence of issues, assumptions, governmental management schemes and policies. These linkages reflect an *upward* aggregation of authority and responsibility. With respect to fishery policy, this upward aggregation is characterized by management decisions farther and farther removed from the resources and people who make a living from fisheries. This type of linkage is the focus of Section 1.

Such an examination must also focus on the dynamics of technical, social and economic adaptations to governmental change initiatives, particularly at the community level where the impacts of policies are most often felt. Thus a second focus is on the flow of activities as decisions and policies are implemented. We based our discussions in this area on the notion that while the aggregation of issues and information which consitutes the *formation* of policies has an *upward* thrust, the thrust of their *implementation* of those policies is *downward,* through regional, state, and local networks. One result of this process is the emergence of structural strains in the networks of implementation. Assumptions upon which the policies are based are not always isomorphic with the realities of the situations with which they were meant to deal—and problems associated with implementing policies on a day-to-day basis are often different from those associated with their formation. The community organizational properties and processes which function to filter change initiatives and policies are of particular importance, and the chapters in Section 2 address these issues.

The title of the book, *Modernization and Marine Fisheries Policy,* is indicative of a second task; the application of sociological and anthropological perspectives to the study of marine resource management. Our substantive focus is on modernization among fishing peoples and communities. In accordance with our definition of modernization, we have chosen to examine the process of fishermen and their communities coming to grips with an ever increasing myriad of formalized regional, national and international fisheries management schemes. With few exceptions, fisheries and fishermen the world over are presently involved in a web of interrelationships which weaves its way upward and outward across regions and nation states. The systemic problems that such a web presents are at least as important as specific innovations, local economic structure, or culture change which are the usual issues we find discussed in the modernization literatures of sociology and anthropology.

The focus and format we have chosen for this volume are products of a concern for the gap between the increasing mass of initiatives for change and our working knowledge of the sources and consequences of those initiatives, specifically with respect to selected issues of marine policy. There have been similar approaches in other areas of policy concern such as transportation and welfare reform which have been helpful, but they have not gone far enough in explicating the critical juncture between national policy and local community. The rapidly changing nature of contemporary social and economic systems, in our view, dictates the use of a framework where social organization as the purveyor of social policies is the central, key unit of analysis. Sociology and anthropology, combined, offer a unique perspective on social policy and social organization, and the comparative methodology which is so crucial to build and document that perspective. Indeed, social analysis is mandated in such concepts as *optimum yield* and *limited entry* which are embodied in the U.S. Fishery Conservation and Management Act of 1976, and other legal mandates. The attractiveness of a combined sociological/anthropological approach is that it forms a rhuberic under which both the formal and substantive components of social behavior may be considered. It is the inclusiveness of the approach we have chosen which makes it advantageous. Some traditional natural resource managers have considered social analysis complicated, unwieldy, and difficult; but such is the nature of the problem. Many of our national goals for resource conservation are unmet because it is difficult for scientists and policymakers to deal directly with the complexity of social organization. We offer the combined tools of sociology and anthropology as an aid to their task.

We did not attempt even geographical coverage either at the conference or in this volume. There are many more countries whose coastal areas are experiencing rapid modernization and the effects of new social policies than are discussed here. Rather, we have concentrated on displaying the range and nature of the problems and issues involved in such situations, and some of the ways social analysis can aid in the explication of these situations.

Marine Fisheries Policy

The recent history of fisheries management has been a process of the upward aggregation of responsibility and authority. This tendency toward the involvement of people and entities increasingly farther removed from the fishery resources, fishing activity and fishing communities themselves is clearly recognizable, pervasive in fishery systems throughout the world and likely to become a permanent aspect of fishery management regimes. This process, the impetus behind it, and the implications for government policy and modernization fit together in the following way. (See Eisenstadt [1] for a statement which relates to this process.)

A primary justification for the extension of national jurisdiction over fishery resources by coastal nations, in addition to the desire for sound resource conservation, was the desire to reserve the right to the benefits deriving from the use of those resources. More simply put, there was an overwhelming desire to "kick the foreigners out." The sight of huge fishing vessels from foreign nations in fleet formations scouring the waters and bottom within sight of one's shores resulted in overwhelming, and often biologically and economically justifiable, personal and national outrage. Under extended jurisdiction, even if the foreigners would not be excised, they would be licensed and taxed so that the economic benefits of their activity would provide sustenance for the "host" nation. These were not matters which could be addressed and redressed at a town meeting. Rather, they were matters which required sensitive negotiations among government leaders at the highest levels from both friendly and unfriendly nations, and the commitment of significant amounts of national-level resources. Just as a local community could not exercise the muscle to prohibit a foreign trawler from fishing within 200 miles of the coast, neither could that community muster the resources to ensure that proper surveillance and enforcement were carried out. These situations form the basis for the push toward the involvement of a broader and more removed range of individuals and entities in fisheries management.

A second issue in the extension of jurisdiction is that of legal ownership of fishery and other marine resources. There is on the one hand a desire to capture formal control over valuable resources, but on the other a reticence to abandon traditional "freedom of the seas." The development of national legislation concerning fishery resources does not, in most instances, imply actual ownership of those resources. The issue of ownership is one which is still hotly debated not only in the United Nations Law of the Sea Conference (UNCLOS) meetings, but also among different political jurisdictions within a single nation. In the United States, for example, the geographical divisions are clear among the Fishery Conservation Zone (FCZ), the territorial sea (from 0 to 3 miles offshore) and within the territorial sea itself between the waters of different states. The division of responsibility and authority over fishery resources within and across these boundaries, however, is much less clear, even in the legislation written to address such issues. Whether from a realization that an attempt to address ownership, either between nations or within one nation, would result in severe impediments to rational management in the short run, or from an inability on the part of legal experts to agree on the principles, precedents and judgments that might flow from those attempts, the issue of ownership is conspicuously absent from most fishery management legislation with one significant exception. In almost all cases such legislation contains the explicit assumption that the resource shall be managed so as to provide the "maximum social benefit" to the *nation*. This aspect of justification for federal action—that the right to the benefits deriving from the resources are held in common by all citizens—is a problematic one. While it is necessary as a principle on which to base federal action, it often carries the connotation of the usurpation of local power, authority or privilege. As strict *legal* principles, even these rights of the general populace are somewhat soft-pedaled in the legislation, even though the *concept* of common ownership is a basis for federal involvement.

A third impetus behind the upward aggregation lies in the self-generating and self-perpetuating properties of bureaucratic systems, an observation made by organizational theorists and substantiated by empirical research (see for example, Selznick [2], Hall [3], Maiolo [4], Sills [5], Etzioni [6] and Champion [7]). From analysis of bureaucratic structures, their enacted rules for conduct, and activities of their participants, one may derive the following principle: once a precedent in law, policy (extrapolated from law) or administrative form is established, structural forces are set in motion that tend to perpetuate activity pursuant to the precedent. This principle seems to be universally applicable to all forms of formal organizations, e.g., government agencies (local, national and international), corporations and even social movements [8]. In the case of fishery management, for example, if a national body is called on to intercede in a fishery dispute, a precedent is set for those involved in which their involvement becomes prescribed behavior. Part of this is social systems inertia, and part is social systems momentum. Once a pattern of reasoning and behavior is established for authority or intervention in a large system with many players, it takes a tremendous amount of time and effort—in addition to the innovative effort required to develop and disseminate a *new* line of reasoning—to either strike or redirect that reasoning or activity. So it is with fishery management under extended jurisdiction. "Kicking the foreigners out" required the development of a pattern of reasoning, significant commitments of time and resources, and large amounts of personal and collective involvement on the local, national and international levels. A bureaucratic pattern of upward aggregation was established.

Although there are many other factors behind this aggregation process, there are only two more to which we shall refer here. One of these is very pragmatic, while the other is somewhat altruistic. With increases in technology, the development of new and expanded markets for fishery resources, and increases in labor mobility, the patterns of fishing activity in a given fishery and among fisheries have become more fluid, and the geographical movements of individual fishing units themselves much more wide-ranging. This fluidity and mobility forces the management process beyond local political boundaries, and therefore beyond the pale of local authority or control, and into the larger management arena [1]. For example, when a multipurpose fishing boat from San Diego, California, fishes part of the year for crab in Alaskan waters for sale in Japanese markets, no single local, or even national, entity has complete authority or responsibility for management or regulation. This kind of fishing system requires an umbrella under which proper coordination of the management systems can take place, an umbrella which transcends individual social and economic systems.

The final factor is the issue of efficiency and full utilization of fishery resources. Most of the national fishery legislation—for example, the Fisheries Conservation and Management Act (FCMA) in the United States—contains prescriptions that the resource be used in an efficient manner, and in a manner which assures, to the extent possible, that the protein and other benefits that the resource could yield be used fully. As a practical matter, however, efficiency and full utilization may be either impossible to interpret and implement or of less importance than was the common impression a decade ago. Efficiency is a muddled concept, especially when the notions of satisfaction or cultural values are introduced. The nutritional benefits to be derived from the sea are not what they were presumed to be in earlier, more expansive periods of man's investigations into the potential of the oceans. However, these two concepts still appear in virtually all national and international fishery legislation, and remain important cognitive forces in the development of national management regimes.

But what does this process of upward aggregation have to do with modernization? In making this connection, we will modify somewhat the traditional notion of modernization. The term "modernization" almost invariably assumes an underlying value structure against which materials, objects, societies, cultures and behaviors are measured in the process of judging them "modern," or whatever one assumes to be the opposite of "modern." We will use the term modernization a bit differently, in the sense of adapting to new or different requirements or constraints, and utilizing available knowledge and resources to meet those requirements or constraints. This sense of modernization is similar to the notion of acculturation, the process of adapting values, beliefs and behaviors to new and different situations. It avoids any judgment of goodness between given objects, ideas or behaviors and the uses to which they must be put, except perhaps that of the goodness of fit between these items and the total context within which they are found.

For fishing peoples, communities and industries, then, modernization is not only the process of adopting new physical materials, objects and organizational technologies in their occupation and in their lifestyles, but also the process of learning to work within the new political and administrative constraints and requirements imposed by the upward aggregation of management regimes [9]. No longer can a fisherman go to his buyer, a fishing cousin or even a local magistrate to air a grievance, obtain information or settle a dispute. Now a piece of gear lost to a Soviet trawler goes before an international claims board; information concerning a closure of salmon fishing of Coos Bay, Oregon, must be obtained from Washington, D.C.; a Spanish trawler wishing to take squid far out of sight of the Atlantic coast of the United States will send representatives to a meeting of the Mid-Atlantic Fishery Management Council in Dover, Delaware. Most importantly, any fisherman who wishes to be a part of the process through which decisions affecting his livelihood will be made must learn, if not adopt, the styles, procedures and principles that are used by vast numbers of other people in immensely varying locations and contexts.

Fishermen, and their communities and industries, must "modernize" in that they must acculturate themselves to the ideas and behaviors of those at all levels to which the authority and responsibility for the management of fisheries have been aggregated. This process of adaptations is not as unidirectional as it may appear; that is, it involves not only the fishermen adapting to the manager, but also the manager to the fisherman. As was evidenced by the creation of regional fishery management councils under the FCMA, to whom the responsibility for the development of management plans was assigned, managers may rely to a significant extent on the opinions, efforts and support of those at all levels in the systems, including, of course, the fishermen themselves. In becoming an effective participant in the management system, one must adapt to the new and different requirements of the larger political arena, and that arena itself must undergo a metamorphosis. Overlaid onto the economic, technological and social change that must occur to maintain the extraction of fishery resources as a self-sustaining enterprise, acquisition of skills necessary in dealing with the new, aggregated management structure constitutes modernization in the broadest sense. This is the sense of modernization with which we shall view the chapters in this book.

The final connection which must be made is between the aggregation of authority and responsibility, modernization and government policy. This connection is in many ways the most simple of all. The upward aggregation process in almost all cases places authority and responsibility in the hands of governmental or quasigovernmental bodies. The acculturative, or adaptive component of modernization involves adaptation to constraints imposed by these bodies. These bodies must use principles of management, scientific information, and public and user group input to make management decisions concerning conservation, allocation and utilization that are intended to be consistent, rational and tailored to the requirements of particular situations. These principles, which solidify information and other inputs into management regimes, and which are subject to but significant expansions on the basic requirements of legislative mandates, constitute fisheries management policy.

This is the context within which we hope that the chapters in this section will be read. Each chapter deals with a set of assumptions used by managers, which in some form constitute management policy, and which reflect the process of upward aggregation we have described above.

THE CHAPTERS

Andersen

It is a common observation that fishery policy and fishery management decisions have historically been made by biologists, with biological data being the only formal, documented information available on which to base decisions. Although factors other than biology have, by the nature of political and administrative processes, always had a place in fishery management, in the first paper in Section 1 Andersen cogently argues for a more formal and structured use of sociological and anthropological data in the fisheries management equation, and consequently in the formation of fisheries policy. He argues that the concept "fisheries" itself must be expanded to incorporate all of the "activities through which people link themselves with aquatic environments and renewable resources." His chapter provides a great deal of analysis of access to fisheries resources, and compliance with crescive and enacted norms, to support his contention that we must rigorously think beyond the biological issues when fisheries management questions are examined.

As an example, controlled access is one of the principles upon which much fishery policy is based. But, as Andersen points out, controlling access through extended jurisdiction or any other means is not a new solution to competition for space and resources. Indeed, it may be as old as fishing itself. What is new is the formalized, governmental process for controlling access based on the declaration of marine resources as "public goods." He notes that "where the resource is limited..., a need develops to control access," and proceeds to show how, in Newfoundland, fishermen have historically developed community-based management through controlled access to fisheries by both public and private strategies.

It is the prevailing view among government managers that protection of fisheries resources by traditional methods of controlling access have not worked. Because these traditional methods have in many instances been unable to control significant increases in harvest levels or competition for fishery resources, fishery managers have gravitated toward broader and more formal controls. Many resources have been overharvested, and one of the rationales for extended jurisdiction is to allow stock recovery and to manage fishing effort to prevent future stock depletion. In addition, many management measures under extended jurisdiction are intended to address matters other than the state of the fish stock or the physical ecosystem, such as the allocation of fishing rights or harvests. The newly developed management schemes supersede, in many cases, traditional access controls, both crescive and enacted.

There is good reason to believe, however, that within these new schemes the absence of guidelines that would be sensitive to such things as community and regional variations, inshore vs offshore fishermen needs and vulnerabilities, and large vs small (in terms of levels of capital) operations portends a set of problems—created by the new management policy itself—which are potentially as harmful as they may be beneficial. In reiterating his claim for better management practices based upon sociological/anthropological data, Andersen argues that controlling access "before and after extended jurisdiction is inseparable" from the socioeconomic and political factors which shape allocation. And he clearly points out that the socioeconomic and political factors are based first and foremost within community settings, a matter which is crucial for management programs which emanate from *outside* of, but affect, a community.

Further, the awareness of this fact is equally important, if more complex to analyze and address, in management problems that affect a number of communities whose histories and traditions exhibit variation. If the direction of extended jurisdiction is clear, to wit, "fisheries should grow to the socially optimum level of newly bounded stocks," so must be the imperative for social scientists to analyze these fisheries and to provide information to the policy makers upon which informed decisions can be made about "alternative pathways and their wider human consequences..."

Britan

Because of the increased information, communication and physical mobility brought about by technological, economic and social change, the question of migration and occupational choice in fisheries has both intrinsic and policy value. Migration is one of the key variables that affect population size, distribution and composition. These factors, in turn, constrain or stimulate social structural changes in communities and societies. Knowledge of occupational preferences and choices as antecedents and effects of migration are especially crucial to the larger picture of coastal zone and fisheries management activities, as Britan's chapter shows. For example, classical theoretical formulations on migration focus on models which connect "abstract economic pushes and pulls to the character and strength of migration streams and counterstreams." Other research has focused on a more micro-level, analyzing migration effects on sending communities or individual migration experiences and adjustments. Britan notes that this level of "analysis has emphasized either culturally idiosyncratic decision-making...or the external realities of political and economic pressure..." His approach to a more balanced analysis is to synthesize the economic, political, cultural and social factors that affect behavioral choices. He asserts that, rather than being made in isolation, migration decisions are made in relation to a particular context which provides an ever changing range of alternatives.

With evidence from his study of migration patterns in St. Brendan's, Newfoundland, Britan empirically supports this hypotheses. In cases where other theoretical formulations would have predicted out-migration, it did not occur, and vice versa. In fact, in the face of strong economic pulls for emigration during the late nineteenth century, immigration occurred. The family context and its adaptation to the nature of the local fishery was revealed to be the crucial intervening variable in these situations. Indeed, the importance of family organization to the community as a whole is best seen in its capacity to respond to resource availability and economic system changes irrespective—or in the face of—government intervention. In this case government intervention, as expressed through a resettlement program, became such a focal point that a major consequence was the unification of St. Brendan's "dispersed families into a corporate community for the first time," although a sharp schism was created as well. Public pressure arising from social structural changes of this sort resulted in an alteration of the resettlement program itself, transforming the requirement of a community-wide move or no move at all into a provision for choice by individual households. Through an analysis of this issue, Britan is able to demonstrate the importance of the sociopolitical context. If this context had been taken into account by policymakers at the outset of the resettlement program, a more reasonable accommodation might have been made to both the plans of the government and the needs of the outports.

In tracing the progression of events in St. Brendan's, Britan has made a strong case for his claim that "adaptation is continuous. Environmental shifts alter individual decisions, thereby creating new behavioral patterns which in turn transform both culture and environment." His chapter provides us with examples of both the effects of a particular policy stance on a discrete community, and the way in which a careful analysis of those effects can lead to effective policy reassessment.

Smith

With the passage of the FCMA in 1976, the United States created a comprehensive scheme to manage fisheries resources within 200 miles of its shoreline. It thus defined a FCZ, and announced to other nation states that the United States felt it had preemptory rights to the fisheries resources within that zone. The foci of the FCMA were to protect the resources from depletion, to protect the rights of U.S. citizens to harvest the resources within the conservation constraints, and to develop an effective and equitable use pattern for those resources. If the U.S. harvest fell short of the level of yield that would be possible without endangering the resources, then, and only then, could foreign fleets enter and fish in the U.S. FCZ. Although certain other countries had claimed extended resource control zones for many years, unilateral preemption by the United States had significant ramifications around the world. Japan, the Soviet Union and other countries had invested large sums of money building fleets specifically to exploit fisheries in the very water now covered under the FCMA. The debates that have and will occur over territoriality and resource control will illuminate the political and scientific literature for years to come.

Another set of problems has accompanied the FCMA, problems that were largely unforseen by both scientists and policymakers who sponsored the FCMA. Those problems center on the differential perceptions and behaviors of those who must implement the FCMA; specifically, differentials among those involved in the creation and activity of the eight Regional Fishery Management Councils. Smith's chapter focuses on those problems, to provide us with an interesting examination of the dynamics of the New England Fishery Management Council, which has primary responsibility for fisheries in the FCZ from the New York bight to the Canadian border. She points out, among other problems in the development of management schemes, a fundamental difference in the perceptions of the purpose of the FCMA by those who would participate in the management process. Members of the fishing industry on the Atlantic coast of the United States antici- pated expansion of the fisheries once foreign effort was curtailed. Fisheries administrators and scientists, on the other hand, perceived the purpose of the FCMA as conservation, even if it meant cutbacks in total fishing effort, including the effort of U.S. fishermen, once foreign effort was put in abeyance.

Smith's candid treatment of these issues and their implications for policymaking and the behavior of policymakers themselves is enlightening. The grueling scenarios enacted by the New England Council to meet the required mandates of the FCMA leave one exhausted and awed at the seeming impossibility of making such a broad, flexible, yet complex law work in the public interest. The plurality of forces that tug and pull to achieve special interests; the unintended and overwhelming legal framework that disproportionately allocates advan- tages or introduces potentially crippling constraints; the confusion created by a phone call, a whisper or even something as simple as a required motel checkout time—these and other features and incidents are discussed by Smith as factors which appreciably shape the ways in which marine fisheries policy is hatched and developed, in the shadow of the FCMA, through the management councils. Once again the social scientist is reminded of the critical distinctions between manifest and latent goals and consequences, which were pointed out a half cen- tury ago by Malinowski and others [10]. We are also reminded of the task of urging the policymaker to embrace an awareness of those con- cepts and their behavioral and structural implications in the creation, monitoring and adjustment of national policies under such statutory mandates as the FCMA.

Langdon

Social scientists have historically had two interrelated challenges in the development of governmental social policies. The first is to con- vince policymakers that the public interest is better served if social scientific data are formally incorporated into the policy equation. Second, once the principle of the use of the data is accepted, the problem becomes one of obtaining and applying data from appropriate, but often disparate disciplines and sources. In the realm of fisheries management, as Andersen points out, biological sciences and scientists have dominated until very recently, when the social sciences have begun making major inroads into the area. As in so many cases when social science breaks through, the discipline of economics has had greater success than other social sciences in permeating the management arena, and has done so more quickly. Economics has a language, a method and, for many, a track record that are more impressive to the nonsocial scientist than sociology, anthropology or other social science disciplines.

Somewhere along the historical path of social science involvement in a policy area, however, the formal models such as those used by economists generally run into difficulty. Although they embody appealing language and method, production functions, indifference curves, and presumed elasticities or inelasticities somehow fail to predict the necessary range of consequences of policies. Indeed, in some cases, e.g., welfare programs, behavior proceeds in a direction opposite to that predicted! Such seems to be the case in many areas of fishery policy.

Langdon's rather pointed chapter represents a critique of the assumptions and uses of a formal economic model in the management of the salmon fisheries of Alaska. As evidence of the influence of the formal paradigm, he examines the limited entry system enacted there in 1973 in terms of the system's rationale, presumed purpose and unintended consequences. In this respect the chapter is very much like Smith's study, except that Langdon concentrates on the specific economic consequences for fishermen of such regulatory systems.

With respect to the formulation of regulatory schemes based on economics, Langdon notes that formal economic models ignore a variety of internal relations of production, and thus the usual treatments of capital and labor found in those models do not apply. He points out that the pragmatic variations from normal assumptions about capital and labor significantly structure the fishermen's motivations toward harvesting and their attitudes toward compliance with protective regulations. A further weakness is inattention to the probability of improved technology, which would undercut the presumed results of limited entry. Finally, Langdon severely criticizes the hypothesized distribution of economic yields within the formalist paradigm.

In each case, Langdon provides data demonstrating ways in which the execution of the formalist model has not produced the intended results in Alaska. Limited entry has resulted in somewhat of an economic dualism in the fishery; overexploitation promises to continue to be a concern, and inequitable distribution of the benefits accruing from the fishery has been exacerbated. It is clear that any management scheme that utilizes economic theory in its policy formulations must take into account the fact that fisheries efforts are embedded in existing social and cultural networks. Langdon provides us with yet another example similar to those of Andersen, Britan and Smith.

Berleant-Schiller

It is generally assumed that fishery development plans are based on the realities of the marine environment. Berleant-Schiller's paper examines a succession of fisheries development projects in the Caribbean. She argues that the projects were based as heavily on the prevaling political environment (e.g., newly emerging nations, such as Trinidad, seeking means to strengthen political independence) as on the conditions and potential of the marine environment itself. In the cases that she cites, very little consideration was given to the prevailing technological and economic constraints.

Political pressure for fisheries commerce often translates into hurried commercial development at the expense of local traditional fisheries. As examples, the author cites some of the effects of the introduction of modern technology in the Caribbean: a concentration of the means of fishing; traditional fishermen and less productive fishing sites rendered useless; markets glutted by oversupply; and fish stocks endangered. A traditional fishing style, with balanced technological constraints and opportunities on the one hand and an adequate though not overabundant supply on the other, was effectively overrun under such conditions.

Berleant-Schiller then turns her attention to Barbuda and an analysis of the traditional fishery there. Her purpose is to "show how the fishery is balanced with marine resources and their economic possibilities; how fishing technology suits the nature and quantity of fish resources and how neither economy nor resource can support technological change in fishing." Although this assertion calls to mind the "functional equilibrium" hypothesis, the author's portrayal is interesting and informative. Berleant-Schiller characterizes the fishery as one with traditional technology which sufficiently meets local needs, incorporates a cash nexus to outside markets, operates well within yield limits which conserve the resource, and facilitates occupational pluralism, i.e., involvement in a range of productive activities in addition to fishing. From her viewpoint, large-scale technological innovation, the infusion of large sums of investment capital, and other associated events would negatively affect the biological and sociocultural dimensions of the fishery. She appeals for, instead, development based on policy principles that would "involve and benefit a local population," and require the "effective use of the resources and facilities already present and apply only that technology which is suitable for local conditions, social and cultural, as well as economic and environmental."

In discussing their respective subjects and situations, all of the authors comment on a theme of central concern to this first section; the explicit and implicit assumptions used by governments to formulate and implement their fishery policy. These assumptions, and the general principles which result from them and on which regulatory and management schemes are based, are not always articulated or clearly set. There are two generic problems here. One is that in not pausing to articulate principles and assumptions—and thereby not forcing them to be clearly thought-out or questioned—much of the rational, documented process of policy formulation is denied. The second problem is that, in the resulting absence of communication of clear policy, the constituents of that policy do not have an opportunity to comment upon or provide feedback to the policymakers, or to adjust their expectations and perceptions to new events and behaviors. One can see a mixture of these two problems in the situations and events described in each of the chapters in this section.

REFERENCES

[1] Eisenstadt , S. N. "Bureaucracy, Bureaucratization, and Debureaucratization," *Admin. Sci. Quart.* 4:302-320 (1954).

[2] Selznick, P. *TVA and the Grass Roots* (Berkeley, CA: University of California Press, 1949), pp. 258-259.

[3] Hall, R. H. *Organizations: Structure and Process* (Englewood Cliffs, NJ: Prentice-Hall, Inc., 1972), p. 331.

[4] Maiolo, J. "Organization for Social Action: Some consequences of Competition for Control," *Sociol. Quart.* (Fall 1970), pp. 463-472.

[5] Sills, D. L. *The Volunteers* (Glencoe: The Free Press, 1957).

[6] Etzioni, A. *Modern Organizations* (Englewood Cliffs, NJ: Prentice-Hall Inc., 1964), pp. 5-19.

[7] Champion, D. J. *The Sociology of Organizations:* (Englewood Cliffs,

NJ: Prentice-Hall Inc., 1964), pp.9.

[8] King, C. W. *Social Movements in the United States* (New York: Random House, 1964), pp.39-57.

[9] Smith, M. E. "Fisheries Management: Intended Results and Unintended Consequences," Chapter 3, this volume.

[10] Maiolo, J. R., Ed. *Highways and Communities* (University Park, PA: Institute for Land and Water Resources, Pennsylvania State University, 1966).

CHAPTER 1
EXTENDED JURISDICTION AND FISHERMAN ACCESS TO RESOURCES: NEW DIRECTIONS, NEW IMPERATIVES

Raoul Andersen
Department of Anthropology
Memorial University of Newfoundland

This book is about modernization and marine fisheries policies. In this chapter, I think it necessary to note that much of anthropology, and the social sciences generally, involves basically the same concept, formulation and ordering process faced by other scientists from which they are held separate. The scientific process employed by fisheries biologists in, for example, their studies of the behavior and life cycle of various species, and stock assessments, is familiar and intelligible—even if the biologist's taxonomic jargon is not. The canons of Baconian science are a common ground. Social scientists are not pursuing a separate mythos.

A further common ground, again with biology, lies in the fact that anthropologists readily acknowledge the complexity of ecosystem relationships and have themselves a developed body of science knowledge on man-ecosystem relationships. Indeed, about a decade ago two anthropologists specializing in cultural ecological studies argued for the development of a "single science of ecology with laws and principles that apply to man as they do to other species"[1]. The scope and character of this "common ground" continues to be developed.

I think it is necessary, also, to stress that the fisheries conceptual equation has long suffered from failure to seriously embrace human factors in thinking about fisheries management and development. Social science contributions to fisheries administration in Canada have been largely confined to economic studies—and there are very few fisheries economists in Canada. I suspect the same is true of the history of fisheries in the United States. If my impression of the situation in anthropology reflects general trends, ten years ago it would have been very difficult to identify more than a handful of social scientists outside economics with fisheries expertise. Neither the push nor the pull were present to draw them into fisheries studies. What I and others have seen to be a shortcoming in science effort and knowledge use in this respect now seems to have changed, at least in the United States. Science support from the Sea Grant program has been important in this change, but the matter merits a more protean explanation than is my purpose here.

This increased involvement of anthropologists in fisheries related research suggests that our rubric "fisheries" is the same as that of fisheries and other aquatic scientists, fishermen, the industry, administrators and enforcement personnel. My experience indicates this is not true. It is necessary to define our basic terms before proceeding.

Fisheries are activities through which people link themselves with aquatic environments and renewable resources. Given their marine environment and its biological resources, the meaningful aspects of these activities include technology (extractive, transportation, folk and scientific techniques for guiding extractive efforts), economic organization (e.g., patterns of access to resources, production incentives, capital formation institutions, markets, middlemen and entrepreneurs, and consumers and their preferences), organized groups (e.g., fishermen, their communities, processor-enterprise operators and workers, conservation and protection agencies and associations, industry associations—union, marketing groups and trade councils, with power and authority to shape decisions affecting resource extraction, processing, distribution, cost and profit determination, and investment and planning decisions), and values and myths (about the "right order" of things that rationalize the power and decisions of individuals and groups that compose and depend on fisheries).

These human components are identifiable in all fishing societies or fisheries adaptations. The form they take is only partly explained by proximity to different marine environments and resources. Their variances embrace different technological levels, different relationships between primary procedures, capital, markets and governments, and different institutions integrated with fisheries.

Our concern, however, is with modernity and contemporary fisheries. Fisheries have undergone a remarkable transformation from prehistoric to contemporary times, and perhaps the most profound change of all has occurred in this decade through extended jurisdiction. Through time, fishing and navigational technologies have expanded man's use of living marine resources. A complex division of labor and widening gap between structurally advantaged and disadvantaged fishing interests has developed in the shift from subsistence to modern labor production. Also, modern fisheries are highly complex in their linkage with local, regional, national and international markets, often as not mediated and determined by controlling corporate organizations with sometimes "global reach" powers. But these trends have carried us to the post World War II "tragedy of the commons" and relentless competition for increasingly decimated stocks. Fishing interests have brought fisheries to a precipice through ill-controlled application of increasingly effective catching technology.

World fisheries today share a common plight which seems part of the greater litany of the contemporary "human ecological predicament" [2], which requires a very different approach to resources everywhere. This larger human ecological predicament is some of the background of the Newfoundland and Atlantic coast fisheries. Perhaps it is also wisely conceived of as part of a major break or discontinuity in human history or, as Wertime [3] has argued, "the end of the world's golden age," when exponential growth, prosperity, and rising expectations must greatly decline. Canada's fishery-stock allocation and management scheme for 1977, under extended jurisdiction, marks its first major move from growth-oriented to steady-state (but not static) fisheries.

THE ACCESS PROBLEM

If a fishery begins with access to the resource, whether production is for subsistence or commerce, where the resource is limited and fishing is susceptible to economic and social changes, a need develops to control access and/or harvest. Thus we have the beginnings of fisheries *management,* although it need not imply the biological conservation of stocks. At any rate, access may be conceived of as confined to decisions about who has the right to fish in a given area over which a coastal or river people claim jurisdiction. Thus, decisions about access to fishery resources presume some jurisdictional authority. Such powers have been visited in coastal communities, fishing families, feudal lords or seigniors, companies, cooperatives, provinces, colonial and central governments, and international bodies such as the International Commission for the Northwest Atlantic Fisheries (ICNAF).

In practice, access controls are asserted by a combination of customary, enacted and private restrictions. But what form have such restrictions taken within the specific empirical framework of the Newfoundland fishery? And what is their place within extended jurisdiction and development of steady-state fisheries?

Newfoundland fishermen manage access to extractive opportunities in two major ways: (1) by public or explicitly delineated, and sometimes legally enacted regulations, and direct or indirect enforcement; and (2) by private strategies. The latter are relatively secret and independent access controls used in areas where public restrictions obtain and access is otherwise unrestricted.

A View Inshore

Before cod traps and gill nets were introduced in Newfoundland waters in the late nineteenth century, inshore, largely within the three mile zone, fishing units were family enterprises of one or two men, often agnatic relations, closely tied to some fishing merchant in a truck system. They engaged in seasonal and daily competition for access opportunities on the fishing grounds within one or two hours of shore and safety. Open sail-and oar-powered dories of 12-23 feet and the danger of bad weather gave little freedom. Some communities had overlapping fishing space, but most had little opportunity to encroach on other's ground.

Local residence and economic dependence on local marine resources gave the minimal right to share a common operational base and compete for fish. Each day men sought to work their handline and/or trawls from the most advantageous positions. On occasion it was necessary to defend their waters when, for example, dories operating from wide-ranging schooners appeared and failed to establish a basis for a trade-off. Cutting trawl lines was an undesired but ultimate recourse. It would typically be spontaneous, yet I surmise it was publicly established, for there was no effective immediate recourse to a higher authority or the promise of such support before wireless communications. The boundary would be indefensible without some general local support.

How were spatial access privileges asserted *within local waters?* Given that some places are better than others for fishing and positioning often requires very precise knowledge to be productive, differential individual learning skills and the value of proving oneself an effective fisherman encouraged men to develop private strategies through information management (e.g., concentration of informational capital in patrilineal fishing groups), through and mastery of techniques designed to outfox competitors without evidencing intent.

The handline and jigger complex predates the trawl in Newfoundland waters as it does in New England and elsewhere in the North Atlantic. Early experimentation on grounds used by handliners revealed the trawl's superior catching potential and that it justified increasing the extent of bottom areas fished. Handline vs trawl technological specialization emerged and gave rise to technologically based disputes over access to fishing space. Competition focused on placement in prime fishing locations. For example, Martin [4] writing of the stormy history of the trawl in the Fermeuse, Southern Shore, fishery, held that the handline and jigger fishermen "deeply resented the high yield operations with their 'long strings of gear' encroaching upon established handline and jigger areas."

Men adopted private access controls in a perpetual guessing game over the time of departure to the grounds. Short of common sense understandings of what constitutes sufficient space to prevent undesired entanglements between individual trawls and other gear, the area controlled by an individual fisherman is a changing function of his aggressiveness (dominance)—offensive and defensive—the productivity of the location itself and personal discretion. Informal spatial rules therefore involved a dynamic which minimized destructive clashes while also permitting adjustments in the face of competitive pressures and situational conditions.

Their only practical recourse being immediate, individual defense of territorial rights, striking differences in their catch success and conflicting interests between groups of narrowly adapted handliners and spatially more versatile trawlmen posed a persistent challenge to informal rules and private strategies developed around use of different technologies in the same waters. Too frequent disputes led to public sanctions for the allocation of large tracts or blocks of territory, e.g., handline sanctuaries and access tradeoffs.

Apart from international restrictions limiting foreign fleet access to its coastal waters, public management of Newfoundland inshore fishing space was therefore initially locally defined and enforced by fishermen themselves. When their efforts proved ineffectual or too disruptive, external governmental support through legitimation and enforcement was sought. In Fermeuse, for example, and it may be a special case, the gentleman's agreement to the effect that no trawls were to be set within three miles of the shore on Fermeuse ground (thus creating a handline sanctuary within) proved untenable. A government mandate was obtained to back this allocation agreement, and it was established as law under the Newfoundland legislative acts of 1892 [4].

Such recourse to external legal authority on the part of Newfoundland fisherman communities may reflect little-developed local political institutions and an established dependence on paternalistic patrons. The latter ostensibly embody neutral application of the law in fishing disputes and indirect sanction. One may wonder at what stage, under what conditions, and at what costs such communities develop, if ever, the capacity to directly regulate regulations among and between fishing technologies in their waters without recourse to higher political authorities. The Maine lobstermen described by Acheson [5] would seem archetypic of such self-reliance.

I have confined the foregoing to some mobile fishing technologies used in Newfoundland inshore waters at least since the 1850s. The modern introduction of monofilament gill nets, which require control over great extents of fishing space, and the Danish seine technique used by longliners, involved minor variations on the control patterns outlined. They were regulated so as not to deny other technologies their opportunity to capture a part of the various migrating species entering local waters. Since World War II, the average size and quantity of inshore catches of cod declined dangerously, primarily under the impact of a growing offshore fishery which intercepted the cod. In 1961 a minimum 5-inch mesh size limit was introduced by Canadian fisheries authorities (The mesh limit went to 5.5 inches in January 1981). Despite growing fears of "ghostfishing" by lost gill nets, however, there remains no restriction on the number of nets individual fishermen might use.

The cod trap [4], a stationary gear introduced to Newfoundland and Labrador waters in the 1880s, inspired new control measures. The cod trap promised and required catch returns at a level sufficient to support crews of at least four men. Patrilocal fisherman groups or trap crews became preferential. The cod trap is ideally placed with the hope that, except for minor positions and repair adjustments, placement is for the entire season (the Labrador floater cod fishery is an important exception). Investments in boats (about 35 feet), gear, and crew are considerably greater for this technology than those mentioned above. The trap is set at high risk, and its effective use demands a good knowledge of the relative productive advantage of different locations or berths in nearby waters, guarantee of tenure, and some assurance that the movement of fish to the trap will not be obstructed. A scale of relative spatial advantages was developed around handline and jigger, and trawl fishing in many areas after years of experience. But there was no assurance that it would fit the cod trap. That required extensive testing over many seasons.

In the now resettled community of Port Elizabeth, Placentia Bay, for example, a high of about 50 named berths was reached. Only 22 were regarded as prime; there was no particular competition for the other. But even the prime berths could prove a total failure, so many fishermen employed two or three traps, thus spreading their chances over several berths.

In the early years of cod trap use, however, positioning followed the pattern set by the more traditional and mobile techniques. The right to compete for berth space was restricted to the local community, and vacated or temporarily unfilled berths could not be usurped by outsiders without first obtaining local permission. A reasonable time was allowed in the early part of the season for men to set their gear without competitive pressure. The first man to set his trap in a given location held the location for the season or until the trap was moved (whether intentionally or by sea action). Where there were few desirable berths and many seeking them, competition led to conflict and undesirable risks against seasonal uncertainties. One could never be certain that the last of winter storms had passed, yet one could not wait too long before berthing his trap lest someone else take the desired berth.

Where competitive pressures and risks were high, fishermen devised a public draw for named berths in advance of each season. The draw procedure was sometimes delineated and enacted under Newfoundland Fisheries Regulations. But where the ratio of berths to fishermen was high, some berths were obtained through patrilineal inheritance [6]. But fishermen-to-berth ratios and related allocation arrangements change, often with controversy that fuels Newfoundland's oral tradition and literature. For example, Scammell [7] wrote,

> It was the best berth in Sloops Tickle and the Martins had become fairly well-to-do from the fish it gave them, with hardly a year missing. Sid knew there was a lot of discontent among the fishermen over it. Good trap berths were scarce in that locality and why a few men should hog the best berths year after year just because their fathers had traps there, the less fortunate trapmen couldn't understand.

The development of customary and enacted public controls did not end private strategies designed to gain positional advantages or continuation of subtle strategies or maneuverings designed to refine gear efficiency and, via various tricks, to manipulate lottery rules and outcomes to individual advantage. The lottery frequently provoked disputes, and court adjudications [4].

The inshore spatial access strategies noted above apply to cod, a migrating groundfish species. Inshore approaches to migrating *pelagic* species (caplin, herring, mackerel, squid, and pothead whale), on the other hand, include inherited locations for stationary short seines (for herring and caplin); mobile beach and bar seines for the same species; stationary traps (especially for squid); individual castnets; and communitywide drives, chiefly for pilot or "pothead" whales.

The movements of many pelagic species, more than those of demersal, are felt to be affected by human interference or disturbance. There is, therefore, often an incentive favoring integration of extraction efforts above the individual level; private access management was less applicable. This incentive toward cooperative endeavor is expressed in the pothead whale fishery of Bonavista and Trinity Bays. It was impractical for both individuals and groups of inshore fishermen of communities in these areas to attempt to capture the whales outside their local waters. Their boat and gear technology was unsuitable for such endeavor, and their quarry might be driven off or broken up and scattered prematurely. Long experience with the characteristics of their environment favored driving them down long, narrow bays and onto stranding beaches. Once a pod of whales of a size deemed economic entered local waters demarked by headlands, right of access to them was usually available to any and all local fishermen willing to cooperate in their capture. Men from an adjacent community who happened to be the area when the drive began could also participate and receive a full share. But a direct share of proceeds depended on cooperative participation. One had to be in the drive from the start.

A View Offshore

Favoring an examination of extreme adaptations, I omit from this discussion the operations of longliners (35-60 ft. or more) which operate to some extent in both the inshore and offshore spheres. They are described elsewhere by Stiles [8,9] and Andersen [10]. In earlier papers [11,12] I described the basic access management practices employed prior to extended jurisdiction by modern Newfoundland offshore fishermen. The essence of this adaptation is given below. The case of the now extinct dory-banking-schooner adaptation which preceded and provided many contemporary trawler fishermen with an important experiential comparison with modern trawling is given in Andersen and Stiles [13] and Andersen [14].

Modern trawler operations from Newfoundland ports date to the late 1940s, when the first two steel-hulled side trawlers were brought up to St. John's from New England. Today there are 3 companies which together control about 9 fleets of up to 12 nonfisherman-owned side and stern trawlers ranging in length from about 120 to 210 ft. The larger vessels have a capacity of up to about 450,000 lbs. These fleets are vertically integrated with fish plants located primarily on Newfoundland's South Coast.

Each vessel is equipped with some of the most modern navigational, fish detection, and ship-to-ship and ship-to-shore communication gear. Their crews of 12-18 men range on trips of about 10 days over the fishing grounds of the Gulf of St. Lawrence and Grand Banks, seeking flounder, cod, sole, redfish and haddock. Their operations are legally and typically conducted in offshore areas beyond the three-mile limit. Competition for fish in this area is intense; for example, the number of trawlers (50 tons and over) operating north of Cape Hatteras increased from 798 in 1959 to 1410 in 1969.

The crews are recruited from virtually the same areas where the banking schooner fishery developed. They are, by and large, heirs to an almost century-old deep-sea fishery occupational tradition. Economically, until recently they were contracted as "co-adventurers" on a trip-by-trip (hence, casual worker) basis, where their remuneration was largely, if not solely, determined by a share of the landed value of fish taken by their vessel alone. At this writing, most are now unionized and better thought of as employees, although the "share system" of remuneration prevails. The share system follows a pattern long and widely established in commercial fishing operations, although it has many variations. (The share arrangement used in the Newfoundland trawler fishery since 1975, for example, is somewhat unusual in that, annually, fish prices are established through collective bargaining on a principle of a negotiated minimum income level [15].)

Vessel owners reckon their trawler skippers the key element in the success of fishing operations and, accordingly, they reward them with earnings 2-4 times that of the deckhand. But the skipper's tenure is precarious. He must bring fish to his vessel to maintain his position before management, his crew and other Newfoundland trawlers.

The modern trawler skipper's responsibility for production differs considerably from that of the banking skipper, who had to rely heavily on his small fleet of dory fishermen to take fish and, where circumstances demanded, act discreetly and independently when fishing to preserve or exert any positional advantages when working a ground in the company of other schooner-dory crews. Trawler operations, in contrast, although conducted largely out of visual contact with the other trawlers in one's company fleet, involve regular contact with other vessels by means of ship-to-ship, and ship-to-shore radio exchanges. Since the trawler is highly mobile, and the skipper shoulders major responsibility for catch production, it is logical that he (and his crew) is concerned with what information passes over the radio between it and other trawlers, on one hand, and their homebase or fish plant on the other. Each skipper controls the information flowing out over his radio to other ships and to plant management ashore; this forms an informational circle in which any party to a radio transaction may expect his words to reach any other fleet unit or management and vice versa. To a lesser extent, he also controls incoming information by shutting down his receiver for periods and by subtly interpreting what comes in for his crew (see Orbach's [16] discussion of the information system in San Diego tuna seiner fishing).

Given that the marine ecology is highly variable and that fishermen are able to discern patterns in this variation over many man-years of concentrated fishing effort, trawler skippers develop individual stores of information about the location and occurrence of various species at various times of the year. Some skippers become specialist in specific bottom areas; some even have them named after them, e.g., Marty's Hole and Bob's Patch. But distances and intense competition for their mutual quarry create a high premium on information revealing the current distribution and catch experience of other units. To fulfill this informational need involves the skipper in a fundamental contradiction: he can only give "good" information to other skippers (whether in his company or outside) or his management (with the expectation that it will be circulated to his competitors) at risk to his present or future performance. Thus, if he is presently taking, or knows where fish may be taken in quantity, giving this information may jeopardize his success through immediate encroachment by other units nearby and the loss of privileged access to a good fishing location he discovered at considerable cost of time and labor and which he might want to use in the future.

All masters require more information than they can possibly acquire alone. So they strike some balance between information management designed to preserve positional informational privileges, and accurate, nonessential (to the donor) information exchange which keeps minimally essential data coming in. I am unable to specify precisely what the relative quanta are, and confine my observations to those information practices bearing on the problem of access management.

The weapons in the skipper's spatial control arsenal are varied and may be used to merely protect one's positional exploitive advantages, or to bring a competitor to grief; literally, to injure his productivity in various ways by causing him to lose time steaming about in search of nonexistent bonanza locations or, at worst, to tear up and lose his gear fishing unfamiliar bottom areas. As skippers are competitive for both men and boats within and between Newfoundland trawler fleets, some try to improve their relative position in the catch statistics at the expense of others. But such endeavor is dangerous as it inspires grudges and retribution if one is found out. The more common practice involves information management, usually through understatement of catch returns that works to discourage other units from moving to one's position. Indeed, listening to the radio banter on the banks, the expression "Fish are scarce," repeated *ad nauseam,* inclines one to think they are scarce *everywhere.*

The fish plant ashore, which the trawler supplies, is also subject to misinformation about catch. As much as 50% or more of actual catch may be withheld at any time before the vessel makes its last daily report before returning to port. This, of course, limits management efforts to achieve maximal fleet productive capabilities and creates problems ashore should unexpectedly high landings glut the processing line with fish. In this regard the distortion is not systematic; one cannot easily compute how far the information deviates from veracity. Even where one discerns seeming inconsistencies in information received, there always remains the possibility that these are purposefully made in a subtle effort to lure others to waste their fishing time.

Functionally speaking, these private strategies favor a spacing rather than concentration of units in particular areas. One might also follow the view taken by Forman [17] that such private strategies help to forestall overfishing of particular locations. That sounds reasonable on the surface even if substantiation is lacking, but it must be recognized that they also contribute to wasted fishing effort (time and labor) and material. In an effort to compensate for these deficiencies individual skippers frequently form alliances with "code-partners" with whom they share information and plan fishing strategy. These alliances may last for years, and they occur both within and between company fleets.

Even in such alliances the main concern is to develop and assert spatial privileges serving one's crew rather than to injure the prospects of others. All skippers engage in a serious economic game, of course, but their play is girded by important moral restrictions. These are evident in the commonly heard dicta: "Take care of your crowd first," but "Never lie to hurt a man." Or, at least, never get caught, let alone admitting it, which impugns one's reputation for both skill and morality. Likewise, to be manifestly deceived reflects on one's repute for cunning in an information game all trawlermen feel they understand. It also inspires directed retribution, and "Then, nobody don't get nothing!"

The problem of technological competition encountered in our earlier discussion of the inshore fishery also occurs in the modern offshore sector. Here, we meet spatial competition generated by differences in scale and technique. One such case is represented by the seeming highly coordinated fleet operations of European socialist fishing nations, in which large numbers and the "front" they cover represent a perceptible and formidable threat to the typically solitary Newfoundland trawler. Having no radio communication with them, defense of space opportunities through information management is impossible. The solitary trawler may even be forced out of the minimal publicly acknowledged space enjoyed in international fishing, i.e., his fishing fairway (the path immediately ahead of the towing trawler), when a large trawler, or several, disregard the rules of the road. Collisions and near misses are a well established hazard.

Another case, one involving major technological difference, is exemplified by Portuguese fishermen who recently attempted to use long blankets of gill nets, presumably well marked with radar-reflective buoys, on banks long used by trawlers. Newfoundland fishermen, and others, object to this technology on the grounds that such gear is easily lost to become ghost nets on the bottom which continue to kill fish for an indefinite period, as they do not deteriorate, thus endangering future stocks. Involved also is the view that such a technology could block off or encompass vast areas of the grounds now fished by trawlers. It takes space needed by others. I cannot verify this point, but such Portuguese gear was reportedly purposely torn up by one or more Canadian trawlers put to this action by their management. It seems this was done with some reluctance on the part of knowledgeable fishermen for it was an action which, in effect, directly challenged the right of others to their living. Nevertheless, it seems to have been successful. The Portuguese ceased the use of this technique on a major scale.

Another seasonally varied pattern of spatial encroachment by foreign and Newfoundland trawlers occurs in connection with the summer run of cod, feeding on dense caplin shoals, into coastal waters, the territory of the inshore fishermen. At this time, violations of the three-mile boundary occur. As one skipper remarked to me privately, "Why, I've taken more fish within the three mile limit than anyone's taken there...in 1963 I made three tows of Cape Race and took 20,000, 25,000 and 30,000 lbs." Perhaps only a few skippers made these incursions, usually under cover of night and/or fog. The threat of being caught by Fisheries Protection Service vessels and fined inhibits them. (Under extended jurisdiction, federal fisheries observers are increasingly common aboard trawlers and surveillance is more rigorous; violations have become more difficult.)

The owners of their vessels, of course, reward their enterprise in returning a good catch. Specific origins are unverifiable anyway. And the rationale is that the fish are there to be taken. The inshore fishermen cannot possibly catch them all. The trawler skipper knows he may destroy some of the inshore and/or longliner fishermen's gear; and this may be done unknowingly. But, anyway, he may rationalize that "those fishermen lose their nets on purpose many times just to collect some money off the government." In short, encroachment gains legitimacy from a self-serving definition of the other fishermen as less committed than oneself.

NEW DIRECTIONS, NEW IMPERATIVES

Beginning in January 1977, the Canadian government undertook to control the harvest of stocks within its 200-mile coastal management zone. This has been done with increasing vigor. All foreign and domestic fishing vessels now require licenses, and traditional stocks are exploited under close areal, seasonal, quota and technological restrictions. Pressures on traditional species have been reduced in most cases and larger operators are encouraged to develop nontraditional species. Surveillance, enforcement, onboard vessel inspections and observers have all increased, as have fisheries biological science efforts, and arrests and fines for infractions have become a reality with the threat of increasingly severe penalties.

Simultaneously, fishery scientists prognosticate general stock recovery will take about 9-10 years, and the industry is charged to respond to the opportunity to take an increasing proportion of the catch available within the management zone consistent with the principle of preferential fishing rights for the coastal state and gradual phaseout of foreign effort as Canadian catching capacity increases. Federal fisheries rhetoric strikes one as somewhat Utopian in this regard, and it is not clearly consistent. On the one hand fishing interests are told that

Canadian fisheries will now be managed for "maximum social benefit" to the nation. Yet, on the other, they will be regulated "in the interest of those who depend on the fishery," which strikes one as more *regionally,* if not provincially, oriented.

For Newfoundland's some 15,300 (1976 figures) fishermen, about 1000 of them offshore fishermen, extended jurisdiction has not been a panacea for their long-term problems. Extended jurisdiction in 1977 and predictions of revolutionary improvements in income prospects for Canadian fishermen have encouraged an upsurge of interests in the Newfoundland inshore fishery. By 1980 Newfoundland inshore fishermen approached 30,000. Federal authorities are moving to introduce restrictions to bring these numbers in balance with available fish. Initial steps involve classification of full-time and part-time fishermen. The control process and objectives are highly controversial.

Access to high-value fisheries, especially herring, shrimp, crab and salmon, is now largely controlled by federal fisheries officials. In most, if not all, cases, federal officials have undertaken to create management committees whose members include concerned fishermen, fishery scientists, and trade representatives. All fishermen must be licensed. Residence in a fishing community alone is not enough to assure continued access to traditional resources. Just how far this expansion of federal fisheries dominance over local level access politics will go remains to be seen. There is an uneasiness among many former bona fide fishermen, especially those often disparagingly termed "part-timers," and seasonal fishermen, about their future access to fisheries. This uneasiness must be taken seriously, not only because of the serious implications any withdrawal of access might have in a province with the highest levels of unemployment in Canada, but also because the socioeconomic implications of most regulatory systems have yet to be given the close study they require. Put bluntly, we are in the initial stages of a highly experimental period in fisheries access management under extended jurisdiction. More basic social science information is needed—and soon. We have not dealt with such management situations in fisheries on such a scale before.

Offshore fishing interests are now subject to unprecedented constraints on areas and species they may harvest and at what levels. Some company spokesmen have opined that this reduced freedom will lead to disaffection among their best skippers, who are forced to give up supposed free-ranging fishing styles to the detriment of their customary productivity. I have seen no evidence of such negative effects as yet, though the daily prospect of being boarded and inspected, and federal regulations which now reportedly require all trawler skippers to keep accurate daily records of catch by species and their specific areal movements, make them subject to closer scrutiny than heretofore. Has this caused skippers to abandon their information management practices? They may be less easy to continue, but I have no reason to think so. They seem inherent in the distinctive role skippers occupy in a highly competitive industrial-corporate enterprise. The relations of production have not been modified, nor do such radical changes seem to be on the horizon. Beyond that essentially structural question, it is reasonable to expect that fishermen, inshore and offshore, share a continuity in the premium placed on demonstration of their fishing acumen by successful relative performance. Are such values also operative in the performance of socialist trawler and inshore fishermen? Perhaps we will learn one day.

Finally, I have risked a somewhat taxonomic recapitulation of some of the ethnography bearing on access management in the Newfoundland inshore and offshore fisheries. Candidly, this ethnography is fragmentary and dated. Only three accounts [4, 9, 12] merit consideration as case studies. They vary in depth and directedness, and all were done prior to extended jurisdiction. More important, apart from its value as historical background on a rejected regime in man-sea relationships, this discussion has not brought us to a forthright examination of one of the most serious issues facing Canada's Atlantic Coast fisheries, namely the future relationships between inshore and offshore fishing spheres.

These spheres tend to be conceptualized in terms that are rather too polarized and superficial, for neither are static and unchanging and both seem necessary to long term Canadian fisheries development. Their interrelationship, perhaps especially in Newfoundland and Nova Scotia, and elsewhere in Atlantic Canada, is highly politicized for many reasons. The failure of fisheries management under ICNAF to prevent domestic and especially foreign trawlers fishing in offshore waters from intercepting and overfishing stocks essential to the inshore sector is one important reason. Its disastrous economic and social consequences are believed to include the failure of the east coast Newfoundland and Labrador inshore fishery prior to 1977.

How might such protection be accomplished under extended jurisdiction and coastal state management? Some Nova Scotian inshore fishing interests argued in 1977 for a 50-mile (protective) limit. Its ecological logic and enforcement feasibility aside, the concept is familiar as a sanctuary designed to protect one technological class from another.

Precisely how such techniques should be agreed on, and how various interest groups should or may participate more directly and effectively in the management (and development) decision-making process remain to be resolved specifically and generally. The absence of clear guidelines and objectives sensitive to regional variations which define the future role of small vs large capital fishing interests in Canada's coastal society and economy inclines us to be uneasy about the future of small producers. Many people opine that the greater gain to Canada which preferential fishing rights enable through an expanded domestic fishing effort favors offshore fishing interests, at least in the short run. Some take the further expansion of vertically integrated fleets as an absolute certainty. Modernizing and enlarging catching capacity to realize this opportunity will be a major problem, but planning for and realizing large capital ventures are familiar tasks for large corporate offshore interests, particularly if government finds this path the easiest way to go administratively. What the socially optimal fleet mix should be, however, is widely in doubt.

Access management before and after extended jurisdiction is inseparable from considerations of the economic, social and political implications of any measures employed to shape allocation. The general direction under extended jurisdiction seems clear enough: domestic fisheries should grow to the socially optimum level of newly bounded stocks. The imperative for anthropologists and other social scientist is to supply the information needed to define alternative pathways and their wider human consequences as we move to this end.

ACKNOWLEDGMENTS

This chapter is based in part on ideas first advanced in "Public and Private Access Management in Newfoundland Fishing" [10], and "The Need for Human Sciences Research in the Atlantic Coast Fisheries," Science Background Study No. 15 [18]. St. John's, Newfoundland

REFERENCES

[1] Vayda, A. P., and R. A. Rappaport. "Ecology, Cultural and Non-cultural," in *Introduction to Cultural Anthropology: Essays in the Access and Methods of the Science of Man,* J. A. Clifton, Ed. (Boston: Houghton-Mifflin, 1968), pp. 477-497.

[2] Ophuls. W. *Ecology and the Politics of Scarcity* (San Francisco: W. H.

Freeman & Company Publishers, 1977).

[3] Wertime, T. A. "Is This the End of the World's Golden Age?" *The Guardian* (Manchester), May 15, 1977, pp. 17-18.

[4] Martin, K. O. "The Law in St. John's Says..." MA Thesis, Memorial University of Newfoundland (1973).

[5] Acheson, J. M. "Variations in Traditional Fishing Rights in Maine Lobstering Communities," in *North Atlantic Maritime Cultures,* R. Andersen, Ed. (The Hague, Mouton, 1979), pp. 253-276.

[6] Firestone, M. "Brothers and Rivals: Patrilocality in Savage Cove," Institute of Social and Economic Research, Memorial University of Newfoundland, St. John's, Newfoundland (1967).

[7] Scammell, A. R. "Trap Berth," in *My Newfoundland* (Montreal, Quebec: Harvest House, 1966).

[8] Stiles, G. "Reluctant Capitalists: Technological Change and the Domestic Role of Production in a Newfoundland Fishing Community." Unpublished manuscript.

[9] Stiles, G. "Fishermen, Wives, and Radios," in *North Atlantic Fishermen,* R. Andersen and C. Wadel, Eds. (St. John's, Newfoundland: Institute of Social and Economic Research, Memorial University of Newfoundland, 1972), pp. 35-60.

[10] Andersen, R. "Public and Private Access Management in Newfoundland Fishing," in *North Atlantic Maritime Cultures,* R. Andersen, Ed. (The Hague, Mouton, 1979), pp. 299-336.

[11] Andersen, R. "Those Fishermen Lies," *Ethnos* 38:153-164 (1973).

[12] Andersen, R. "Hunt and Deceive," in *North Atlantic Fishermen,* R. Andersen and C. Wadel, Eds. (St. John's, Newfoundland: Institute of Social and Economic Research, Memorial University of Newfoundland, 1972), pp. 120-140.

[13] Andersen, R., and G. Stiles, "Resource Management and Spatial Competition in Newfoundland Fishing," in *Seafarer and Community,* P. H. Fricke, Ed. (London, England: Croom Helm, 1973), pp. 44-66.

[14] Andersen, R. "The 'Count and the 'Share': Offshore Fishermen and Changing Incentives," in *Proceedings of the Canadian Ethnology Society Meetings, 1977* Mercury Series (Ottawa, Ontario: National Museum of Man, 1978), pp. 27-43.

[15] MacDonald, D. A. "Process and Change in the Newfoundland Fishery: The Trawlermen's Strike of 1974-75," MA Thesis, Department of Anthropology, Memorial University of Newfoundland, St. John's,

Newfoundland (1978).

[16] Orbach, M. K. *Hunters, Seamen, and Entrepreneurs* (Berkeley, CA: University of California Press, 1977).

[17] Forman, S. *The Raft Fishermen* (Bloomington, IN: Indiana University Press, 1967).

[18] "The Need for Human Sciences Research in the Atlantic Coast Fisheries," *J. Fish.Res. Board Can.* 35(7) :1031-1049 (1978)

CHAPTER 2
MIGRATION, MODERNIZATION AND GOVERNMENT POLICY IN A CHANGING NEWFOUNDLAND COMMUNITY

Gerald M. Britan
Department of Anthropology
Northwestern University

INTRODUCTION

Since World War II, anthropologists have been abandoning the description of cultural statics to analyze modernization and change. However, a comprehensive perspective on culture as a framework for adaptive human coping is only now emerging (e.g. Barth [1], and Bennett [2]). This perspective attempts to synthesize the social, psychological, biological and ecological variables that are involved in the survival of human populations and the fulfillment of their wants. Its greatest challenge has been the development of a theory adequate for interrelating phenomena from such disparate domains.

One promising approach has centered explicitly on individual decision-making as an interface between material conditions and social and cultural trends. Such an approach translates the macroteleology of "cultural coping" into a micropurposive rationality of individual actors, whose choices, while reflecting existing social and ecological conditions can also modify them [3, 4]. Recent studies [5-8] have considered the specific factors affecting productive decision-making in particular empirical settings, but little progress has been made in relating types of decision processes to more general social and cultural classifications.

This chapter explores the relationship between behavioral choice and productive organization in the Newfoundland fishing community of St. Brendan's. The specific focus is on migration; spatial mobility as a means of coping with the environment that improves both individual and community fitness. Such adaptation has been important on St. Brendan's from initial settlement in the early 1800s to the present, although the nature and magnitude of migration and the locus of migration decision-making has varied markedly over this time. These migration changes reflect broader shifts in St. Brendan's economy from a traditional local fishery, to a schooner fishery, to individualized cash fishing and wage labor, to increasing immersion in the political bureaucracy of an intruding state. Thus, although the fact that St. Brendan's is a fishing village tells us little, the nature of production organization in its fishery has a strong influence on other behavioral choices and on the community's participation in modernization and change.

THE TRADITIONAL COMMUNITY

St. Brendan's has always been a somewhat isolated community located on a small island off Newfoundland's northeast coast, 200 miles from the capital city. Although the island seems windswept, it provides easy access to prolific fishing grounds and has enough fertile soil to support extensive subsistence farming. Many of the details of early settlement are lost, but the first European immigrants arrived in the Bonavista Bay Archipelago early in the nineteenth century as part of a general migration from communities to the south. Population growth was rapid and by the mid-1800s more than 20 island communities, including St. Brendan's, were well established. On St. Brendan's, high rates of fertility combined with continuing immigration to push the population to more than 500 by the turn of the twentieth century and over 800 by the 1950s [9-16].

Early St. Brendanites pursued a typical Newfoundland *outport* economy, in which economic activities fell into interdependent market and subsistence spheres. Whereas purchased goods such as salt, line, sailcloth and metal were required for fishing, coffee, tea, tobacco, sugar, kerosene and alcohol were culturally defined necessities. The island's marketable products were limited almost exclusively to codfish and, since low prices and uncertain catches made fishing a high-risk, low-yield occupation, subsistence production was essential to keep cash needs low and to provide a reserve of flexibility.

The organization of work for both fishing and farming was structured by age, sex and seasons, not by outside markets. The social matrix for these activities was found in patrilineal groupings, the core of agnates who combined as a crew [17-19]. However, changes occurred early on St. Brendan's, and migration was an important factor from the start.

By the mid-1850s, regional population growth began to exert

Population

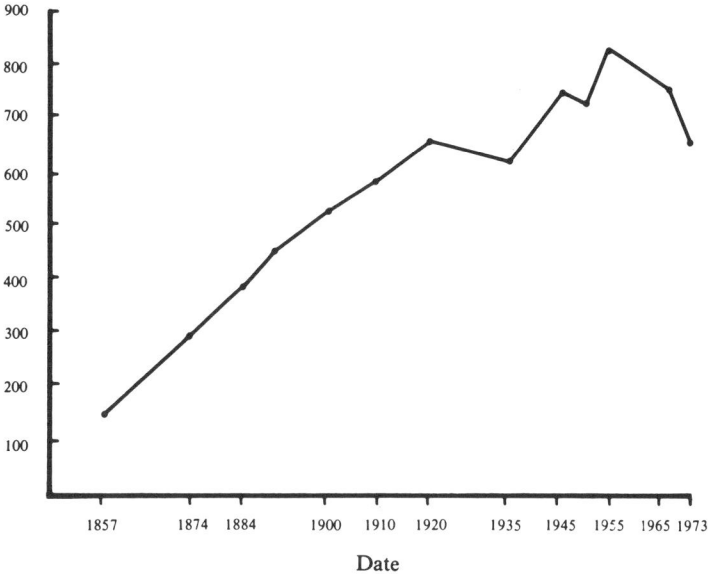

SOURCES:
Census of Newfoundland & Labrador 1857—1945
Census of Canada 1951—1956
Field Notes

Figure 1. The Population of St. Brendan's, 1857—1973.

severe pressure on the limited number of locally available fishing sites. New resources were needed, but economic options were limited. The technology to exploit offshore fishing grounds had not yet been developed, and nearby areas suitable for permanent emigration were already settled. A solution was found, however, by emulating communities to the south that had already responded to population pressure by building large sailing schooners for seasonal *voyages* to fishing grounds off the Labrador coast.

Between 1850 and 1950, the people of St. Brendan's built dozens of sailing schooners. These ships ranged from 60 to 110 feet in length and each carried several smaller boats that were used for inshore fishing in Labrador harbors. Schooners departed St. Brendan's in early June, just after the spring thaw. Fish were caught with the same kind of equipment—jigs, longlines and traps—that were used at home, and then heavily salted for storage. The ships returned to St. Brendan's in the fall, leaving Labrador when their holds were full or when the weather became inclement. When the schooners arrived home, everyone joined in to rewash the fish, lightly salt them, and lay them on wooden *flakes* to dry in the sun. Once the fish were made and sufficiently dried for shipment, they were reloaded on the schooners for delivery to merchant sponsors in larger towns who had supplied capital for shipbuilding and outfitting (for more detailed discussion see Britan [5, 12]).

The advent of fishing schooners precipitated major changes in the organization of production on St. Brendan's. The agnatic core of the nuclear family, which had previously supplied labor for the purely local fishery, could not supply enough manpower for the increased scale of the Labrador voyage. Although nonkinsmen occasionally worked as sharemen on the schooners, changing patterns in the fishery were soon reflected in broader social and economic alterations. Extended households, called "crowds," developed, supported by more diffuse, agnatic ties that linked neighboring crowds into common "gardens," which engaged in balanced exchanges of labor and goods.

The crowd typically consisted of a father or a group of brothers and their adult sons who coordinated production in fishing, subsistence farming and other economic endeavors. Its head was the skipper, ideally the father or oldest sibling. In theory, the skipper controlled all of the crowd's income, purchased supplies for fishing and consumption, scheduled work and selected economic strategies. However, since cleavages in the crowd were a constant worry, consultation and a guise of egalitarianism were maintained.

The crowd's organizational functions quickly transcended the schooner fishery, for in St. Brendan's high-risk, low-yield environment, flexibility and the ability to exploit all possible alternatives were essential. The crowd was the locus of a common enterprise that could combine a range of productive strategies, including those involving migration, and which could thus minimize the repercussions of one alternative's failure. For example, while most male members of a crowd migrated to the Labrador fishery each year, others remained at home to fish locally and to farm. The returns from all of these activities were pooled and, over time, the number of men pursuing each alternative was adjusted to select past success to ensure sufficient profits.

The Labrador fishery, and the extended family system within which it was embedded, was the basis for a flexible economic adaptation on St. Brendan's which persisted for nearly a century. The crowd was able to encompass significant changes in fishing technology, work patterns and economic activities, while maintaining the same basic structure. Throughout this period, migration alternatives, first summer fishing in Labrador and later seasonal work in winter lumbering, had a continuing importance. Such spatial mobility did not, however, involve individual decisions so much as social assessments of economic alternatives by the agnatic group. Yet, when wage labor opportunities later increased, migration decisions did become individualized, and social relationships were altered in turn.

CHANGING PATTERNS OF LABOR MIGRATION

Wage-paying activities that could be combined with fishing and farming were always avidly sought by St. Brendanites, but jobs were scarce during most of the nineteenth century. It was not until the 1890s that development of regional lumbering and mining enterprises provided anything more than occasional off season employment. By 1900 temporary and permanent labor migration had become more realistic options, but the decision to migrate remained grounded in the productive organization of the fishery. Two distinct periods of wage migration can be identified (Table 1) [9-14, 21, 22]. Between 1890 and 1940, migration was only an occasional alternative, and migration decisions

Table 1. Migration Rates: St. Brendan's 1890—1970

Time Period	Emigration Rate (Outmigrants/1000) Year
1890—1900	-3.9
1900—1910	3.8
1910—1920	11.0
1920—1935	15.0
1935—1945	-0.4
1945—1950	41.0
1950—1955	2.3
1955—1960	28.0
1960—1965	36.0
1965—1970	39.0

Sources:
Census of Newfoundland and Labrador 1890—1945
Census of Canada 1951—1966
Parish Records
Field Notes

were made within the continuing social context of the extended family. Between 1940 and 1960, however, migration decisions became individualized as part of a thorough economic change that undermined the traditional social fabric and helped bring about the Labrador fishery's demise.

Labor Migration from 1890 to 1940

Before Newfoundland's confederation with Canada in 1949, St. Brendan's remained isolated from more developed North American labor markets. Until the 1890s, local wage labor alternatives were nearly nonexistent, and permanent emigration primarily consisted of out-marrying women and a few out-marrying men. By the end of the nineteenth century, however, the growth of mining and lumbering in the Bonavista Bay region opened a wider range of nonfishing options. As a result, both permanent and temporary labor migration rapidly increased.

Migration data for St. Brendan's were obtained from parish records and government censuses [9-16, 21, 22] and were cross-checked for accuracy against elicited genealogies. Equally precise information on the availability of wage labor during this period is not available, but government reports and informant accounts clarify the general trends in the regional economy.

Conventional migration theory would correlate these changing St. Brendan's migration rates with the strength of economic pushes and pulls (Figure 2). Thus, outmigration would be expected to be high when outside job possibilities were good and when fishing profits were bad, and outmigration would be low when conditions were reversed. This, however, was not the case. The reasons lie in the social and economic context within which decisions to migrate were made.

Despite the strong regional economic pull of rapidly growing lumbering and mining enterprises at the end of the nineteenth century, a net immigration to St. Brendan's continued. Moreover, when there was a sharp decline in the number of locally available jobs between 1900 and 1915, outmigration from St. Brendan's began to rise steadily, a trend which continued when strong economic pulls reappeared during the 1920s. Outmigration from St. Brendan's did drop sharply and remain at low levels during the depression of the 1930s, but there was a significant lag before this shift occurred. On the other hand, increases in emigration associated with the war years boom of the mid-1940s took place quite rapidly.

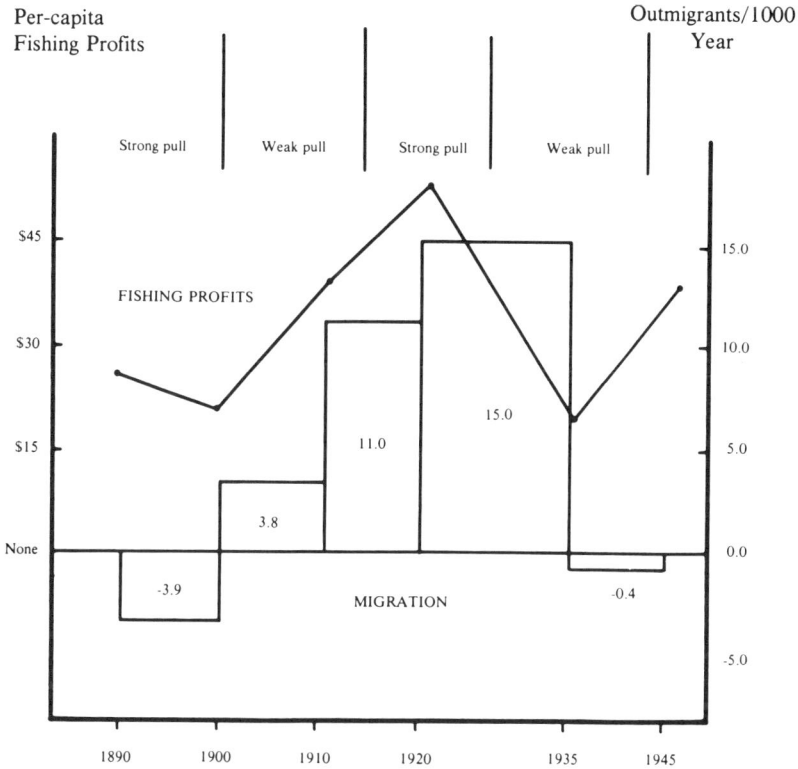

Figure 2. Migration, Fishing Profits, and Economic Pulls: St. Brendan's, 1890—1945.

The relationship between migration and economic pulls on St. Brendan's was, at best, somewhat irregular, and one might hypothesize that these discrepancies resulted from variations in local economic pushes. In traditional St. Brendan's, the best single indicator of economic failure and success was per capita fishing profits, which encompass variations in both catch size and fish prices. Informant accounts, schooner records and government censuses provided a basis for fairly accurate fishing profit calculations, which could then be compared with migration trends.

Between 1890 and 1900, declining fishing profits were unexpectedly associated with declining levels of outmigration. This reversal continued between 1900 and 1920, when rising local fishing profits were associated with steadily increasing rates of outmigration. Indeed, when the number of outmigrants peaked in the early 1920s, St. Brendan's fishing profits peaked as well, which is just the opposite of what would be expected. Between 1920 and 1935, declining fishing profits were more normally associated with high levels of emigration, and a net immigration in the early 1940s occurred during a period of steadily rising fish prices.

Abstract economic pushes and pulls clearly do not provide a satisfactory explanation for historical patterns of migration on St. Brendan's. This does not mean that economic pushes and pulls had no effect on migration. However, the productive organization of the Labrador fishing economy involved a social structure based on extended family relationships, in which migration incentives were assessed not by individuals alone, but by individuals acting as members of social groups. These seemingly contradictory data make sense when they are considered within this broader social context.

During the Labrador fishery, migration decisions involved more than individuals assessing the immediate profitability of wage-paying alternatives. Although people viewed migration as a possible source of greater earnings and greater social freedom, it was always a risky alternative. An analysis of sample migration histories shows that only a quarter of all migrants could expect any long-term success. If employment failed, a migrant would be forced to return home where he was dependent on his crowd for support.

The economy of the crowd was not based on individuals maximizing profits, but on extended households which strove to satisfy their domestic needs. When times were bad, all economic alternatives were pursued and all labor was mobilized, even if marginal, to insure that basic subsistence needs were met [23,24]. Informants accounts and sample migration histories reveal that at such times the crowd was unwilling and unable to absorb the risk of letting some of its members migrate. In good times, on the other hand, there was a surplus of labor, and the crowd could absorb the risk that increasing outmigration implied. Therefore, it becomes understandable why emigration rates were highest at times when both the local economy *and* outside wage labor possibilities were good.

In the Labrador fishery adaptation, extended kin groups were the minimal economic unit. Profit and loss were not individualized. The crowd organized production and social life and translated the individual aspirations of its members into corporate decisions. Descriptions of this decision-making reveal that it was the crowd, through consultations among its skipper and other male adults, which weighed the balance between workers and consumers. The crowd as a corporate whole decided whether it could survive the loss of labor that migration involved, support a larger proportion of nonproductive hands, and reabsorb outmigrants if their economic strategies failed.

Labor Migration from 1940 to 1960

Beginning with the World War II, labor migration from St. Brendan's increased markedly. The local demographic shift resulting from increasing rates of emigration undermined the social basis of the Labrador fishery and helped transform the entire adaptation. In a remarkably short time, the extended family fishery was replaced by individual households that were competing in a wage and cash economy. The process of continuing modernization had begun.

The initial stimulus for this change was the construction of a number of military and communications bases throughout Newfoundland and Labrador during the 1940s. The associated need for local workers created a much stronger and more stable labor pull than had ever before existed in the area. Migration was no longer a poorly understood, high-risk alternative, but rather a realistic opportunity, especially for the young men whose labor was most eagerly sought. Yet, if these same young men remained at home, they would be socially and financially dependent on their crowd for many years. Under the pressure of continuing acculturation, migration for the first time offered clear advantages, and the decision to migrate quickly became individualized. As risk declined, the crowd could no longer hold the personal aspirations of its individual members in check.

The organization of production in the schooner fishery, however, was based on the availability of a continuing pool of dependent labor. As the number of young men working off the island increased, the labor pool of several agantic crowds became too depleted to provide complete schooner crews. Alternative recruiting methods were tried, such as the use of nonkin "sharemen," but few men were available. By the mid-1940s, several skippers were forced to beach their ships. This released older men into the labor pool, whose entry into the migrant work force was made easier by already developing networks.

By the late 1940s, the initial spate of construction work finally began to slack and, although some younger men stayed away permanently, other migrants quickly returned to St. Brendan's. For a time the Labrador fishery resurged, but the extended family had already been weakened and the agnatic core of the schooner crew was often supplemented by sharemen outsiders. When jobs, primarily in

construction and coastal freighting, again increased in the years following Canadian confederation, outmigration increased as well. Schooners
were beached once more and the Labrador fishery ground to a rapid
halt.

However, while the seasonal voyages to Labrador ceased, fishing
continued to be an important economic alternative for St. Brendanites.
Regional outmigration to wage-paying jobs relieved population pressure and reopened niches in the local fishery. Older men, who had a
difficult time finding wage labor (or who had large investments in
fishing gear and agnates available as fishing partners), returned to the
local fishery using smaller trap skiffs with crews of two to four men.
There were also sporadic attempts to reorganize the Labrador fishery
as a rational economic endeavor using 40- to 60-foot longliners and
nonkin based crews, but these failed when fish catches declined under
the influence of foreign offshore trawling.

The shift in productive organization from large kin-bound enterprises to smaller-scale fishing and migratory wage labor wrought major
changes in the social and cultural life on St. Brendan's. As the environment changed, the locus of economic choice shifted from the corporate
crowd to a growing number of individual-decisionmakers, and other
accoutrements of the Labrador fishery economy began rapidly to disap-
pear. Soon the common fields, root cellars, and dwellings of the crowd
were only a memory. Residence became neolocal. Informal visiting
extended beyond the confines of the family to encompass workmates
and friends. Traditional gatherings, the family-centered "times," were
soon replaced by islandwide socials. And a newly built community hall
became the center of village life.

The 1950s and 1960s were trying decades for the people of St.
Brendan's, as continuing acculturative forces combined to create a
"modern" community. In the face of the new options and pressures
from growing regional and national bureaucracies, new community
institutions were founded such as the parish council, the school board,
the roads committee and the community development board. In these
formal associations, important decisions were again deindividualized,
but the old kinship idiom was replaced with political forms dictated by
the requirements of outside bureaucracies. In this new St. Brendan's,
migration strategies retained a continuing importance, but individual
behavior choices were supplemented by new decisions that the community had to make as a whole.

THE RESETTLEMENT ISSUE

Despite the increasing pull from wage labor opportunities, St.
Brendan's population continued to grow throughout the 1950s and

early 1960s. While net emigration was increasing, most of those leaving were young unmarried men. Former migrants returned during the slack period of the early 1950s to marry, start families and create a miniature baby boom (see Table I). These men were satisfied with seasonal wage employment and valued the security that St. Brendan's provided through subsistence farming and fishing. Soon, however, government programs of economic development and community resettlement injected new factors into the situation.

By the mid-1950s, the Newfoundland government had decided that its economic development program would require isolated fishing villages to relocate to areas of anticipated industrial growth. Early government resettlement programs were quite restrictive. Grants were provided to individual families, but only if they moved to designated growth centers and only if at least 90% of the community left at the same time. Vacated land became the property of the government, and continued economic use was, at least in theory, prohibited. (For a detailed discussion of the nature and problems of resettlement, see Iverson and Matthews [25].) Despite these restrictions, a number of island communities began preparing to move. Indeed, some left even before the program went into effect.

The government resettlement program was remarkably ineffective. Numerous migrants arrived in growth centers not only without jobs, but without housing. Relocation grants quickly evaporated as merchants charged exorbitant rates for the transportation of personal belongings. Facing dismal prospects in their new surroundings, many families turned to government relief or, when possible, to the old fishing sites they had left behind. St. Brendan's did not relocate, and today it is the only island community that remains in Bonavista Bay.

Resettlement remained a hot issue on St. Brendan's throughout the early 1960s. In many ways, the debate united the islander's dispersed families into a corporate community for the first time. A number of meetings were held to discuss the pros and cons of moving and staying before residents finally decided that if the community moved, it should move en masse to a single new site. A committee was established to investigate possible places for relocation, but progress toward an ultimate decision was slow.

There are several reasons why the people of St. Brendan's resisted resettlement more strongly than their neighbors. The island traditionally supported one of the most successful fisheries in the bay, and many residents saw little advantage in relocating. Moreover, as Catholics living in a primarily Protestant region, St. Brendanites felt isolated and strongly attached to their traditional ways. The resettlement experience of neighboring communities reinforced the feeling that opportunities in "growth" centers were for the most part illusory; meanwhile, the economic opportunities at home were improving. Regional population decline and improved marketing networks made the local fishery more profitable. Soon, fishermen were able to sell flounder, herring, salmon and lobster as well as the ubiquitous cod.

As time went on, the formal community groups which had crystallized around the issue of resettlement turned their attention to obtaining improvements in local services. By the mid-1960s, government aid was galvanized to build roads, schools and power plants, and to provide ferry, telephone and medical services. Instead of moving to a modern community, the accoutrements of a modern community were brought to St. Brendan's.

The government resettlement program spurred this change by translating the individual idiom of adaptive choice that had emerged in the 1940s and '50s into a political process that encompassed the entire community. Factions and informal leaders emerged within a decision-making structure that reflected the requirements of an external bureaucracy. Certainly, such organized, communitywide decision-making was without precedent on St. Brendan's.

From the beginning, moreover, the issue of resettlement created a sharp schism in the community. Migration was not equally advantageous to all. It was most profitable for people whose skills would enable them to find regular wage work in a new locale. Thus, a sizable minority, mostly younger families, wanted to leave the island, but a nearly equal segment of older households adamantly refused to budge. The majority was in between. They would prefer to find wage paying jobs and move to the mainland, but doubted that their search for employment would be successful.

The problem was resolved in the late 1960s when the government resettlement program was itself altered. Instead of requiring a communal move, support was provided to individual households. In the new program's first year, ten large families left St. Brendan's, a significant portion of the proresettlement vote. Since then, a few additional families have left each year. Thus, spatial mobility decisions on St. Brendan's have again been individualized. Yet, at the same time the political idiom of formal communitywide choice has expanded to encompass a growing range of activities.

THE CONTEMPORARY COMMUNITY

Except for the rotting hulks of beached schooners, there is little to remind a modern visitor to St. Brendan's of the Labrador fishery, which was so important less than a generation ago. Although nearly a quarter of the households still fish and more than half engage in at least some subsistence production, the economy is strongly based on wage labor and cash. Modern social and political institutions, e.g., a post office, a central school, a community hall, development committees and public works projects, are beginning to emerge. St. Brendan's has become a place of nuclear households, market decisions and formal associations much like any other Canadian or American town.

Migration today does have a continued importance, but in a social and economic context that is greatly altered. Individuals now see permanent wage work as their ideal, yet there are only jobs at home for 10% of the population. Given the region's perennially high unemployment (seasonally as much as 25%), unskilled jobs are difficult to find off the island as well. People, therefore, pursue flexible and spatially mobile economic strategies (Figure 3), seeking a variety of employment in a range of locations for varying periods of time. The most promising options have historically included seasonal construction work in Labrador and work on coastal freighters, but skilled St. Brendanites have migrated as far as Boston and Toronto in search of work.

Young men, especially if they have technical skills, have the best chance of finding permanent off-island jobs. As a result, during the past decade the bulk of each high school class has left St. Brendan's in search of work. Except for occasional visits, most of these migrants leave permanently. Thus, St. Brendan's migration rates have remained high, averaging more than 30 persons per year. With falling birth rates, the island's population has begun to decline rapidly. After reaching a peak of more than 800 residents in 1960, there are no more than 650 St. Brendanites today (see Figure 1).

However, even young men migrants face an insecure future. Each year at least three or four young men lose their off-island jobs and return to St. Brendan's, if only for a short interval. These men rarely turn to fishing or subsistence production, but bide their time, collecting unemployment insurance while waiting for personal networks to communicate word of new job openings. These men are committed away from the island.

Older or less skilled men find the search for permanent off-island employment even more difficult. if they are lucky enough to find full-time jobs, these men are likely to leave permanently. But most St.

```
┌─────────────────────────────────┐
│ BUSINESSMEN                     │
└─────────────────────────────────┘

┌─────────────────────────────────┐
│ MEN WITH PERMANENT              │   PERMANENT
│ OFF-ISLAND JOBS                 │   OUTMIGRANTS →
└─────────────────────────────────┘

┌─────────────────────────────────┐
│ MEN WITH PERMANENT              │
│ LOCAL JOBS                      │
│ ─ ─ ─ ─ ─ ─ ─ ─ ─ ─             │
│ SKILLED SEASONAL                │
│ WAGE LABOR MIGRANTS             │
└─────────────────────────────────┘

┌─────────────────────────────────┐
│ UNSKILLED SEASONAL              │
│ WAGE LABOR MIGRANTS             │
│ ─ ─ ─ ─ ─ ─ ─ ─ ─ ─             │
│ FISHERMEN/SUBSISTENCE           │
│ FARMERS                         │
└─────────────────────────────────┘

┌─────────────────────────────────┐
│ RECIPIENTS OF                   │
│ GOVERNMENT AID/                 │
│ SUBSISTENCE FARMERS             │
│ ─ ─ ─ ─ ─ ─ ─ ─ ─ ─             │
│ RECIPIENTS OF                   │   PERMANENT
│ GOVERNMENT AID ONLY             │   OUTMIGRANTS →
└─────────────────────────────────┘
```

(left vertical axis label: INCREASING INCOME)

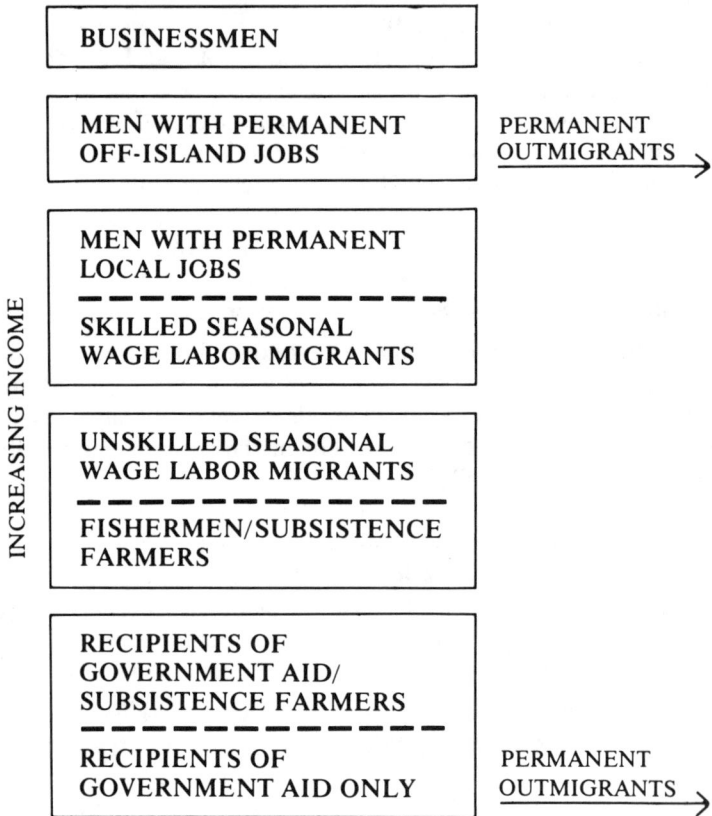

Figure 3. Economic Strategies on Contemporary St. Brendan's

Brendan's men are unable to secure year-round or even seasonal employment. While nearly all St. Brendan's men seek summer wage work, only about 70% find jobs in a given year. For those who fail, local economic resources provide useful options. It is these men, along with older retirees, who turn to local fishing and farming as a more profitable and, in their view, dignified alternative to government relief.

During the Labrador fishery period, adaptive decisions occurred within the social context of the crowd , which often severely restricted an individual's choice of alternatives, including migration. Later, in the face of new government programs, resettlement became a community-wide political choice. Today migration has become an individualized strategy for seeking personnel benefits. The social restrictions of the past, however, have been replaced by a new set of stark economic realities. Migration is now not simply possible, but often necessary. Change has ignored local development possibilities in the fishery and created a large, flexible and underemployed work force. Despite, or perhaps because of, the government's efforts, the people seem little better off than they were before.

MIGRATION, DECISION-MAKING AND COMMUNITY CHANGE

Migration has been the subject of intensive study at least since Ravenstein's classic writings [26], and a range of alternative viewpoints has developed. The predominant geographic and demographic perspective, generated primarily in the West, focuses on quantitative models that relate abstract economic pushes and pulls to the character and strength of migration streams and counterstreams [27, 28]. Anthropological studies, on the other hand, generally concentrate on particular migration processes, examining the effects of migration on sending communities [29-31] the experience of participants [32, 33] or the adjustment of migrants to new urban settings [34, 36]. This microlevel analysis has emphasized either culturally idiosyncratic decision-making [37, 38] or the external realities of political and economic pressure [29, 39-41]. It has rarely synthesized the broad range of political, economic, ecological, social and cultural factors that underlie any particular situation of behavioral choice.

Migration decisions are not made in isolation, but rather in relation to a wide range of behavioral alternatives that exist in any political and economic context. Individuals evaluate these alternatives in terms of their payoffs in the environment, their accessibility through existing social arrangement, and their congruence with established cultural values. Behavioral decisions vary to cope with ecological and economic stress in a continuing adaptive process.

This chapter has examined the changing nature and implications of migration in St. Brendan's for individuals and their community. In so doing it has tried to integrate an analysis of spatial mobility into a more general appraisal of St. Brendan's changing social and economic structures. The basis for this approach can be found in Firth's [42] definition of social organization as the patterns that arise from independent behavioral choices, and from Barth's [1] elaboration of that theory to include goal oriented actors constrained by environment and society. This involves:

reasoning people who weigh the alternatives available within existing social and economic conditions, selecting those activities that best meet their needs . . . . a synthetic model of social process that integrates the analysis of environment and choice in both stability and change [3].

Bennett [2] recently clarified this adaptational framework as a major alternative to interpretive approaches in anthropology. The adaptational model focuses on human "coping, dynamic human purposes, wants and needs," and the decision-making processes through which humans seek to achieve them [2]. This involves not only the environment in which the alternatives are manifest and the results are determined, but also the cultural knowledge through which options are perceived and evaluated. Adaptation is continuous. Environmental shifts alter individual decisions, thereby creating new behavioral patterns which in turn transform both culture and environment.

Over the past 150 years, a variety of adaptive strategies have emerged on St. Brendan's, and the community and its productive base have altered enormously. Migration, however, has retained a continuing importance. While changes in migration alternatives came from external conditions such as the fishery environment, developing markets and intruding bureaucracies, internal factors still influenced individuals as they purposely selected strategies to achieve personal ends. Their choices were conditioned by existing social and cultural contexts, and those contexts were altered by their decision in turn.

Thus, migration represented very different decisions for St. Brendanites as local adaptations varied over time. Although choice was ultimately individual, it was embedded in existing productive arrangements and political groupings. Three major periods and types of migration decisions can be identified.

During St. Brendan's Labrador fishery, production, distribution and consumption were designed to satisfy the needs of corporate extended families and not to maximize individual profits. Patterns of migration reflected the needs of the agnatic crowd and the nature of the household economy, within a high risk, low yield environment. As a result, migration levels were highest not when local economic pushes were strongest, but when the crowd could best afford to absorb the risks of increased emigration.

When opportunities for wage labor expanded, however, latent tensions in the traditional social system were expressed in rising migration rates among the young and the demise of the traditional fishery. A new cash-oriented, nuclear family community emerged in which economic decisions were, for the most part, individualized. In this context migration decisions centered on individual profit and risk, reflecting the abstract pushes and pulls of the geographic theorists. In concert with other acculturative forces, these changing migration patterns spurred the creation of a modern community.

By the early 1960s, however, migration became embedded in a new social reality. External bureaucracies began intruding. They offered new alternatives and benefits, but required new local social forms before they could be obtained. The migration decision was translated into an issue of community resettlement, and individual choice was embroiled in a formal, political arena of communitywide debate. This shift was mirrored by similar alterations in other domains of social and economic behavior.

An analysis of adaptive coping must account for material reality, that is, environmental alternatives as they actually exist. Yet, in all of the situations we examined, strategic choices were only understandable in terms of the social and cultural forms through which environmental possibilities are perceived and implemented. While modernization and change are manifest in the decisions and behavior of individuals, these are only understandable in terms of the broader social and economic context within which individual choices are made.

CONCLUSIONS

In St. Brendan's, migration decisions were an integral part of community modernization and change. Yet, migration on St. Brendan's is incomprehensible outside of its broader context of social relationships and economic alternatives. This fact has important implications not only for migration and decision theory, but also for an understanding of the relationship between government policy and community change.

Whereas most migration theory seeks to isolate general factors that affect spatial mobility in any setting, we have attempted precisely the opposite. Broad economic forces may account for the flows of people across entire regions, but they cannot explain variations among particular ecological and cultural contexts. Thus they tell us little about the place of migration in community change. An anthropological approach, on the other hand, seeks to account for local change outcomes by viewing migration in terms of the alternatives and constraints that affect specific populations within particular social and economic settings.

In this sense, however, the nature of migration decisions is itself variable. As we saw, the decision to migrate from St. Brendan's is in some instances a choice for each individual, but at other times the choice belongs to a group, e.g., extended families during the Labrador fishery, and formal political associations in modern times. In each of these cases the process of decision-making can only be understood when related to the social organization in which decisions were embedded and their place in a wider political and economic setting.

This point is equally applicable to other decision-making domains. Even in modern industrial societies, most behavioral choices are not individualized market decisions, but social decisions that take place within the particular organizational context of a family, a firm, a university, or the like. Decision-making theorists, therefore, cannot assume that social process is directly reducible to individual dynamics. They must also consider the varying social structures that translate individual decisions into social facts.

The same, of course, is true of government policymakers who seek to direct the course that social process and modernization takes. Until recently the government policies affecting St. Brendan's paid little heed to existing productive forms, and instead imposed a new style of decision-making that was congruent with the formal bureaucracies' own needs. St. Brendan's, as a result, has become a modern town, but a town that is increasingly dependent on government largess and increasingly divorced from its old economic base in the fishery. The situation might be different if government agencies tailored their policies to local resources, local groupings and local aspirations and supported the redevelopment of a modern, but independent, local fishery. This has, in fact, become the government's attitude in recent years.

The fact that St. Brendan's was a fishing village seems to have had little impact on its course of migration and fishing production at any point in time. The extended family schooner crowd as opposed to individualized local fishing did have a significant effect, not only on migration decisions, but on the course of change as a whole. The findings suggest that despite variations among maritime communities, similarities in their fishing organization may well imply further similarities in adaptive decision-making and modernization processes. Maritime ethnography, therefore, provides a favorable setting for testing broader propositions about the relationships among productive organizations, behavioral decision-making, and community change.

It seems clear that a practically applicable theory of social change cannot focus exclusively either on macrolevel social and economic forces or microlevel individual decisions. While broad political and economic shifts may be ultimate causes of change, they tell us little about process within particular communities. Conversely, individual adaptive coping is necessarily idiosyncratic when divorced from the community institutions within which environmental possibilities are realized. What is needed is a synthesizing approach which translates broader change forces into particular patterns of individual choice and community change. This is the kind of model upon which our analysis of migration, modernization and government policy in St. Brendan's is based.

REFERENCES

[1] Barth, F. "On the Study of Social Change," *Am. Anthropologist* 69:661-699 (1967).

[2] Bennett, J. W. "Anticipation, Adaptation, and the Concept of Culture in Anthropology," *Science* 192:847-853 (1976).

[3] Britan and Denich 1976 (see manuscript pp. 1 & 18).

[4] Boehm, C. "Rational Pre-selection from Hamadrayas to *Homo sapiens:* The Place of Decisions in Adaptive Process," *Am. Anthropologist* 80:265-296 (1978).

[5] Britan, G. "Fishermen and Workers: The Processes of Stabilty and Change in a Rural Newfoundland Community," PhD Dissertation, Columbia University, New York (1974).

[6] Chibnik, M. "Economic Strategies of Small Farmers in Stann Creek District, British Honduras," PhD Dissertation, Columbia University, New York (1975).

[7] Ortiz, S. *Uncertainties in Peasant Farming* (New York: Humanities Press, 1973).

[8] Rutz, H. J. "Individual Decisions and Functional Systems: Economic Rationality and Environmental Adaptation," *Am. Ethnologist* 4:156-174 (1977).

[9] "Census of Newfoundland and Labrador," Newfoundland Printing Office, St. John's, Newfoundland (1890).

[10] "Census of Newfoundland and Labrador," Newfoundland Printing Office, St. John's, Newfoundland (1900).

[11] "Census of Newfoundland and Labrador," Newfoundland Printing Office, St. John's, Newfoundland (1910).

[12] "Census of Newfoundland and Labrador," Newfoundland Printing Office, St. John's, Newfoundland (1920).

[13] "Census of Newfoundland and Labrador," Newfoundland Printing Office, St. John's, Newfoundland (1935).

[14] "Census of Newfoundland and Labrador," Newfoundland Printing Office, St. John's, Newfoundland (1945).

[15] "Census of Canada," Government Printing Office, Ottawa, Ontario (1951).

[16] "Census of Canada," Government Printing Office, Ottawa, Ontario (1956).

[17] Faris, J. C. "Cat Harbor: A Newfoundland Fishing Settlement" Institute of Social and Economic Research, Memorial University of Newfoundland, St. John's, Newfoundland (1972).

[18] Firestone, M. M. "Brothers and Rivals: Patrilocality in Savage Cove," Institute of Social and Economic Research, Memorial University of Newfoundland, St. John's, Newfoundland (1967).

[19] Nemec, T. F. "I Fish with My Brother," in North Atlantic Fishermen, R. Andersen and C. Wadel, Eds. (St. John's, Newfoundland; Institute of Social and Economic Research, Memorial Univerity of Newfoundland, 1972).

[20] Britan, G. "Environment and choice in Rapid Social Change," Am. Ethnologist 3:55-72 (1976).

[21] "Census of Canada," Government Printing Office, Ottawa, Ontario (1961).

[22] "Census of Canada," Government Printing Office, Ottawa, Ontario (1966).

[23] Chayanov, A. V. The Theory of Peasant Economy (Homewood, IL: Irwin Press, 1966).

[24] Sahlins, M. "The Intensity of Domestic Production in Primitive Societies," in Studies in Economic Anthropology, G. Dalton, Ed. (Washington, DC: American Anthropological Association, 1971), pp. 30-51.

[25] Iverson, N., and D. Matthews. "Communities in Decline: An Examination of Household Resettlement in Newfoundland," Institute of Social and Economic Research, Memorial University of Newfoundland, St. John's, Newfoundland (1966).

[26] Ravenstein, E. G. "The Laws of Migration," J. Roy. Statis. Soc. 48:167-235 (1885).

[27] Lee, E. "A Theory of Migration," *Demography* 3:47-57 (1966).

[28] Gade, O. "Geographic Research and Human Spatial Interaction Theory," in *Migration and Anthropology*, R. F. Spencer, Ed. (Seattle, WA: University of Washington Press, 1970).

[29] Harris, M. "Labor Migration among the Mozambique Thonga," in *Social Change: The Colonial Situation*, I. Wallerstein, Ed. (New York: John Wiley & Sons, Inc., 1959), pp. 91-106.

[30] Philpott, S. B. "The Implications of Migration for Sending Societies," in *Migration and Anthropology*, R. F. Spencer, Ed. (Seattle, WA: University of Washington Press, 1970), pp. 9-20.

[31] Van Velsen. "Labor Migration as a Positive Factor in the Continuity of Tonga Tribal Society," *Econ. Devel. Cultural Change* 8:265-278 (1960).

[32] Block, H. "Changing Domestic Roles among Polish Immigrant Women," *Anthropol. Quart.* 49:3-10 (1976).

[33] Mayer, P. *Townsmen and Tribesmen* (Capetown, South Africa: Oxford University Press, 1971).

[34] Denich, B. "Migration and Network Manipulation in Yugoslavia," in *Migration and Anthropology*, R. F. Spencer, Ed. (Seattle, WA: university of Washington Press, 1970).

[35] Elken, W. *Migrants and Proletarians* (London, England: Oxford University Press, 1960).

[36] Little, K. *West African Urbanization* (Cambridge, England: Cambridge University Press, 1965).

[37] Douglas, W. A. "Peasant Emigrants: Reactors or Actors?" in *Migration and Anthropology*, R. F. Spencer, Ed. (Seattle, WA: University of Washington Press, 1970).

[38] Wolpert, D. "Behavioral Aspects of the Decision to Migrate," Regional Science Association Paper No. 15 (1965).

[39] Amin, S. "Introduction," in *Modern Migrations in Western Africa*, S. Amin, Ed. (London, England: Oxford University Press, 1974), pp. 65-124.

[40] Berg, E. S. "The Economics of the Migrant Labor System," in *Urbanization and Migration in West Africa*, H. Kuper, Ed. (Berkeley, CA: University of California Press, 1965), pp. 160-181.

[41] Mitchell, J. C. "The Causes of Labor Migration," *Bull. Inter-African Labor Inst.* 6:12-47 (1959).

[42] Firth, R. *Elements of Social Organization* (London, England: Watts, 1951).

CHAPTER 3
FISHERIES MANAGEMENT: INTENDED
RESULTS AND UNINTENDED CONSEQUENCES

M. Estellie Smith
Department of Anthropology and Sociology
State University of New York at Oswego

The implementation of the Fisheries Conservation and Management Act (FCMA) of 1976 created a Fishery Conservation Zone (FCZ) under the control of the United States. (It should be noted that we actually only extended our conservation zone 188 miles, not 197, since at time of the implementation of FCMA the United States already exercised economic control over a total of 12 miles beyond the shore.) Along with the FCMA came the mandate to create, along with other administrative structures, regional fisheries management councils (RFMC). The FCMA does not apply to economic resources other than the fisheries, and the FCZ is not part of our "territorial waters" as the term is defined by international jurists. This distinction is important since it reflects the government's fundamental stance that the FCMA is designed to protect national economic interests and the food resources of the world commonweal, but not to interfere with military, scientific or other activities. The position is explicit that the United States will, when feasible, manage the fisheries in this FCZ in terms of international equity based on historical precedent, international law and treaties, and human need. Its congressional proponents stressed this in the legislative debates, and thus laid the groundwork for the FCMA to be seen not as a move to appropriate and preempt a historically common resource of mankind for the sake of national greed so much as to conserve for all and protect from a few man's future access to those resources. This primacy of the need for immediate conservation measures, as opposed to the secondary consideration of immediate economic benefits, proved to be a stumbling block in the implementation of management plans as will be elaborated below.

This chapter focuses on the dynamics of the current formative period, the beginning of which was signaled by the formation of the RFMC. It will concern itself with delineating the transactions of the New England council especially, as that council conducts its affairs in an interface with the public in the open arena of monthly meetings and periodic hearings. The dynamics of these encounters as they affect the production of management plans for the fisheries in the New England region will be set forth in the hope that others will be able to understand better the complexities of the process. In tracing this process, I will attempt to show that the differing positions that are held by those engaged in formulating management details and principles tend to generate unforeseen consequences.

Assumed here is that underlying the diversity of interests are two technological components. On the one hand, we have artifactual industrial hardware, the purpose of which is to expand and increase the capacity of the involved sectors to control exploitation of ecozone resources. The most obvious hardware is, of course, that of the industry itself, i.e., vessels, gear, equipment, and processing and packaging machinery. Not so obvious, but equally important is the hardware of the administrative and scientific sectors, e.g., computers, databanks, and information retrieval equipment.

On the other hand is the mentifactual, conceptual software, the design of which is aimed at expanding the capacity of the involved sectors to conserve ecozone resources. Software here will be defined as the concepts and/or conceptual and human organizational systems that are specifically designed tools used to implement an exploitive technology. Examples are not only such scientific tools as the concepts of maximum sustainable yield (MSY) and optimum yield (OY), statistical analysis, sampling procedures, computer programs, systems analysis and similar tools of technicians as well as professional personnel, but also the constructs of organizational and associational entities such as government bureaucracies, the RFMC and special interest groups like the Massachusetts Inshore Draggerman's Association (MIDA).

The position that technology includes not only material tools (artifacts) but also conceptual and organizational constructs (mentifacts) departs from the dominant traditions of the social sciences which favor a sharp distinction between the two [1]. Very recent literature, however, especially that emanating from those who have a special concern for technology, its workings and broad sociocultural impact, is beginning to favor such a stance. Wenk [2] for example, points out:

When we combine the purely technical or hardware ingredient

of technology with the softer ware and when we examine the full arena of social and environmental impacts, we uncover an exceedingly subtle but potent attribute of technologies: they have the capacity to produce two types of consequences.

> The first-order *results* are intended, usually narrow and explicitly. But the second-order *consequences* are intangible, indeterminant, and often unsuspected (emphasis added) [2].

There are two justifications for this statement. First, it has certain analytical strengths and is productive, i.e., it generates new insights. Second, there is a substantial body of data supporting its legitimacy on ethnoscientific grounds. For example, the only place in "A Legislative History of the FMCA of 1976" [3] in which the word "tool" is used is in the section on definitions which states:

> The underlying management concept of this Act is embodied in the term "optimum sustainable yield." This concept is the cornerstone of the Congressional Findings and Statements of Policy and Purpose set forth in Section 2 of the Act....
>
> Optimum sustainable yield is a refinement of, and takes as a point of departure, the traditional fisheries biology concept of maximum sustainable yield (MSY). MSY is simply a *tool* by which the level of harvest of a given stock can be determined...
>
> The measurement of MSY as a scientific *tool* has been refined dramatically in the past decade...On the other hand, a responsible body of opinion supported the proposition that the Committee should not give statutory recognition to MSY since it was felt that the concept had been discredited as an effective management *tool*.... The Committee believes that the failure of ICNAF has not discredited MSY as a management *tool* but rather points up clearly the fact that MSY is only a tool....[3].

Two more examples drawn from my field data:

> "Organizations like MIDA and CCCFC [Cape Cod Commercial Fishermen's Coalition] are the tools that the fishermen will have to use if they're going to survive" (September 1977); "The Council is simply a tool of NMFS [National Marine Fisheries Service] and Kreps [Secretary of Commerce Juanita Kreps]" (December 1977).

Thus, to use standard anthropological terminology, it is clear that in the cognitive view of the folk (whether they be congressional representatives, scientific advisors, or fishermen and processors) a componential analysis of technological ethnoscience stresses two main elements: machinery and equipment, and concepts and human organizational systems (see Smith [4-6] for other statements utilizing this perspective of technology in a maritime setting).

Data for this chapter have been gathered from three sources: fieldwork in several New England ports since 1971; attendance at the general sessions and public hearings held by the New England Regional Fishery Management Council (June, 1977 to present); use of archival and governmental documents as well as industry periodicals, especially the *National Fisherman* and *Fishing News International;* and assorted statistical reports by NOAA and NMFS.

HISTORICAL BACKGROUND

A brief introduction to the historical events of the hardware technology explosion which has so devastated the world's fishing stocks is in order here. It will provide the *raison d'etre* of the FCMA and the RFMC. It is difficult to grasp the full extent of this aspect of the technological revolution but a few examples may serve to illustrate it. The world's first major commercial net factory was built in 1883 [7]. Otter trawls first appeared in New England in 1905, and were not widely adopted until after World War I. Industrial fishing with integrated fleets centered around factory ships became common only in the late 1950s. It has been little more than a decade since the majority of new commercial fishing vessels have had gear and equipment costs in excess of hull costs. The rise and fall of fisheries has been accelerated in accord with the expanding exploitive capacity of the industry. Fishing communities are still generally rural, and are still considered among the most conservative and slow to change. They are increasingly faced with boomtown rises and declines similar to that which accompanied the growth of the anchovy industry in Peruvian coastal communities. Typical of the process is a description of the Atlantic City fishing industry:

> A commercial fishery was first established in Atlantic City in 1911. In the early years it was a seasonal operation, harvesting local fish, packing them, and then distributing them to nearby eastern markets in spring, summer, and fall. Vessels of the day were powered by sail and oar. This type of fishery continued until the advent of motorized vessels, which increased the range over which the fishermen could operate.
>
> In the 1920s the motorized vessel in combination with the otter trawl increased the efficiency of the fleet to a degree previously undreamed of. Fishermen were able to follow fish on their offshore migration and could fish the wintering ground at the edge of the continental shelf....Between 1955 and 1965...packing the catches and catering to the needs of the fleet were five fish docks and three marine supply dealers. Box factories were born, ice houses expanded existing facilities, and trucking companies developed refrigerated

trailer units. Docking facilities expanded their refrigerated holding facilities, fillet houses were established to better serve the expanded markets in the industry.

As a result of over fishing....As a result of the decline in the industry, personnel sought other fields of employment.

Consequently, the undermanned vessels deteriorated physically, and the owner-operators sold them in other areas, and in some cases lost them at U.S. Marshal's sales.

In the subsequent years no new capital has been investing in fishing vessels in Atlantic City. As a result there are now only eight offshore fishing vessels and ten skiffs operating out of this port. Personnel are difficult to obtain. Because of the loss of income, the docks have deteriorated and are in need of major repairs and improvement [8].

It is significant that humanity's growing technological ability to exploit the stocks was a subject of concern as early as 1893 when a Select Committee of the House of Commons noted that catches and sizes of fish were diminishing in the North Sea fisheries because, "appliances for catching them have of recent years been greatly increased in size and efficiency and the fishing grounds have been largely extended in area" [9]. It was this same concern which led the Swedish government to invite various countries to a conference in Stockholm in 1899, and this in turn led to the formation of the International Council for the Exploration of the Sea in 1902. This was the first of many such organizations concerned with the problem of stock maintenance in the face of the industry's increased technological ability to exploit the resources of the sea. The conclusions were always the same. Expanded research and improved technology were leading to a potentially dangerous situation in depleted stocks.

In describing the evolutionary pattern, a former Fisheries Secretary for England and Wales commented as follows:

The first sign would be the same as that which was already beginning to attract notice in the report of 1893..namely, that the fishing effort required for a given catch would increase....Fishermen would find that by carrying on with the old methods, their catch per boat was taking more time to get and even so, might be declining. The more progressive would search for new and better methods to increase their efficiency, and so their catching power. For a time these more progressive men would do well. They would be securing for themselves a larger share of the available cake. The others would find their catches steadily getting worse, and they would be forced either to take all kinds and sizes of fish, the small and uneconomic as well as the larger and remunerative or themselves have to adopt more modern fishing methods. But as more and more fishermen turned over to more and more efficient fishing methods, total fishing power would increase in relation to the same or probably depleted fish stocks, and the vicious circle would start to turn once more [9].

Thus, we have had repeated warnings concerning the problems which arise when increased technological exploitive skills make man capable of increasing productivity. But, as Aldous Huxley has stated in a warning sounded at the conference on the technological order in 1962: "Evidently we have to have a great many tremendous kicks in the pants before we can learn anything" (cited by Florman [10]).

Despite such danger flags, the post-World War I era saw a tremendous expansion of the industry to exploit the stocks that had managed to rebuild during the low catch period of the war years. But, by the beginning of World War II, the stocks had again declined to significantly marginal levels though, again, a crisis was averted by a second crisis, World War II, which like its predecessor curtailed fishing and allowed the stocks to recover.

The years following the end of the war witnessed an intensified repetition of the earlier drama, and on a wider geographic scale. History did repeat itself, and the same componential growth in fishing effort, due to the same formulas of technological expansion, the same search for new grounds and marketable uses of underutilize species, within the same framework of fleet and vessel size increase, took place once more. Government played a far more significant role in encouraging this expansion than they had in the earlier phase. All nations, whether combatants or not, were faced with the need to deal with shattered, stifled or war-based economies. Not a few benefited from the ready availability of capital through foreign aid programs promulgated by both national and international agencies and the more prosperous Euroamerican countries were anxious to rebuild their own internal industrial and employment structure by providing equipment and machinery to other nations. The governments of many countries began to look to the fisheries as a source of national income as well as needed protein.

Further, the end of colonialism and the emergence of Third World countries, some newly independent and all anxious to break free of foreign economic domination, led these nations to look to the development of the fisheries as a necessary step before those resources were depleted by foreign fleets capable of taking in a single day what their own small, primitive, artisanal fisheries could not land in a year. Protein needs, a desire to build an export base so as to achieve a more favorably inclined balance of payments, and the implications which both of these held for the internal economy and political stability of the ruling government all contributed to the growing thrust of certain countries into the world fisheries scene.

The first inkling of what was to come occurred less than a decade after the war. Britain developed the first factory ship at the Salvesen Yards in Leith, Scotland. The Fairtry I served as an innovative spark and prototype vessel. In a few years, other countries, particularly those of Eastern Europe and Japan, not only copied but rapidly improved the design, as well as expanding the vessels' exploitive capacity by building on the nineteenth century concept of an integrated fleet, complete with logistical support vessels. Rationalized, centralized fleets, in vast armadas of sometimes over 100 units, began to roam the seas. These distant water fleets, complete with catch vessels, processing ships, supply, repair, refueling and hospital units (and even spotter aircraft when appropriate) became usual, familiar sights in the hitherto local fishing grounds of other nations. The tragedy of the commons [11] was unfolding.

By the early 1970s world catch, till then taking significant annual leaps, began to decline, reflecting the inroads made on the resources. Mexico had extended her jurisdiction as early as 1945, and several other Latin American countries had followed her lead. Other countries began to move in similar directions and this led to the United Nations Conferences on the Law of the Sea (UNCLOS), which some say were given their initial impetus by the wealthy nations desiring to maintain de facto control of ocean resources, in whatever capacity (transport, strategic, mining, fishing). Despite the negotiations, not a year passed that some nation did not declare and/or increasingly enforce extension of their territorial waters or resource and economic controls of contiguous zones, particularly the continental shelf area.

Perhaps overconfident that some 25 percent of the world's known stocks lie in North American waters, the United States and Canada resisted such unilateral declarations, publicly pinning their hopes on the UNCLOS conferences culminating in an internationally sanctioned conservation and regulatory scheme. However, by 1972 approximately 3000 foreign vessels representing 23 flags were sighted off the New England coast alone (mostly in the Georges Bank area near Cape Cod) in a one-year period. This wholesale decimation of the stocks, particularly on the Grand Banks and Georges Bank, finally led first Canada and then the United States to move independently.

It had taken less than a decade for the new technology to massively deplete the world's fisheries. The technique of pulse fishing especially wreaked havoc on the stocks, as well as having a domino effect on the entire biomass. Three additional factors probably played an important role in forcing the government to move unilaterally in 1974-1975, after years of ignoring U.S. industry pleas and despite continued strong resistance to such a move by the State Department, the military, and certain sectors of the fishing industry itself.

First, criticism of the International Committee for North Atlantic Fisheries (ICNAF) management attempts grew intense. Second, UNCLOS negotiations gave rise to increasing concern by private corporate interests regarding the future of offshore mineral deposits. Third (and related to the second factor), the oil companies began a *sub rosa* but massive lobbying effort for such a declaration to facilitate their own plans for oil drilling on the continental shelf areas.

Public hearings conducted by a Congressional subcommittee were held in various key locales around the country throughout 1974 (see Reference 12 for a transcript of ten such meetings). The final congressional debates began in 1975 and culminated in the FCMA of 1976, which became law on March 1, 1977.

The FCMA was based on recognition of multiple national and international interests in a multiple-use zone, and the management scenario was designed accordingly. Regional fishery management councils especially reflect that multiplicity of interests and incorporate the concept of the interplay of actors representing special interests against a backdrop of economic, political, social and cultural values, within a technological infrastructure setting.

It may be noted here that the deceptive unity demonstrated by those various sectors during the pre-FCMA hearings was taken as indication that these groups, e.g., NMFS, fishermen of various types, conservationists, shoreside industry representatives, law enforcement and scientific personnel, linked by a common concern for conservation of the stocks and protection of the U.S. fisheries, could work together effectively. Given that, and an underlying theme of the democratic ethos, it was deemed necessary to incorporate all sectors in the decision-making processes which would generate management plans. What was ignored was the fact that it is a common phenomenon that diverse interests band together when faced with a common enemy or the desire to achieve a common goal, but return to sectorial conflict when the one aim has been accomplished. One particular area of dissonance is usually the best way to proceed to the next phase after the initial goal is achieved.

The simplistic view, especially of the industry, that all would be well if only extended jurisdiction would remove foreign fishing from traditional U.S. grounds, bears a striking resemblance to reports on cargo cults, i.e., nativistic, millenarian movements, based on the belief that there will arrive great ships (in this case, our own) loaded with cargo (fish) and bringing happy and prosperous times, after the foreigners are expelled.

> Cargo cults, like other revitalization movements, develop in situations where there is extreme material inequality between societies in contact. Cargo cults in Melanesia, for examples, attempted to explain and erase the differences in material wealth between natives and Europeans [13].

Just so, it was widely believed that inequalities in wealth, resulting from the differences between the antiquated, wooden vessels of the Americans in relation to the high technology ships and gear of the foreigners, would be erased if only "the natives" could regain control and sovereignty over their own territory once again. Once rid of the foreigners, our own fleet could modernize and rebuild and one would see a growth in catch, prosperity, and general well-being.

But the "catch 22" that would face the actors lay in the fact that the industry saw expansion of the fishing effort as the solution to their problems, while administrators and scientists were concentrating on the need to retrench and conserve existing resources. One group was thus concerned with exploitation and *growth in the fisheries,* and the other was aiming for *preservation of the stocks.* One side saw expulsion of the foreigners as the way to gain greater access to the resource. The other side saw that same end as a necessary precondition for gaining regulatory control over the fishing effort. When the Hallelujah Day arrived, one group anticipated halcyon days of expansion, and the other saw an indefinite period of "bite-the-bullet" contraction.

Because anticipated results were in opposition, neither the industry people, on the one hand, nor the administrative and scientific personnel on the other, could fully anticipate the consequences of achieving their goal of gaining jurisdiction over the major portion of the continental shelf and its resources. The FCMA itself, designed with deliberate open-endedness so as to achieve flexibility is, rather, a source of dissonance and frustration as a consequence of its ambiguity. This is particularly true of Section III of the FCMA, which deals with the Fishery Management Plan, as it is designed and implemented by the RFMC, the Department of Commerce officials, scientists, technicians, et al., in cooperation with industry people specifically and the public generally.

Table 1. Technical Aspects of the Regional Fishery Management Councils

---

Members
    Voting
        The principal state official (or his designee) responsible for marine fishery management in each constituent state of the FMC region.*
        The Regional Director of NMFS (who is also the designated federal official responsible for ensuring operational conformity to the FCMA and for appointing a second official who will be responsible for administrative details of that conformity.
        A designated number of individuals† who have knowlege or experience with regard to the fishery resources of the FMC region.
    Nonvoting‡
        The regional or area director of the US Fish and Wildlife Service (or designee).
        The commander of the Coast Guard district for the FMC region (or designee).
        The executive director of the Marine Fisheries Commission for the FMC region (or designee).
        A Department of State representative (or designee).
Staff
    Executive Director
    Staff assistants to Director, as appointed and assigned duties by the council and/or the Executive Director. Staff may be full-time or part-time.

Committee and Panels
    Scientific and Statistical Committee, which must be chartered in the same manner as the RFMC.
    Advisory panels (see above charter provision).

---

*There are eight regions total. The number of states within each region varies.
† For example, 11 for the New England council; 12 for Mid-Atlantic; 8 for South Atlantic; 4 for Caribbean; 11 for Gulf; 8 for Pacific; 7 for North Pacific; and 7 for the Western Pacific.
    Total voting members for each of the above eight councils, respectively, is 17, 19, 13, 7, 17,13, 11, 7.
‡ The Pacific council has one additional nonvoting member appointed by and serving at the pleasure of the Secretary.

This introduction has attempted to lay a framework for the presentation of the structure and process of the council for the New England region, as that council is evolving due to internal and external vectors essentially derived from technologically based cognitive models. The presentation of data and analysis which follows is, by necessity, crude. In addition to the limitations of space, there are the far more significant boundaries imposed by limited access to the workings of the council and other agencies involved and, most importantly, because the entire program is less than a year old at this time and is a fast changing scene with participants still feeling their way into the situation. Finally, it has been outlined with a broad brush because, although limited to observation of one regional council, and therefore containing biases peculiar to that set of data, there is an attempt to blur specifics in order to present material with relevance beyond the confines of New England.

GENERAL ORGANIZATIONAL STRUCTURE OF THE COUNCILS

The FCMA explicitly gives latitude to each regional council to work out actual organizational details (though certain procedures and structures are fixed), especially in the degree of qualitative emphasis which each council chooses to place on the input of the various structural components. Guidelines for the councils' operations are furnished by the Secretary of Commerce, via an Operations Manual [14] provided by NMFS, plus the need for the councils to conform to national standards and the provisions of the Federal Advisory Committee Act (Public Law 92-463), narrow the latitude which specific councils have, particularly in what shall be defined here as the formal (conceptual principles) and technical (specific operational procedures) aspects (see Smith [15] for an expanded statement and analysis of the formal, technical and informal aspects of governing systems).

In general the structure is as shown in Table 1. The production of a management plan is outlined in Figure 1. Suffice it to say here that the formal and technical objectives of the council are summed up in the following excerpt from the joint explanatory statement of the Committee of Conference appended to Public Law 94-265:

> Each Regional Fishery Management Council is authorized and directed, *inter alia,* to develop fishery management plans and amendments to such plans; to submit periodic and other reports to the Secretary of Commerce; to continually review and revise assessments as to optimum yield and allowable foreign fishing; and to conduct other necessary and appropriate activities, with respect to the management and conservation of the fisheries over which it has authority.

> Each Council shall conduct public hearings with respect to the development of fishery management plans and amendments, and with respect to the administration and implementation of the provisions of this legislation. Each Council is directed to establish scientific and statistical committees and necessary advisory panels

to assist in the development or amendment of any fishery management plan. Each advisory panel shall be composed of persons who are either actually engaged in the harvest of, or are knowledgeable and interested in the conservation and management of, the applicable fishery or group of fisheries. The regional Councils and their committees and panels should receive maximum public input. The provisions of the Federal Advisory Committee Act apply, and therefore meetings must be open to the public, with few exceptions.

Thus, the council is charged to:

1. be aware and cognizant of the existence, significance, and present/future implications of raw data (e.g., NMFS landing and market figures) and other relevant reports/analyses, whether such materials deal with biological, economic, social or political factors, on a local, state, regional, national or international basis;

2. develop fisheries management plans and amendments (henceforth in this paper shortened simply as "plans") through the use of such materials available the council also being authorized to

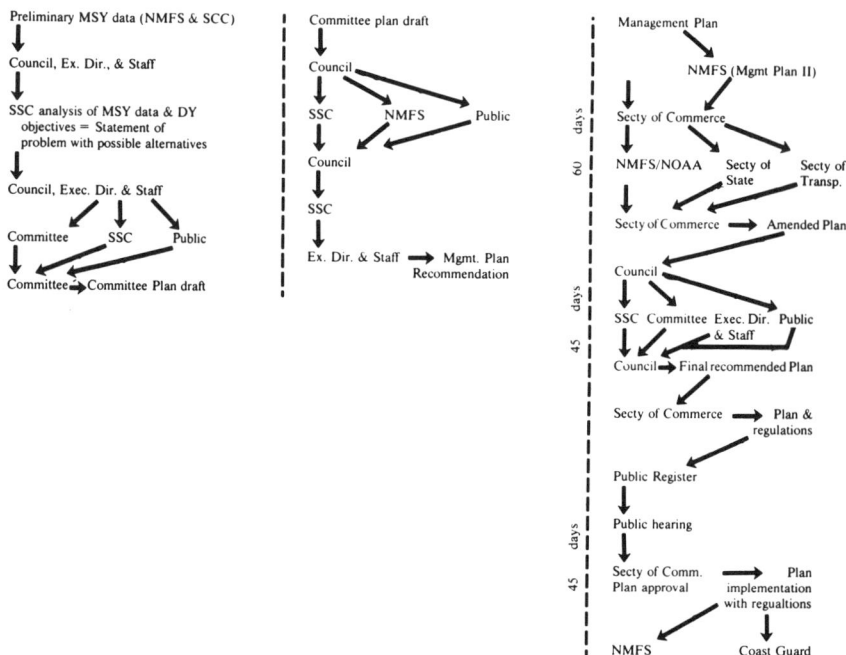

Figure 1. Council Planning.

initiate, design, accumulate and analyze additional material through the use of council staff, other federal agencies, committees, panels, contract consultants and public input;

3. formulate such plans (1) in terms of OY when possible or MSY when necessary (in either case the plan must satisfy environmental impact requirements in the environmental impact statement [EIS] which accompanies the plan) and (2) so that the immediate needs and long-range objectives of biological, social, economic and political concerns are consonant with each other;

4. satisfy as completely as possible the total range of affected persons, the biomass, and existing statutes, regulations, treaties, etc.;

5. take special care that the biological basis of the stocks is conserved and the socioeconomic viability of the fishing industry et al. is enhanced;

6. conduct any other necessary and appropriate activities, and

7. accomplish its work as expeditiously and economically as possible but with a maximum of public and scientific input. Such work is to be done within a total systemic network of the following components:

a. federal and state agencies/sectors: the Department of Commerce (NOAA/NMFS especially), State and Interior (e.g., Bureau of Indian Affairs); the department which directs the Coast Guard law enforcement activities; the Environmental Protection Agency; Congressional members and committees (e.g., the Senate Committee on Commerce, Science and Transportation, which is in charge of drafting legislation on ocean policy and fisheries resource management); the judicial system; state marine fisheries agencies, other RFMC, etc.;

b. scientific, technical, and professional sectors: pure and applied physical and social science (as well as the scientists); professionals and technicians attached to the industry, government, research, and academic centers, lawyers and jurists, engineers, regional planners, market analysts, statisticians or other disinterested purveyors of knowledge as well as committed spokesmen for special interests, etc.;

c. the fishing industry and related shore-based sectors: lobsterers, gillnetters, longliners, trawler fishers, seiners, fixed-gear, inshore, offshore, distant or foreign water fleets; seasonal/year round and full/part time fishermen; small, medium, large boat owners; mixed and single species fisheries; owner-captains, "ten percenters", crew; buyers, processors, packers, wholesalers, retailers; fishery or fishery-focused firms that are or may be vertically integrated, investment-oriented (e.g., Gloucester banks) or involved in international trade and import/export; fishermen's cooperatives, cannery workers, labor unions, common interest groups (e.g., fishermen's wives and seafood buyers' associations); transportation industry representatives, bait buyers, longshoremen; suppliers of ice, fuel, repair services; boat, gear and equipment manufacturers; ship chandlers, etc.;

d. the recreational sector: party and headboat operators, sportfishermen and anglers, marina operators, hotel and restaurant owners, Chamber of Commerce representatives, shoreline development interests, and all those who look to fishing and the fishing town or seaside milieu to attract the tourist dollar, etc.;

e. environmental and species conservationists;

f. national economic protectionists and expansionists;

g. alternative marine environment utilizers: oil, mineral, shipping, sand and gravel mining, flood and shoreline control engineering, landscaping, offshore waste disposal interests, etc.; and

h. consumers: retail shoppers, institutional seafood wholesalers, and the public generally, in whatever guise that amorphous entity presents itself.

This is only a partial listing of the various sectors that were represented in the 889-page volume of the House hearings on extended jurisdiction [12].

In sum, "to the extent practicable," the diversely constituted councils are charged to produce complete descriptions for each fishery within its jurisdiction, from which can be generated plans in which political processes that "drive the administrative entities do not erode the quality of scientific advice" [14], while producing a plan design, "(tempered) with real world knowledge of what is acceptable to society" [14], but which meets every need, satisfies every requirement of as many sectors as necessary, in minimal time and at minimal cost. One can only conclude that the even partial capacity to accomplish these objectives is facilitated by the council's collective ability to walk on water. And it is clearly to the advantage of those in the department, at whatever level, to place the responsiblity for producing such plans on the regional council.

PROCESS IN THE GENERAL PUBLIC MEETINGS AND HEARINGS

Up to this point the emphasis has been on the formal conceptual framework and the technical organizational structure. Because the first year was a formative period in which the *implicit* conceptual and organizational foci were only beginning to emerge, and because the technical structure was deliberately left flexible, it is difficult to present a rigorous analysis. Not only is sheer quantitative data lacking because of the brief life span of the council thus far (the data were gathered 3/1/77 to 2/15/78) but, despite theoretically open access to all deliberations (except a few), no one person could attend all the meetings, observe all staff activities, meet with all the people, in all the places, all the time. What is amenable to analysis, however, is the public face which has been presented thus far at the public monthly meetings of the council. Further, it is important to deal with this public face, since it is the part of the council's performance that plays a large role in establishing the identity of that body for nonmembers and their interactive behavior with it. This is true particularly for the fishermen because (1) the industry as a whole is the special concern of the FCMA and (2) as the council's current voting membership is constituted, it is heavily weighted with representatives of shoreside industries (buyers, processors, cannery owners, etc.). Informal as well as business ties among this group allow for a dissemination of information among this group even when they are not members, providing data on and rationales for publicly vague activities.

Fishermen, however, have limited access to such knowledge, and must base their perceptions and analyses (and the strategies devised on the basis of that cognition) primarily or even solely on what they see or have reported to them as occurring in those public meetings. Thus, the public behavior of the council has an attitude formation potential for fishermen (the primary clients of the council at present) far beyond that which seems to be recognized by the council, the government, scientists and other sectors of the industry. This is why the main concern of this chapter is the limning out of the FCMA as it is managed in this one sphere.

The council receives public input in a variety of ways. First, since it is constituted by design of the FCMA, as that delineates the identity of the voting and nonvoting members and staff, the council is itself a source of public input. Individuals for whom council participation is secondary to their primary work activities are, presumably, *intended* to bring to the functioning of the council the loyalties and attitudes, the assumptions and goals, which they have developed as participating members of that primary work focus.

Second, both NMFS and the council are required to conduct public hearings on proposed management plans. For example, when the groundfish plan for the New England region was being prepared, a series of well-publicized meetings was held around the Northeast region, to which the public was invited and at which scientists explained the manner in which stock sizes were calculated and the ways through which the projected MSYS were derived. The audiences could then engage in a dialog (often quite pointed) with those individuals who were at the front to represent NMFS and the council. Charts, graphs, statistical concepts and the like were used to demonstrate to the audience the validity of the database and rationale for the plan features. As is the case at the general public meetings, the audience at these hearings, mostly commercial and recreational fishermen probed, debated and responded with catch and market figures of their own which, like the scientific statements (though at a different level), varied widely in degree of sophistication and relevancy.

A central concern of the fishermen was whether the initially proposed council plan was, in fact, the most reasonable solution. They questioned, among other things, the accuracy of the MSY calculations from NMFS which formed the basis for the OY quota plan produced by the scientific and statistical committee (SSC) and Groundfish Oversight Committee of the council. Ad hoc committees from fishermen associations on Cape Cod and Gloucester prepared counterproposals that, they explained to the audience, were more practicable, realistic and sensitive to the needs of the industry.

The council provided for the audience copies of the plans and related relevant material (e.g., newspaper articles, graphs and tables of catch statistics) which were photocopied and circulated among those in attendance. Various features of the discussion led the individual chairing the hearings to ask for an expression of the majority will through a public vote, the results of which he would report back to the council so as to give them a sense of which plan was most and least favored. This input would, the audience was told, help the council to refine the proposed plan prior to submission to the secretary.

Although meetings were scheduled from 7 to 10 PM to facilitate public attendance (and all continued much later than the planned cutoff time), it was clearly impossible for many working fishermen to attend. Thus, it was critical that those forced to be absent be represented by officials of such associations as the Cape Ann (Gloucester) Chamber of Commerce, CCCFC and MIDA if the purpose of the hearings was to be accomplished. Still, individual fishermen did cancel trips to attend, despite the fact that this resulted in an economic loss to boat owners and crews. The motel/restaurant meeting rooms were filled to capacity or even overflowing as 100 or more people jammed in at each hearing. Some individuals, such as the President of the CCCFC or MIDA, attended more than one such meeting to have maximum input to the council and a wider forum in relation to other fishermen. Council and NMFS/NDAA staff added extra travel and evening work to their extended job schedules, just as the fishing industry personnel did, though, again, the fishermen had the added burden of lost revenues. Though there was no public circulation of minutes from these hearings, newspaper coverage informed the public at large of discussion highlights.

The third and most genuinely public input is accomplished through the mechanism of the periodic general council meetings. The FCMA states that such meetings may be determined, in time and format, by the council or any voting member thereof but must be held at least quarterly. The New England's Council's pattern has been to meet approximately every four weeks,e.g., the 1978 schedule revealed meetings scheduled for January 18-19, February 8-9, March 1-2, March 22-23, April 19-20, May 17-18, June 7-8 and 28-29, and so on through December. Meetings are advertised in the *Federal Register* at appropriate times, and mailings to those on a regular mailing list give prior notice of time, place and agenda. One is placed on the mailing list by a phoned or mailed request to have one's name added, or by signing the register list of attendees when participating in the meeting itself. Meetings are held in a public meeting room at the Holiday Inn in Peabody, MA. Past meetings have been patterned to take place on Wednesday and Thursday. The first day begins at 10 AM and ends at about 5:30 PM, with breaks for lunch and afternoon coffee. The second day follows approximately the same schedule except that it begins at 9 AM and includes a morning as well as afternoon break. Scheduled commencement times not uncommonly slip 15-20 minutes behind, e.g.,a 10-minute break lasts 25 minutes because council members are scattered and do not return because they are engaged in some other activity. Occasionally, there have been first and/or second day evening sessions running from about 7 to 9 PM.

Council members sit at a U-shaped table facing the audience. Some seats are fixed and constant, but much of the seating arrangement shows regularity only because of the personal spatial needs of the individuals. A major complaint during this initial period was the audience's inability to hear due to the poor acoustics and inadequate public address (PA) system. The council staff recognized the problem and each meeting has been marked by attempts to improve the situation. So, for example, the original microphone equipment of the council was designed simply to facilitate the taping of council proceedings; an improvised system that plugged the recorder into a PA system had many flaws and even now inhibits clear transmission of the proceedings for many, especially those beyond the fifth or sixth row of the audience who are additionally hampered by audience discussion around them. There are microphones around the council table (one for every three or four members), and one in front of the audience for their use. The number of council microphones, however is inadequate. In addition to purely mechanical problems members will often obscure transmission by speaking away from the microphone, deliberately leaning away, speaking too softly, or placing their hands over the mikes so as to limit the range of their remarks, (whether deliberately or not) conveying to the audience that they wish to keep the comments inaudible to the public. At the March 1-2, 1978 meeting, general complaints concerning an inability to hear were addressed from the audience to one member in particular. Later, that member, in responding to an individual who had been one of the complainants, began his reply with, "Why don't you clean the dirt out of your ears?", which many in the audience angrily commented to each other was offensive, uncalled for and out of place.

Other ways in which effective dialog is diminished result from members walking around the table to talk to another member, or moving into the audience to huddle with an aide or staff member. As might be expected, these "openly covert" discussions are accompanied by the kinesics of gestures and facial expressions (such as grins, frowns, nods, raised eyebrows and other-directed glances) which transmit messages to the audience and are freely interpreted as to their sense; the interpretation is often negative.

There are certain inadequacies in the current council procedures which inhibit the communication flow. Each member of the audience is required to identify himself before addressing the council, but those on the council are not always identified nor are they required to do so. Thus, even regular audience participants, let alone first-time attendees, are not always sure who is speaking, what the speaker's background is, or to whom they (the audience) should specify their comments are addressed. This identification problem is compounded by the fact that (1) nameplates of council members are not visible to most in the audience and (2) not all designees or regular members have nameplates. This might seem a trivial point but improper identification or one based on some hastily chosen identifying aspect of the member can cause confusion, and worse, laughter, the latter embarrassing some speakers to the point that they lose the thrust of the comment or question they wish to raise.

Another difficulty arises from time limitations. Obviously, the council members must be allowed to explore an issue to the extent they believe necessary. Comments from the floor are not permitted (except as they are solicited by the council as a point of information) until there are no more questions or comments from those on the council. This not only limits time for the audience portion (in one situation they were allowed only about a few minutes vs the more than three hours consumed by the council,) but occasionally completely prohibits public input.

On one such proposal recently, no discussion, questions or comments were allowed the audience prior to the vote. When the audience, surprised by the sudden decision to call the question without the expected public input, began to call objections to this action from the floor, the chairman responded that the council was required to follow Robert's rules of order which stated that, once the question had been called and seconded, a vote must immediately be taken. A casual observer might have felt that this was a relatively minor displacement of the intentions of the FCMA, but the audience became incensed with the action, and a little background information will indicate why.

The council had announced in the earlier morning session that it had only just received word from Washington (11:45 AM) that the Secretary of Commerce and her staff were to decide on a particular fishery management plan that very afternoon. For various reasons, the appropriate committee had not yet forwarded a recommended plan to the secretary and, as a result, perceiving the need to have some input into the secretary's plans, the group had to convene during the luncheon period and hastily formulate a series of recommendations. These were to be submitted for general council discussion, modified if necessary, and received in Washingtion D.C., no later than 3:30 that day if they were to be included as considerations in the formation of the management plan.

Despite the council's public indication that members had been caught unaware by the announcement from Washington and responded as effectively as they could, many in the audience later claimed that they had come to this particular meeting because they had heard rumors that this issue was liable to be a point of crisis. So, presumably, the council should have been similarly prepared.There was also a high degree of cynicism concerning a report that the Northeast Regional Director of NMFS, when asked a question just prior to the morning announcement concerning the possibility of such an issue arising, had skirted the question and replied to a reporter that he had no knowledge of any particular problems concerning that agenda item.

The elimination of audience input, though justified by a few on grounds of necessary expediency, aroused intense feelings among the audience. Members of the council heard many negative comments during the coffee break which immediately followed the vote, and responded defensively to what they considered unfair and unjustified charges. The audience, however, felt they had been stifled and cheated; the council members believed they had been placed in an untenable position but had done their best; and both thought the behavior of the other group unreasonable. The informal political dimensions of the governing situation resulted in dissonance, conflict, and another brick being laid in the rising wall of misunderstanding due to differing expectations.

In sum, the mechanics of deliberations are both inadvertently and deliberately modified and subverted, thus providing the basis for distrust, inadequate review and subversion by the industry. Whether haste is induced by last minute recognition of need, inadequate foreknowledge of the plans of the Secretary and her staff, or even (as once occurred) such trivial circumstances as a motel-imposed deadline on the use of the meeting room ("We have to decide on this proposal in the next six minutes because that's when the hotel says it's going to throw us out"), it is clear that a primary problem at this point in the Council's maturation, especially vis-a-vis the public, arises from difficulties in the communication flow at all levels and involves the consequences of insufficient information as well as unintended and/or ambiguously interpretable over-information.

Second, the publically observed dramas of a private caucus, particularly by council members, should be avoided as much as possible. It will continue to be (and probably increasingly so) a source of much suspicion when meeting participants see it occur at crucial points in management plan debates.

Third, humor, a part of most deliberations and certainly a part of these, while an admittedly essential part of most debates, should be used with care. Though usually serving as tension-relaxing and group-reintegrating mechanisms, such displays can be interpreted negatively as ridicule, lack of appropriate seriousness and concern, or expressive of disdain for others or cynicism. The audience has shown itself to be particularly sensitive; members have shown themselves not to be immune to jibes from the public or the news media.

Moving to a look at the council members per se, we see, as one might expect, that their performance on the council varies considerably. Some three or four are dominant in all discussions; another three to five are active in debates whenever one or two particular areas are under discussion; some only enter the dialog when called; and at least one rarely participates, often letting whole sessions pass without contributing at all. Further, since council participation is only an activity secondary to their primary subsistence occupation, some are required to forego attendance to attend to other duties. Thus, members have differing patterns of attendance and thus varying degrees of input on decisions.

Some rarely leave the table to talk with other members. Others are in constant movement during the sessions, walking around to talk to this or that council member, moving into the audience or outside hall to discuss something, leaving to make phone calls, and the like. Occasionally, such movements remind one of theater-savvy actors who know how to upstage another performer and distract the audience at critical times.

Members also bring differing attitudes to the conduct of council affairs. There are those who believe it is their prescribed role and/or public responsibility to represent the interests of a special group or point of view; others also accept this position for discussion purposes but abstain from voting on those issues in which they believe a conflict of interest ethically requires they refrain from influencing the outcome; and still others have stated that, although they have special interest and knowledge which allow them to bring certain points to general attention, they believe themselves duty bound to take a disinterested, objective stance which elevates the common good over that of the few for whom they have a special concern.

A number work for compromise. A few stick to unalterable principles. Occasionally some are flippant, usually most are serious, one or two can be rude and, at times, a few have become angrily intransigent. At one end of the spectrum there are those who do a lot of homework and thoughtful preparation for agenda topics, and at the other end are those who appear to be considering matters under discussion for the first time. Some members are rapier-sharp, going to the heart of the matter, asking pointed questions, raising subtle but critical issues, and grasping complex ramifications. But here, too, one finds a continuum. Finally, there are members who seek out information from the public, the industry representatives, scientists and the like, while other members appear to use only those materials which come to them from the staff or elsewhere, unsought and and possibly even unwanted.

The council is not simply a collectivity of individuals even at this formative stage. Each meeting shows networks within the group operating. Some of these networks are the result of committee work together since the formation of the council, but others stem from earlier friendships and associational memberships. Others form because of common perspectives or shared interests and at least one seems to have emerged because of a common concern about the apparent domination of council activity by federal agencies. It is far too early to tell which such groups are, in fact, only short-term cliques and which are stable, extending even beyond the members' council service or terms of office. Such networks or cliques are discouraged by the FCMA, which designated one-, two- or three-year terms of office to the initial set of voting members, to maintain continuity but also, theoretically, assuring a new slate at the beginning of every fourth year. In reality, what will probably happen is that some members will be elected to another three-year term, and some former members will retain more than a casual influence on and connection with the council as a whole and with individual members.

Important here is that the voting and nonvoting federal and state officials, and the Executive Director of the council, have the capacity to exercise a disproportionate (and undoubtedly intended) degree of authority and power. So long as they hold the designated bureaucratic position they remain permanent members of the council, capable of constructing influence and power bases. It can be noted here that there is a surprising unanimity concerning the excellence with which the Executive Director at the time of this research was carried out performed his job. Even those who found the council a cause for dismay qualified hostile remarks with praise for the "objective," "self-effacing" and "informed" performance which consistently marked the work of this Executive Director. As one fisherman put it, "Even when I'm yelling at him, I'm not really yelling at *him*. He's probably the only guy in the whole setup, from Washington down, who looks out for the other guy instead of his own tail when push comes to shove." A number of informants have expressed pleasure that there was continuity and stability in his presence.

Several other members have earned the praise of the audience. One, expected to be provincial in his knowledge and narrow in his interests, has frequently been cited as being "surprisingly good on the council," "fair" and "doing a damn good job." Since the remarks often come from members of the audience who have marked difference of opinion with said council member, this would seem to indicate the ability of the public to make reasonably objective evaluations of a member's performance.

Another word is needed concerning the permanent members.

These state and federal personnel, as a result of their position in the bureaucracy, usually have aides and other support personnel available to them. Such supportive persons are not infrequently in the audience and are called on to provide necessary information during council discussions. This is useful for the audience as well as the council, since such expertise can eliminate unnecessary quibbling, introduce new considerations and generally help in the decisions which must be made. However, it can also function negatively simply because some members have such assistance in scoring or obscuring a point. Such staff can make it possible for the official to get off the hook and, more significantly, also permit him to participate in an exchange of views without personally having to have the specific, relevant data at his fingertips. Other council members and the audience, who lack such a substantive data bank to call upon, can be overwhelmed or have their arguments whittled to seeming trivia, fantasy, ignorance or paranoia by such experts "who have the figures to prove it" (not to mention the jargon). At least a few of the members have shown a marked decline in participation following an exchange in which they were unable to substantiate their point with the same degree of rigor. It was after one such exchange that I heard one member say to another, "I felt foolish. I knew I was right but I didn't have the figures. I guess if I don't come here armed with enough information there's no sense in pushing anything."

In theory, of course, all council members can call on the staff to provide necessary information but here is where we get into the matter of committee-type stylistics, bureaucratic experience, and the confidence of public participation gained from longterm exposure to this participatory demand. All of these play an important role in assisting a member to think on his feet. For some members this is the first time they have served in such a capacity, and they are still learning how to play the game.

Committee participation is an important part of council membership, though here again some members do their job better than others. Membership on a number of committees is no criterion of excellence. Narrowness of choice in filling slots seems to play as much a part as any measure of potential performance and capability. There are 15 standing committees (with one having four subcommittees) and 13 permanent (oversight) committees, two of which are ad hoc. The committees are made up of council members or the designees of such members to the council. Two members are on fifteen committees each, and the remaining members serve on zero to five committees. The average number of committee memberships is seven but, obviously, the range of variation is so wide that such a figure says nothing. Further, what is really significant is on which committee one serves, some being relatively insignificant and requiring only minimal service, while others, such as the groundfish oversight committee, are central to the New England management scheme and requiring almost constant attention.

Although the FCMA is broad enough to include a wide range of activities (and members of the industry are especially interested in seeing the council begin to work in the area of positive assistance, such as subsidies, boat purchase loans, etc., rather than negative regulatory functions), the main concern of the council to date has been the production of management plans. It is this, of course, which has been so disappointing to the industry which sees itself, to quote one representative, "as having to bear the brunt of the rebuilding, and of being regulated out of business to help the rebuilding, while the foreigners get off scot free."

An important element of the FCMA was the emphasis on public input when considering the social, political and economic implications of the plans. The vehicle for many such concerns is the environmental impact statement (EIS) which must be developed with each plan. The theory of this has been considerably altered in practice. In the first place, since OY quotas are also to be calculated on the basis of such sociocultural implications, the EISs are sometimes viewed as simply replicas of considerations already taken into account when designing the proposed plan and, as such, are simply abstracted from relevant material within the body of plan, summarized and appended as brief two or three page outlines. The other extreme has appeared also, however; some EISs are several thousand pages in length and become to cumbersome for anyone to consider seriously.

Second, the concern for public input, especially as that is reflected in the EIS and hearings which attend those statements, may have the consequences of restricting innovation. For example, at one meeting the remark was made, "that will require a whole new EIS and hearings and we don't have time for that if we want to get a plan accepted by the deadline, or unless you want to face the possibility of emergency regulations during the interim." The comment was based on the fact that altering a plan from one already submitted requires an EIS and an accompanying lengthy series of public hearings, and routings through various parts of the bureaucratic structure. So, rather than go through all of this red tape, attempts are sometimes made to have revisions of present plans conform closely enough that a new EIS will not have to prepared. This kind of pressure has obvious consequences in the evolutionary development of fisheries management. (For another variant of this same problem, see Moore [16].)

Turning now to the other major group of participants in the public meetings, the audience, we see, first, that membership is far more diverse (e.g., a wide age span, the participation of women). Second, effective participation is more limited. Most if not all in this group follow every phase of the activities going on at the front of the room though such intensity is probably related to the fact that we are dealing with a highly selective sample of the public by mere virtue of their attendance.

Surprising to me (though considering my own presence I should have expected it) are the numerous observers who are present at each session, at times constituting a majority of the audience. In the early months, such individuals said little, remained aloof, and presented an anonymous identity. Most began attending because of specific, problem-oriented business, scholarly, technical, administrative, or other professional fact-finding motivations. Objectivity was (and still is to some extent) the theme, as when watching a play; one may be amused, puzzled, annoyed or intrigued, but not involved or commited. At the beginning this aura of objectivity was aided by being a stranger. Students working on papers and projects, consultants (or would-be ones hoping to use gained knowledge to find employment), natural and social scientists, professional and technical persons attached to some ongoing project such as the coastal zone management (CZM) progress or port studies came to observe, knowing few others in the audience, if any, and making copious notes which were jammed into the briefcases which often identified them from other members of the audience.

As the meetings have gone on in time, however, those who regularly attend have tended to lose their objectivity, such as it may have been. They have entered or been drawn into one or more of the networks which have formed in the audience and on the council. Some observers have voluntarily joined certain subgroups, others have been coopted by the fishermen, the processors, the commercial interests or other observer sets, the cooptation occurring when some question, or some remark explains their presence at the meetings and gives notice that they can be used in some way by a subgroup. Thus, for example, a professional formerly employed by the federal government in Washington (and currently on a postdoctoral research project) has been recently employed as a parttime consultant for the council; a biologist working on a CZM program has donated her time to a fishermen's association to help them assemble and present in appropriate style relevant data for an alternative management plan. Sometimes such people are used on an ad hoc basis, contributing comments and strategy suggestions over luncheon, at the coffee break in the hall, or in the bar following the meetings. Sometimes they become regular links, as in the case of the Provincetown librarian who is now funded by her town council to attend and report back on the meetings. Moreover, they become involved; what is interesting is the degree to which such individual have become active participants rather than passive observers. And what is significant for this analysis is that members of this group are performing the same data bank service the staff and aides of council members perform for their chiefs.

Related to the observer group, yet constituting a distinct and peripheral part of the intended public, are the news media representatives. Although there are usually only three or four such people, they have a significance far outweighting their numerical standing for it is through their eyes that most of the nonattending public (and even some of those present) receive information and develop their attitudes about the council, the industry, government and sciences, and the actions of these sectors.

Newspaper reporters do a much more thorough and accurate job than television personnel. The latter tend to cover the meetings only intermittently (usually when one of the council's news releases has indicated that some notable will be in attendance) and then only for, say, an hour or so with the resultant public film coverage often being no more than a minute or two in viewing length. Newspaper personnel, however, often stay for the entire two-day session, observe and ask questions based on background knowledge gained by repetitive attendance. At least two of the regular writers have special expertise in coverage of fisheries news, as well as a broad range of information about their reading constituency which allows them to focus on and analyze the proceedings from a popular perspective. Yet they, like the other observers, form opinions, have biases and skew their emphases and omissions for various reasons. Thus, the picture that the public receives, and on which its opinions and actions are based, are influenced to a large extent by what the news media choose to present. In addition to these conscious or unconscious slants there are factors such as the broader concern of the editor as to how much coverage, what budget costs, and reporter allocation the agency should give, where and when the article or film footage appears, and even such attention-getting devices as what typeface will be used for the headline, all of which influence the public's awareness of and significance assigned to the news item.

Perhaps the greatest strength that the atomistic and often factionalized industry possesses lies in the ability of the news media to formulate and concentrate opinion and action in the community at large, as well as increasing the sensitivity or even the vulnerability of the council, the government, and scientists to the public impact of their actions.

The most obvious audience sector is that made up of those linked directly to the industry. This segment may be divided into two major groups; those who harvest the product (the fishermen) and those concerned with the results of that harvesting (the wives and daughters of fishermen as well as representatives of fishermen/ vessel owners associations, and spokespersons for shore-based industries).

Individual fishermen representing only themselves are few in number and rarely attend consistently. This underrepresentation stems from such factors as: (1) the economic difficulties which arise when one must give up fishing time; (2) the historically grounded cynicism which most fishermen have concerning the extent to which they are heeded by government of scientists, and (3) the high level of frustration felt when faced with what is perceived as the constant blocking of attempts to communicate with and influence the council. It is increasingly obvious to most fishermen that individual voices carry little weight. The number of fishermen and vessel owners' associations that have been forged in recent months, and particularly in the way such groups are increasingly transcending local float, port or fishery parameters, gives evidence for the extent to which fishermen are beginning to recognize that the greater the number for whom one speaks the more weight is given that utterance by the listeners.

A common pattern has been that those who began coming as individuals have now become spokespersons for a group, or even organized such a group themselves, serving both as speaker for and reporter to their membership.

A very real problem for the fishermen is best analyzed from a sociolinguistic perspective. There has been a tradition in New England of the town hall meeting, and one might expect representatives of this tradition to be verbally facile in a public forum. However, in the age-old fashion of such shore activities being structured to fit the work/time patterns of shore people, fishermen have not played as active a part in such arenas as might be predicted. Indeed, they often vocalize distrust of such proceedings; rather, distrust of their ability to make any significant impact on such deliberations. Even those whose families have lived in a particular community for generations will often use a phrase such as, "Those town people don't give a damn for what the fishermen want." As a consequence of this many fishermen who are vitally concerned with the workings of the council do not attend, attend but keep silent during the meetings or, even when attending and attempting to enter into the public dialog, find it difficult and even painful to express their position. In the difficult public role not a few are conscious of deficiencies as a speaker. They are sensitive about perceived dialect stylistics, aware of vocabulary differences or insufficiencies both in sending and receiving messages, awkward at being required to move to front center of the audience and speaking into a microphone in front of large numbers of strangers. They are often unskilled in verbal exchanges and debates, especially when the ground rules favor the format used by administrators and scientists. And, it must be pointed out, some council members have been less than fair in their dealings with the fishermen, seizing on some personal aspect of the speaker's presentation to diminish the substance of the comment through a subtle or not so subtle *ad hominem* response.

The women in fishing families are also active participants, particularly those from Gloucester, who have sent at least two members, and usually more, to every council meeting. The role of such women is important because many fishermen explicitly relinquish their own participatory role to the females of their family on the grounds that this allows them to continue to pursue the business of making a living. Precedence for this allocation has appeared in recent years, especially as increased government paperwork has led many fishermen to utilize the services of the family females as bookkeeper, payroll clerk, secretary, etc. Additionally, the introduction of the citizen's band (CB) radio has further allowed the women to participate in and be aware of events surrounding the lives of the fishermen when they are at sea. This vicarious experiencing has given women a greater empathy for, as well as involvement and stake in, the act of fishing itself. Thus, particularly in the last decade or so, women have been much more involved in the actual daily business of fishing than in earlier times when men tended to keep such transactions private and their womenfolk isolated from all except the economic result of the process.

Women make few public statements on the floor, however, tending to conduct their business in the forum of their local communities, through petitions and delegations to congressional representatives, letter writing or other representations to the news media and, most importantly, through preparation of materials which fishermen's associations can use in their attempts to get backing from various sources of influence. For example, an economic impact study owed a great deal of its success to the Gloucester fishermen's wives who collaborated on the gathering, assemblage and collating of data for the report.

Though tending to make few public statements in council meetings, the women are having a great deal to say off the floor as a result of their audience role. What they see and hear at the meetings is reported back to the fishermen with whom they have contact, and appears to have a substantial influence on the actions which fishermen take as a result of this information. The obviously subjective reports can affect, for example, future fishing strategies as when a wife reports on the flounder situation and possible impending closures as she interpreted the direction of council discussion. Or it may determine what stance the fisherman will take at the next meeting of the association to which he belongs. In sum, though keeping a low profile the fishermen womenfolk are a force with which to be reckoned and must be considered an important part of the council's public.

Representatives of shore-based industry associations are themselves a lesson in the conservation of resources. Unlike the fishermen, who participate on a generalized basis, industry representatives focus and speak out on primarily those management problems which deal with their special concerns. As one said to me, "You've got to keep the punch where it matters; talk too much and they stop listening." This seems to be the strategy followed by most such agents. Recreational boating interests, for example, address the council only when the topic at issue affects party and headboat fishing patterns directly. They come to the meetings well prepared with reports and statistics (although at this stage no one is ever well prepared enough.) Such materials are undoubtedly produced from the records which such associations or (more likely) individual businesses themselves maintain.

There is also a greater commonality of communicative stylistics between this group and council members than between the fishermen and the council. Processors, cannery operators, chambers of commerce representatives and the like are used to the board meeting format, meeting with government officials, and conversations with technicians and professional people of various training. They are more effective in this mode of interaction.

Unlike the fishermen, who tend to emphasize the technological hardware of management plans (favoring, for example, gear regulation of mesh size as a way of managing the catch), the shore industries, in common with the council, administrators and scientists, lean in the direction of software management plans, stressing systems analyses, market stimulation/depression designs and other managerial types of fisheries regulation. Here, again, one portion of the audience finds it easier to talk to the point of the council's emphases. This also has the negative effect of making the fishermen communications seems even more irrelevant by comparison. Following a rather heated and broad ranging series of comments by several fishermen, I heard one such industry representative despairing say, "They just don't understand. We don't even talk the same language!"

There is a weighting in representation among the 11 optional voting members, with the skewing towards members from the shore-based industries. These industries also have closer associational links with the council than those represented by membership on the council alone. Industry colleagues meet in the course of other daily business activities and during informal social contacts, or they meet with other people who are intermediate links and transmit information back and forth with the network. There is nothing illegal nor even vaguely unethical about this. Council business is open to the public. Discussion within the trade on the workings of the council is normal and expected. However, some people have greater access to information of the straws in the wind variety and thus have a better feel for where things are going and what may be about to happen.

It is unclear how much, over the long haul, this additional knowledge and additional input will really affect the outlines of management plans and the decisions surrounding those plans which, after all, are ultimately determined in Washington. Equally uncertain is the extent to which the shore industries will be able to deal successfully with the increasingly restrictive quotas. Though alternating between gloom and optimism, most business representatives currently seem to hold the attitude that *some* accommodations, whatever the conditions of the stocks, will have to be made to keep things going. The industry presentations on the council floor, therefore, are presented in a communicative framework of reasonableness, common goals of rational economic design, and, more covertly, indications that the industry has a few cards of its own to play if the council gets "too independent." If my interpretation of this pattern is correct there should be, for example, no total closure of the 1978 herring fishery, despite what has been called the dangerously low stock levels. It is more likely that the persuasive powers of Maine packers, especially when they remind the council of the impact of unemployment in the factories that closure would bring, will prohibit such a recommendation. Rather, the council can be expected to ask for quotas only slightly less than catches of earlier years, though they may have to do some fancy footwork of ICNAF area allocations.

There is more diversity of style among the representatives the fishermen's associations than among those of the industry. The individual styles of orientation towards the council's purposes, the way each interacts with council members, and the particular presentation methodologies are sharply distinctive. Their attitude towards the fishermen are often widely different, one from the other. One member of such an association has, on several occasions, privately indicated that he believes fishermen incapable of the kind of sophisticated, objective, dispassionate understanding which must be brought to the problems of the region if the New England industry is to survive. For him, the major task of his association is to act *in loco parentis* for the fishermen. This is a rare extreme, however, and other representatives vary between serving only as speakers for their members to being active providers of alternative programs, a kind of minority voice in council decision-making.

Practically all of these agents have gained in assurance and skill over the past months. At least two such individuals initially commented in rather belligerent, emotionally colored, advocacy terms, but have gradually shifted to a more open style marked by a lean prose and substantive data. That this alone, however, is not enough to give one entry to the council is indicated by the fact that two other individuals, outstanding for their reasonable but determined attempts to represent the fishermen on the basis of data-oriented arguments, have failed in attempts to get appointed to the council. Informants differ as to whether the nomination was blocked by the council, rejected by the Secretary after recommendation by the council, or was made impossible due to technical restrictions in membership. There is consensus, however, that both men would be threats to the current domination of management programming by Commerce/NMFS.

As the council continues its work it will be interesting to see what counteractive changes will be wrought on such associations and the individuals who emerge as dominant personalities in them. Indications are that there will be a growth in the number, inclusiveness, interlocking and cooperative nature, and membership of such groups, and that they will take an increasingly flexible line with the councils, preferring nonpublic negotiation and discussion on the really significant problems in hammering out proposed management plans, while reserving the public forum for position statements. The monthly meetings, in other words, will be used more to broadcast to the public (and one's membership), and bring some public pressure on the council rather than serve as the forum for actual negotiation.

One last comment about the public's role in these meetings is necessary. It is interesting that two groups are notable for their absence. I have not heard anyone identify himself or herself as a consumer. Nor have I encountered any representative of the shoreside laborers, e.g., longshoremen or cannery workers.

The consumer groups, so prominent in other such public meetings, appear totally unconcerned with the deliberations that are occurring here. There have been no voices raised as to possible effects of landing limitations or stock declines on retail fish prices. Pleas from the fishery factory workers concerning the potentially devastating unemployment which lack of supplies would create are also missing. This seems even more unusual than the lack of consumer input, since labor has a long history of active involvement on matters which concern workers. In a relatively narrow economic base such as Maine has, cannery employment plays a significant part in the overall labor picture.

To summarize the problems of public input, the following difficulties seem to be applicable whichever sector (fishermen, spokesmen, or distaff) is involved:

1. Many reject not only the validity of certain fundamental propositions of current fisheries management needs, scientific knowledge pertaining thereto, and the internally controlled hierarchies of administrative systems. Time which could be better spent is thus utilized in what appears to be quixotic attempts to alter positions and patterns which are entrenched and/or fundamentally unalterable.

2. They frequently present arguments so all inclusive and sweeping that they lack focus.

3. Their arguments not uncommonly have no substantive basis.

4. They fail to recognize the extent to which the industry itself has altered old attitudes, values, work and associational patterns relating to traditional fishing life in order to accommodate the vastly different exploitive patterns of twentieth century fishing patterns. They argue for the anciently rooted freedom to be an entrepreneurial maximizer at a time when any real value of personal skill, laboriously obtained through limited apprenticeship openings (which worked to inhibit new entries) has already been replaced with a reliance on tools of the trade available to the highest bidder, outsider or not.

5. They defeat themselves by letting differences divide them, e.g., floor arguments in which inshore/offshore fishermen/processors, or commercial/recreational fishermen engage in charge and countercharge, and validate the statements and positions of those who make the same charges when arguing the need for external regulation.

6.   They, like the council, allow themselves to be forced to assume positions where they are reacting to a predetermine crisis scenario designed by others, rather than a self-determined, initiatory programmatic stance.

7.   They lack sufficient knowledge of parliamentary procedure to control any of the managerial aspects of the proceedings.

8.   They lack a stable supply of resources (human and monetary), information, and regional, even national, coordinating back-up services.

CONCLUSION

As repeatedly stressed, the council is going through a formative period, and the industry is being subjected to rapid change, both imposed and self-generated. Because of this the structure and process of the council and its participating sectors are in a state of constant reformulation, adaptation, and solidification. However, it is in this formative stage that the components and processors are especially clear and amenable to observation. Who can do what, where, when and how are under constant examination by the participants themselves and therefore are more explicit and capable of review by an observer. Features which will later become more understood and habitual (and thus more covert) are now the subject of open debate and discussion. These conditions make it an ideal time to observe the interface among the various sectors which are integral to the micro- and macrolevels of all segments. Mutual needs, areas of common goodwill and consensual goals, as well as points of friction, conflict, and real or potential cleavage are revealed in overt formal statements, explicit examination of technical structure and organizational format, and the informal give and take process that goes on in the caucuses and confrontations away from the public forum of the meeting.

Fundamental to this analysis has been the position that technology, as hardware and software, generates both the problem and the solution. Each sector tends to view the technology of the other sectors as the source of difficulties. Boats, gear and equipment multiply, which leads to overexploitation, often because the investment costs force fishermen into an ever upward-spiraling fishing effort. Economic concepts of rationalization lead businesses to manipulate buying and pricing patterns. Computers and systems analyses technology are used by technicians in various spheres to see these tools as proving optimal production solutions though they deal with a narrow range of human variables. Conceptual models and canonical principles of methodology gull scientists to have an unscientific faith in their findings. Accretive bureaucratic/regulatory growth is seen by government to be the best tool for humanity's control of its future.

Within each sector, obviously, these same "evils" are seen as the appropriate technology, and the productive effort increases. Thus Congress designed an act, which manufactured a council that produces plans, so as to manage the fishing effort. We therefore have created a tool that gives us an instrument to produce tools to control the use of technology.

I have also stressed that a fact of human existence appears to be that strategies designed to produce intended results inevitably lead to unforeseen consequence. So, for example, support of the extended jurisdiction formula which was based on recognition of the stock decline led to an acceptance of the position that the resources of the sea are no longer a common resource. Rather they are to be closed, first to foreigners, and then to anyone designated as a predator dangerous to the biological survival of the stocks. We have shifted from believing that the multiple use of the ocean is available to all who have the capacity to exploit, and are free to indiscriminately maximize that exploitive capacity. Although the sea and its resources are no longer a common resource, however, they are still within the common domain, i.e., diverse users with competing objectives have lost the *right* but retain the *privilege of access*. Under this new commonwealth perspective the U.S. government sees itself mandated to hold the resources in trust for all; to restrain any, so as to insure for everyone, the most equitable distribution of the resources. A fisherman translated the consequence of this position as, "Face it. As soon as that 200 mile limit went into effect the Feds owned the fish."

Clearly, even within the narrow temporal and spatial limits of this study, more research is needed (how familiar that phrase!), especially if the management plans are to succeed in attaining their complex goals. A major problem, however, is that all of the actors know just enough to try to achieve grandiose results with primitive tools. As is so often the case, rising aspirations have preceded the materialistic capacity to achieve the desired ends. Multistranded management planning and implementation is complicated in and of itself, but is further convoluted when different sectors of industry, administration, science and society at large differ as to the proper and appropriate functioning and function of management. It all becomes more involved when one adds such dimensions as long-term goals vs short-term needs, the ways in which attempts to satisfy short-term needs may alter long range planning, the means we have to achieve either set of purposes, and the fact that present actions and unknown variables alter the calculated future upon which strategies and decisions are based, thus making the future essentially undeterminable. This is why the results of decisions not uncommonly become transformed into unforeseen consequences and why solutions themselves usually seem to create new problems.

It is partially for these reasons that, at this point, this paper offers no solutions or even quasisolutions framed in the manner of alternatives. This abrogation of responsibility will disappoint some (and relieve others). It is not because I believe that pragmatic problem solving is best left in the hands of those in the industry and/or government who are structurally in the position of working out such answers. Such decision-makers are no better or worse than we scientists. We have a somewhat broader and (theoretically) more objective view of the situation possibly because, as one fisherman pointed out at a recent council meeting, "The damn scientists get paid no matter what they do, and whether they're right or wrong." But we are often deficient in the knowledge of practical problems of implementation and necessary tradeoffs in the realm of *Realpolitik.* Industry and government, on the other hand, may be better equipped to deal with problems of realistic funding, personnel needs, and required compromises, but often lack the ability to divest themselves of special interest parochialism.

This document is best seen as one which will serve its purpose if it acts as a catalyst for discussion and further exploration, and as a base for further research. If the caveats presented here are noted, they may at least serve to brace one for tomorrow's problems which will arise because of today's solutions.

ACKNOWLEDGMENTS

The research reported here was supported with funds from the Pew Memorial Trust; the Department of Commerce, NOAA Office of Sea Grant under grant number 04-7-158-44104; the Marine Policy and Ocean Management Program of the Woods Hole Oceanographic Institution; and by sabbatical funding from the State University of New York.

REFERENCES

[1] Andersen, R. C., and C. Wadel. "Comparative Problems in Fishing Adaptations," in *North Atlantic Fishermen,* R. Andersen and C. Wadel, Eds.

(St. John's, Newfoundland: Institute of Social and Economic Research, Memorial University of Newfoundland, 1972), pp. 141-146.

[2] Wenk, E. "Oceans and the Predicament of Humankind," in *Technology Assessment and the Oceans*, R. D. Wilmot and A. Slingerland, Eds. (Boulder, CO: Westview Press, F. A. Praeger, 1977), pp. 9-17.

[3] "A Legislative History of the FCMA of 1976," Congressional Research Service, Library of Congress, Ocean and Coastal Resources Project, U.S. Government Printing Office, Washington, DC (1976).

[4] Smith, M. E. "Don't Call My Boat a Ship," *Anthropol. Quart.* 50:9-17 (1977).

[5] Smith, M. E. "Introduction," in *Those Who Live from the Sea*, M. E. Smith, Ed., American Ethnological Society Monograph Series (Minneapolis, MN: West Publishers, 1977).

[6] Smith, M. E. "The Utility of the Total Institutional Model for Maritime Studies," in *Exploring Total Institutions*, R. Gordon and B. Williams, Eds. (Champaign, IL: Stipes Publishing Co., 1977), pp. 151-163.

[7] *Fishing News Int.* 16(9):12.

[8] McGarrigel, H. "Statement before the Subcommittee on Fisheries and Wildlife Conservation and the Environment, of the Committee on Merchant Marine and Fisheries," H.R. Serial No. 93-97, U.S. Government Printing Office, Washington, DC (1974), pp. 247-248.

[9] Engholm, E. "Fishery Conservation in the Atlantic Ocean," in *Atlantic Ocean Fisheries*, G. Borgstrom and A. Heighway, Eds. (London, England: Fishing News Ltd. 1961), pp. 49-54.

[10] Florman, S. C. *The Existential Pleasures of Engineering* (New York: St. Martin's Press, 1976).

[11] Hardin, G. "The Tragedy of the Commons," *Science* 162:1243-1248 (1968).

[12] "Hearing before the Subcommittee on Fisheries and Wildlife Conservation and the Environment, of the Committee on Merchant Marine and Fisheries," H.R. Serial No. 93-97, U.S. Government Printing Office, Washington DC. (1974).

[13] Green, E. "Cargo Cults," in *Encyclopedia of Anthropology*, D. E. Hunter and P. Whitten, Eds. (New York: Harper and Row, 1976).

[14] "Operations Manual, Regional Fishery Management Council, Initial Draft," Extended Jurisdiction Planning Office, NMFS, Washington, DC (1976).

[15] Smith, M. E. "Governing at Taos Pueblo," *Contributions in Anthropology Monograph Series* (Portales, NM: Eastern New Mexico University Press, 1969).

[16] Moore, R. C. A. "Fisherman Say Unenforced Rules Are Worthless," *Nat. Fisherman* 12/77:36a (1977).

CHAPTER 4
MANAGING MODERNIZATION: A CRITIQUE OF FORMALIST APPROACHES TO THE PACIFIC SALMON FISHERIES

Steve Langdon
Department of Anthropology
University of Alaska, Anchorage

INTRODUCTION

The Pacific salmon stocks of Alaska helped the United States feed itself and Western Europe during World War I and later helped the United States weather the Depression of the 1930s. Alaskan salmon became a staple on dinner tables in American homes of all socioeconomic classes. From a peak production of 137 million salmon in 1936, Alaskan salmon production slumped to less than 20 million in 1967. By 1976, the harvest had climbed back to 37 million fish, still a far cry from average production over the period 1925 to 1940. This 40 year decline precipitated tremendous expenditures on biological investigations of salmon as well as a number of regulatory and management schemes designed to prevent the total destruction of Alaska's salmon stocks. Crutchfield and Pontecorvo [1] analyzed these salmon fishery regulations and suggested that they can be divided into three major categories: "selectivity controls that affect the size and/or the age at which fish can be taken; controls affecting the aggregate sweep efficiency of the gear employed; and fixed quotas." The authors conclude that few of the regulations promulgated according to these principles "bear any relationship to conservation in either physical or economic meanings of the word." As a result of the failures of these principles, as measured by the continuing decline of Alaskan salmon stocks, a new principle of fisheries management has emerged in the past few years based on formal economic theory. The formalist approach has not only become the dominant regulatory paradigm for Alaskan salmon fisheries management, through the limited entry legislation enacted in 1973, but also in national and international fisheries management (albeit at significantly different levels of human society) as testified to by the Fishery Conservation and Management Act (FCMA) of 1976 and the interminable United Nations Conferences on the Law of the Sea (UNCLOS).

Despite the widespread acceptance of the formalist paradigm, in some form or other, there are a number of shortcomings at both the conceptual and operational level in its application to the Alaskan salmon fisheries, some of which I suspect are equally as prevalent in its use on other fisheries. In this chapter, I will show the formalist treatment of the Alaskan salmon industry to be inadequate, particularly in its conceptualization of the relationship between labor and capital, incomplete in its assessment of the roles of competition and indebtedness in the fishing fleets, and shortsighted in ignoring technological change. I will also display the critical failure of the formalist paradigm to deal with issues concerning the distribution (geographic, ethnic and occupational) of the net economic yield derived from the Alaskan salmon fisheries. Finally, I will show that the adherence of formalist approaches to presently constituted juridical/political institutions and economic modes of production leads to significant retreat from their own fundamental principle of economic maximization.

THE FORMALIST PARADIGM AND ITS APPLICATION

As proponents of the formalist paradigm, Crutchfield and Pontecorvo [1] have claimed to advance a model of salmon fisheries conservation that pays specific heed to the *economic* factors inherent in production and management. In particular they state, "Our central theme is that rational fishery management must evolve from the objective of maximizing net economic yield of the resource". Taken in toto, their work makes a compelling and sophisticated analysis of the processes that promote overcapitalization and overexploitation of open access resources, both of which they see as "responses to an improvement in earnings as a result of a positive income elasticity of demand." In pure formalist terms, they show that "exploitation is pushed to the point where average unit costs are equal to price exclusive of rent. In these circumstances, the economic rent inherent in 'superior situations' is dissipated to pay the opportunity incomes of additional entrants." Further, they contend that traditional regulatory objectives couched "in purely physical terms" have not provided "a vital basis of choice."

The authors go on to note that there are several reasons for promoting

an integrated fishery program aimed at economic maximization of benefits from the resource.... First, it is one of the most valuable of North American fisheries, and ranks high in value among individual fisheries of the world. The stakes, in terms of regional welfare, are sufficiently high to make this study more than an academic exercise, *particularly in Alaska* (emphasis added).

Elsewhere they note "the vicious and continuous political infighting [over depleted stocks] that has plagued conservation authorities," a situation they would like to alleviate. Moreover, they see these processes as threatening all fisheries since "the prospective growth in the demand for animal proteins, coupled with the tremendous impact of new capital investment in modern fishing vessels and gear in European and Asian countries" promises to multiply the incentives for overexploitation. They argue that

Failure to develop regulations based on economic calculus leads to the ad hoc, "hole-plugging" hodge podge of regulations now characteristic of many fisheries. it is important to realize that the need for regulation of open access fisheries arises from economic reaction of profit-making units. If this fact is realized, a simple, consistent, and readily enforceable program can be developed.

The crux of their program is to limit entry into the fishery. This plan has been adopted in Alaska and British Columbia, although in slightly different forms.

The Alaska limited entry program was implemented in 1973 by establishing a point system to rate applicants applying for permits to enter those salmon fisheries designated as "distressed." The designation of "distressed" was arrived at by assessing the status of the stock being harvested and the number of units per year engaged in harvesting stock in a particular area. In southeast Alaska, both purse seining for salmon and power trolling for salmon were designated as "distressed." Applicants for permits to enter these fisheries were rated on longevity in the fishery, investment in the fishery, dependence on the fishery, and availability of alternative sources of employment. In general, persons who held vessel and gear licenses for a particular fishery during the 1972 season (the season prior to the enactment of the legislation) were able to accumulate enough points to obtain permits for that fishery. The chief problem cases in initially implementing the program involved men who had been crewmen most of their adult lives but never held vessel and gear licenses and those with a long history of participation in the fishery who had not been active during the period 1970-1972. Active participation in those years was given extra weight in the point system. Permits could be bought and sold as long as they were transferred to an individual with the ability and intention of actively participating in the fishery. In effect, then, what limited entry did was to turn the right to fish into a capital asset for those who were active in the fishery just prior to the legislation. Although the law provides for a determination of the maximum number of units of gear necessary to harvest fully the commercial take of the fishery resource and to allow a level of income to fishermen that is capable of sustaining a professional fishery, and for a gradual reduction of excess gear capacity, the program as implemented allocated significantly more permits for both purse seining and power trolling than were optimally needed, because of the "history and traditions" of those fisheries. The Alaska legislation, in effect, prohibited *new* entry into the fishery but did not reduce what was considered excess capacity.

PROBLEMS IN FORMALIST ANALYSIS

Because the purse seine fishery for salmon is by far the most important in Southeast Alaska in terms of dollar value of catch, men employed and number of salmon caught, I shall focus this analysis on the operation of that component of the fishery.

The formalist paradigm and analysis presented by Crutchfield and Pontecorvo [1] essentially uses aggregate concepts such as yield, rent, total costs, receipts and fishing effort. However, they do also attempt to analyze the internal relations of production between the owners of the canneries (capital) and the fishermen (labor). Although the economic relationships between labor and capital are not central to Crutchfield and Pontecorvo's aggregate level analysis, certain flaws in their model stem from inadequate conceptualization of the structure and operation of labor-capital relations. The real world of labor and capital in the salmon industry is actually organized into a wide variety of relationships. These can be conceptualized along several dimensions. First, one can look at the structure of the processors when one finds entrepreneurial ownership, in various forms, and cooperative ownership, also in various forms. Second, one can look at the structure of the fishing vessels and discover entrepreneurially organized and cooperatively organized vessels. Third, one can analyze the integration between the vessel and the processor, which reveals a number of different kinds of relationships.

In my analysis of the purse seine fishery operating on the west coast of the Prince of Wales Archipelago in Southeast Alaska [2], I discovered four different types of integration between captains of fishing vessels and the processors to whom they sold their fish. These were (1) cannery-owned vessels leased to a captain for some period longer than

Table 1. Vessel-Processor Organization Integration:
A Partial Typology

| | Type of Processor Organization | | | | |
| | Cooperative | | Entrepreneurial | | |
Type of Integration	Independent	Dependent	Cooperative	Independent	Dependent
Cooperative	1	3	5	7	9
Entrepreneurial	2	4	6	8	10

one fishing season, (2) cannery-owned vessels with captains hired by the cannery for the fishing season only, (3) vessels with captains purchasing vessels mortgaged through the cannery and (4) captains who independently own their vessels. These by no means exhaust the total range of possible types of integration.

Table 1 provides a partial typology of the vessel/processor organizational integration I found operating on the west coast of the Prince of Wales Archipelago. It assumes, first, that both the fishing vessels (producers) and the canneries (processors) can be organized either cooperatively or entrepreneurially. It assumes, second, that a vessel can be independent of the processor, dependent on the processor (mortgage, debt, lease or hired-hand relationships) or cooperatively integrated with the processor. It should be logically impossible for a vessel, however organized, to be cooperatively integrated with an entrepreneurial processor, but it is quite possible for an entrepreneurial vessel to be cooperatively integrated with a cooperative processor. A description of the economic relationships found in each cell is as follows:

Cell 1:
The vessel is organized cooperatively and stands in an independent, profit-maximizing relation to a cooperative processor.

Cell 2:
The vessel is entrepreneurially organized and stands in an independent, profit-maximizing relation to a cooperative processor.

Cell 3:
The vessel is cooperatively organized and stands in a dependent relation to a cooperative processor through mortgage, debt, lease

or hired-hand status.

Cell 4:

The vessel is entrepreneurially organized and stands in a dependent relation to a cooperative processor through mortgage, debt, lease or hired-hand status.

Cell 5:

The vessel is cooperatively organized and is cooperatively integrated with a cooperative processor. This is the pure communal case with total and equal integration of fishing and processing sectors as well as complete accountability by labor for the direction of the organization. Vessels of Sweden, Poland and Russia variously approach this case.

Cell 6:

The vessel is entrepreneurially organized and cooperatively integrated with a cooperative processor. This is the form usually taken by North American fishermen cooperatives, in which a group of vessel owners organize to take over the processing and marketing of their products. The label "cooperative," as defined above, is probably improper, as there are always forms of labor, both on the vessels and in the plants, that are formally excluded from the direction of the organization.

Cell 7:

The vessel is cooperatively organized and stands in an independent, profit-maximizing relation to an entrepreneurial processor.

Cell 8:

The vessel is entrepreneurially organized and stands in an independent, profit-maximizing relation to an entrepreneurial processor.

Cell 9:

The vessel is cooperatively organized and stands in a dependent relation to an entrepreneurial processor through mortgage, debt, or lease.

Cell 10:

The vessel is entrepreneurially organized and stands in a dependent relation to an entrepreneurial processor through mortgage, debt, lease or hired-hand status.

By far the most common of the variants on the west coast of the Prince of Wales archipelago are those of cells 4 and 10, which account for 32-35 of the estimated 45 vessels fishing for west coast canneries. Variants 3 and 9 occur but rarely, and in all instances vessel cooperation is based on kinship. Variants 5 and 6 do not occur because no cooperative processor in the area is so organized; the cooperatives developed under the Indian Reorganization Act in the 1940s and 1950s were influenced by forms existing elsewhere in the United States when they were established. The few vessels that might be assigned to cells 1, 2, 7 or 8 (the Independents in Table 1) have in fact departed from full independence by accepting processor prices on fish in exchange for certain benefits such as discounts on equipment, cheap repair costs, lowered rates of vessel insurance and availability of extra equipment in times of emergency.

This analysis reveals a mode of production characterized principally by entrepreneurially organized vessels in dependent relations with either entrepreneurially or cooperatively organized processors is dominant on the west coast of Prince of Wales Island. These various kinds of relationships have significance in a number of ways including the economic structuring of motivation, willingness to disobey regulations designed to protect the stocks and the distribution of the fruits of production. With regard to the economic structuring, Cove [3] suggests in his study of 35 British Columbia purse seiners that there is generally higher productivity among captains with mortgaged vessels, as a group, than among any of the other groups defined by their economic relationship with the processor, i.e., hired-hand captains, independent captains, etc. Cove attributes this pattern to a greater motivation to produce brought on by the need to make boat payments. Data from the west coast canneries provides support for Cove's suggestion. For three years (1973, 1974 and 1975) I compared mean rankings based on total pounds landed for each vessel and discovered that in 1973 and 1975 the captains with mortgaged vessels were the most productive.

One might additionally expect that in a fishery characterized by economic and biological decline due to overcapitalization there will be a greater willingness to ignore regulations designed to protect salmon stocks among captains with mortgaged vessels. This would result from the fact that failure to make boat payments would result in the loss of the vessel and all of the payments already invested in it. Thus the potential of financial ruin would be more urgent to captains with mortgaged vessels than either independent or hired-hand captains and provide them with considerably more incentive to violate regulations when it appeared they might not be able to make their boat payment. The economic interrelationship of overcapitalization and captain dependence can thus be seen to structure a situation for further degradation of stocks. It is important to note that it is this type of dependent relationship that canneries like to structure, because in this fashion they can commit captains to fish for them for extended periods. The aggregate level analysis of the formalists fail to reveal this variability and its implications.

The purse seine fishery, like many fisheries of the world, is characterized by the share system. The essential logic is that everyone shares in the windfalls and risks the production effort. Cove [3] terms this a "co-adventure system" and Hawthorn et al. [4] contend that British Columbia Indian fishermen have accepted this production system because "Even in those types of fishing that required hired crews working under a skipper, the division of labor and the methods of sharing the income are along cooperative rather than authoritarian lines." Thus, conventional understandings see the share system as a cooperative arrangement. I shall take this point up again momentarily.

The production that must flow through the structure of the share system depends on the price paid for the fish by the processor. The aggregate level analysis on Pontecorvo and Crutchfield [1] does not take into account the wide discrepancies that one finds in the prices paid for fish precisely because they do not attend to the structural arrangements outlined in Table 1. Table 2 reveals wide discrepancies paid for fish by canneries operating within a roughly 60-mile radius. The west coast canneries pay less for fish than do their Ketchikan counterparts. The cause for this is that the predominantly Indian-captained fleet operating on the west coast is more tightly bound to the canneries, i.e. more captains in dependent relationships, than is the predominantly white-captained fleet operating out of Ketchikan. Thus the rewards that are passed through the share system to the crew differ substantially depending on the captain's relationship to the processor.

The formalists' inattention to the differences in the relationship between canneries and captains in terms of their differential impact on the mechanisms of the share system lead them to fail to specify who (what) is labor and who (what) is capital in the various captain/processor relations. For example, Crutchfield and Pontecorvo [1] note that various types of bonuses accounted for between 12-15% of the total gross receipts of fishing vessels. They interpret this information as follows:

> In effect, the entire economic rent from the fishery (and at least some part of the quasi-rent accruing to capital equipment in the canning sector) has been transferred to labor input in the fisheries in order to maintain existing catch levels [1].

Captains, the primary recipients of various kinds of bonus payments, are regarded by Pontecorvo and Crutchfield as labor. As I have noted, several kinds of relationships are possible between processors and captains. When the captain is a hired hand on a company-owned boat, he is clearly labor, albeit with a special interest in the conduct of the enterprise. However, when the captain is the owner of a vessel mortgaged through the cannery, the "bonus payments" mentioned above became investments in his capital, the vessel. Elsewhere the

Table 2. Average Price per Pound Paid for Salmon by Species and Year West Coast Prince of Wales Archipelago (WC) and Ketchikan-Area (KA) Canneries Compared, 1970-1974*

Species	Cannery Location	1970	1971	1972	1973	1974
King	WC	.18	.18	.18	.35	.40
	KA	.18	.34	.27	.98	.67
Coho	WC	.14	.20	.20	.35	.40
	KA	.23	.21	.25	.49	.50
Sockeye	WC	.27	.27	.27	.50	.60
	KA	.29	.28	.30	.53	.67
Pink	WC	.121	.15	.15	.24	.30
	KA	.15	.15	.17	.25	.34
Dog	WC	.101	.13	.13	.27	.35
	KA	.15	.14	.17	.45	.42

*Because of the way the Alaskan Department of Fish and Game collapses the cannery price data, the figures for Ketchikan-area canneries include the west coast Prince of Wales canneries so that prices in Ketchikan-area canneries other than those of the west coast of the Prince of Wales Archipelago were even higher than these data indicate.

Source: Ketchikan Area Annual Management Reports, (1971-1975). Unpublished documents. Ketchikan: Alaska Department of Fish and Game.

authors allow as much: "Only the hidden 'incentive payment,' which did not go through the share mechanism, enabled the boats to cover contractual operating costs" [1]. Finally, the independent captain is clearly not labor at all but rather a secondary entrepreneur extracting labor from the crew to invest in capital. This capital can in turn be used as collateral for further capitalization or for other production. In these last two circumstances, the "co-venturers," as Cove [3] and Crutchfield and Pontecorvo [1] term them, are not the captain and the crew, as when the captain is a hired hand, but actually the captain and the processor. They are engaged in a joint entrepreneurial venture.

What is of even greater theoretical import, for the historical materialist perspective, is that the captain of a vessel mortgaged through the processor is both labor and capital at the same time. An analysis of the flow of revenue (which is more completely documented in Langdon [2]) shows that the processors are able to extract surplus value from (1) labor through the low prices, and (2) capital through the share system. In the case of the captain of a mortgaged vessel, he is exploited (along with his crew) by virtue of the low price for fish paid by the processor. However, the captain in turn exploits the crew through vessel and equipment shares used to pay off his indebtedness and transfer ownership of the means of production to himself. In the mortgage relationship, then, the captain is but a junior partner of the processor in joint entrepreneurial enterprise. He agrees to long-term participation in the system, with substantial, although decreasing exploitation, in exchange for a portion of the value appropriated from the crew.

Partially as a result of this misunderstanding, but also I think from lack of a full investigation of the different structures involved, Crutchfield and Pontecorvo [1] mistakenly conclude that the share system, whereby "the individual worker becomes a co-venturer with the vessel owner," acts in the long run as "a further deterrent to more capital intensive techniques." It appears to me that a share system acts as a deterrent only when there are additional demands on the captain from an experienced crew for redistribution either through strong kinship or friendship bonds. In such cases, particularly where alternative employment is not available, Crutchfield and Pontecorvo's interpretation seems valid. On the other hand, where such ties do not exist and the captain becomes "an employer of casual, part-time laborers," who are inexperienced and unsophisticated, then maximum extraction, with minimum redistribution, leading to further capital investment becomes possible. In either case, low levels of profit will inhibit any capital investment as captain and crew (in the first case) or the captain himself (in the second case) require(s) the extra shares for mere survival. Thus, the share system, per se, does not inhibit more capital intensive techniques. Given appropriate conditions, in fact, it may be seen to foster them. Net profit and the nature of the social relations of production determine how the share system actually works.

The final conceptual oversight regarding levels and types of economic structure stems, once again, from the authors' failure to delve fully into the economic ramifications of captain/processor relations. From the external perspective of the economist concerned with maximizing net economic yield [1], it appears that within the industry there is "irrational competition for fish" leading to "sub rosa payments of skippers and subsidized construction of new boats" motivated by "the dominating fear of being cut off from sufficient supplies of fish." Competition is irrational in that it leads to overall excess capacity, but even they see that from the standpoint of individual processor, such behavior is completely "rational" if the end is getting enough fish to stay in business. This leads us to an important point regarding rationality and formalist analysis. How is one to decide what level of, and whose, rationality is more appropriate in this situation? Formalist analysis cannot provide an answer without recourse to social values and mechanisms upheld by legal-political forces. I shall return to this point later.

From the standpoint of the processor there is yet a further benefit of overcapitalization that Crutchfield and Pontecorvo fail to note, namely, that it keeps the great majority of captains in debt to canneries. They will therefore be dependent on the canneries and subject to the pricing policies of the firms. This prevents the development of much stronger bargaining units in the fishing fleets. It might be imagined that the result would simply be higher prices and fewer units with no particular jeopardy to the processors. But in fact the processors would lose their iron grip on the fishing end of the industry. And with that gone, it is not a very large step to "forward integration" through the formation of cooperatives by the larger number of independent vessels. This would cut down on the processors' access to fish and introduce a totally new and unknown factor into their market. Thus, the maintenance of a debt-ridden fleet keeps the number of independent vessels below the critical level at which they might coalesce and break away.

Although the history of the salmon fisheries of North America shows that a tremendous amount of technological change has occurred, one of the problems quickly discovered in Crutchfield and Pontecorvo's analysis is that "no further technological change was forecast" in their limited entry model. As a result, their limited entry proposals do not address themselves to the possibility of innovation leading once again to overcapitalization and threats of overexploitation. This in turn would require a new regulatory step of some kind, as the present systems have no flexibility for responding to such eventualities. Smith [6] has suggested that one of the "failures of success" in fisheries management programs is precisely this phenomenon. He writes, "the implications of the failure of management success...indicates that with time fishermen's innovations and factors outside the control of managers will erode the regulatory, territorial, and investigational scope of management programs." In terms of his metaphor the scope will not actually erode but rather will not expand to include the necessary new information. As an example pertinent to the formalist limited entry programs, he notes that "fishermen exchanging small boats for large ones forced British Columbia to change from a vessel-for-vessel limit to a ton-for-ton limit" [6]. In the Alaskan case, one of the areas on which the Limited Entry Commission wished input as they drafted legislation to cover all fisheries, not just salmon, was how to manage continuing technological change since the formalist aim of economic maximization seeks to utilize the most efficient means at hand.

THE DISTRIBUTION OF ECONOMIC YIELDS

Understanding the distribution of economic yields has long been recognized as one of the weak points of various varieties of formalist theory. Greenberg [7] has noted that problems of equity and the roles of institutions in distribution have been shied away from by formalists, not so much for their lack of interest but because of the difficulties involved. Crutchfield and Pontecorvo [1] also declined to face directly issues of distribution of the "maximized net economic yield" their proposals are designed to produce. Yet, throughout the volume are statements which clearly indicate their position. For example, they seem unconcerned as to how economic yield is distributed although from their treatment of the share system commented on above it would appear that they regard it as inefficient in important respects. In fact, Crutchfield and Pontecorvo are supportive of the present structure of production and mode of distribution, as is clear from their remark that a step-by-step reduction in fleet size would generate $1.5 million in savings which "would permit substantial increases in incomes to *boat-owners* and *share fishermen*" [1] (emphasis added). In addition, note the direction of integration that is suggested in the following passage: "Even if there were a tendency for *packers to integrate backward into direct operation of fishing vessels,* however, it is not certain that the economic results would be entirely undesirable" [1] (emphasis added). As Richard Cooley has written, [8] the canning company's control over fishing operations in Alaska is a fact (not a tendency), resulting from early steps cannery operators undertook to organize and finance fishing operations on a large scale in order to assure themselves an adequate supply of fish in the face of the seasonality of the industry, and the necessity to import qualified fishermen to work in the remote fishing areas. Cooley's interpretation is best applied to the Bristol Bay fishery of western Alaska and is not relevant to Southeast Alaska where the Tlingits and Haidas quickly became proficient with white fishing techniques. For further discussion of this, see Chapter 5 of Langdon [2].

I have also shown that this circumstance of fishermen's dependence leads to lowered fish prices and enhanced control over surplus value by the cannery owners, which is partially redistributed to captains to obtain their compliance in the system. Thus Crutchfield and Pontecorvo's proposals can be seen to buttress this economic mode of production.

Nor do they seem to be concerned as to where the "maximized net economic yield" is put back into the economy. They are not supportive of a distribution system constructed on any geographical basis.

In their discussion of the irrationality of limiting technological efficiency, Crutchfield and Pontecorvo sarcastically comment that Alaskan limits on vessel length in the purse seine fishery "had nothing to do with conservation; it was simply a device to keep the larger Puget Sound purse seiners out of the Alaska fishery" [1]. Other evidence of their attitudes toward geographically based distribution is found in the following:

The only real difficulty might come in the allocation of licenses between resident Alaskan fishermen on the one hand, and cannery owned units operated by non-resident fishermen on the other. There is no doubt that there would be great political pressure in Alaska to throw the burden of the adjustments on "the outsiders." If this sentiment could be overcome, overall efficiency suggests that a parallel reduction would be more acceptable [1].

On this same topic, they write elsewhere:

And, in all honesty, it appears in retrospect that the basic political conflict was not entirely between the canners and the proponents of sound management, but also between the canners and local residents over division of the spoils [1].

And finally, consider the following:

The state constitution contains a provision specifically guaranteeing access to the fisheries for all citizens of the state: unquestionably a reaction to what Alaskans regard as serious abuses by absentee owners of traps during the early days of the Alaska fishery [1].

Other writers exhibit a considerably different perspective. For example, Rogers [9] wrote of Kasaan:

Although a salmon cannery, a mine, and a logging operation have been located in the neighborhood of Kasaan, the management of each enterprise has neither drawn labor nor bought fish from local residents and the local fish runs have been severely depleted by the nonresidents. The accelerated depopulation of the village reflects the stronger influence of economic forces in this case over aboriginal geographic ties.

Of the Bristol Bay case, Cooley [8] wrote

Fishing was under such tight control by a few large corporations and the nonresident union that until the 1930s only a few residents were able to fish in the area even though they were willing to become company employees.

Crutchfield and Pontecorvo themselves [1] write that:

Much the same comments would apply to southeastern Alaska. Many of the vessels sampled in the Puget Sound survey also fish in that area....

The evidence presented by Rogers [9], Cooley [8] and Gruening [10] all make it absolutely and abundantly clear that huge economic benefits were taken out of Alaska as a result of the canned salmon industry. Substantial amounts continue to be. Crutchfield and Pontecorvo seem to be unconcerned about what appears to be a maldistribution. One might even point out their own internal contradiction on this question, as we have already noted their admission that "the stakes, in terms of regional welfare,...particularly in Alaska" are very high.

Their disdain for geographic-based distributions does not end with Alaska vs outside concerns. Of Alaska's current regional registration, they write:

> After the worst of the pressure has been relieved, however it should be possible to restore a greater degree of interregional flexibility without running a grave risk of excessive concentrations of gear at any single point -- a situation which brought about the use of area restrictions [1].

The implications of comments such as this, which run throughout the study, include a tendency toward establishment of a highly efficient, technically advanced, professional fisherman, with full year-round employment, who has no ties to any state, regional or local fishery but instead is spatially mobile. I shall return to this point, but turn now to consider how Crutchfield and Pontecorvo address themselves to the question of to whom "maximized net economic yield" is going to be distributed.

In their initial presentation, it was noted that "limited entry" was conceived of as a "simple, consistent" program. Elsewhere they take great pains to emphasize their concern that "limited access to the fishery (be) administered without discrimination" [1]. From both the "consistent" and "without discrimination" characterizations, one gets the impression that, as we've seen with the how and where, once again Crutchfield and Pontecorvo may want to avoid the point of to whom the revenue goes. Only in passing do they hint that one would not want "a disproportionately large part of the total catch (to) go to the least efficient units in the fishery" [1]. Given those promises, the proposals offered by Crutchfield and Pontecorvo pay virtually no attention to the circumstances of Native American fishermen in British Columbia, Alaska and Washington. Any extended consideration of the fishery rights of Native Americans are further constrained by the fact that Crutchfield and Pontecorvo's gear reduction program is guided by "the objective to enhance the general welfare of the state residents" [1].

In addition, they see as a "mild problem...that grows to really serious proportions in Alaska and in British Columbia" the following: "the heavy reliance of some Indian tribes on salmon fishing, and the fact that they are, in geographic, cultural, and economic terms highly immobile" [1]. In the following statement they offer their only commentary on the issue of Indian fisheries:

> As in all problems dealing with structural immobility arising out of unequal economic opportunity, there are no easy short-run answers. It is suggested, however, that there are more efficient ways to provide better economic opportunity for isolated Indian groups than to maintain them in an inefficient fishery incapable of generating either means or incentive for change [1].

Despite this understatement, the value premises of the authors come through, to wit, geographic, cultural, and economic immobility are unacceptable and detrimental to the rationalization of salmon fisheries; we shall therefore proceed as if they do not exist in the hopes that by so doing they will, in fact, not exist [1].

One further outcome of Crutchfield and Pontecorvo's disinterest in the "to whom" of distribution should be noted. Smith [6] notes that the implementation of a limited entry law in British Columbia has, in the course of seven years, made vessel owners extremely wealthy men. In Alaska, the adoption of the limited entry program created an initial value of $15,000-20,000 for a purse seine permit. Thus one of the social stratification outcomes by governmental limitation of entry in Alaska, as in British Columbia, has been the virtual overnight creation of a rich and privileged class with added economic clout and incentive to enter the legislative lists and do battle for themselves.

DISCUSSION

At this juncture one might ask why we should be concerned about where the net economic yield from the Pacific salmon fisheries is going to end up. There are several important reasons to be concerned about these issues, including the long-term welfare of the resource and that of the human population making use of the resource.

Although limiting entry does alleviate the problem of continuing to attract further entry into a fishery already overcapitalized and overexploited, it does not provide any necessary incentive not to overharvest for those who remain in the fishery. Thus fishermen might continue to overharvest and take their net economic yield and invest it where the return on their investment is more attractive, rather than restraining their present harvest levels and accepting sustained but lower levels of return. I view this as a type of frontier economics problem [11] that results in resource degradation, but Clark [12] goes so far as to argue that extinction, resulting from maximization of profits is a "definite possibility under private management of renewable resources."

This implication does direct us to the question of whether territorial control or some other form of property right to the resource makes any more sense than limiting entry. Recently Acheson [13] and Wilson [14] have investigated the Maine lobster fisheries in an effort to find evidence of a solution to Hardin's [15] "tragedy of the commons." Both studies convincingly demonstrate that lobster fisheries claimed by a group of men on a territorial basis, which Acheson [13] describes as "perimeter-defended," are characterized by high and stable yields, by larger lobsters, and by healthy stocks with normal age grade distribution. By contrast open access or "nucleated" lobster fisheries are characterized by declining or unstable yields, by smaller lobsters, and by unhealthy stocks with abnormal age grade distributions. in addition both studies indicate substantial economic benefits accruing to fishermen of "perimeter-defended" or "controlled access" areas. Further, Acheson's [13] historical sketch indicates that the perimeter defended system used to be nearly universal on the Maine coast, and persists where there are territorial ties of fifty years or more and only slight impact from expanding urban centers. Thus the Wilson [14] and Acheson [13] studies strongly support the principle that long-term, sustained productivity of renewable resources is enhanced by parcelling resources into territories delimited and controlled by discrete groups. This principle makes solid sense when applied to the Alaskan salmon fisheries, but the territorial unit must be meaningful in both salmon terms, i.e., constructed with regard to spawning systems and migratory routes, as well as human terms.

Despite this and other evidence for territorial control, the theoretical problem of the "frontier" remains unsolved. If the economic benefits from extinguishing a resource are sufficiently attractive, what is to stop such action? Margolis [11] analyzed "frontier" economic behavior, especially in "frontier" agricultural systems. She suggests that a set of economic conditions composed of (1) readily available credit, (2) cheap factors of production (resources), (3) strong demand, and (4) unstable price conditions combine to produce an ecological outcome of degradation. In her analysis, Margolis contends that uncertain environmental conditions help account for the unwillingness of frontier agriculturalists to invest in fertilizers and conservation measures designed to enhance soil productivity. The set of economic conditions she cites were all present during the "frontier" phase of the Alaskan canned salmon industry from 1878 to 1900 on the west coast of the Prince of Wales Archipelago. One of the critical flaws in Margolis' argument is that "unstable price conditions" do not mean low prices but rather fluctuating prices with periods of windfall profits followed by abrupt collapse. On the west coast of Prince of Wales Island I discovered that the two frontier canning firms operating both netted the entire costs of their operation (vessels, equipment, buildings, supplies, labor, etc.) in one year, 1896 [2]. Thus, the returns to "frontier" economic behavior could be substantial. The trick, of course, was to know when you had extinguished one resource so you could take your profits and invest them elsewhere.

The history of the Pacific Steam Whaling Company, which erected a plant on the west coast of Prince of Wales Island in 1896, is an exemplary case of an expansive, nonterritorially committed, "frontier"-type firm. Prior to locating on Prince of Wales Island, this firm had canneries in three other Alaska locations with only slight periods of temporal overlap. Moser [16] reports the major sockeye systems in all those areas to be in a state of dramatic decline by 1896. Thus this firm would use profits derived from overexploitation in one area to build plants, extract profits, and overexploit elsewhere. Interestingly, the destruction of salmon runs in streams near their plants caused the Pacific Steam and Whaling Company to go out of business in 1901. They had run out of salmon frontier [17].

Lurking offstage as each of these acts of overexploitation the frontier drama are played out is the spectre of "irreversibility" [18]. The early overharvesting of southeast Alaskan sockeye stocks appears as yet to be "irreversible," as they have shown no signs of revitalization since their precipitous decline nearly 50 years ago. Margolis has taken for granted one of the essential structural features of frontier economic expansion in the American West, that is, the right to reinvest your profits where you could get the best return. The problem of frontier economies clearly remains because no matter what the institutional arrangement, local production groups whose product is consumed elsewhere cannot escape immersion in the world economy. The unbelievably flexible capacity of the world economy to shift resources as well as its seductive lure of profit-making pose dangerous threats to high levels of sustained production from renewable resources everywhere. For the foregoing reasons I am more than a little concerned when I read formalist analyses which indicate that "institutional barriers" are problems in "fisheries development and technology transfer" [19]. The data on fisheries decline throughout the world would seem to indicate that we are close to Flannery's "hypercoherence" situation than we are to a lack of integration, and perhaps what we need is more institutional barriers, not less [20].

In closing, let use return to the formalist approach to the Pacific salmon fisheries to assess, in light of the argument presented, whether or not Crutchfield and Pontecorvo [1] have given us "a radically new concept of regulation." The accumulated evidence, I submit, suggests otherwise. Rather, what they have brought forth is clearly a proposal designed to shore up a capitalist, entrepreneurial mode of production based on common property principles, which as Christy and Scott [21] note "has been a firmly based American tradition," i.e., grounded in social values and political power, not economic rationality. If the reader will permit yet another tired analogy to the processes described by Thomas Kuhn [22], what Crutchfield and Pontecorvo propose is a further refinement of economic "normal science" operating within the economic paradigm of capitalism. More critical as a theoretical failing is that, in the end, Crutchfield and Pontecorvo's adherence to already established institutions and modes of production leads to a bastardization of their own fundamental principle: "the optimal rate and method of fishing is that which maximizes the net economic yield from the resource" [1]. On the west coast of Prince of Wales Archipelago I traced the processes of technological innovation, economic competition, and governmental regulation which led to the harvesting of salmon ever farther from the stream mouth. Of this process, Crutchfield and Pontecorvo write, "In brief, the tendency to push the fishery farther from the stream mouth has steadily decreased efficiency in the fishery" [1]. In addition, they write elsewhere,

> The analogy that best describes this process is to compare the transition (of salmon) from the salt to freshwater to a funneling process. Clearly, fishing effort is more efficient if applied in the area of greatest fish density, the neck of the funnel; and in any program that considers economic rationalization of the fishery, the efficiency criterion is of great importance [1].

Note how they shift away from the full implications of their own analysis. They present several objections which "stand in the way of its (their program) full implementation"; one of these "is institutional and, to a certain extent legal. *Management on this basis would involve complete reorganization of the fishery and economic regulation at a level of sophistication beyond that implicit in the mere erection of barriers to entry*" [1]. The implications of their analysis, raised to its ultimate conclusion, is a salmon fishery based on principles of private property, as opposed to common property, and stream mouth harvesting. Such a management paradigm would likely favor populations which have geographic-based identities and long-term, cultural commitments to salmon. The policy implication of Crutchfield and Pontecorvo's analysis is that such populations are pawns to be shifted about through the manipulation of economic forces legitimized by political legal power. For those populations limited entry is bitterly ironic in that the net economic yield to be maximized from the resource will not be directed their way, and they will likely be eliminated from the Pacific salmon fishery.

REFERENCES

[1] Crutchfield, J., and G. Pontecorvo. *The Pacific Salmon Fisheries: A Study of Irrational Conservation* (Baltimore, MD: Johns Hopkins University Press, 1969).

[2] Langdon, S. "Technology, Ecology and Economy: Fishing Systems in Southeast Alaska," PhD Dissertation, Stanford University (1977).

[3] Cove, J. J. "Hunters, Trappers, and Gatherers of the Sea: A Comparative Study of Fishing Strategy," *J. Fish. Res. Board. Can.* 30:249-259 (1973).

[4] Hawthorn, H., C. Belshaw and S. Jamieson. *The Indians of British Columbia* (Berkeley, CA: University of California Press, 1960).

[5] "Ketchikan Area Management Reports," Alaska Department of Fish and Game, Ketchikan, AK (1971-1975).

[6] Smith, C. "The Failure of Success in Fisheries Management," *Environ. Manangement* 1:239-247 (1977).

[7] Greenberg, M. "The New Economic History and the Understanding of Slavery: A Methodological Critique," *Dialectical Anthropol.* 2:131-141 (1977).

[8] Cooley, R. *Politics and Conservation: The Decline of the Alaska Salmon* (New York: Harper and Row, 1963).

[9] Rogers, G. *Alaska in Transition: The Southeast Region* (Baltimore, MD: Johns Hopkins University Press, 1960).

[10] Gruening, E. *The State of Alaska,* 2nd ed. (New York: Random House, 1968).

[11] Margolis, M. "Historical Perspectives on Frontier Agriculture as an Adaptive Strategy," *Am. Ethnologist* 4:42-64 (1977).

[12] Clark, C. "The Economics of Overexploitation," *Science* 181:630-634 (1974).

[13] Acheson, J. "The Lobster Fiefs: Economic and Ecological Effects of Territoriality in the Main Lobster Industry," *Human Ecol.* 3:183-207 (1975).

[14] Wilson, J. "A Test of the Tragedy of the Commons," in *Managing the Commons*, G. Hardin, Ed. (San Francisco: W. H. Freeman, 1977), pp. 96-111.

[15] Hardin, G. "The Tragedy of the Commons," *Science* 162:1243-1248 (1968).

[16] Moser, J. "Salmon and Salmon Fisheries of Alaska," U.S. Fish Commission Bulletin No. 16 (1899).

[17] Cobb, J. *Pacific Salmon Fisheries*, 4th ed., Bureau of Fisheries Document No. 1092, U.S. Government Printing Office (1930).

[18] Krutilla, J., and A. Fisher. *The Economics of Natural Environments* (Baltimore, MD: Johns Hopkins University Press, 1975).

[19] Gates, J. "Economic Data Needs in Fisheries Management under Extended Jurisdiction," in *Establishing a 100-Mile Fisheries Zone* (Washington, DC. Office of Technology Assessment, 1976).

[20] Flannery, K. "The Cultural Evolution of Civilizations," *Ann. Rev. Ecol. Systemat.* 3:339-426 (1972).

[21] Christy, F., and A. Scott. *The Common Wealth in Ocean Fisheries* (Baltimore, MD: Johns Hopkins University Press, 1965).

[22] Kuhn, T. *The Structure of Scientific Revolutions* (Chicago, IL: University of Chicago Press, 1962).

CHAPTER 5
DEVELOPMENT PROPOSALS AND SMALL-SCALE FISHING IN THE CARIBBEAN

Riva Berleant-Schiller
Department of Anthropology
University of Connecticut, Torrington

The colonial and post-colonial history of the Caribbean can be read in part from the continuous and abundant flow of surveys, reports, proposals and development plans directed to the area. The succession of fisheries development projects since the 1940s is not exceptional, and reflects a succession of political realities from changing metropolitan-colonial relations after World War II to growing independence and the emergence of new states. This chapter examines the changing goals of Caribbean fishing development projects and discusses them in relation to fish resources and the nature of small traditional fishing communities. I shall show that fishery development plans are related as much to their political environment as to their marine environment, and very little to the economic and technological conditions of the majority of fishermen. I use the fishery of Barbuda, West Indies, as an example of an artisanal fishery that satisfies local needs, and whose present functioning strongly implies the damage that could result from attempts at commercial development. No such development has ever been attempted in Barbuda, but I shall show that a changing political situation in the immediate future places the fishery at risk.

In the Caribbean, as elsewhere, traditional fisheries exist side by side with developing commercial fisheries. These traditional fisheries are unmechanized and mainly associated with inshore reef and demersal fishing. Plans for developing commercial fisheries, on the other hand, focus on mechanized pelagic fishing. The two fisheries are distinct, yet related. Some of the development problems of commercial fisheries involve the nature and future of traditional fisheries, problems such as choosing development priorities, ensuring local food supply, and estimating the effects of change upon traditional fishing. The differences and the relationships between the two fisheries are made explicit in the following discussion.

DEVELOPMENT PLANS AND CARIBBEAN POLITICAL STATUS

In 1944 the Anglo-American Caribbean Commission set up a project for the development of Caribbean fisheries. The commission, organized during World War II, institutionalizd the fact of growing U.S. strategic interest in the Caribbean. This interest fitted neatly into British efforts to handle postwar problems with its Caribbean colonies. The work and the attitudes of the new commission did not depart from British Colonial Office policies. The commission encouraged intraregional cooperation, but its intent was less to foster independence than to ensure food supply and a measure of self-support. The reports of the fisheries development project reflect the colonial nature of the commission.

The U.S. Fish and Wildlife Service provided a project investigator and a purse-seine vessel for exploratory cruising [1]. The other investigator had already worked in the southern Caribbean and understood the need for research [2-4]. The two investigators tried to devise sensible and limited ways in which artisanal fishers could use commercial gear. Their work was not meant to expand the inshore demersal fishery, but to determine whether artisanal fishers, given some simple innovations in gear and craft, could move offshore with their existing knowledge and technology [5].

The innovations were tested locally in the waters of Trinidad and Guyana (then British Guinana), using a purse seine vessel adapted for trawls, lines and gillnets. The idea of supplying local food need governed the research throughout. Whiteleather and Brown [5] found that otter trawling for bottom species in the Gulf of Paria yielded a consistent catch that compared favorably with catches from other tropical waters, but they also recognized the need for conservation. Therefore they recommended small motorized craft only, with light seines to be used cautiously on the rough bottoms. They recommended no development along the Guiana coast; although it was relatively unexploited, they found conditions unsuited to small boats and only questionably worth the justification of larger vessels.

The publications that emerged from this commission project reiterate the themes of careful management, limited resources and the desirability of local self-sufficiency in food supply. They emphasize cautious application of limited technology to increase catches without straining stocks [5-7]. These common-sense and conservationist qualities are not vitiated by the colonialist origin of the project. Perhaps the only deficiency in the work was in its lack of thought as to how fishers might finance even the modest technological innovations recommended.

Although a third investigator working in Belize (then British Honduras) at the same time was less conservative and proposed some commercial development [8], the tone of the fisheries work of the 1940s echoes the British preoccupation with her immediate colonial problems. But a new movement was beginning during this period, a movement toward West Indian regional federation and independence.

After 1945 the movement toward a West Indian regional and internally controlled political body went on simultaneously with the work of the essentially colonial Anglo-American Caribbean Commission. During the 1950s the federation movement and the commission had few motives in common, but shared the practical concern of establishing regional cooperation and regional economic autonomy. Fishery development plans of the 1950s expressed the new attitude in projects that looked toward a mechanized, pelagic, commercial fishery. This does not, however, mean that local food supply was totally neglected. For example, the FAO demonstrated the workability of fish culture in the irrigation canals of British Guiana between 1953 and 1960 [9].

In 1952, for example, the commission held the first of three fisheries conferences in Trinidad, principally to consider the commercial development of a shrimp and tuna fishery. As a result, private surveyors began to explore both the shelf and the deep-water areas of the Caribbean for these comparitively profitable resources [10]. The private surveys turned up no new possibilities for the expansion of a shelf fishery. The most likely possibilities for commercial exploitation appeared to lie in pelagic stocks of such species as tuna, swordfish and marlin, although research on the size of these stocks was yet to be done.

The theme of regional cooperation persisted through further fisheries work in the 1950s [11], culminating in 1959 with the last of the three commission conferences. In 1958 the West Indies Federation had materialized out of the postwar federation movement [12]. This last conference, therefore, took place just as the commission was relinquishing its roles to the new federation. Its proposals exhibit a sensitivity to certain issues that are later lost in emergent nationhood, notably the importance and vulnerability of traditional fisheries, the needs of artisanal fishers, and the real differences between Caribbean nations in resources, potential, and economic conditions [13]. Chapelle, for example, explained that individual fisheries must each determine their own degree of mechanization according to economy, boats, capital required of fishers and natural conditions. He warned, prophetically, that fishery technology is not "a matter that should be decided by local pride or desire but by the hard economic facts" [14].

The general recommendations of the conference included the keeping and publishing of fisheries statistics in each country; a search for dependable pelagic stocks; the expansion of fish culture; the development of chilled storage and distribution; caution in proceeding with mechanization and processing; and finally, a committee to continue fisheries services until another organization could succeed the commission, the most likely being the FAO. At the same time, the conference recognized the need for positive efforts to preserve artisanal fishing. Thus the conference bridges the schemes of the 1940s and the schemes that follow, especially the ambitious United Nations (UN) Development Program-Food and Agricultural Organization project of the 1960s and 1970s.

In 1960 and 1961 the West Indies Federation received from the FAO, under a program of technical assistance, the services of a naval architect to study and improve local fishing boats. The architect, Knud Rasmussen, undertook the project in new political conditions. The West Indies Federation wanted to expand its economic potential. Some of its members, soon to be independent, were concerned with their own political and economic interests. The research on vessel design appears to have been undertaken to stamp a development decision that had already been made, rather than to contribute to its making. In Trinidad, for example, the transformation of local fishing had already begun; an artisanal fishery was rapidly changing into an industry that required marketing organizations, fishermen's associations, and loans to finance the investment in vessels and gear [15]. Rasmussen saw that innovations in craft must be accompanied by means of using those innovations. Therefore the recommended research on market expansion and on fish movements. Here is a situation where technological innovation was to lead, while research and infrastructure were to follow its direction. It is quite different from 1945, when technological innovation was to be fitted into known resources and the local economy.

Following the recommendation of the commission's last conference, a group of caribbean governments sought help from the UN

Special Fund (UNSF) in organizing a regional fisheries project. The Federation countries—Antigua, Barbados, Dominica, Grenada, Jamaica, Montserrat, St. Kitts-Nevis-Anguilla, St. Lucia, St. Vincent, Trinidad and Tobago—joined with British Guiana, Netherlands Antilles, Surinam, Puerto Rico, Dominican Republic and Haiti. But by 1962, when the project report was submitted to the UNSF, the Federation had just dissolved. Some of its members were still colonies. Independence for Jamaica, Trinidad and Tobago, and British Guiana was scheduled within the year. Only Haiti and Dominican Republic were independent states at that time.

The UNSF survey report proposed that the UNSF support a regional fisheries program that might also include the French West Indies, Colombia, Venezuela and British Honduras. It recommended exploration and oceanographic research. It also proposed a program of market research and development that would include intra-Caribbean trade, demonstration marketing with the use of ice, and a program for the training of fisheries officers and master fishers. It did not recommend the development of fish processing [16].

The kind of fishery meant to grow from these proposals was a commercial pelagic industry for supplying the region and for export. Attracting capital, "private or public, domestic or foreign" was an essential part of the plan. The plan was conceived in two phases: a one-year organizational phase and a three-year phase of exploratory fishing, market research and training. The surveyors proposed five research vessels equipped with modern gear to look for tuna grounds, flying fish stocks, live bait grounds and areas where large pelagic species could be taken by mechanized trolling. Trawling research was not recommended. The vessels were to include four 65 and one 45 foot vessel, large enough for efficiency and small enough for potential local use.

This plan completed the movement toward an expanding, mechanized, commercial fishery in the Caribbean with a marketing system to suit. The traditional demersal fishery was not totally ignored, however. The surveyors recognized its importance and envisioned the new fishery gradually and cautiously absorbing the old. Nevertheless, the report included no suggestions for gradual absorption, let alone for preservation or development. The report did not admit that the traditional fishery might be an irreplaceable community food resource that should be preserved.

This report was the foundation of the fisheries project of 1965-1971, which was sponsored by the UN Development Program, a part of the UNSF, and administered by the FAO. The members of the project were Antigua, Barbados, Dominic, Dominican Republic, French Republic (French Guiana, Guadeloupe, Martinique), Grenada, Guyana, Jamaica, Montserrat, Netherland Antilles, Puerto Rico, St. Kitts-Nevis-Anguilla, St. Lucia, St. Vincent, Surinam, and Trinidad and Tobago. This project was a large and ambitious project that reflected the new independence of some Caribbean states and the anticipated independence of others. The basic development decisions were built into the project; they did not emerge from its research phase. They included plans for pelagic fishing, mechanization and large vessels, commercial marketing, and large capital investment plans less conservative than the suggestions made in the 1962 report.

The first phase of this new Caribbean Fishery Development Project (1965-1969) provided for the simultaneous beginning of marketing development, pelagic exploration and personnel training. It was geared to future hopes rather than present realities. For one thing, the five modest but well-equipped research vessels proposed in 1962 became two large vessels and one modest vessel, 82 and 56 feet, respectively. The large vessels could not indicate their potential usefulness for Caribbean waters as well as the smaller ones originally proposed. Although research had been focused mainly on pelagic stocks, the most successful cruise returned from demersal trawling, not recommended at all in 1962, between Trinidad and Surinam [17]. It yielded enough to encourage commercial investment [18]. Live bait fishing was inconclusive, and tuna longlining was abandoned before the end of the phase [18, 19]. The most valuable fish resources appeared to be on the Guiana Shelf; the second phase of the project therefore added plans for attracting private investment to a commercial trawl fishery in that area as well as for marketing and processing development. In short, the entire project emphasized the exploitation of new fish resources at a scale large enough to attract private investment. The results of the project in 1971 were equivocal. Although the Guiana Shelf had yielded the largest catches, it appeared that there was still hope for a pelagic fishery and, contrary to initial results, tuna longlining. One excellent result of the project's marketing demonstrations was an increase in consumption of locally caught fresh fish, but the catches were not large enough to sustain a new local marketing system [20]. It is notable too that no estimate was made of how long the Guiana Shelf stocks might last under commercial exploitation, nor any provision for oceanographic or ichthyological research to answer that question.

The waters of the Guiana Shelf are not typical of all Caribbean waters, nor are they the home of the pelagic stocks on which hope was originally centered. Very little of the Caribbean Sea includes continental shelf, the most productive type of fishing location. Shelves are part of youthful ecosystems in which the great fluctuations in species populations benefit fishers [21]. Most Caribbean bottoms are quite different. They are parts of a mature ecosystem, which is characterized by stability and diversity of species rather than by flux. Tropical waters are also less productive than temperate waters because they lack the convection that encourages the growth of phytoplankton and brings nutrients up to the surface [5].

These natural conditions suggest that the waters surrounding most of the small islands of the Caribbean could not support a commercial trawl fishery, even if the bottoms were smooth. Indeed, there is evidence that these waters are already yielding what they can to local pot fishers using artisanal technology [22, 23]. A commercial fishery for such islands as Antigua or Montserrat would mean long-distance, deep-sea vessels, cold storage facilities and a new marketing system. Can the society and economy of small islands support such development? Is investment from the outside desirable? How would a commercial fishery affect the local artisanal fishery that provides local food?

Commercial development as envisioned by the UNDP-FAO might work for some project members. Trinidad, Puerto Rico and Guyana, for example, have both suitable waters and sufficient economic resources. Nevertheless, much smaller members share the same way of thinking about fisheries development, as the platform of Antigua's Progressive Labour Movement of 1971 will illustrate. The platform says that plans to help local fishers within the existing fishing system are not the answer to development. The party envisioned a Japanese trained trawling fleet, export catches, cold storage, and canneries [24]. Barbuda, as part of Antigua, was to participate in this development.

The report of an economic survey of the Eastern Caribbean made in 1967 betrays the same way of thinking: " A major breakthrough into much larger-scale operations is required, new types of vessels and equipment back by fresh enterprise, larger-scale commercial organization and capital"[25].

Such national aspirations are understandable and explain much of why the goals of recent fisheries projects, unlike those of 1940s, are directed toward mechanization and commercial development. These aspirations, stimulated by cooperative schemes such as the UNDP-FAO project, contribute to the formulation of development plans that are not always soundly based on ecological realities.

Evidence of the damage done both to fish and fishers by the over-application of technology in the Caribbean is indisputable. It has been shown by the mechanization of the lobster and conch industries in the Grenadines, which now threatens the lobster and conch stock [26-27]. It has also been shown by the introduction of gillnetting into Barbados [28]. Although the Barbadian flying fish catch increased almost threefold between 1955 and 1962, the higher cost of fishing with powered craft concentrated the means of fishing among fewer owners, many of whom were not fishers themselves, while less productive fishing sites and presumably the artisanal fishers who had used them fell out of use. Mechanization created market gluts, fishers' indebtedness and strain on the flying fish population.

Many researchers have pointed out that the low yield for effort in Caribbean reef fishing, especially in the Leeward Islands, is a consequence both of natural scarcity and intense exploitation [5, 7, 23, 29, 30]. It is not a consequence of limited technology, which is apparently adequate for local needs and as much as the stocks can support.

The traditional fisheries, then, are barely balanced with the fish supply. Technological limitations and other cultural controls prevent overstraining. Craig, for example, describes the three subsistence coastal fisheries of Honduras, each belonging to a separate cultural group, and argues that in each of them culture shapes the conservative working habits of fishers [31]. However, the taking of spiny lobster increased greatly as a result of the introduction of export by air. Craig suggests that the aspirations of the state and its desire to increase export may induce fishing practices that endanger stocks.

The desire of developing states to maximize economic and political returns from their resources is understandable. Still, at least one economist has argued what anthropologists usually recognize—that there is social maximization as well as profit maximization. Copes argued that the socially optitmum management of fisheries encourages entry for those whose technological and financial capabilities maximize immediate resource rent [32]. Export fishing and large private investment impinge on traditional fisheries. Preserving the one while developing the other is a difficult problem. As Epple points out, fishing systems include technological, cultural, economic and social components. A change in one component affects the others [33]. Commercial development has already had adverse effects on small-scale fisheries both within and outside of the Caribbean.

The development of offshore fishing in Venezuela since 1945 has included fleets of trawlers and longliners, processing plants, and government loans [34]. Artisanal inshore fishers tried to mechanize also. Their engines proved cranky and uneconomical, but still displace sail. Meanwhile, the commercial fishery took over the largest share of the internal market, leaving coastal fishers to the dried mullet trade with other poor people and a lot of increasing poverty. The solution that Flores [34] proposes is the development of fish culture and the incorporation of artisanal fishermen into the commercial fishery. I cannot agree with his second proposal if it means, as he says it does, the elimination of artisanal fishing.

In the Persian Gulf, a shrimp fleet development plan resulted in declining catches after the first few years, while a growing opposition between traditional fishers and a commercial fishery in the same area resulted in lower protein intake for the local population [35]. Such a result would be tragic in the Caribbean, where fish are essential to nutrition and where 75 percent of the fish consumed must already be imported [20].

Yet, the UNDP-FAO project has already attracted a great deal of private investment in commercial fishing [20]. This means danger for small artisanal fisheries. But why should these fisheries be preserved, especially when, as the project showed, local fish consumption increased with demonstration marketing? We need to examine such a fishery, and try to assess its value and its functions within the community.

I should like to turn now to the artisanal fishery of Barbuda. The Barbudan case is instructive not because it demonstrates conclusively that small local fisheries are inevitably destroyed by mechanization and intensified exploitation, but because it has never been mechanized or developed and is still an effectively functioning element in local society and economy. Further, Barbuda faces at this moment grave political change. In the following sections I will show how Barbudan fishing technology suits the nature and quantity of the fish resources; and how neither economy nor resource can support much technological change. I will also describe the current political situation and its implications for the fishery.

BARBUDA AND ITS FISHERY

Barbuda is one of the Leeward group of the Lesser Antilles. Until 1977, when Barbuda achieved a measure of self-government, it was fully a dependency of the British Associated State of Antigua. The population of about 1400 supports itself by a range of activities that include fishing, lobster diving, shifting subsistence cultivation, stock keeping and charcoal burning. These provide both subsistence and money. There is little opportunity for paid labor on the island, and about half of the 234 households are assisted by remittances sent by relatives abroad. Cultivation, wood cutting and stock keeping are carried on under a customary system of land tenure that gives all Barbudans equal rights to the use of common lands outside the village. Emigration keeps the population small enough so that no disputes arise over these rights to Barbuda's 160.5 km. Marine grounds are also open to everyone, and their use is not usually a matter of conflict, although fishpot theft is a problem.

The Barbudan economy and modes of subsistence have changed little since the late eighteenth century. Even before emancipation Barbudans carried on the same occupations that they carry on today, and have always considered the island to be their own [36, 37]. Codrington, the single village, may be described as a peasant community in which two-thirds of the population subsists by direct use of land and sea. Both of these are essential in the total range of complementary productive activities that supports individual households and constitutes the island's internal economy. It was, for example, only when I began to investigate fishing that I could discover some of the patterns of plot choice among swidden cultivators, who try to choose grounds en route to favorite fishing areas. All productive activities must therefore be considered as related parts of the total household economy and of seasonal and daily rounds. Fishing is an essential part of this complex.

Furnished with an artisanal technology, fishing supplies local needs, redistributes cash within the island, does not pressure the resources beyond what they can bear, and permits Barbudans to spend time on other necessary productive activities because their cash investment in fishing equipment is minimal. The work organization of fishing also reinforces village social organization, as I have shown elsewhere [38].

We shall see that mechanization is more profitably applied to lobster-diving, because lobsters command a much higher price on the outside market. Fishing and lobster diving are complementary in the Barbudan economy. Fishing supplies household subsistence and small cash, whereas lobster diving establishes links to the outside world, brings money into the island, and carries the potential for entrepreneurship and change.

Agricultural development schemes have a long history of failure in Barbuda [36], but fishery development schemes have never been tried. In his development report of 1968, Bryden did not plan for fishing development. He recognized the importance of the inshore fishery to the local population [39], but considered that the development of an offshore industry was restricted by law. In 1971 another report on the economic potential of Barbuda admitted that " in terms of breeding safe catching quantities, size limits, etc., nothing is known about one of Barbuda's prime resources [40]."

Even this cautious statement begs the question, for it seems to imply that fish are a "prime" resource in some other way than in their local dietary and economic importance. The report admits that intensified reef fishing stimulated by proposed tourist development and marketing facilities might seriously deplete fish stocks even while it temporarily encourages larger catches.

Yet, development need not mean the maximization of export production by a mechanized offshore fishery. If development is to involve and benefit a local population, it must foster the effective use of resources and facilities already present and apply only to that technology which suits local conditions; social, cultural, economic and physical. The technology, economy and ecology of the Barbuda fishery constitute a test case, the consideration of which is particularly apt in an uncertain political situation.

BARBUDAN FISHING TECHNOLOGY

Barbudan fishing technology is simple: traps, nets, sailboats and poled rafts. It is adequate for supplying the local market. A few fishermen use lines and spearguns, but the fish caught by these means are for the household rather than for sale.

Barbudan trap fishermen use the fishpot that is known throughout the Caribbean. Their pot is an oblong box of variable size made of chicken wire fitted around a withy frame. These wire oblongs have only in the last 15 years or so replaced the traditional hexagonal pot made of woven straw.

Pot fishing is for comparatively shallow waters—the lagoon on which the village is situated and some offshore reef areas. The lagoon is the most heavily used area because it is the area most convenient to the village. Sailing trips outside it and around the island take too long and present problems in returning the catch quickly to the village. Some fishermen who set pots among the reefs surrounding the island leave their boats or rafts on shore near the potting area and carry the catch overland to the village by donkey.

The kinds of fish attracted to the pot vary according to the area in which the pots are set and to the length of soak [23]. In the lagoon, grunt *(Haemulon* sp.) predominate, but snapper *(Lutjanus* sp.), chub *(Kyphosus* sp.), and small barracuda *(Sphyraona* sp.), sometimes enter the pot too. Outside the lagoon among the reefs surrounding the island the principal pot fish are cavalli *(Caranx* sp.), larger snapper species and a small bony doctorfish *(Acanthurus hepatus).* Fishermen set their pots in favorite places, hauling them again after a week or two.

The other important fishing method is seining. The Barbuda net is a simple seine, a single-layer oblong net meant to hang vertically in the water, its lower edge lined with stone sinkers and its upper edge with floats of wood, cork or styrofoam. There are 12 seines in Barbuda, used by their owners and also lent out in return for a share of the catch. Seines last five years or more, if holes are carefully mended and lines and floats are replaced.

The seine is used in the lagoon, where depths do not exceed two meters, and in the "flashes," shallow salt ponds just inside the shore-line among the mangrove. Lagoon seining yields mostly mullet *(Mugil cophalus)*, but also "tenpounder" *(Elops* sp.), ladyfish, barracuda, snapper and "shad" *(Gerres anereus* and *Eucinostemus* sp.). On nights when there is neither groundswell nor full moon (which means high water) to drive the fish away, the crew sets out at about 1:00 a. m., trailing behind their sailboat a dinghy into which the net has carefully been folded. At the right spot, the crew climbs into the dinghy and rows a great circle around the fish, paying out the seine. When the fish are encircled, the fishermen draw the seine in tightly and load it full of fish into the dinghy, which is again towed home behind the sailboat.

Seine fishing in the flashes follows the same principle. It is good after a high tide strands the fish in the shallow flashes, where they can easily be seen. The fishermen encircle the fish on foot in the shallow water, and draw the net in tightly. They carry the catch home by dinghy or donkey.

There is still another way of using the seine. This technique creates an artificial environment on the lagoon bottom to lure the fish into a position where they can be netted. The fisherman cuts a clump of a certain variety of mangrove and places it in a bare spot on the bottom. Vertical shoots grow downward from its branches to the bottom, making a shelter of tangled roots and branches that attracts grunt, chub, red snapper and small barracuda. After about two weeks the fisherman can surround the mangrove with a seine, pull up the mangrove, and catch the fish [31].

The seines are about 180 meters long. The ideal crew is three men, each of whom receives a share of the catch, along with shares for the owners of boat and net. These are usually, but not necessarily, crewmembers too, and receive two shares if they are. Owners sometimes lend boats or nets in return for their share of the catch, but no one keeps equipment specifically for that kind of profit.

The fishing boats themselves are open sloops between 4 and 5.5 meters in length. There are 15 of these in Barbuda along with one decked sloop of almost 9 meters, and some small rowing and sailing dinghies. The sloops show variety in beam and freeboard, but have in common carvel-built hulls, shallow wooden skeg-like keels that require the boats to carry ballast, and comparatively short masts and long booms. The mainsail is fairly small in relation to the length and weight of the boat. Their size allows the boats to handle well in the strong, steady trades, but makes them useless in light and puffy winds, a failing that affects the catch at certain times of the year. The shallow keels suit the lagoon, where reefs bring water depths to less than a meter in some spots.

None of the sailing vessels has an outboard engine, although engines are used for lobster-diving, which is profitable enough to pay for them. Not only does diving earn the money to buy engines, but anyone who could buy one would turn it toward lobster-diving outside the lagoon rather than toward fishing.

Those fishermen who do not own a boat often set and haul their pots from a simple raft called a "dagger" [41, 42]. Daggers are made from the stems of the dagger plant (*Agave karatto*, century plant). They are built at the place where they are to be used. Twelve mature dagger stalks are pegged together by a wooden pole passed through a hole bored in each end of each stalk. The pole is secured and the stalks forced together tightly by a figure-eight lashing. The raft is propelled by poles, a shorter one to get the raft offshore and a longer one for maneuvering in deeper water. The dagger raft is an efficient craft for carrying fishpots and for use as a diving platform from which a fisherman may gather conchs for home use. Its disadvantage is that hand propelling limits its range, and it must be used with some other means of transporting the catch to the village. But it is not dependent on wind, it costs nothing, and it is easily built and replaced.

EFFECTIVE ENVIRONMENT AND THE CATCH

Studying fishing requires long, continuous observation, for there are many difficulties and a great deal of vagueness inherent in the activity itself [43]. These are related to the nature of the fish and to the multiplicity of factors affecting fish, fishermen and observer. In Barbuda they have also to do with the fact that fishing is only a part of each fisherman's activities and household economy. There are also variable environmental conditions that affect the behavior of fish and fishermen. Technology enters too, for whatever piscine riches lie beyond its reach might as well not exist.

In any environment, only those resources that can be reached by culture and technology count as resources at all. Culture and technology carve out what Steward called the "effective environment" from natural possibilities. The Antiguan agricultural report of 1963 illustrates perfectly the distinction between environment and effective environment in its single comment on Barbudan fishing: " Fish remained a scarce commodity on the island, although Barbuda is noted for plenty and excellent fishing. There is need for fitting fishing boats with engines...which would facilitate...deep-water fishing " [44]. Barbuda's effective environment does not include much deep water for fishing, since deep water cannot be reached by sailing boats in practicable one-day trips and the few engines on the island are more profitably turned to lobster-diving. Thus the "plenty and excellent" fishing does not exist, except in some ideal way unrelated to the realities of Barbudan economy and technology. It is perhaps a sporting ideal that has no bearing on the subsistence and cash needs that Barbudan fishing must meet.

Sport fishers do occasionally visit the island because of its obscure reputation as a fishing paradise. These infrequent visitors leave in the warden's "Visitors' Book" a repetitive record of disappointment. For every disappointment there is some special condition to blame for the day's failure: strong winds, weak winds, groundswell, tide, season, poor boats, lack of proper bait. Yet the observable reality in the form of fish caught is the only reality worth bothering about.

Technological as well as environmental limits affect West Indian reef and demersal fishing elsewhere, too. Wherever the fishpot is the principal tool, both total production and yield in return for effort are low and cannot supply more than local needs [22]. Yet this is not the fault of the pots, which are probably well-suited to supplying local needs while conserving resources. A study of fishing in the Leewards and Windwards done around 1945 indicates this likelihood:

The mainstay of Leeward Island fisheries is demersal (bottom) communities of fish associated with coral reefs down to thirty fathoms, where the fishpot is perhaps the most efficient method of capture, and is the dominant method...These reef fisheries cannot be pressed too hard without serious reduction of yield [6].

Barbudan waters reachable by sail in one-day round trips do not even approach 30 fathoms (55 meters) [45]. When a month in Barbuda passes in which only three pot fishermen think it worthwhile to fish, and bring in daily catches of less than 10 kg, we may suspect that the environment is already yielding what it can to the technology. Research in Jamaica confirms that the low density of fish among near-shore reefs is a consequence of local pot fishing, and not a cause of low pot yields [23].

Some of the environmental factors that affect the movements and therefore the availability of fish are wind, tide, groundswell, breeding needs and the migrations of the fish food supply. Thus, no matter what the fish numbers, a proper conjunction of weather, season and moon phase is necessary to make them available. The best season for Barbudan seine fishing, for example, is said to be from January to June, when mullet are abundant in Barbudan waters. In order to net mullet, fishermen must have wind enough to sail, through not so much wind that maneuvering the net is difficult. Yet this is the very season of puffy and variable winds, for the usually strong trade winds falter in Barbuda during February and March. The comparative calm encourages the fish, but discourages the fishermen, who depend on sail. And so it is the very time of abundant fish that fishermen, knowing that the winds are undependable, beach and repair their boats.

Heavy groundswell also appears during this time. It drives mullet into deeper water, beyond sailing range. Further, 5 of every 28 days are spoiled for fishing by full moon, which affects the water and therefore the movements of fish. This is folk belief as well as environmental fact [23]. The catch is therefore limited by natural, behavioral and technological realities during the very season when mullet are plentiful in the waters. I observed this situation in February 1973, when only one seining crew bothered to go out at all, and made only two catches the whole month totaling 300 kg. The numbers of fish were there, but they were unobtainable because of winds, rainfall, groundswell and tides. Mechanization of boats would bring these fish into the effective environment, but it is the simple technology itself that prevents oversrtaining of the resource while it satisfies local food needs.

Environmental factors also affect potfishing, which is supposedly best from July to December, when absence of groundswell allows grunt to come close to shore. Yet the strong, steady winds of this season that are good for sailing make handling rafts and pots difficult. This is also the season of cutting and burning swiddens, and of planting and cultivation after the onset of the rainy season in September. Fishermen must coordinate fishing with the other pursuits that contribute to their livelihood. Only 7 out of Barbuda's 36 fishermen fish full time without engaging in other productive activities, although the income from fishing is essential to all of them.

Catches, then, have little to do with the numbers of fish or with the desires and industry of fishermen. They are dependent on factors that cannot be controlled or even predicted with certainty. For the observer who tries to estimate the catch or to assess the economics of fishing, this vagueness in the activity presents as many problems as it does to the man who tries to earn a living at it. Catches can be known only after years of continuous observation. Epstein could not keep track of catches in Matupit through the seining season, and so could not assess the contribution of fishing to income [46]. Firth was forced to generalize his annual figures from six months of observation, from known seasonal variation, and other factors [43].

Brown arrived at an average of 200 lbs. (90.8 kg) a week for 50 weeks for the Leeward Islands pot fisherman who uses sloop or outboard-equipped dinghy [6]. The Barbudan fishermen that I observed rarely approached half that amount. Brown's estimate for Barbuda, 60,000 lb/yr (27,240 kg/yr) is perhaps closer to reality, but still must be regarded cautiously.

Davenport suggests that it is better to estimate time spent on fishing than to try to estimate catch, and gives a figure of 30 hours a week as the yearly average at spent on fishing at Negril, Jamaica [47]. However, it is not possible to estimate or observe the time that Barbudan fishermen spend, since many apparent fishing trips are combination trips on which more time may be spent harvesting pigeon peas or tending charcoal kilns than is actually spent hauling and getting fish pots. Remembering that the data must be used and generalized with caution, let us see what can be drawn from them.

One seine crew of three members made three trips during February and caught 300 kg of fish on two of them. Since the price of mullet in 1973 was East Caribbean (EC) $0.60/kg (US $0.30/kg), each share for the month yielded EC $36. Although the crew had told me that they fish twice every week, I could see that their actual behavior was determined by conditions and not by their ideal. Five nights of high tide, eight nights that closed the rainy season, and heavy groundswell kept the boats on the beach and the fishermen indoors. The fish were there, it is true, but they were not available to fishermen. Because conditions kept most fishermen at home, the 300 kg caught by this crew were all sold, but large catches of mullet often were not sold and must be dried and salted in the hope of later sale.

During this same time, four pot fishermen made a total of 23 trips, but only one caught anything. It was, after all, the seine season. He brought in about 76 kg of fish at EC $0.70 kg, earning EC $53.20 for the month. His earnings were therefore greater than those of the two seining crewmembers who received a share each, but less than those of the crewmember who also owned the boat and net. The pot fisherman, however, puts in far more labor. Yet, his returns are more certain for small amounts of fish. Ten or so kilos on each trip are always sold immediately.

In fact, fishing income seems to average out to about EC $26 per week. These observations, cautiously as they must be used, tend to confirm Firth's observation among Malay fishermen that there is a general equilibrium in the returns of various kinds of fishing, and that the more regular kinds, in this instance pot fishing, yield a lower *rate* of return, or, as I have expressed it, require a greater investment of labor.

Although fishing income is never great, fishing is essential to the household, to the Barbudan diet and as a means of redistributing money on the island. It seems clear that such an income could never support mechanization, and that mechanization is probably not desirable if the fish resources are to be preserved. Lobster diving, on the other hand, is the Barbudan marine industry that brings money into the island from outside and yields a greater return for effort. It is not surprising that mechanization, still on a small scale, is turned toward that pursuit.

LOBSTER DIVING IN BARBUDA

Because lobster prices are much higher than fish prices, lobster diving has drawn off technological resources in the Caribbean. In Bequia, lobster diving emerged as an important activity when the price of lobster rose to two and a half times the price of fish. Mechanization, capital, and manpower were invested in lobster fishing until it could not easily be given up, although catches began to decline as a result of over exploitation. Development of the lobster fishery through technology was self-defeating [27]. Because lobsters are part of a succession of fauna that will enter pots according to their placement and length of soak, the pot owner has a choice [23]. The pot fills more slowly with lobster than with fish, however, and ultimately yields about the same income for the sailing pot fisherman. The divers using powered boats have a greater earning potential, and diving offers the possibility of entrepreneurship as well.

Lobster divers go out in teams of three, sharing equally their catch of about 900 kg. They earn about EC $150 a week, a sum far above the fisherman's income. But because their income is so great, divers work less. They earn about EC $3000 a year for 100 days of work, still a large income by Barbudan standards. A local lobster dealer relieves the divers of managerial tasks by purchasing the catch for export by air to Puerto Rico.

While it may appear that divers have a large unrealized earning potential, we may see their limited activities and limited mechanization as a response to practical knowledge of what the grounds can produce. Beyond a certain investment of time and equipment, the return may not be worthwhile. Meanwhile, the divers' limits on their own work have the effect of conserving the resource, as have their practices of free diving only and of sparing female lobster about to reproduce.

POLITICAL CHANGE AND FISHERY DEVELOPMENT FOR BARBUDA

We have seen that the changing goals of fishery development schemes in the Caribbean are associated with changing political statuses. The movement toward independence that began after World War II continues, as does the weakening of any federation imposed by former colonial powers. In 1969 Anguilla declared her independence from the Associated State of St. Kitts-Nevis-Anguilla [48]. At present, Nevis agitates for separation from St. Kitts, and Tobago from the state of Trinidad and Tobago [49]. Tiny island secession appears to be the political movement of the 1980s in the Caribbean [50]. Recent events in Barbuda epitomize this trend. (Statements about Barbuda's present condition that are otherwise unreferenced emerge from my own conversations and correspondence with Eric Burton, Barbudan representative to the Antiguan parliament; Hilbourne Frank, chairman of the Barbuda Council; Derek Knight, legal counsel to the Council; and Russell John, publisher of the *Barbuda Voice*, from November 26, 1979 to June 26, 1980.)

In January 1977 Barbuda achieved its first self-governing council after a long history of dependence that included periods of a family fief leased from the British Crown, as the leased holding of private developers, as Crown Colony, and as ward of Antigua under the administration of an Antiguan appointee aptly named "the Warden" [36, 37, 51, 52]. This was the first achievement of a secessionist movement that began in 1971, after Antigua, recently moved from British colony to British Associated State, began to anticipate complete independence. Since then the Barbuda Council, whose members have twice been elected as independents on secessionist platforms, has flatly declared that Barbuda will not remain part of an independent Antigua. In the fall of 1979 the Council entered into negotiations on the matter with the British Foreign Office, and expects to continue talks in 1980. According to one British constitutional lawyer there is no legal reason why Barbuda should not be separate from Antigua, and many reasons of custom, history, society and ideology why it should [53, 54].

Antigua expects full independence in late 1980. Whether Barbuda goes into independence alone, as part of Antigua (which seems unlikely), or works out some alternative solution with the Foreign Office, the fishery will be affected. Antigua has long regarded it with interest [44]. Some Barbudans also see an export fishery as part of the economy of an independent Barbuda [55].

The question of fishery development in Barbuda is not only academic, since the Barbuda Council has contracted for an economic development study to be carried out as part of the case to be presented to the Foreign Office. What kinds of development might possibly be applied to Barbuda's finfish and lobster fishery?

It is not just a matter of the comparative abundance of the resource that lobster diving rather than finfish fishing is the marine activity that links Barbuda to the outside economy and brings new money into the island. It is also a matter of economics and technology, for the price of lobster makes powered boats and air transport worthwhile. But there is no evidence that the lobster fishery can support intensified exploitation with new technology. In fact, the evidence from Bequia suggests the dangers of stimulating production [27]. But mechanization is not the only way that development can proceed. Conservation, management, the services of a marine biologist and ultimately the possibility of lobster culture may be alternatives [39, 40, 56]. Lobster culture is not yet a workable reality, but as research continues it may become a significant alternative to long-distance refrigerated vessels.

Demersal fish, on the other hand, have a comparatively low commercial value, although their subsistence value is crucial. Their low market value makes mechanization, cold storage, and quick transport unworkable. Fish therefore remain a resource for subsistence and internal sale, a use suited to the nature and quantity of the resource. Both seine and pot fishermen might be helped by outboard engines, which would overcome the difficulties of too strong and too weak winds, and would extend the range of fishing boats into deeper waters. Bottom trawling, purse seining for pelagic schools, gillnetting and true trammel netting might then be introduced [5].

However, even these modest innovations have disadvantages. Fishing income cannot provide for the purchase of engines or different kinds of nets and boats, and it is not known whether catches would offset indebtedness. It is not known how long the waters could sustain purse seining, gillnetting and bottom trawling, or whether the yield would justify the investment in equipment. Further, the bottoms of the waters surrounding Barbuda are not smooth and would be destructive to bottom trawling equipment. Clearly one requirement for the development of the Barbudan fishery is prior research into stock sizes and fish movements and into optimal equipment within the means of Barbudan purchase and maintenance.

One very modest innovation that might make a great difference in catch is the stackable S-shaped trap. Because a traditional boat can carry six or seven times more of these than of ordinary pots, mobility is increased and fishermen may exploit offshore banks. The pots catch fewer fish, but compensate by using less space and labor [30]. Another alternative to the application of technology to existing stocks is fish culture, a kind of development that might be quite workable and productive in the mangrove flashes along the shore [9, 57].

CONCLUSION

The Barbudan fishery has shown us the need for considering effective environment and local conditions before implementing plans for economic change. So far, an interaction of environment, artisanal technology, and economy has protected the fishery from depletion and preserved it for local use. However, this working balance could easily by upset by mechanization aimed at expanding production. Even the minimal innovations that I have suggested require cautious testing and evaluation. At the same time it is necessary to recognize that the fishery exists to fulfill Barbudan needs, and that these needs may change as Barbuda's political status changes.

I have argued that the changing emphasis of Caribbean fishing development proposals toward commercial production reflects changing political status and the national aspirations of Caribbean states. The former concern of colonial authorities for local food supply has given way to the concern of emergent states for their own economic autonomy. The importance of small fisheries to local diet and local economy is unequivocal, yet the needs and aspirations of emergent states are also important. How these differing development needs are to be reconciled and made mutually supportive is one of the critical problems in economic development.

REFERENCES

[1] Poole, B. L. *The Caribbean Commission: Background of Cooperation in the West Indies* (Columbia, S.C.: University of South Carolina Press, 1951).

[2] Brown, H. H. "The Fisheries of British Guiana," Development and Welfare in the West Indies, Bull. No. 3, Advocate Co., Barbados (1942).

[3] Brown, H. H. "The Sea Fisheries of Barbados," Development and Welfare in the West Indies, Bull. No. 1, Advocate Co., Barbados (1942).

[4] Brown, H. H. "The Sea Fisheries of Trinidad and Tobago," Development and Welfare in the West Indies, Bull. No. 2, Advocate Co., Barbados (1942).

[5] Whiteleather, R. T., and H. H. Brown. "An Experimental Fishery Survey in Trinidad, Tobago and British Guiana, " Anglo-American Caribbean Commission, Washington, DC (1945).

[6] Brown, H. H. "The Fisheries of the Windward and Leeward Islands," Development and Welfare in the West Indies, Bull. No. 20, Advocate Co., Barbados.

[7] Thompson, E. F. "The Fisheries of Jamaica," Development and Welfare in the West Indies, Bull. No. 18, Barbados (1945).

[8] Thompson, E. F. "The Fisheries of British Honduras," Development and Welfare in the West Indies, Bull. No. 21, Barbados.

[9] "Onverwagt Brackishwater Fish Culture Station, British Guiana," Fisheries Division Bull. No. 3, Department of Agriculture, British Guiana, La Penitence, British Guiana (1960).

[10] Whiteleather, R. T. "Another Look at the Caribbean Fisheries," in *Proceedings of the Seventh Annual Session of the Gulf and Caribbean Fisheries Institute* (Coral Gables, FL: University of Miami, 1955), pp. 180-183.

[11] Salmon, G. C. "Report on the Fisheries Industry in the Countries Served

by the Caribbean Commission," FAO Report No. 781, UN Food and Agriculture Organization, Rome, Italy (1958).

[12] Lewis, G. K. *The Making of the Modern West Indies* (London, England: MacGibbon and Kee, 1968).

[13] Caribbean Commission. *Report of the Third Caribbean Fisheries Seminar,* St. Maarten, Netherlands Antilles, July 3-9, 1959 (Trinidad: Central Secretariat, 1959).

[14] Chapelle, M. I. In: *Report of the Third Caribbean Fisheries Seminar,* St. Maarten, Netherlands Antilles, July 3-9, 1959 (Trinidad: Central Secretariat, 1959), pp. 12-13.

[15] "Report to the Government of the West Indies Federation on Fishing Boats, Based on the Work of Kjeld Rasmussen, Naval Architect," Expanded Program of Technical Assistance, No. 1409, UN Food and Agricultural Organization, Rome, Italy (1961).

[16] Kasahari, H., and C. P. Idyll. "Report to the Managing Director, United Nations Special Fund Caribbean Fishery Mission," United Nations, New York (1962).

[17] Rathjen, W. F., M. Yesaki and B. Hsu. "Trawlfishing Potential off Northeastern South America," in *Proceedings of the 21st Annual Session of the Gulf and Caribbean Fisheries Institute,* J. B. Higman, Ed. (Coral Gables, FL: University of Miami, 1971), pp. 86-110.

[18] Dibbs, J. L. "Review of the UNDP/FAO Caribbean Fisheries Development Project, Phase I, 1965-1969," in *Proceedings of the 22nd Annual Session of the Gulf and Caribbean Fisheries Institute,* J. B. Higman, Ed. (Coral Gables, FL: University of Miami, 1970), pp. 106-109.

[19] Winsor, H. C. "Progress Report on the UNSF/FAO Caribbean Fisheries Development Project," in *Proceedings of the 19th Annual Session of the Gulf and Caribbean Fisheries Institute,* J. B. Higman, Ed. (Coral Gables, FL: University of Miami, 1967), p. 127.

[20] Ripley, W. E. "The Caribbean Fishery Development Project," in *Proceedings of the 23rd Annual Session of the Gulf and Caribbean Fisheries Institute,* J. B. Higman, Ed. (Coral Gables, FL: University of Miami,

[21] Gines, H., and F. Cervignon. "Exploratory Fishing in the Southern Caribbean and Northern Atlantic Coasts of South America," in *Proceedings of the 20th Annual Session of the Gulf and Caribbean Fisheries Institute,* J. B. Higman, Ed. (Coral Gables, FL: University of Miami, 1967), pp. 145-158.

[22] Juhl, "Status and Potential of the Fishery in the Caribbean," in *Proceedings of the 23rd Annual Session of the Gulf and Caribbean Fisheries*

Institute, J. B. Higman, Ed. (Coral Gables, FL: University of Miami, 1971), 175-183.

[23] Munro, J. L., P. H. Reeson and V. C. Gaut. "Dynamic Factors Affecting the Performance of the Antillean Fish Trap," in *Proceedings of the 23rd Annual Session of the Gulf and Caribbean Fisheries Institute,* J. B. Higman, Ed. (Coral Gables, FL: University of Miami, 1971), pp. 184-194.

[24] "P. L. M. Election Manifesto," Progressive Labour Movement, St. John's, Antigua (1970).

[25] "Report of the Tripartite Economic Survey of the Eastern Caribbean, January-April, 1966," Ministry of Overseas Development, London, England (1967).

[26] Adams, J. E. "Conch Fishing Industry of Union Island, Grenadines, West Indies," *Trop. Sci.* 12:279-288 (1970).

[27] Adams, J. E. "The Lobster Fishing Industry of Mt. Pleasant, Bequia Island, West Indies," in *Proceedings of the 24th Annual Session of the Gulf and* Caribbean Fisheries Institute, J. B. Higman, Ed. (Coral Gables, FL: University of Miami, 1972). pp. 126-133.

[28] Bair, A. "The Barbados Fishing Industry," Publication No. 6, Geography Department, McGill University, Montreal, Quebec (1962).

[29] Brody, R. W. "Fish Poisoning in the Eastern Caribbean," in *Proceedings of the 24th Annual Session of the Gulf and Carribean Fisheries Institute,* J. B. Higman, Ed. (Coral Gables, FL: University of Miami, 1971), pp. 100-116.

[30] Munro, J. L. "Large Volume Stackable Fish Traps for Offshore Fishing," in *Proceedings of the 25th Annual Session of the Gulf and Caribbean Fisheries Institutes,* J. B. Higman, Ed. (Coral Gables, FL: University of Miami, 1973), pp. 121-128.

[31] Craig, A. K. *Geography of Fishing in British Honduras and Adjacent Coastal Waters,* Louisiana State University Studies, Coastal Studies Series No. 14 (Baton Rouge, LA: Louisiana State University Press, 1966).

[32] Copes, P. "Factor Rents, Sole Ownership and the Optimum Level of Fisheries Exploitation," *Manchester School Econ. Soc. Studies* 40:145-163. (1972).

[33] Epple, G. M. "Technological Change in a Grenada West Indies Fishery, 1950-1970," in *Those Who Live from the Sea,* M. E. Smith, Ed., American Ethnological Society Monographs No. 62 (New York: West Publishing Co., 1977), pp. 173-193.

[34] Flores, J. E. "Changes in Traditional Fishing Technology of

Northeastern Venezuela," paper presented at the Ninth International Congress of Anthropological and Ethnological Sciences, Chicago, IL, August-September 1973.

[35] Keddie, W. H. "Fish and Futility in Iranian Development," *J. Devel. Areas* 6:9-28 (1971).

[36] Berleant-Schiller, R. "The Failure of Agricultural Development in Post-emancipation Barbuda: A Study of Social and Economic Continuity in a West Indian Community," *Bol. Estud. Latinoam. Caribe* (26):21-36 (1978).

[37] Lowenthal, D., and C. G. Clarke. "Slave-Breeding in Barbuda: The Past of a Negro Myth," *Ann. N.Y. Acad. Sci.* 292:510-535 (1977).

[38] Berleant-Schiller, R. "Production and Division of Labor in a West Indian Peasant Community" *Am. Ethnologist* 4:253-272 (1977).

[39] Bryden, J. M. "Report on Barbuda," Ministry of Finance, St. John's, Antigua (1968).

[40] "Barbuda: A Report to the Government of Antigua," British Development Division in the Caribbean, Foreign and Commonwealth Office, Overseas Development Administration, Bridgetown, Barbados (1971).

[41] Forman, S. *The Raft Fishermen* (Bloomington, IN: Indiana University Press, 1970).

[42] Hammel, E. A., and Y. D. Haase. "A Survey of Peruvian Fishing Communities," *Anthropol. Rec.* 21:211-299 (1960).

[43] Firth, R. *Malay Fishermen* (London, England: Kegan Paul, Trench, Trubner, 1946).

[44] "Annual Reports," Department of Agriculture, Lands, Marketing, and Credit, St. John's, Antigua (1949-1964).

[45] "Chart 1484, Island of Barbuda," revised ed., U.S. Department of the Navy, Oceanographic Office, Washington, D.C. (1970).

[46] Epstein, A. L. *Matupit: Land, Politics and Change among the Tolai of New Britain* (Berkeley, CA: University of California Press, 1969).

[47] Davenport, W. H. "A Comparative Study of Two Jamaican Fishing Communities," PhD Thesis, Yale University (1956).

[48] Parry, J. H., and P. M. Sherlock. *A Short History of the West Indies,* 3rd ed. (London, England: Macmillan, 1971).

[49] Thorndike, A. E. "National Identity and Secession: The Case of Nevis," paper presented at the Fifth Annual Meeting of the Caribbean Studies

Association, Curacao, Netherlands Antilles, May 7-10, 1980.

[50] Smith, L. "Secession: The Problem of the Eighties," *Bull. East. Caribbean Aff.* 5:29-30 (1979).

[51] Berleant-Schiller, R. "Land Tenure and Political Change in Barbuda," in *Proceedings of the Middle States Division, Association of American Geographers* (in press).

[52] Hall, D. *Five of the Leewards* (St. Laurence, Barbados: Caribbean Universities Press, 1971).

[53] Lowenthal, D., and C. G. Clarke. "Island Orphans: Barbuda and the Rest," *J. Commonwealth Studies* (in press).

[54] Macdonald, J. "the Constitutional Position of the Island of Barbuda," Unpublished manuscript (1979).

[55] Burton E., Personal communication (December 3, 1979).

[56] Ingle, R. M., and R. Witham. "Biological Considerations in Spiny Lobster Culture," in *Proceedings of the 21st Annual Session of the Gulf and Caribbean Fisheries Institute,* J. B. Higman, Ed. (Coral Gables, FL: University of Miami, 1969), pp. 158-162.

[57] Weatherly, A. H., and B. M. G. Cogger. "Fish Culture: Problems and Prospects," *Science* 197:427-430 (1977).

SECTION 2
SOCIAL DYNAMICS AND
TECHNOECONOMIC ADAPTATIONS

INTRODUCTION

In the introduction to Section 1, we alluded to the upward aggregation of marine fisheries management responsibility and authority to governmental and quasigovernmental bodies. People in these bodies must make decisions concerning conservation, allocation and utilization of marine resources that are based on certain principles, natural and social scientific data and information, and public and user group input. These principles, and the policy decisions that result from them, are intended to be consistent, rational and tailored to the requirements of particular situations.

It is the dialectic between the need for general systemic principles and the need to tailor management decisions to particular situations which defines the context of Section 2. As we move from the high levels of responsibility and authority discussed in Section 1 to the more specific analyses of sociocultural dynamics and technoeconomic adaptations in Section 2, we will pick up a thread which we began in the introduction to Section 1. Policies, and the decisions that result from them, change in character as they are implemented down through the system. A national policy is altered somewhat by each lower level governmental entity which must actually implement the policy. A regional policy, whether it is agreed on among nations or among townships, will be expressed differently in each economy, each culture, each political sector which is subject to the authority of the policymaker.

Just as a statement in a foreign language must be translated into the vernacular to be understood and complied with in another, when resource management principles must finally be translated into action they must be expressed in a form which is understandable to those who are expected to alter their behavior. Further, that form must carry the possibility and probability of compliance within the range of alternatives and constraints of the subject population. Thus when, as Löfgren

141

points out, a Swedish bureaucrat decides as a matter of principle that it is best for a fisherman to have a single, year-round occupation, he may have to implement that decision among a population of crofter-fishermen for whom year-round fishing is not a feasible economic alternative, and whose familial structure, land tenure system, and social and political relationships conform to a system of occupational pluralism.

In most cases, in fact, the formulator of the original policy principle may never become aware of the reasons for the success or failure of the implementation of that policy. The reason for this is twofold. First, the implementation itself must often transcend so many layers of the management structure that it is not possible either for the effects of the policy to reach the subjects intact, or for information concerning the ill-fit or necessity for alterations in the policy to reach back up to the policymaker. Second, there is most often no rigorous, documented evidence of the full range of factors relevant to the implementation of a given policy in a particular situation.

It is this second problem to which Section 2 of this volume is addressed. These articles explore specific examples of sociocultural dynamics and technoeconomic adaptations. They are examples of the particular aspects of economy and society which are relevant to policy formulation, and they comment on the policy principles and management measures that have affected fishermen, fishing communities, and fishing industries in the past.

To provide a transition from the policy principle orientation of Section 1 we have arranged the chapters in Section 2 in increasing order of specificity in their social scientific analysis. Thus Löfgren's chapter begins the section in a vein similar to Section 1, with considerable discussion devoted to Swedish fisheries policy. Each chapter thereafter delves more deeply into empirically-based social and economic questions, ending with Acheson's heavily quantitative analysis of innovation in the Maine lobster fishery. These papers, with their unique levels and styles of analysis, are intended to demonstrate the different kinds of social scientific analysis that can both inform policymakers of the effects of their policies and, more importantly, can form the basis for input which can guide the formation of policy in the first place. Thus we are not aiming at a set of tools which are useful only in evaluation after-the-fact. Rather we propose that the modes of analysis and types of data and information collection exhibited in the following papers are necessary adjuncts to a consistent, rational, socioculturally and economically appropriate process of initial policy development.

THE CHAPTERS

Löfgren

Löfgren offers a comparative historical analysis of maritime adaptations in the area known as the "Atlantic Fringe." He focuses on changes in peasant fishing and crofting villages that have been transformed into small-scale trawling communities, and illustrates how local communities have become integrated into wider social and economic systems.

Three points bridge the gap between policy principles and social and economic analysis. The first is Löfgren's treatment of occupational pluralism as a successful adaptation to conditions such as seasonality and existing economic opportunities. He points out that criticisms of such adaptations from policy levels—criticisms which label these adaptations as conservative in a pejorative sense—ignore the fact that the explanation of occupational pluralism is not to be found in the conservatism of the fishermen but in the very nature of the process of industrialization in rural and semirural areas. He points out that pluralism should not be viewed as an example of economic marginality, but rather as one of a progression of links between maritime communities and general industrial development.

The second point concerns the role of the middleman and entrepreneur in development. Often the middleman is viewed as a parasite, firmly in control of the market and distribution of goods and services to the detriment of the local population. Löfgren points out how critical this role is in regard to the modernization of the fisheries, a role expanded on by Pollnac in a later chapter in this section, and how, contrary to popular belief, the middleman may be subject to strict and productive local normative controls in a "moral economy" context.

The third issue of importance is Löfgren's treatment of the family in the fishery economy. In many analyses there has been a tendency to overstate the role of kinship relations in preindustrial fishing, and understate them in industrial economies. Löfgren argues that in preindustrial Sweden fishing labor recruitment patterns were based on neighborhood and friendship links as much as on kin ties. With the capitalization of fishing production, problems of ownership, inheritance and management emerged, but in fact the increased reliance on kinship networks offered a partial solution to these problems. For example, modernization in the form of an increasingly capital-intensive industry places a great deal of pressure on the family as an effective economic unit, but the necessary working knowledge of taxation and legislation can often be developed with just such a corporate kinship structure.

As fish stocks in the North Atlantic have become depleted, many fishermen have left the industrial fishery. Many of these have left only to return to an occupational motif similar to the preindustrial one, namely, that of the crofter/fishermen which represented the starting point of Löfgren's analysis. Anyone suggesting during the prosperous 1960s that a return to such a composite, small production unit had a future would have been severely criticized. Now, however, such an alternative seems to be feasible in the Scandinavian countries. Löfgren's clear analysis of these and other timely and crucial occupational issues in fisheries management present useful examples of the considerable overlap among matters of both scholarly and policy interest.

Faris

The character of fishery policy is determined by the paradigm within which that policy is developed. This paradigm defines the nature of the "problem" which requires the formulation of the policy in the first place. How one defines the problem, and what one perceives as the symptoms of the problem are critical variables in the policy formula.

Faris suggests that fishery policy in Newfoundland developed under an inappropriate and incorrect paradigm; that of a capitalistic, class-separated economy. What were considered problems by fishery authorities in the Newfoundland case—production flows, employment, profit, capital accumulation, price structure, and so on—were in fact only symptoms of a more basic problem, which was the maldistribution of the ownerships of means of production and of the accrual of the benefits from fishery activity. The inability or unwillingness of those involved in fishery management to address these root problems, Faris argues, inevitably led to a situation where the government became involved more and more in supporting through artificial constraints what was an unproductive and maldistributed system of resource exploitation in the first place.

There are many value systems which may underlie policy formulation, and Faris criticizes a prevalent form of value structure involved in modern fishery activity—that which underlies the capitalistic economic model. The salience of this argument will vary from case to case, but the general point is important; that one must not only be aware of the symptoms which signal trouble in resource exploitation and distribution systems, but one must also question the basic values and beliefs which underlie the system itself. Faris presents ample ethnographic and economic evidence to demonstrate this point.

Maiolo/Tschetter

Traditional treatments of social and economic change trace sequences of change primarily within fishery systems themselves. The sequences usually involve fishing innovations, fishing organization, and adjustments at the institutional/community and cultural levels. In their paper on infrastructure changes in North Carolina, Maiolo and Tschetter argue that such analyses ignore the consequences of changes which may occur in entirely different settings but in a way which affects fishing organization and technology even when such effects are indirect and unintentional.

Their chapter focuses on community infrastructure investments such as the construction of highways, railways and bridges during several periods of development in Carteret County, North Carolina. County development, including changes in fishing organization and technology, could not accurately be explained without a recognition of such factors as the existence, or lack of, railroad lines to the state's interior, the continuous improvement of the highway network within the county and to the rest of the state, and the construction of bridges between communities formerly separated by waterways. In addition to a period of steady development of the tourist trade during the last quarter of the nineteenth and the first half of the twentieth centuries, infrastructure investment made Carteret County the major commercial fishing area in the state and one of the leaders in the south Atlantic region. In association with these developments, changes occurred in the occupational structure, organization and technology of the fishing industry. These trends resulted in a bifurcation in county development: tourism and transport in the west and fishing in the east. Infrastructure investments eventually grew out of this period of bifurcation, creating the county economic links which established the bases for a trend toward social and political integration.

The authors suggest that an inclusive model of maritime adaptations and modernization must explicitly allow for the possibility that changes can be initiated from a wide range of sources, even sources far removed from fishery systems. From a policy standpoint, they suggest that a more inclusive model of structure and infrastructure will result in broader understanding of coastal social and economic processes. Concerning the trend toward tighter controls in coastal zones, for example, existing approaches in the literature on maritime adaptations are not as useful as they could be because they are too limited in scope. What would the effects be on fisheries of restricting recreational housing to limit pollution in coastal areas, as opposed to converting from ground-absorption waste systems to treated waste and allowing housing construction to take place? Questions like this are difficult to answer until a broad, multidimensional model of change and adaptation is established. The synthetic anthropological/sociological approach is needed for the development of such a model.

Pollnac

Small-scale fisheries do not generally have significant impacts on national economic aggregates. When examined on a global basis, however, the number of people in such fisheries and supportive occupations is very impressive (over 13 million people), and these occupational alternatives contribute to the welfare of people in situations which are very difficult to address via large-scale or highly sophisticated economic or technological development approaches. In attempts to improve the productivity of these fisheries, among other goals, policy formulation and implementation have repeatedly run into difficulty. Pollnac argues for the use of a more informed approach than those of the agrarian and industrial sectors, which have often created unnecessary and potentially crippling economic, social, cultural and psychological dislocations.

Pollnac points out that the development of distribution systems and the role of the middlemen (and women) are necessary consequences of developing fisheries. Following the initial comments by Löfgren, Pollnac provides us with additional insights into the increasing complexity of modernizing fisheries. Typically, there are unsettling effects of change stimuli—for example, new technology, ownership patterns and workgroup and community stratification. Even when the intent of a policy stance is to mitigate these effects, unforseen resistance may develop to the effect of management decisions on traditional social organization. A government loan program, for example, may require the establishment of fishermen's cooperatives. The intention may be to break down or prevent the development of what is perceived by a policymaker as an inequitable distribution of economic benefits. In cases where the cooperatives take the form of managing the marketing of fish products, the perceived target is often the economic position of the middleman. But the role of the middleman is frequently viewed too narrowly by policymakers. It is many times a role which involves the provision of many personal and community benefits to fishermen, such as loans and flexible credit, which cannot be offered by cooperatives.

Pollnac utilizes existing data from a wide variety of cultural settings in order to build his model, and illustrates specific reasons for the success or failure of certain features of planned programs for change which may aid in broadening the perspective of the policymaker.

Christensen

Government aid programs experience some of the most subtle and perplexing impediments when key features of the cultural context of their subjects remain unexplored. A government-sponsored low-interest loan program in West Africa in the 1950s failed miserably while, at the same time, an indigenous lending pattern operated successfully at a 50% interest rate! Christensen details the cultural features which account for this and other phenomena which accompanied the introduction of motor power in West African fisheries.

The strong role of women in the marketing and entrepreneurial process is a distinctive feature of West African fisheries. The matrilineal organization of many West African cultures has profound effects on the patterns of capital formation and distribution. Working back to Langdon's discussion in Section 1 of the applicability of formalist economic paradigms, the West African case which Christensen describes is one in which many of the basic tenants of formal economic theory apply, but in which it would be impossible to utilize the formalist paradigm because of the unique social and economic organization of the fishery system.

In comparing the plight of the Fanti fishermen who remain in Ghana with the success of those who migrate temporarily to fish in Liberian waters, it is interesting to observe the adaptive social organization which emerges in the Liberian setting. To be sure, it can be argued that the migration is selective, and that much of the success can be explained by the individual characteristics of those who migrate. Yet Christensen presents solid evidence of the development of structural features which increase the probability of successful ventures in Liberia, features which could perhaps be fostered in Ghana through informed policy development.

Acheson

Innovation in the construction of lobster traps in New England produced an aluminized trap which was said by many to be superior to both vinyl-coated and traditional wooden traps, although this innovation was not uniformly adopted in that fishery. In the final chapter in Section 2, Acheson presents the results of a study intended not only to empirically test the effectiveness of these various gear types, but also to search for the reasons underlying their differential rates of adoption.

Based on careful data collection and analysis, Acheson shows that variables other than trap materials had much more influence on catch rates; namely, season, trap length, skill and bait. Even with those variables controlled, the aluminized traps produced higher catches. Did not the fishermen, with all their experience, share this information? If they did, why was the adoption of the aluminized traps not uniform in the fishery? Much of the answer to these questions lies in the fact that Acheson performed his analysis with the aid of considerable resources: time, money, statistical analysis and computer technology. These resources, and the information they can produce, are not generally available to fishermen. Even with their experience in the fishery, fishermen cannot be expected to produce this kind of comparative analysis.

Irrespective of the actual productivity of various gear types, however, is the complex of social and economic relationships within which the Maine lobster fishery is embedded. Harbor gangs, highliners and cash flow are all concepts which have determined, to a much greater extent than biological productivity, the rate of adoption of various gear types. Although the realization of the information limitations under which fishermen operate is important, it is Acheson's analysis of the social and economic context of innovation which is crucial to policy analysis.

When the eventual adoption of more efficient technologies, such as aluminized traps, result in overwhelming pressure on fishery resources, the resulting regulation and allocation decisions which must be made will rely heavily on the kinds of analysis which Acheson and others in Section 2 have supplied.

All of the papers in the following section explore the sociocultural dynamics of specific situations whose character and economic well-being are subject to the effects of marine fisheries policy. Each provides not only a picture of an arena within which those effects will be played out, but from which attentive policymakers can glean certain basic relationships and phenomena upon which to base their policy principles.

From Löfgren we learn that pluralistic occupational patterns can be a productive and adaptive enterprise, and that the corporate family may be a very effective unit for small-scale trawler fishing. Pollnac advises us that middlemen should not automatically be considered pejorative entities, either economically or socially. Christensen confirms the existence and usefulness of cultural keys to participation in organizational labor migration patterns and badly needed financial assistance programs. In these and other ways each author points out, as a result of careful, documented anthropological and sociological analyses, specific precepts which will work to the aid or to the detriment of modernization and change brought about by marine fisheries policy.

CHAPTER 6
FROM PEASANT FISHING TO INDUSTRIAL TRAWLING: A COMPARATIVE DISCUSSION OF MODERNIZATION PROCESSES IN SOME NORTH ATLANTIC REGIONS

Orvar Löfgren
Department of European Ethnology
University of Lund, Sweden

INTRODUCTION

The North Atlantic region offers excellent opportunities for a comparative analysis of maritime adaptations. Here we find fishermen with highly diverse cultural backgrounds operating with different technologies within varying economic frameworks. No other maritime region of the world has been studied so intensively by anthropologists, historians and other social scientists.

Such a situation provides a good testing ground for general problems of social and economic development. The wealth of historical information enables us to study adaptive processes over long time spans. This research material provides us with unique possibilities for an historical perspective on developmental changes which just have started in other coastal regions of the world.

The aim of this chapter is to discuss some of these comparative problems. I will restrict myself to the development of the North European region labeled "The Atlantic Fringe". More specifically, I will focus on the situation in the Scandinavian countries with comparative examples from Ireland, Scotland, Newfoundland and Eastern Canada.

Furthermore, my discussion will center on one kind of fishing community and one sector of the fishing industry, namely, peasant fishing and crofting villages which have been transformed to small scale-trawling communities during the last century. The company trawler fleets of urban ports have a different history and a different structure that fall outside the scope of this paper [1].

Although we have an abundance of maritime community studies from the North Atlantic region, relatively few attempts have been made at a comparative analysis [2, 3]. My own attempt will be highly tentative. In looking at some patterns and trends of socioeconomic change in Scandinavia I am deliberately taking a bird's-eye-view of the last two centuries. I am well aware of the risks of making complex patterns simple, and ignoring the many regional and local variations. Such an approach is necessary, though, to a discussion of structural similarities in modernization processes. I have singled out a few topics for my analysis, problems I find crucial for our understanding exactly how the traditional structures of many coastal communities have been transformed during the last century and why some traits in these traditional structures have shown such a great persistence. I will focus on the ways in which these local communities have been integrated in wider social and economic systems. The long historical perspective makes it easier to discuss problems of cause and effect, and thus give us a better theoretical framework for general discussion of modernization processes in the North Atlantic and in maritime settings in general.

In the Scandinavian and British regions we can study the life cycle of many fishing communities: their gradual emergence, the development of a peasant fishing economy and the adaptation to industrialization and urbanization during the last century. By depending upon the historical perspective we may also question some of the popular myths about rural fishing communities along the North Atlantic Fringe. They have often been described and analyzed as traditional pockets in an industrialized world, as marginal adaptations almost untouched by social and economic changes in the larger society. These myths of traditionalism and marginality persist among those who are responsible for planning regional development.

Again, I want to stress that my discussion is highly selective. I have tried to isolate four main topics for comparative study. My starting point is the kind of adaptations we find under the label "peasant fishermen." This is followed by a discussion on the persistence of occupational pluralism in these maritime settings. The next topic concerns the role of the entrepreneur in the modernization of peasant fishing. Finally I turn to the problems of capitalization and professionalization in the later stages of economic development and the emergence of trawler fleets.

The empirical material for this discussion is mainly drawn from my book *Fangstman i Industrisamhallet* (Maritime Hunters in Industrial Society) [4], where I have used my study of a Swedish fishing village over the period 1800-1970 as a starting point for a comparative discussion of economic change in some North Atlantic regions [2, 5, 6]. Apart from my own field work on the Swedish west coast, I have had to rely on written sources, mainly in the form of community studies. The elaborate reports of nineteenth century fishery commissioners, which are available both in the Scandinavian countries and from Ireland and Scotland, have constituted an important additional source. I have also drawn heavily on an ongoing, interdisciplinary research project, in which I collaborate with the economic historian Rune Bunte, also at the University of Lund, in analyzing the economic profiles of a sample of Swedish fishing communities during the period of 1870-1970, using both quantitative and qualitative material.

A MARITIME PEASANTRY?

If we search back into history for a period of stable and traditional maritime settlement in Scandinavia we will be disappointed. As far back as historical records will take us we find a dynamic pattern, in which waves of economic expansion and regression succeed each other. Fishing communities grow and stagnate, and the size of the maritime population varies greatly from time to time depending upon market fluctuations and the availability of other economic opportunities in the coastal region.

This is a picture we meet already in the Middle Ages, but for the purpose of this paper I will restrict the historical perspective somewhat. My starting point is the period of about 1700-1850, the period preceding industrialization in Scandinavian history.

At the beginning of the eighteenth century, most coastal regions of Scandinavia were relatively sparsely populated. Fishing was dominated by coastal peasants, who combined maritime activities with farming. The number of specialized, full-time fishermen was small indeed. By a complex combination of land and sea resources, these coastal peasants could maintain a high degree of subsistence. A great many niches were combined to a form a well-balanced production year, which gave the household labor a steady, full-year employment and made it possible to minimize the dependence on market exchange.

We often find these coastal village to be part of a regional economic system which was based upon a kind of ecological symbiosis.

All over Scandinavia coastal peasants exchanged fish for other commodities with inland villages. We can describe this as a system which
integrated different ecotypes or production patterns [5]. In exchange for
their fish, coastal peasants got grain from inland farmers or timber,
wood and berries from woodland peasants.

On the whole these coastal peasants were often in a more favorable economic position than their agrarian or woodland counterparts.
The fact that they had access both to a maritime and a land based
ecosystem meant that they could exploit a wide range of resources and
keep up a high level of subsistence production. They stood with "one
boot in the boat and the other in the field," as a local Swedish saying
put it.

During the eighteenth and nineteenth centuries these regional
economies were radically transformed. This was a period of rapid
growth in peasant populations in Scandinavia and other North European countries. The population boom was closely linked to the emergence of the type of production system labeled agrarian capitalism.
Landowning peasants turned into cash cropping farmers, and the competition for land got tougher. Hand in hand with the demographic
expansion went a total transformation of the socioeconomic structure.
Through a gradual process of proletarization, the class of landless
peasants expanded rapidly, and in many Scandinavian regions it came
to dominating the social structure toward the middle of the nineteenth
century.

The landless class expanded in the phase between the dissolution
of a traditional peasant economy and the emergence of industrial population in Scandinavia. This meant that the landless usually had to make
a living within their local, rural setting. Industrial opportunities were
still few, and the other main alternative was emigration to North America.

It is against this dramatic background of social and economic
change that we must view the new maritime settlements which grew up
during the period of 1750-1900 all over Scandinavia. In many coastal
regions the population doubled during the first half of the nineteenth
century. Although farming was fragmented into smaller and smaller
holdings, the number of landless peasants continued to grow. For these
new proletarians the maritime resources became an important
economic alternative.

Parallel to mass migration across the Atlantic to the United States
we thus find another wave of population movement, which has often
been ignored by historians. Stagnating fishing communities started to

expand and new maritime communities were born as landless peasants moved out to the coast and became fishermen.

What made fishing such an attractive alternative? First, the entry into the occupation was relatively easy. The inexpensive technology needed to carry out small-scale coastal fishing demanded very moderate investments. Secondly the sea was often the only common property resource left in the peasant ecosystem, the only niche not controlled by landowners. (In some regions where landowners had established control of the marine resources, the entry into fishing became more complicated.)

It would be wrong, however, to view this new adaptation as a strictly maritime one. It is, rather, a case of a complex crofting and fishing economy. Few of the settlers could make a living out of fishing alone. Poor marketing possibilities, lack of local capital, absence of sheltered harbors and use of small open boats made fishing a highly seasonal activity. The fishermen had to fall back on other types of subsistence. Most of them tried to become smallholders by renting a patch of land from local landowners or by clearing new fields in the barren coastal landscape. This strategy was made possible by the fact that the land along the seashore often represented a very marginal resource for the landowners. Soils were sandy and of poor quality.

A contemporary innovation made this combination of fishing and small-scale agriculture easier. The potato plant turned out to be ideally suited for these types of marginal soils. It can be argued that it was the combination of two high-value food stuffs, fish protein and potatoes, which facilitated the rapid expansion of new maritime settlements during this period.

This expansion took place on terms dictated by the local landowners. In many Scandinavian regions we find the new class of fishermen crofters tied to the farmers, to whom they usually were subordinate in both political and economic terms. The fishermen were far more dependent upon the farmers than vice-versa. For the farmers the crofters were first of all an agrarian proletariat, a labor reserve which could be tapped seasonally. As farming came to be dominated by cash crops, the need for extra manpower during the peaks of the agricultural year grew.

Thus it was no longer a question of an ecological symbiosis between maritime and agrarian ecotypes, but of a marked economic dependence. Not only did the farmers control much of the crofters resource base, be it arable soil, grazing land, or even fishing rights. They also represented the most important market outlet for the two commodities the fishermen could sell, namely, fish and their own land. Added to this was the fact that crofters often had to turn to farmers for a loan to build a cottage or buy a boat. The asymmetrical character of these transactions can be illustrated by Figure 1, which depicts the flow of goods and services between the two groups.

This exchange system was facilitated by the fact that while the landless expanded toward the sea, we find a reverse movement among the coastal farmers. Their economic focus was gradually transferred from the complex subsistence pattern described earlier to a more specialized cash cropping. Marginal activities like coastal fishing were abandoned and left to the crofters to develop. This new market orientation among the landowning farmers thus created a vacant space for the landless, who not only took up fishing but also many other traditional

LANDOWNING FARMERS →   ← CROFTER/FISHERMEN

Leasing of land for house-building,   Fish
small scale farming and harbour
facilites, fishing and grazing rights

Leasing of sheep and cattle   Seasonal labor
(often on a half-share basis)

Part ownership in boats and   Sea transports
fishing equipment

Provision of credit and cash   Local crafts
loans

Farm products (mainly grain
and meat)

Land transports

Fodder

Timber and fuel

Figure 1. Transactional Flow Between Farmers and Crofter Fishermen.

subsistence activities abandoned by the farmers.

Let me summarize some characteristics of this new adaptation which took place in the periphery of the farming economy. Quite often it was based on a coastal ecosystem with distinct features: a landscape of sandy beaches, marshy fields and poor soils, where the heather often had replaced earlier forests. This ecological setting was exploited with an inexpensive technology. Lack of capital was compensated by intensive use of household labor. Coastal fishing was carried out from small, open boats with equipment manufactured at home. With the use of the potato plant and animals like sheep and goats, marginal land resources could be utilized. Driftwood and seaweed was collected from the beaches. Peat and cow dung constituted two main sources of fuel. The spade had to be used instead of the plough, and for transport one had to make do with wheelbarrows and carrying. Few crofters could afford to keep a horse and cart.

This maritime economy, based on fishing, gardening and gathering, was nothing special to Scandinavians. We find it in most coastal regions along the North Atlantic Fringe [4]. The general process behind these maritime settlements is the same. The growth of the fishing population must be seen as a result of profound changes in the economic and demographic structure of the rural communities which preceed the development of new production systems like agrarian, and later industrial capitalism.

The timetable of this transformation of peasant society varied greatly. The development took place much earlier in the coastal regions of the British Isles than in Scandinavia, while Iceland underwent the same process even later. Other regional variations depend on differences in the economic framework. In areas where industrial expansion occurred almost parallel to the rural population growth, we should expect to find less of this maritime expansion. Again, the British Isles can be used as an example. It is no coincidence that the fishing population of Scotland and Ireland grew much faster during the eighteenth and nineteenth centuries than was the case along the coasts of southern England, where industrialization and urbanization had been in full swing for two centuries.

The Irish and Scottish settings also differ from Scandinavia in that local resources more often were controlled by feudal landlords rather than a class of farmers. This influenced the relations between maritime and agrarian sectors of the regional economy, although the whole pattern of maritime expansion was very much the same. Fishermen were recruited from the lowest social and economic strata in the region, and both their social standing and economic position remained weak. For a general discussion see Lofgren [7], and for regional examples Ansom [8], Darling [9], Evans [10], Goodlad [11], Grant [12], Hunter [13], and Smith [14].

THE PERSISTENCE OF OCCUPATIONAL PLURALISM

One very dominant feature of these nineteenth century communities of crofters and coastal fishermen was their occupational pluralism, an economic trait which has been characteristic of many coastal communities up to the middle of the twentieth century. Most households have combined a number of economic activities, and we often find individuals switching between different occupations during their life cycle. There are many reasons for the emergence and persistence of this economic adaptation. Although the pattern itself may look remarkably alike in a nineteenth and twentieth century setting, the underlying factors can be very different.

First of all there is the periodicity of both farming and fishing activities, which is more marked in the North Atlantic region than in many other coastal areas of the world. Climatic conditions, the habits of marine species and the technology available to exploit them interacted in a way which made fishing a highly seasonal activity. In some regions we find that the production rhythm of fishing and farming overlapped, which gave the household unit problems of coordination. It is against this background that much of the sexual division of labor in the fishermen's household can be explained. In other areas the ecological conditions made combinations easier, for example in Northern Norway, where the important winter cod fishery fit in nicely with the intensive husbandry and fodder collection during the short summer season.

More important was the economic security and flexibility which this composite household economy gave the fishermen. Hardly any nineteenth century fishermen could rely exclusively on maritime activities in these rural settings, especially with the given technology and the uncertain market conditions. A comment from the commissioner for the Irish fisheries in 1866 illustrates this dilemma: "who ever knew Irish fishermen, *exclusively fishermen,* provident? Political economists may say what they please, but I have seldom seen an Irishman exclusively fisherman prosperous for two seasons, *without the bit of land* to occupy him in boisterous weather and to give his family a more certain prospect of food. Numerous illustrations of this theory may be found in Ireland [15]."

It is against this background that we must view the great amount of time and resources many landless fishermen devoted to secure a small holding. The combination of land and sea resources gave both a certain security and an important flexibility to the household economy. A bad fishing season or a failure of the potato crop did not need to have catastrophic consequences for the family. To some extent it could be compensated by a more intensive exploitation of alternative resources. We meet this dynamic pattern of movement between marine and agrarian niches in many nineteenth century coastal settings.

During this period, specialization meant greater dependence on a market where the element of risk-taking was marked. Economic pluralism was part of a highly rational strategy to maintain some degree of economic autonomy and independence of the market fluctuations. The rationality of this strategy, however, was not seen by many contemporary economists and government officials. Instead, economic pluralism was viewed as an economic evil, a stubborn peasant tradition preventing economic development. Two quotations can exemplify this common type of lament.

The first one stems from a report by a fishery commissioner inspecting a Swedish coastal region in 1897. He writes that "the combination of fishing and farming has here, as elsewhere, paralyzed the development of the two livelihoods." His thoughts are echoed in an economist's report on the crofter-fishermen in Lewis in the Scottish Hebrides from 1919: "No land used as land is used in Lewis would pay... specialize and separate the crofter and fisherman. Either can be made profitable if well understood. Both lead to double failure when combined...."

During the nineteenth century, the economic pluralism of crofter fishermen was structured mainly with an agrarian setting. Gardening, agriculture and husbandry were important subsistence activities, and when Scandinavian fishermen took wage labor they mainly worked for local farmers.

With the expansion of industry new opportunities emerged in the coastal economy, but most industrial wage labor came to be of a periodic nature. Again, the explanation of occupational pluralism was not founded in peasant conservatism, but rather in the very nature of early industrialization in marginal and rural areas. The demand for labor tended to very enormously from season to season. One reason for this was ecological condition and the problems of transport. Jobs like logging, floating and work at saw mills were of a seasonal nature, and this was the type of industry that dominated in many Scandinavian regions. We find the same pattern in many construction industries of this period. The demand was not for a full-time industrial work force, but for a manpower reserve that could be employed seasonally and that could take care of itself during the rest of the year. For these early industries, the crofter fishermen constituted an ideal labor force in many ways, and their economic pluralism was an asset rather than a drawback. In this way industrial expansion came to maintain the composite economy, which an earlier generation of government officials had combated.

For many crofter fishermen, wage labor in local industries or seasonal migration to industrial centers became a niche that could be combined with others to spread the incomes over the year, a means of maintaining the traditional adaptation rather than changing it. In many North Atlantic regions, forestry was the most important of the industrial alternatives, especially as this was a winter job which did not interfere with summer fishing and agriculture.

An example from Northern Sweden of the 1920s illustrates this new type of occupational pluralism within the framework of an industrialized economy. Even if fishing supplied the main cash income of the household, the family had to fall back on other sources of income, especially during the winter when very little fishing could be carried out.

> One called oneself "fisherman," but to this title other ones had to be added: log driver, stevedore, mason, logger, seal hunter, carpenter, boat builder, industrial worker, shoemaker, rope-maker, bicycle repairman, etc., just to mention some common sidelines to fishing. A fisherman was usually a jack of all trades [4].

Pluralism remained an important characteristic of many Scandinavian coastal economies up to the middle of the twentieth century. There was a constant mobility between fishing and industrial work. For many of the men who left fishing to work in local industries, the maritime expertise remained a latent capital which could be activated in times of industrial depression or booms in the fisheries. During the depression of the 1930s many unemployed turned back to fishing. In the same way the spectacular fishing boom of the World War II made former fishermen turn to their original occupation.

It is important that we do not analyze these patterns of occupational pluralism as examples of economic marginality or peasant traditionalism. It is obvious that many coastal areas were marginal to early industrialization in a geographical sense, but in economic terms there exist many links between these isolated maritime communities and general industrial development. It would be misleading to talk of dual economies. If we focus on the ways in which the economic pluralism of the fisherman's household was shaped by the restraints and opportunities of the macrosystem, we will reach a better understanding of why this pluralistic pattern persisted for such a long period and why it disappeared so rapidly from the scene during the 1950s and 1960s in Scandinavian and many other north Atlantic regions.

MERCHANTS AND MARKETS

It is obvious that the label "peasant conservatism" does not have any greater explanatory value in discussions of the maintenance of occupational pluralism than in discussions of its origin. The same type of label was also used by government authorities who found it difficult to persuade crofter-fishermen to abandon their small scaled coastal fishing for a more intensive deep sea fishery. Another quotation from a Swedish fishery-commissioner in 1886 may illustrate this cultural stereotype: "The reserved and stubborn personality of the West Coast fisherman has made him distrustful and insusceptible to innovations...."

Such cultural and psychological explanations rarely show any deeper understanding of the fisherman's situation, although they may well reflect the frustrations and bewilderment of planners who cannot make a local population understand "its own best interests." There are many Scandinavian examples of this resistance against the modernization of fishing among crofter fishermen of the late nineteenth and early twentieth centuries. New technologies based upon the use of bigger, decked boats, driftnets, seines and boat engines were often very difficult to introduce. The main reason for this resistance was of a structural rather than cultural nature.

These new, more highly capitalized technologies demanded a type of risk-taking which few crofter fishermen could afford, especially since a lack of capital usually meant that new equipment had to be financed with outside credit, often on unfavorable terms.

A changeover to a more intensive deep-sea fishery also meant greater involvement with the market, and here the fisherman's possibilities of influencing prices and other market conditions were small indeed. Although most Scandinavian crofter fishermen exploited a common property resource and owned their means of production, their control over the distribution and marketing of the catches was negligible. In such a situation the fisherman's reluctance to increase production for more distant markets may well be a highly rational strategy. He is better off within the traditional system of local trading and bartering of fish combined with the pattern of economic pluralism discussed earlier. The fact that modernization of peasant fishing always involves a greater dependence upon the market makes a discussion of exactly how fishermen become linked to external systems of exchange important. In the following paragraphs I will focus on one aspect of this economic integration, i.e., the important role played by fish merchants and middlemen in the modernization process.

During this transitional period (1850-1930) we find merchant and local traders occupying a key position in the economic structure of many small fishing communities, not only in Scandinavia but also in Scotland, Ireland and Newfoundland [4]. Views of exactly how this position of economic brokerage has affected the development of local fisheries tend to vary. Sometimes the local trader is depicted as an important prerequisite of economic growth, in other cases he is seen as an exploiter and an obstacle to sound economic development. A discussion of his role first of all calls for an overview of the problems of distribution and marketing which faced fishermen in small, rural communities.

In preindustrial fishing the problems of distributing surplus catches to a wider market was an important constraint on fishing. The fishermen faced a greater dilemma than the agricultural peasant. Fish, unlike corn or cattle, demands rapid handling and processing. The alternative to a quick and local economic exchange was preservation, but to transform fish into a storable product through smoking, drying or salting was a time-consuming process. Larger quantities of fish could not be handled by household labor in this way. Consequently, the bargaining position or withholding power of the fisherman was weak [16, 17]. The peasant fisherman had to make sure his catches were preserved or markered immediately.

Fresh fish could only be transported in small quantities within a rather narrow region. In many fishing communities where the marketing of the catch was done by fishermen's wives or small-scale dealers, this region was restricted by the distance a person could reach during a day by horse and cart. If there existed marketing possibilities along the coast, fishermen could, of course, transport larger quantities of fish themselves.

The development which turned crofter fishermen into full-time deep-sea fishermen called for an expanded market as well as an intensified pattern of production, often with a new and expansive technology. This development brought along a new division of labor. The work of the fisherman and his family became restricted to a few stages in the production and distribution processes. A more complex organization was needed to handle, store and transport large quantities of fish to a wider market. The distance between the fisherman/producer and the consumer grew in both physical and economic terms.

This new division of labor could be structured in different ways. The many steps from the actual fishing operations out at sea to the final marketing of the catches could be managed by a long chain of economic units. In some cases we find a whole network of middlemen developing. In other instances a vertical integration of the whole process emerges in which trading companies took control of fishing, curing and marketing. This type of integration has been more common in the British Isles than in Scandinavia, though the development of fishermen's marketing cooperatives constitutes a different form of vertical integration. This type of organization is a recent twentieth century phenomenon in North Atlantic fishing.

In most coastal regions it was a new body of fish merchants who came to link the fishermen to the market, but their position in the local fishing economy varied a great deal. At the one extreme of the continuum we find the ambulating buyers who lacked a steady clientele of sellers. In this case trading usually consisted of a relatively simple economic transaction. Fish was exchanged for cash or other goods with no further obligations. The next time one traded with another dealer. Many of these ambulating traders came to develop a steadier contact with the fishermen, but their position was usually different from that of the locally integrated trader or merchant. Among the latter category we usually find a very complex set of transactions emerging between buyer and seller. These relations were not only complex but also, like those earlier relationships between crofter fishermen and farmers, asymmetrical. The uncertainties of fishing, the unpredictable changes in fishing luck and the low withholding power put the fishermen in a weak bargaining position. These weak points could be exploited by the trader, who thereby could diminish the considerable element of risk-taking in his own marketing activities. Against this background it is not surprising to find a general pattern in the way relations between fishermen and local traders were structured in most North Atlantic regions.

First, the merchant could offer fishermen a wide range of goods and services in exchange for their catch, such as consumer goods and fishing equipment. This often helped to turn fish trading into a credit system. By providing generous and long-term conditions and credit, traders could secure a debt bondage system and a stable network of sellers. These "running credits" were often partially settled on a yearly or a seasonal basis, to be carried on to the next trading period, and many fishermen came to live in a state of chronic indebtedness. Many traders also acted as moneylenders to the fishermen, whose lack of capital was notorious and constant. It was also common for merchants to combine curing and marketing activities.

In some regions we find the merchants as owners of both harbor sites and buildings in the community. To the debt bondage tie was added the position of tenant, and this system was common in both Scottish and Norwegian settings [4]. These conditions gave merchants a key role in the local economy, although the actual strength of their position, of course, was influenced by many other factors, such as the degree of competition from other traders.

The physical and social isolation of many coastal communities also helped merchants to gain a firm control of the local economy. His profit was not only drawn from the marketing of fishing, but also from the importance of consumer goods and fishing equipment to the community (Figure 2). This double trading role made him less dependent on the fluctuations in the fisheries. He had other sources of income to fall back on.

In some coastal regions we find this position of trading monopoly encapsulated in a feudal structure as, for example, in parts of Latin America and the British Isles. Here the feudal landowners not only controlled the means of production but also the marketing. The fisherman tenant had to sell his fish through the landowner, and also paid rent for the usufruct rights to local land and marine resources [14, 18, 19].

In other regions it was mainly the isolated position of the fishing community and the constant need of an external supply of food and equipment which constituted the condition for such a trading monopoly. This seems to be the case among both Newfoundland truck dealers and the famous Norwegian "nessekonger", for example [20, 21].

This dependence cannot, however, be attributed solely to factors like physical isolation or marginality. In my study of entrepreneurial careers in some Swedish communities I found other social factors of great importance as well. Often the fishermen found it hard to handle relations with the outside world. The rhythm of their work and their poor social and economic standing in the hierarchy of the land-based society opened up another niche for the local merchant. He could

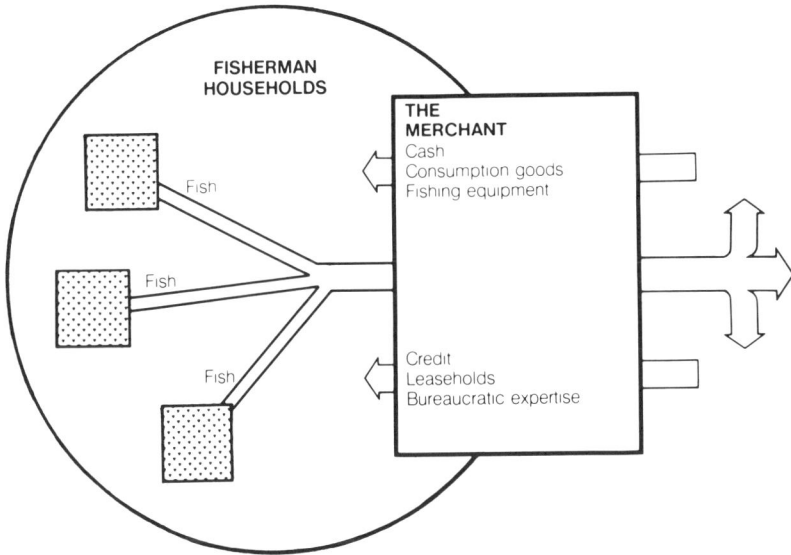

Figure 2. Merchant–Household Interrelationships

become a social broker as well as a trader. This pattern of social and economic brokerage has been amply documented from northern Norway, where we find the same pattern. The merchant controls the economic circulation and acts as a local political leader vis-a-vis the outside world. He can supply the bureaucratic expertise and the social contacts which the fishermen often lack [20].

It would be wrong, however, to paint a picture of the local trader as a constant winner. There are also examples of merchants whose position with the fishermen is weak. He may find it hard to live up to traditional expectations of generous credit, especially if he is competing with buyers who do not feel themselves hampered by these demands. To be a local merchant in a well integrated, isolated fishing community can be a check on as well as an asset to his trading activities. In a tightly knit moral economy he could be the object of considerable social control. He may find that the social costs of a strictly economic profit maximization strategy carried out against obligations of local solidarity, of family and friendship ties can be too great (see, for example, Charest [22] and Paine [23]). In comparative discussions of entrepreneurial careers and strategies this factor of local integration must always be considered.

A dealer in Newfoundland characterized his role in the local community as "a father, and the fishermen, his children," and in many cases we find that relations between the two parts took on a patriarchal nature which no doubt could mask a more systematic exploitation, but which also could be seen both as a fetter and an asset. The patriarchal nature of the relation was stressed in situations where the merchant acted as political broker and link with the outside world. In these instances both merchant and fisherman could also mark more fundamental conflicts between the two parties.

The same ambivalence is evident in the merchant's role as an innovating entrepreneur in the local community. He was often the driving force behind the development and modernization of the fishing. Again we find a point where interests could overlap. There are numerous examples of merchants who, as introducers of new technology and who provide fishermen credit for investments, often became integrated into other business activities when the trader takes on the sales agency for a new type of engine. Such a development is well in line with the economic strategy I have discussed earlier. In the Scandinavian fisheries, this period of classic entrepreneurship lasted up to the World War II in many coastal regions. It was the actual transition from a peasant fishing economy to a fully market-integrated one which created favorable conditions for local entrepreneurs and middlemen like the merchant, the trader, or fish curer. The situation which emerged during the 1940s and 1950s gave the fishermen a far better opportunity for handling their political, social and economic relations with the outside world without the help of brokers. A striking feature of this period of classic entrepreneurship is the tendency for local merchants to develop an *indirect* rather than a direct control of fishing. Although we certainly do not lack Scandinavian examples of traders and curers taking over production through investments in fishing boats and equipment, the overwhelming majority of entrepreneurs did not involve themselves financially in the actual fishing.

There were good reasons for this strategy. By controlling the marketing and/or curing of fish, and by tying the producers through debt bondage and similar means, the merchants secured a firm grip on the local economy without getting involved in the risky and uncertain fishing activities. Unlike entrepreneurial activities in farming and industrial production, there were no greater incentives for such a direct control over the actual production.

Combined with the patriarchal pattern this indirectedness often masked the antagonistic nature of the relation between merchant and fisherman. Against this background it is easier to understand the ambivalence echoed in the fishermen's own view of such local entrepreneurs. They can be described both as benefactors and exploiters.

THE FAMILY CREW: ANACHRONISM OR ADAPTATION?

The transformation of the crofter-fisherman economy not only included the introduction of new technology and new modes of integration with the market economy, but it also made fishing more capital-intensive. As investments in fishing boats and equipment increased, problems of capital management came into the foreground. In the following, I will discuss some of the consequences of this capitalization of production, starting with the pattern of ownership and crew recruitment.

There has been a tendency to overrate the role played by kinship relations in preindustrial fishing. If we look at recruitment and crew formation among nineteenth century fishermen in Sweden, we find a pattern of flexible and loosely structured fishing units. As fishing was a highly seasonal activity and the need for manpower often varied in different fisheries during he year, crews tended to change in size and composition. To put it in the other terms one can argue that the fisherman was a highly mobile element of production. He usually brought his own gear and could easily leave one boat for another. It was labor rather than capital which was the most important factor of production. The actual ownership of boats was of minor importance.

Although family crews were not an uncommon phenomenon in this preindustrial setting, we find recruitment patterns based upon both neighborhood and friendship links as much as upon kin ties [4]. This flexible and fluid social organization is documented from many other preindustrial maritime communities (see for example the discussion in Breton [24] and Norr and Norr [18]). It also appears frequently in the 19th century fishery statistics. In the reports from Swedish and Irish fishery commissioners there are many laments over the loosely structured fishing crews, which make the taking of censuses a troublesome task, as fishermen moved from boat to boat.

As long as fishing was a seasonal activity that demanded very moderate capital investments, such a system of loosely structured and flexible production units would function well. As fishing became much more capital-intensive, the problems of ownership and management of the fishing capital became more dominant. It is during this phase we find the role of the family crew strengthened. The reason for this is, I would argue, that the family crew proved itself to be a most effective type of economic corporation for capital management in this situation. Consequently, it is not surprising that we find a predominance of family crews in those preindustrial settings, where the fishing unit also controlled important means of production, such as fishing rights.

The capitalization of production also made inheritance and succession to the fishing capital a more important question. In traditional peasant fishing, the entry into the occupation was relatively easy. The necessary investments in gear and boats were modest. Furthermore, the perishability of the equipment meant that family inheritance played a far less important role among fishermen than among farmers [4].

As investments in boats and equipment grew bigger during the twentieth century, inheritance patterns became more important for the formation of new fishing units and the fission of old ones. In this process, we find agnatic inheritance and recruitment patterns dominating many regions. In an agnatic crew structure based on fathers, sons and brothers, fission and formation of fishing units was less problematic than in a bilateral system.

In the same way that I talked about a period of classical entrepreneurship, I would like to talk about the heydays of the family crew 1920-1960, a period during which the fishing fleets of most Scandinavian regions were mechanized, and new types of capital intensive equipment like seines and trawls were introduced.

A comparison of 20 community studies from both sides of the North Atlantic [4, 22-33] shows the family crew to be a dominant feature of the economic organization in non-Scandinavian regions as well, *nota bene* during this period. This would perhaps not have been the case had these studies dealt with nineteenth-century conditions. Perhaps more important is the notion that, judging from the Scandinavian scene, a later study of the situation in the 1970s would also show some important changes in ownership and recruitment patterns.

CAPITALIZATION AND PROFESSIONALISM

My argument about the family crew as a feasible and very

adaptive type of economic corporation rests on material concerning the pre-1960s period, and is based upon rural communities with a rather similar production pattern dominated by coastal trawling, seining and long-lining, with crews of four to six men. In these settings the egalitarian and cooperative socioeconomic structure of peasant fishing survived twentieth century modernization without any greater structural changes. Even if the family crew became a much more marked trait of the social landscape, there were few tendencies of economic stratification or a new division of labor *within* the studied communities.

Elsewhere I have discussed the processes which maintained this pattern in most Scandinavian settings [4]. The explanation must be sought in the interplay of many factors: the adaptive strategies among the fishermen themselves, the absence of a direct outside control over production from merchants and middlemen, the establishment of fishing cooperatives, and state legislation.

Today, the picture is different. During the last decade, the pace and capitalization of fishing has quickened to such an extent that traditional units of production and management, like the family crew, often find the problems of capital management overwhelming. Capitalization is not the only villain in the current crisis of the Swedish and Scandinavian fishing industries. This crisis has demonstrated how vulnerable the traditional patterns of ownership and production are, how easily they can be eroded, and how new patterns of economic stratification can emerge in their place.

One would perhaps have expected the sophisticated technology and the safety net of the modern welfare state to have made fishermen less vulnerable to fluctuations in catches and market conditions. On the contrary, it seems as though new types of economic risks have replaced the old ones in many instances. As fishing has become more and more capital-intensive, the ecological and technological insecurity of earlier generations of fishermen has been superseded by a *financial* insecurity.

The new type of financial insecurity is one of many factors behind the Swedish fishing crisis. The herring boom of the early 1960s, which was caused by the development of new, industrial outlets for herring (oil, meal, etc.), led to a rapid growth in the Swedish trawler fleet. As old crews split up and new ones were formed, a different pattern of recruitment emerged. Sole ownership became more common, and the nonowners in the crew were often recruited from outside. They did not always have a local and maritime background. They were attracted by the high shares offered during the boom years, and did not stand in any kinship, friendship or neighborhood relation to the owners. Financing these new units was no problem, as the supply of outside credit was good. A booming trade in new and second-hand trawlers developed, and some skippers even found that they could make more money from trading in boats than from actual fishing.

Overexpansion and overfishing in the North Sea soon put an end to this spectacular boom. During the late 1960s and early 1970s, the exodus from fishing started. Between 1966 and 1976, the number of Swedish fishermen was cut in half. The new owners and skippers were trapped in a vicious circle. To keep up the returns, they had to resort to more intensive fishing, and this, in combination with falling man shares, made many of the "outsiders" leave fishing and return to jobs on shore. The fisherman owner was left not only with a manpower shortage, but also with growing economic problems. As the profitability decreased, it became difficult to keep up with financial obligations to the banks. Repayment of credit in the form of interest and mortgages had been planned for a situation of growing returns and economic expansion. As the slump started, it also became difficult to sell a trawler for a reasonable price. Everybody was trying to get out of a business. Some sectors of the fishing industry survived this crisis better than others. Stable, locally integrated crews based on kinship and friendship ties with joint ownership showed a greater shock-absorbing capacity, especially in those cases where this organizational pattern had been combined with composite pattern of fishing and more cautious investments [4].

In Sweden, there were tendencies towards a more marked cleavage between owners and nonowners. If we turn to Denmark, the situation was slightly different. Here the golden years of the 1960s were not only shaped by new opportunities for fish marketing, but also by new taxation rules which made investments in trawlers a very attractive alternative for nonfishermen. There was a rush to buy shares in new trawlers which often were manned with outside labor. Again the result was a shortsighted overexpansion with overfishing as a natural result [34].

By this somewhat simplified account of the dramatic 1960s and 1970s, I have tried to illustrate how difficult it can be to maintain the traditional egalitarian patterns of ownership and production in a situation of rapid economic growth. Adjustment in the 1970s has been painful. Many maritime communities on the Swedish west coast have virtually ceased to exist as fishing communities, and in Denmark parts of the traditional socioeconomic structure have been eroded as company fishing has expanded.

There are other factors that have threatened the existence of this traditional structure. Management decisions in fishing have become much more complex. Knowing how and where to fish is not enough. To be fisherman owner or member of a family crew on a medium sized trawler is rather like managing a small business firm. To carry out your job you need to know a considerable amount about state legislation, taxation rules and other financial matters. Knowledge about marketing conditions in different ports, restrictions on fishing and quota rules becomes as important a part of the maritime expertise as the traditional knowledge of fishing techniques and the maritime landscape.

Hand in hand with modernization goes not only capitalization but bureaucratization. The traditional type of family crew I have discussed may find it harder to handle all these new aspects of their fishing activities. To be a successful skipper you need a good knowledge of taxation rules and strategies as well as having the knack of finding fish. On the whole it can be argued that state regulations about investments, rentability and taxation have been very important in shaping the development of the Scandinavian fisheries during the last decades.

Another aspect of this development is the marked trend toward a professionalization of fishermen. It is a profession, and the activities of the fishermen's own associations and government policies may put a definitive end to the tradition of occupational pluralism.

With the hardened competition for marine resources and market outlets there has been a growing demand for licensing laws in the Scandinavian countries, laws which restrict access to fishing. For the professional fishermen, one aim of these laws is to keep out competition in the form of industrial workers who fish for leisure and a bit of extra cash. But these laws will strike both ways. They may well make it difficult for fishing to keep up a composite household economy, where fishing remains one of several niches. Such a policy will erode the possibility of occupational pluralism even more.

There are some signs of new development in another direction. During the optimistic 1960s the economic ideology behind developmental schemes was clear. The catchwords were sophisticated and capital intensive technology, large-scale specialized fishing for industrial use rather than for direct human consumption, and a focus on quantity rather than quality. Anyone who would have dared to suggest that there was any future in a composite, coastal fishing with a relatively inexpensive technology and small production units would have been heavily criticized. Today experts seem less sure. There has even been talk of such alternatives as rather realistic in a Scandinavian setting.

It is also clear that those who were forced out of fishing during the crisis are not interested in returning on any terms. Interviews with former fishermen suggest that the type of intensive fishing which calls for long periods away from home is not a realistic alternative for men who have tried a job on shore and had the benefit of a regular home life.

Therefore, it is not surprising that most of the Swedish fishing communities which still are viable have maintained a pattern of composite coastal trawling where fishing activities and the social organization of production are very much integrated in the local community life. According to some planners of the 1960s, these were the types of communities with no future.

CONCLUSION

One danger inherent in discussion of modernization and economic change is the use of a dichotomy where "traditional" and "modern" patterns are viewed within a simplified unilinear model of evolution. An historical perspective can serve as a healthy antidote against such a view of socieconomic change. I have argued that much of what has been regarded as traditional elements in the rural fishing communities along the North Atlantic Fringe, on the contrary, are adaptations to recent changes in the macroeconomic system. Neither the pattern of occupational pluralism nor the family crew can be explained as traditional survivals.

There are other dangers in using a simplified evolutionary model. Modernization can be viewed as the change from simple to more complex structures, from local self-sufficiency and isolation to integration into wider networks. Although anthropological research has shown us how misleading such notions can be, they still survive, often as an unconscious model of modernization in the minds of planners and politicians. If we take for granted that modernization and "rational development" equals the introduction of capital intensive technology, specialization, and large-scale, complex patterns of production, then our prophecies may well turn out to be both self-fulfilling and self-defeating. This "hidden" steering mechanism is very evident in the planning of fishery development in Scandinavia.

I have illustrated the dangers of such a view of modernization and economic growth with the example of the dramatic 1960s and the bleak 1970s in Swedish fishing. The current crisis has at least shattered some of these notions of the benefits of unbridled growth, capitalization and specialization. We have been reminded how dangerous it is to equate modernization with economic growth, and to forget the important questions of "growth for whom, and on what terms?"

The analysis of modernization studies concerns the choice of explanatory models to determine cause and effect. We should be wary of modernization studies in which attempts are made to isolate *the* decisive factor behind socioeconomic change or to find *the* event which acted as a release mechanism. in the search for explanations concerning the lags or bursts of modernization, we often resort to a factor analysis in which the relations between cause and effect often are simplified as, for example, in many innovation studies. By trying to single out factors like new technology, entrepreneurial activities, improved transport facilities, or economic innovations like new methods of obtaining financial assistance or the introduction of insurance schemes and government aid, we may be trapped in a rather futile discussion of the "hen and egg" type.

The alternative is an analysis where structure rather than innovation becomes the key concept. All the kinds of factors listed above may be of crucial importance in explaining why economic change occurs at a particular moment, in a particular way, but these factors interact in such a complex fashion that it is an impossible task to talk about a linear pattern of cause and effect.

A structural perspective forces us to focus on the way these factors are related and integrated. In short, it calls for a dialectic rather than a linear approach. We must also discuss the difference between quantitative changes, which can take place within the existing social or economic structure, and qualitative changes which lead to a total restructuring of the system. For two examples of such structural analysis (although within different theoretical frameworks) see Brox, [35] and Breton [36]. Through such a perspective, we may get a better understanding both of resistance to change and of unforseen consequences of modernization or economic growth.

REFERENCES

[1] Tunstall, J. *The Fishermen* (London: MacGibbon & Klee, 1962).

[2] Andersen, R., and C. Wadel, Eds. *North Atlantic Fishermen* (St. John's, Newfoundland: Institute of Social and Economic Research, Memorial University of Newfoundland, 1972).

[3] Andersen, R., Ed. *North Atlantic Maritime Cultures* (The Hague:Mouton, 1979).

[4] Löfgren, O. *Fongstman i Industrisamhallet* (Lund, Sweden: 1977).

[5] Löfgren, O. "Peasant Ecotypes: Problems in the Comparative Study of Ecological Adaptation," *Ethnol. Scand.* (1976), pp. 100-115.

[6] Löfgren, O. "Maritime Hunters in a Peasant Setting? A Comparative Discussion on Swedish Peasant Fishermen," in *North Atlantic Maritime Cultures,* R. Andersen, Ed. (The Hague:Mouton 1979).

[7] Löfgren, O. "The Potato People: Household Economy and Family Patterns among Rural Proletarians in Nineteenth Century Sweden," in *Chances and Change: Social and Economic Studies in Demographic History in the Baltic Area,* D. Guant et al., Eds. (Odense:Odense University Press, 1978).

[8] Ansom, P. F. *Scots Fisherfolk* (Banff, UK:Banffshire Journal LTD., 1950).

[9] Darling, F. F. *West Highland Survey: An Essay in Human Ecology* (Oxford: 1955).

[10] Evans, E. *Irish Heritage: The Landscape, the People and Their Work* (Dundalk:Dundallan Press, 1958).

[11] Goodladd, C. A. *Shetland Fishing Saga* (Lerwick:Shetland Times LTD., 1971).

[12] Grant, I. F. *Highland Folkways* (London:Routledge, 1961).

[13] Hunter, J. *The Making of the Crofting Community* (Edinburgh:J. Donald, 1976).

[14] Smith, H. D. "The Development of Shetland Fisheries and Fishing Communities," in *Seafarer and Community,* P. Fricke, Ed. (London:Croon Helm, 1973).

[15] "Report of the Inspectors of Irish Fisheries," Parliamentary Papers, London (1866), p. 7.

[16] Firth, R. *Malay Fishermen: Their Peasant Economy,* 2nd ed. (Hamden, CT: Archon Books, 1966).

[17] Wolf, E. *Peasants* (Englewood Cliffs, NJ: Prentice-Hall Inc., 1966).

[18] Norr, K., and J. Norr. "Environmental and Technical Factors Influencing Power in Work Organizations: Ocean Fishing in Peasant Societies," *Sociol. Work Occupat.* I(2):219:251 (1974).

[19] Price, R. "Caribbean Fishing and Fishermen: A Historical Sketch," *Am. Anthropologist* 68:1363-1383 (1966).

[20] Barth, F. "The Role of the Entrepreneur in Social Change in Northern Norway," *Arsbok Universitetet Bergen, Hum. Ser.* (1963), p. 3.

[21] Wadel, C. "Marginal Adaptations and Modernization in Newfondland," Newfoundland Social and Economic Studies, No. 7, Institute of Social and Economic Research, Memorial University of Newfoundland, St. John's, Newfoundland (1969).

[22] Charest, P. "Cultural Ecology of the North Shore of the Gulf of St. Lawrence," in *Communities and Culture in French Canada,* G. Gold and M. A. Treblay, Eds. (Toronto:Holt, Rinehart & Winston, 1973).

[23] Paine, R. "Coast Lapp Society II. A Study of Economic Development and Social Values," Oslo (1965).

[24] Breton, Y. "A Comparative Study of Work Groups in an Eastern Canadian Peasant Fishing Community: Bilateral Kinship and Adaptive Processes," *Ethnology* (1974), pp. 393-418.

[25] Beaucage, P. "Organization Economique et Parents a al Tabatiere," *Rech. Sociograph.* 11:91-116 (1970).

[26] Blehr, O. "Action Groups in a Society with Bilateral Kinship: A Case Study from the Faroe Islands," *Ethnology* 2:269-275 (1963).

[27] Brox, O. "Natural Conditions, Inheritance and Marriage in a North Norwegian Fjord," *Folk* Vol. IV (1964).

[28] Byron, R. F. "Economic Functions of Kinship Values in Family Business: Fishing Crews in North Atlantic Communities," *Sociol.*

Soc. Res. 60(2):147-160 (1975).

[29] Dikkanen, S. L. "Sirma: Residence and Work Organization in a Lappish-Speaking Community," *Semiske Samlinger* Vol. 8 (1965).

[30] Faris, J. C. *Cat Harbour: A Newfoundland Fishing Settlement* (St. Johns, Newfoundland: Institute of Social and Economic Research, Memorial University of Newfoundland, 1972).

[31] Firestone, M. "Newfoundland and Family Structure: Features and Variations," in *North Atlantic Maritime Cultures,* R. Andersen, Ed. (The Hague:Mouton 1979).

[32] Rudie, I. "Household Organization: Adaptive Process and Restrictive Form. A Viewpoint on Economic Change," *Folk* 11/12:185-200 (1969/1970).

[33] Shorthall, D. "Capital Acquisition and Technological Change in the Scottish Inshore Fishery," paper presented at the Annual Meeting of the Society for Applied Anthropolgy, Amsterdam, 1975.

[34] Laegsmand, K. "Nordsofishere," unpublished thesis, European Ethnology, University of Copenhagen (1967).

[35] Brox, O. *Newfoundland Fishermen in the Age of Industry: A Sociology of Economic Dualism* (Toronto: 1972).

[36] Breton, Y. "The Influence of Modernization on the Modes of Production in Coastal Fishing: An Example from Venezuela," paper presented at the Annual Meeting of the Society for Applied Anthropology, Amsterdam, 1975.

CHAPTER 7
MODERNIZATION IN TRADITIONAL FISHING COMMUNITIES: THE EXAMPLE OF CAT HARBOUR

James Faris
Department of Anthropology
University of Connecticut

INTRODUCTION

In Cat Harbour, Newfoundland, Canada, modernization has numerous manifestations. The most significant of these was the resettlement of the traditional community.

I first undertook field research in the traditional community in 1964-1965 [1, 2]. Cat Harbour was resettled in 1967-1968 under the provincial government's policy of centralization. I visited the area again in 1972 to document the effects of resettlement. The first analysis of the material was in a joint paper with Antler [3] in which we critiqued the government's resettlement program and policies toward the fishery.

This chapter is an extension of that study, with further data on the resettlement, and further examination of a theme noted there and pursued in several other papers [3 - 5]:

With the increasing rationalization of capitalism, the productive process of outport fishermen had to be penetrated to force producers to surrender a greater amount of their surplus value (previously captured and held by them inasmuch as a finished produce was offered and not their labor), and, increasingly, to require them to sell their labor rather than the product of it. Thus, whereas a possible capitalist rationalization in agricultural peasantries involves the alienation of the means of production (as well, of course, as control of the forces of production) for increasing proletarianization; in fishing peasantries, capitalist penetration strategy has to await and rely on State intervention [4].

This chapter focuses on the critical role of the government in regard to modernization which occurs in such circumstances, and emphasizes the importance of considering the neglected issue of class struggle in understanding the dynamics of modernization.

THE DYNAMICS OF CAPITAL

Modernization in the Cat Harbour context can only be understood as the rationalization of capital. What is meant by this, what is its measure, how and why is it facilitated? First it is necessary to briefly examine the dynamics of a capitalist economic system as they are relevant to our concern.

Capitalism, as all modes of production, is characterized by a fundamental contradiction between the way in which humans appropriate from nature (forces of production) and the way in which they appropriate from each other (relations of production). In capitalism this contradiction is expressed in private control of the forces of production, which enables the propertied to hire the labor power of those who do not own or control. Thus, we have social commodity production and private ownership. Because the labor sellers thus have no other access to a living, they must respond on terms that are normally unfavorable to them.

Capitalism is specifically distinguished from other modes of production in that labor, too, is a commodity to be bought and sold in its temporal expression. Value under capitalism is created by the action of human labor power on nature, and appropriation by the capitalist consists of extraction of a portion of that value created by labor, namely, that portion above what is necessary to reproduce the labor and the conditions of production. Of course, if the cost of reproducing labor is cheap (low wages, no infrastructural cost of keeping labor) and/or if it is extraordinarily productive (achieved, among other ways, in embodying labor in machines raising the organic composition of capital, i.e., the ratio of such embodied labor to wage labor), profits may be great. However, capitalist competition, locally or internationally, plus the limited ability of consumers to pay exorbitant prices, forces the prices of capitalist commodities down. To maintain rates of profit, the capitalist must expand in command of both resources and markets, in elevating the organic composition of capital, in reducing wages, and in increasing productivity. This requirement to expand, to stimulate growth of the productive forces, of course, often comes into contradiction with the demands of labor as the classes of producers struggle for better living conditions with those who hire their labor power. This, if successful as it always, more or less, must be, creates a tendency for the rate of profit to fall. There are other factors, of course, but ultimately any tendency toward the decline of the rate of profit is traceable to class struggle. There is no "tendency" inherent in capitalism as a mode of production by definition. To suggest so denies, effectively, the role of people in making history. Apart from its teleology, it confuses the concept of a mode of production with the social formation. This form of determinism has too long plagued serious materialist study.

A fall in the rate of profit requires even more frantic expansion and growth. And it is in such circumstances that the state becomes critical, for political hegemony is often necessary before further economic exploitation is possible.

If commodity producers do not sell their labor, but only their product (as has traditionally been the case in outport Newfoundland for at least the past century), capital then can only extract value by keeping low the price offered for the product, keeping high both the rent and the cost of instruments of production (provisioning commodity producers at high prices), and minimizing infrastructure costs in facilitating all this, it behaves, at least in one form, like mercantile capitalism. Antler [6] has recently and cogently argued a contrary thesis, that in fact the traditional inshore fishery in Newfoundland was thoroughly penetrated by capitalism in the nineteenth century, and that the commodity producers are in fact disguised wage laborers, however much control over their product they appear to have. I do not want here to attempt to test this thesis—the implications are very important, and the debate must be informed by very careful data collection and interpretation. I want to leave this issue aside, in fact, by discussing not capitalist penetration, but capitalist rationalization.

Whatever the case, if the relationship of traditional inshore fishermen to capital was as wage labor to capital, or as commodity producer to mercantilist, the changes in this traditional situation since confederation of Newfoundland with Canada (1949) have been without doubt a rationalization of capital, i.e., appropriating a greater portion of value (and changing the production of value) than what was earlier possible.

Capital, in seeking rationalization (greater appropriation of value from labor) may, given the conditions of the determining class struggle, move in several ways such as control over the subject of labor (the means of production), control over the object of labor (the labor process) or more direct control over the product of the producers. Depending on the level of struggle between labor and capital there may be quite different political and ideological implications in local circumstances. This will determine the extent to which the state is necessary to facilitate the movement of capital (or labor to capital).

Of course this struggle is not always visible and it may not be manifest at the level of the local fishing community. The ability of capital to move, to "modernize" (to rationalize the appropriation of value in the traditional fishing community) may reflect the struggle between labor and capital at some other point as in the industrial centers of capitalist nations, for example, where labor demands for an increasing portion of the value they produce (thereby bring down the rate of profit to capital) may force capital to rationalize itself in peripheral areas where labor is not so well organized, is cheaper, and where the struggle against capitalist appropriations not so sharp. This, in my view, began to happen sometime after the middle of the twentieth century in outport Newfoundland, in the example under discussion. This culminated in rapid modernization of the outport fishing communities such as Cat Harbour in the mid-1960s which continues to the present. Of course there has been a long struggle by outport fishermen against capitalists; this is the essence of Antler's thesis [6] (see also Sider [7]). It may not, however, have had the consequences of forcing a significant challenge to the rate of profit in sufficient mass or with sufficient organization when compared to the struggles by metropolitan producers.

In tracing the trajectory of capital's increasing appropriation of value from producers, there may be certain peculiarities. These peculiarities demonstrate the various contradictions within capital itself, in each case brought about by the sharpness of class struggle at one or another place in one or another form and time. There are the conflicts between industrial and commercial capital, for example, and there are the exigencies of local circumstances as well.

It is from these bases, I will argue, we can generate all the facts characterizing the subject under study, namely, the modernization of traditional fishing communities. I propose, demonstrating at every point, explicitly how the social change documented is a response to the wider social forces which dictate local development and change in the social fabric of the community. It has not, of course, been the same in all cases, but one inescapable experience is common. All west Atlantic fishing settlements and enterprises have experienced this rationalization to some extent, in one or another form (save perhaps Cuban fishing communities, about which we have no post revolutionary data). Even those experiments in cooperative structures are not exempt, for we now know that most cooperatives are organized only on terms favorable to market domination if they are to persist, and actually facilitate capitalist rationalization rather than hinder it.

This demonstration requires, then, neither conspiracy theories of causality, mechanical determinism nor capitalist greed. It simply requires understanding the logic of capitalist development, and in the inshore Newfoundland fishery, understanding the necessity of the state; that is, understanding the necessity of political hegemony to effect greater economic exploitation.

CAT HARBOUR: THE TRADITIONAL COMMUNITY AND ITS RESETTLEMENT

Cat Harbour was originally located on a peninsula on the northeast coast of Newfoundland, Canada. Cat Harbour was the original name of the settlement, changed to Lumsden North in the early part of this century by a missionary who was offended by the connotations of the earlier name (so labelled from the large number of young bay seal that frequented the area). In speaking of Cat Harbour resettlement, I speak only of the Cat Harbour portion of the resettled community.

The traditional community for the past 100 years was based about the quite successful pursuit of an inshore fishery involving principally the harvest of cod in fixed traps. This (as well as cod taken in trawls, jigging, and in sunken gill nets) was processed into a salted product sold to fish buyers servicing the world market. These same buyers were also mercantile suppliers. All processing was in the hands of producers.

In the original Cat Harbour description [1, 2] I argued that the particular types of land and property tenure, work organization and kinship were a function of the material circumstances in which people found themselves. This meant primary production units (76% of the men over 17 years of age) organized principally about male agnates, land tenure premised on water access, divisions of labor based on sex in primary production and processing.

Fishermen, while not in control of marketing (except for a period during the FPU under William Coaker, when fishermen held their catch in bulk until a higher price was promised [2]), were in large measure in control of the embodiment of labor in the product and were thus able to command the surplus value in the processing of the finished product. Fishermen were appropriated by mercantilist extraction, that is, the low price paid for their finished product relative to its sale price to consumers. The same merchants also often supplied fishermen, commanding their debt (and thus their fish) and commanding the choice, type and quality of technology available. However exploitative such mercantilist forms of appropriation may have been, capital still had not rationally extended into the processing sector, in capture of value, or in complete dictation of technology and innovation in the forces of production. It is, then, rationalization we are discussing as modernization.

This was facilitated in major part by a resettlement of the community in 1967-1968 to an inland site adjacent to another settlement, in line with government policy to centralize services and to eliminate excess and redundant infrastructure costs [8]. By law, once left, communities could not be resettled, and those moving were compensated for their move (all in the community had to agree to move before compensation could be paid to any).

MODERNIZATION

Returns to Labor

Fishery

Though the gross demographic profiles did not change significantly from the traditional community of 1964 to the "modernized" resettlement of 1972 (Figure 1), the occupational structure shifted dramatically. Whereas in 1964, 65 men of the community over 17 years of age gained their principal livelihood at the fishery, in 1972 only 16 men still remained. I say remained, for no new persons entered the fishery, and only two of the 16 remaining were under 45 years of age. Moreover, of the 31 young men (the total number) maturing into the labor force from 1964 to 1972, not one entered the fishery. This represents a decline in the fishery oriented occupations by over 75% for men. Women's occupational changes, no less dramatic, will be considered below. Antler and Faris [3] compared the decline in Cat Harbour with other settlements on the northeast coast and other areas of Newfoundland to determine the significance of the resettlement itself on the occupational structure. The decline in fishery occupations is not so severe in communities having not been resettled, indicating that resettlement is an important contributing factor in the demise of the traditional inshore fishery, although not the only one.

Not only did men leave the fishery, but there are also several measures of the actual decline in returns to labor. A comparison of the returns to fishery labor of a sample of men in 1964 [2] to the same sample of 1972 is instructive. Fortunately for comparison, five of the

Numbers of Cases

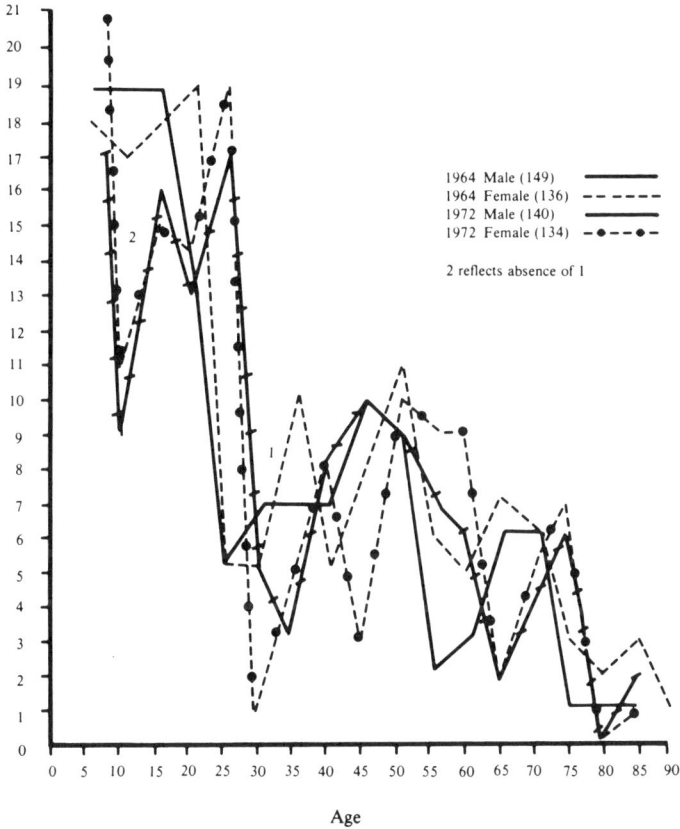

Figure 1. *Population Distribution by Age and Sex: 1964, 1972.*

six men of the original 1964 sample were still fishing in 1972. But counting only those five still fishing, the average percent of fishery income to total income decreased from 81.3 to 60.5%, an average decline of 20.8% in income derived from the fishery. That decline, however, is not simply a matter of occupational choice, for returns to fishery labor fell relative to returns to nonfishery labor, and the value of fishery product returned to the fisherman declined as well. The decline in fishermen is then in part a rational response to labor and product markets.

First, let us look at the actual yield data plotted against men fishing. Figure 2 indicates that the returns to effort declined from 1964 to 1972, with a single year's exception. The catch, then, declined at a greater rate than the number of fishermen pursuing fish. Figure 2 actually reveals an aspect of government policy toward the inshore fishery, for it is the failure of the state to stem the destructive predatory fishing of foreign trawlers that primarily accounts for this decline in catch. This problem is considered in detail elsewhere [3, 9]. Suffice it to say that not only did such unchecked foreign predation aid in destruction of the spawning grounds, but also commonly destroyed local fishing gear which might be set where foreign boats trawled.

The returns to fishing relative to other income can be seen in Tables 1 and 2. On the average, total income of the sample went up by 41.2% between 1964 and 1972, whereas the average income from the fishery increased but by 21.1% during the same period. The lesser increase is only in part a function of declining catches, for during this interval a number of other species became commercially relevant, such as lump spawn, for which there were no marketing provisions in 1964. Moreover, the increased ratio of non-fishery to fishery income does not

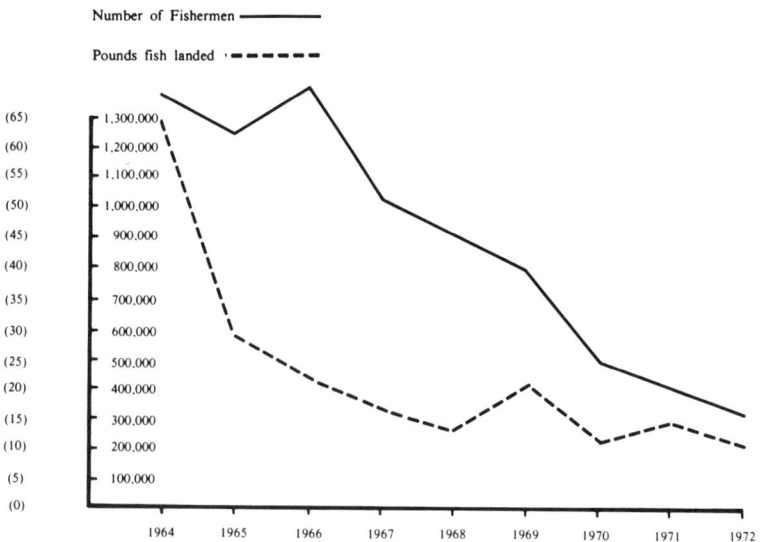

Figure 2. Cod Catch and Numbers of Fishermen: 1964—1972.

Table 1. Income, 1964.
All Sources Except Family Allowances

Fisherman	Fishery Income ($) (Expenses Deducted)	Total Income ($) (Expenses Deducted)	Fishery/Total Income (%)
1	3010	3470	86.7
2	3340	3900	85.7
3	2000	2510	79.7
4	1480	1800	82.2
5	2270	3040	74.7
6	2490	3240	76.9
Average	2432	2993	81.3

alter in the minds of local fishermen their conception of themselves as fishermen, who consider non-fishery income as supplementary and essentially a contribution to reproducing labor power for the fishery. This important fact is lost on Federal Department of Fishery statisticians, who classify fishermen working under five months of the year at the fishery as "casual," five to ten months as "part time," and only those working over ten months each year as "full time" fishermen. As noted elsewhere [2], it may be that fishermen have to spend considerable amounts of time while working at non-fishery occupations actually preparing for the next season's voyage, even though traditional Cat Harbour's trap voyage (often the bulk of the fish caught each year) might be no longer than six weeks with extremes of weather and ice.

A major factor in the loss of fishermen to the inshore fishery is the declining share of the wholesale fish price that is returned to them. The price of fish increased during the period 1964-1972 like most other commodities, but fishermen got a smaller portion of that price, both in salt fish and in fish sold unprocessed. In fact, with government control over salt fish marketing coming during this period, the returns to fishermen from the wholesale of salt fish declined at a much more rapid rate than the decline of the returns of fishermen from the wholesale of fresh fish. The declines are indicated in Figures 3 and 4. Although there is an increase in the price of fish to fishermen, their share of the total wholesale price of fish declines and dramatically so for salt fish.

As noted above, forcing labor to sell itself rather than its product is and has been primary to capitalist rationalization. For in selling its product, labor retains the value embodied in processing. By selling itself, labor gets paid for but the time spent, and the owner of the

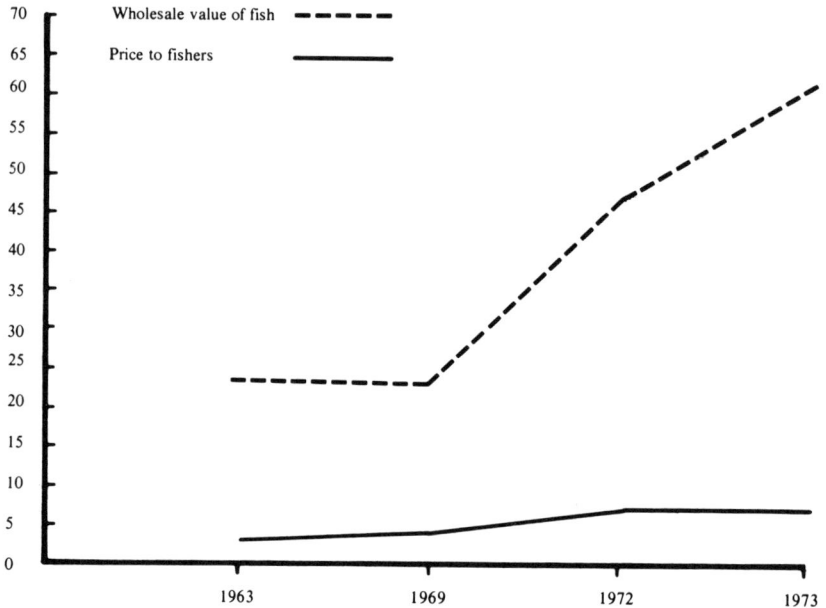

Figure 3. *Fishermen's Share of Wholesale Value of Fresh Cod: 1963—1973.*

Table 2. Income, 1972.
All Sources Except Family Allowances

Fisherman	Fishery Income ($) (Expenses Deducted)	Total Income ($) (Expenses Deducted)	Fishery/Total Income (%)	% Increases in Total Income since 1964
1	3150	4540	69.4	23.5
2	6020	8200	73.4	52.4
3	1780	4925	36.1	49.0
4	725	3095*	23.4	41.8
5		4160*		26.9
6	3680	4666	78.8	30.6
Average	3079	5085	60.5	41.2

(minus Fisherman #5)

*Not fishing. 40 weeks (a $2.60 per hour, 40 hr. week.

means of production retains the rest of the value labor has embodied in the processing of the product. Thus, the sale of fresh fish by inshore fishermen meant a loss in value that is now captured in processing by plant owners paying but a wage. There is, moreover, the traditional advantage of producers being able to hold salt fish until higher prices were available (which, as noted above, happened historically in Cat Harbour). While a fresh fish market developed rapidly with freezing facilities from 1964 to 1972, by no means did the world demand for salt fish decrease. Yet, a host of mechanisms was put into effect to force fishers to sell fish fresh rather than to put it into salt, even though increasingly, as agents of the government Salt Fish Corporation, fresh fish plant owners would themselves put fresh fish purchased into salt! The manner in which the control over processing was achieved constantly reflects such direct government action. Table 3 documents the shift in types of production.

The very creation of the government Salt Fish Corporation—making it the sole marketer of salt fish—was an attempt to rationalize the salt fish market in the face of increasing sales of fish fresh. Even unemployment benefits were calculated in a manner that inhibited keeping fish in salt, requiring it to be sold rather than held. Moreover, with a government monopoly in marketing salt fish, there is no competition in buying, and thus less possibility that holding salt fish for higher prices can be a successful strategy for fishers. The Salt Fish Corporation is not just a monopoly purchaser of salt fish, it actively discourages fishermen salting at all, and hires fresh fish plant owners to

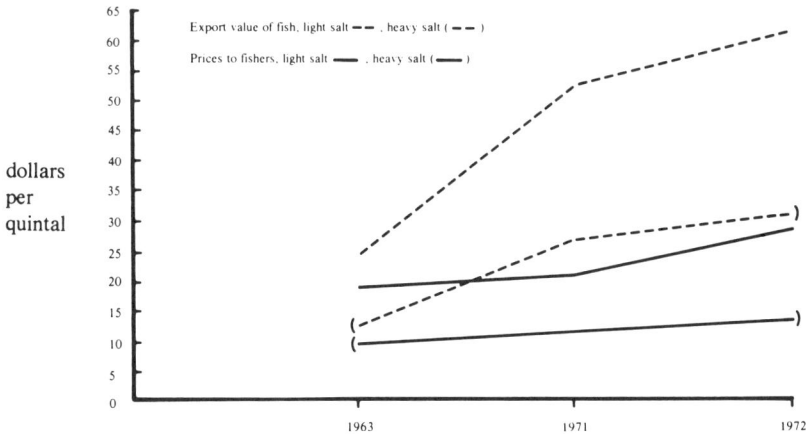

Figure 4. Fishermen's Share of Export Value of Salt Cod: 1963—1972.

salt fish, buying fresh fish rather than salted from fishermen. This is sanctioned by repeated attacks on the quality of fisherman-produced salt fish, e.g., its unhygienic processing, as interpreted by the Salt Fish Corporation in their marketing difficulties.

> Moreover, the Saltfish Marketing Act provides compensation to processors for capital expenditures on necessary retooling, for machinery made redundant, for depreciation, etc. Processors are also reimbursed for use of storage space, packaging and transport costs; in 1971 these three alone were greater than all trans-Atlantic shipping costs of the finished product! These costs are borne by producers—they must come out of "the price of fish"—as the Canadian Salt Fish Corporation is financially self-sustaining. It is small wonder that fresh fish owners are willing to cooperate in the venture [3].

The resettlement itself also aided the decline of salt fish processing by inshore fishermen, for such processing requires a considerable storage facility at or near the point where fish are landed. With the resettlement, it is no longer possible to maintain nor watch such structures (in fact, the specific construction of buildings on a site abandoned by resettlement is prohibited by the Resettlement Act). However, the control of processing of fish by plant owners, their increasing absorption of greater portions of the total value of fish beyond the fishermen's share, is not the only dynamic of capitalist rationalization involving outport fishermen of Cat Harbour. There are also active attacks on their very control over their labor power in general, forcing them out of the inshore fishery altogether. The state's role here may be seen in increasing regulations and prohibitions, and is detailed elsewhere [3, 9].

Non-Fishery

We have documented the increasing capture of value by plant owners of the total value of fishery products, and the concomitant decrease in the total share of the product by fishermen. There is also an extraordinary increase in proletarianization in the outport which is more pronounced in Cat Harbour as a consequence of resettlement, as manifested in the tremendous increase in nonfishery occupations.

Whereas in the sample of Table 1 and 2 only one man left the fishery altogether, 75% of the total number of men of the community left the fishery between 1964 and 1972. Individual 5 of Table 2 is instructive and typical. He worked as a carpenter on a school construction project for $2.60/hour for 40 weeks for a 40-hour week. Even though being able to work as much as 40 weeks of the year is unusual, his total income still ranks next to last of the sample of six, the other

Table 3. Shifts in Types of Processing.

Year	1964	1965	1966	1967	1968	1969	1970	1971	1972
Light salt (quintals)	70	20	30	20	20	15	--	--	--
Heavy salt (quintals)	5120	2396	1700	1330	995	1635	952	–	--
Fresh fish (pounds)	--	--	--	--	--	2500	2000	290,000	210,000
Total weight	1,290,880	598,376	431,640	336,140	253,730	408,500	236,000	290,000	210,000
Number of Fishermen	67	61	68	52	46	40	25	?	1

five individuals still maintaining some fishery income.

Of the 72% (63/88) of the male labor force no longer fishing in 1972, 50 men worked elsewhere but maintained their families and permanent residence in Cat Harbour. These men were primarily employed in hydroelectric, mining construction and industrial sites of Labrador (Churchill Falls, Labrador City) (9), St. John's (4), other cities of Newfoundland (9), Toronto (10), and at other wage labor occupations elsewhere (18). Another 13 were wage laborers at nearby projects so they spent each night in Cat Harbour. Of this entire group, by September of 1972, 18 men were unemployed (an unemployment rate of 36%). But even though unemployed, they were not available to the fishery. This work, then, cannot be considered contribution to the reproduction of labor power for the fishery, unlike the seasonal nonfishery labor of most of the individuals in Tables 1 and 2.

Returns to labor were greatest in Labrador, where wage returns to Cat Harbour men ranged from $3.52/per hour to $4.61/per hour for three-month contracts, the successful completion of which could include round-trip transportation. St. John's wages for Cat Harbour men were a maximum of $2.60/hour, which was also the common wage rate for local men elsewhere in the Province. Union scale at this time was $3.50/hour in St. John's for journeymen, but no local men got this wage. Toronto wages were from $2.65 to $3.20/hour to all local men working there. Local non-fishery wage laborers made far less—$1.65 to $2.00/hour on local federal and provincial construction projects which hired local men. Women's wage labor was from $1.40 at the nearest fish plant, 25 miles from Cat Harbour (see below for more detail treatment of women's labor).

These wages and this return to labor from non-fishery sources, while *at best* only slightly more than the most successful fisherman of Table 2 (fisherman number 2), nevertheless bear scrutiny. Newfoundlanders who work away and maintain their home in the outport do not constitute an infrastructural expense to the industrial center. They are very much like migrant laborers, such as those who travel from Mozambique to the mines of South Africa, and are supported there in large measure by the mining companies. Newfoundlanders are commonly on contract the benefits of which (such as the return fare) require satisfactory completion of the contract. The chief burden of the costs of reproduction of labor power is transferred back to the outport community. No schools, homes or expensive social services need be provided by capital in the population centers. This labor goes home to be reproduced and sent back [10]. Although it might seem possible to make as much money as possible before returning home, labor legislation effectively inhibited this since men making $1.60/ hour must work 56.5 hours before overtime had to be paid, men making $2.00/hour must work for 61.5 hours before claiming overtime, and men making $2.50/hour had to work 73 hours before overtime pay was required!

Again, it can be seen here that the role of the state is critical to the maintenance of this system. Although this is considered in more detail below, the essential point here is that wage labor elsewhere by outport residents is not at their gain. Rather, it is pursued only in circumstances favorable to capital. They furnish a labor force which is unorganized, well-skilled, reliable and, most importantly, captive. Legislation such as the above insures that the captivity will not be at the worker's advantage.

The Social Fabric

Local Organization

The traditional fishing outport in Newfoundland was characterized by fishing units recruited agnatically. The implications of this have been widely noted [4, 11]. Cat Harbour, perhaps more clearly than other areas, had a traditional residential pattern which placed crews of the same surname in adjacent gardens; each garden being a linear extension of fishing premises on the water, and the segmentation and further dividing of gardens a consequence of the developmental cycle, i.e., the establishment of new crews with new fishing premises and gardens [2].

The resettlement of Cat Harbour in 1967-1968 was to an inland site with no access to water (thus eliminating the shorefront gardens of the same surnames paralleling one another), and the demise of the fishery no longer required adjacent agnates. Of the crews still fishing in 1972, only one was composed of patrikins—compared with crews, all of whose members were agnates of 71.4% in 1964, and crews with at least two agnates of 92.5%. The few remaining crews today are composed along lines of friendship and affinity (with friendship being the chief factor even in crews composed of affines).

While this is a distinct change from the traditional recruitment mechanisms, a consequential effect is that it is more difficult to secure labor without the mechanism of agnatic kinship. Recruitment has to be opportunistic, and even the few remaining fishermen are discouraged at the problem of having to recruit crews in such a manner. The economic cooperation of the traditional agnatic units is now gone, along with its resistance to opportunistic recruitment. This is actually a more serious problem in other areas of the province where the fishery is less severely damaged than in Cat Harbour [3]. Another visible consequence of the decline in traditional local organizational structures may be seen in the dramatic changes in the marital and post-marital residential patterns since 1964. Table 4 details this.

Whereas in 1964 over one third of local women married local men, since that time only 9% of local women have married locally. This reflects both the greater absence of local men as they leave to seek work, as well as the fact that local young women are also leaving the community for work. In 1964, 56% of local women married outside the community, over half of these marrying into nearby settlements on the northeast coast. Since that time, almost 70% of local women have married out of the community and less than one fourth of those having married out actually married into nearby settlements. In 1964, 90.2% of local men married and established residence in Cat Harbour (the rest leaving the community). The reverse of these data is even more revealing, for while in 1964 only 4.2% of residential men had married into Cat Harbour (i.e., 4.2% of residential man had origins elsewhere), by 1972, 18.7% of those men having married since 1964 were outsiders having married into the community. None of these men fished, but were away most of the time in wage labor. Their local wives simply maintained residence in their natal home. This will probably be an increasingly common pattern. As men are away wives will

Table 4. Post Marital Patterns: 1964-1972

	1964	1972
Percent local females marrying into Cat Harbour	36.5%	9.0% (married since 1964)
Percent local females Marrying outside Cat Harbour	56.0%	69.2% (married since 1964)
Percent local men married and establishing local residence	90.2%	21.9% (married since 1964)
Percent non-local men marrying into Cat Harbour	4.2%	18.7% (married since 1964)

maintain their natal residence, often in their parents' house, and fewer marrieds will have their own residence than previously. (In 1964, only 4.9% of the conjugal units lived with parents [2]. In 1972 this had risen to 12.5% of conjugal units.) The shift from virilocality to increasing forms of uxorilocality, then, is a direct consequence of the changing occupational structure. One further new pattern is, of course, a completely neolocal postmarital residence pattern totally divorced from the fabric of the outport community.

A final local organizational consequence of the new occupational profiles is this. Since young men no longer fish, they do not have the pressing need to establish a productive unit which incorporates wives and breeds children for the work organization. The critical importance of family labor to the fishery enterprise has been noted repeatedly [2-4, 12], and is quantitatively discussed below.

Conjugal stability and family unity has also changed. Individual well-being is now threatened by alcoholism and drugs and other manifestations of extreme alienation have increased. Divorce, previously unknown in Cat Harbour (a rate of 0.3% [2], has risen by a factor of almost 26. Suicide has doubled.

The consequences of increased consumerism brought about by the demise of domestic production in gardens, knitted woolens, etc., have produced further damage. Automobile accidents and accidents with appliances claim and maim lives. Shopping now requires an automobile rather than a trip to the root cellar. While no one had died since 1964 at the fishery (previously, the sealhunt and various storms while fishing had claimed lives in every genealogy [2]), automobile accidents had claimed three lives (two as a result of drunkenness) during the eight-year period from 1964 to 1972.

Women

One of the most severe shifts in traditional productive organization with modernization is in women's roles and the return to women's labor. One of the consequences of the resettlement program was ostensibly to give women employment in fish processing plants where they could be paid for their labor, freeing them from their work in the traditional fishery stage head where they received no salary [13]. But while there was no pay, a woman's contribution in the stage processing activity made a significant difference to her husband's share of the voyage. In Cat Harbour a woman in heading, gutting, or salting made a difference of four quintals to every one hundred quintals of fish landed [2]. It has been calculated [3] that at 1972 prices (approximately $30.00 per quintal), this would be $360.00 for a 300-quintal total catch, for four to five weeks of work three to four hours each day (maximum), six days each week. The rate was even higher elsewhere, where women's contributions were estimated to be as much as 40% of the value of the trap voyage [3].

Comparing this to fish plant wages to women (beginning at $1.40/hour at the nearest fish plant to Cat Harbour in 1972), women are actually losing value in expending more labor. For an eight-hour day, five days per week for four weeks, a woman grosses wages under $325.00. Moreover, the distance to the fish plant from Cat Harbour inhibits most local women from access to it, although there are insufficient numbers of jobs in any case. Many outport women, then, no longer engaged significantly in the domestic production that created many of the items of food and clothing now bought. Instead, they simply kept house, contributing in this unpaid fashion to the reproduction of male labor power.

The removal of women from the fishery has been total. In 1964, 41 of the women of the community actively worked in processing fish, principally in heading, gutting and salting. In 1972 there were no women in processing. It is not that these tasks are gone since fish are sold fresh, for it must still be gutted. But, unlike the traditional outport where gardens and houses were adjacent to fish landing stages, the resettlement is two miles inland from the fishing premises inhibiting, effectively, women from moving quickly from house to stage and back.

Of the community's young women, 21 had left for jobs elsewhere since 1964 (of a total of 28 women who matured between 1964 and 1972). Only one works in a fish plant. There are four women with local jobs that allow them to return home each night. The remaining three are housewives, joining older local women whose lives have also become increasingly unproductive of value. But not only is their labor missing in productive endeavors (which traditionally amounts to a substantial portion of the "winter's diet"—estimated by Brox at over $1000 [14]), but they must now purchase these goods. Not only, then, has their labor lost value, but it can be measured concretely in rising (and now required) consumerism and increasing debt.

Several researchers have noted that the appearance of transfer payments (family allowances, pensions, welfare, etc.) has also had a destructive and causal effect on the demise of women's productive labor in the outport [12, 15]. Such interpretations must be treated with caution, however, for however much such payments domesticize women they more importantly inhibit class struggle, i.e. for greater demands for a share of the total value of the fishery product. It is a taxpayer subsidy for the profits of those capital firms which buy fish and labor from the outport (contrary to critics who argue such transfer payments, welfare, and subsidy actually maintain the nonviable inshore fishery).

The Role of the State

Local Inhibitions to Capital

The traditional Newfoundland inshore fishing was dominated by capital interests that were principally manifest at the local level as mercantilist.

Thus, rationalization of the fishery, or of outport labor in general by finance and/or industrial capital, required certain critical changes. Capital rationalization of the fishery also precipitated, whether intended or not, the pursuit of nonfishery occupations as fishermen realized their increasing disadvantage. This must be distinguished from specific attempts to recruit and make available outporters for nonfishery labor. We have seen that control over the means of production or over some aspect of the processing of the product constitute the classic mechanisms of capital to increasingly extract surplus value. But control over the resource or over processing to capture surplus value was problematic for several very real constraining reasons.

Control over the resource is particularly complicated. Even though the inshore fishery was essentially a harvest, the mobility of fish and the consequent inability to embody labor directly in the resource meant that extraction of surplus value by ownership of the resource was impossible. Rent could not, then, constitute a form of appropriation. The only means of control of the resource had to be in access such as by regulation of the ability of fishermen to actually fish by licensing mechanisms, restrictions on size, type or means of catch; and by control of marketing factors, freezing, salting, storing facilities, contacts for sale, artificially low prices; altering the source, type, quality and price of capital goods supplied to outfit fishermen, and restrictions on social service transfer payments, unfair unemployment benefits vis-a-vis nonfishery occupations, etc. All of these mechanisms were used but they all required state intercession. The state, then, was critical.

Control over processing was also complicated by the nature of the production of the inshore fishery itself. The production units were scattered, isolated, and independent of each other (unlike, say, farmers in an irrigation scheme). This same phenomenon paradoxically also contributed to an independence and relatively greater comprehension of the nature of mercantile exploitation. Class struggle, then, was often acute. Moreover, the traditional inshore processing was a function of a work organization that consumed much capital in its own reproduction [4]. Crews came about through fragmentation of estates and the centripedal effect of inheritance practices, constantly requiring additional capital in each generation to form new crews with the capital gear necessary to constitute an entire fishery unit. A man, fishing with his father and brother, would find his sons and daughters sufficiently mature that he must establish his own crew. This would mean complete sets of gear (boats, engines, traps, stages, stores, etc.), only a portion of which may be acquired through inheritance, since another portion of the capital gear of the original crew went to each of his brothers as they too established their own production units. Accumulation and differentiation were thus difficult with the continual fractionating of capital.

While not, of course, causal, these factors nevertheless all contributed to the inability of capital to rationalize in common ways, through easy penetration of the processing sector. Economic appropriation was via the abovementioned mercantilist form. Capitalist rationalization ("modernization") in the Newfoundland fishery required and necessitated, perhaps to a greater extent than elsewhere, state intervention and state assistance.

Thus, we see the outport made available, as it were, to such modernization by an entire series of government moves and policies (see Antler and Faris [3] for greater detail). Indeed, it is the thesis of this paper that *only* through the agency of the state could industrial and finance capital rationalize the production process in the Newfoundland traditional fishery (extract greater value from producers), and make labor available to nonfishery occupations. This was not a uniform nor could it be a planned process. Indeed, there are real contradictions in this rationalization between different capitals. Thus the rationalization of the fishery itself, through forcing inshore fishermen to become wage laborers in offshore or midwater capital-intensive fresh fish production was, to some extent, in conflict with the demands for a wage force in other industrial endeavors (in Labrador and other sites on the mainland as well as on the island). There was also the tendency for capital to rationalize in actually providing consumer goods to a fishery that was being destroyed by other capitals (such as in the provisioning of the inshore fishermen with new capital gear while at the same time driving them into offshore trawlers and other wage labor). But capital cannot coherently plan and still be free, so these contradictions are inevitable and expectable. They constitute the evidence that the policies of the government and capital are not conscious conspiracies at all levels, however much it may sometimes appear to be the case. Of course there can be collusion by various sectors. There simply can be no integrated planning.

Finance capital also moved to the relocation and resettlement areas themselves. An enormous amount of capital has been poured into the resettlements. The cost of resettlement has been repeatedly emphasized by critics. It has been characterized as an irrational move on the part of an impotent or blundering government, as an example of the very lack of planning [14, 16] or as the being chiefly of benefit to the fishermen. Here too, the Canadian taxpayer is forced, in the conventional wisdom, to support irrational schemes and wasteful expenditures in attempts to secure Newfoundland voters and extend Canadian franchise. But a closer examination of this state expenditure indicates that far from being some sort of irrational government action, the capital that enters the resettled communities in the form of highly visible projects for water, roads, town halls, and sewers is ultimately of benefit to capital. In resettled Cat Harbour, it is of significance that the federal provincial governments have *granted* only $34,104.17 (as of 1972), while *loaning* the resettlement $683,500.00 (Source: Department of Municipal Affairs and Housing). All the local projects employ local labor at between $1.48 and $2.00/hour, representing the lowest wages for males in the province, and far below union scale for construction projects. Thus the infrastructure necessary to maintain the bedroom community is not only debted to local people, but they are paid the lowest wages for its construction with most of the money going back to the capitalist providers of material. Like USAID, all the capital expense goes back to the metropole and only the low wages remain in the community (in 1968, for example, for every dollar spent in the province of Newfoundland, $0.71 left the province). Also, their traditional society and economy are destroyed in the process.

There are other consequences of this expenditure as well. Many of these projects are indeed ill-advised and initiated (though certainly not irrational or useless from the capital point of view), and the enormous debt that is engendered is all too blindly accepted as largesse rather than debt. Various government functionaries are a conspicuous part of local society. Newfoundland political culture, once confined in people's minds to demagogic struggles about the premiership of the province, now permeates local council elections, where decisions on allocation of government monies, attraction of such monies, etc., are undertaken. For now, political patronage may enable a part time or a temporary job for a relative on a local project. This campaigning is fervent, and individuals previously not involved in community decision-making (because of factors such as literacy requirements and unspoken status distinctions) are now vaulted into candidacy in scrambling for the access to available funds. Tacit discriminations are now thrust into overt consciousness. Status differentials are becoming more marked. Individual successes in the traditional setting were often in the form of simply not being in debt rather than conspicuous display. And there were other dynamics involved in the relatively undifferentiated traditional outport community [2].

Class Consciousness

Let us look in more detail at the explicit way in which class struggle was relevant to the capitalist rationalization documented. I want to suggest that the "backwardness," the resistance to innovation, then, which characterizes so much of the literature on traditional fishing settlements, actually reflects a consciousness and a class resistance to increased or continued mercantilist exploitation.

Consciousness of mercantile exploitation came to be the wedge that was used to usher in a more mature capitalist exploitation. It became the consciousness necessary to industrial and finance capital. These later capitals were made to appear allies against traditional mercantile exploitation about which fishers were so keenly aware.

It was not, however, a consciousness informed by a proletarian awareness, but rather, by a narrow struggle against mercantilist exploitation. The extent to which the state represented these interests which, until the era of Premier Smallwood, it usually did in the minds of local fishermen, was suspect. The thesis here is that since the middle of the twentieth century the state most effectively facilitated the rise and rationalization of industrial and finance capital. Mercantilists that did not adapt, in fact, are now but relics on the Newfoundland scene.

The traditional populist politician in Newfoundland was successful to the extent that he appeared to stand against the fish buyers and provisioners, the merchants that were the visible manifestation of outport exploitation. Indeed, party lines were often ostensibly along the lines of merchant house- associated Conservatives and Liberal "anti"-mercantilists. Smallwood, Newfoundland's most successful demagogic premier, was the archetype Liberal example. Smallwood's history, as it was interpreted to outport fishermen, represented a fisherman's voice against the mercantilists. But rather than altering the buying and provisioning system directly, Smallwood focused appeal on the possibility of nonfishery occupations with which outporters could supplement their income (or escape the fishery altogether). He ushered in monopoly capital as Newfoundland was ushered into Canada.

Most of the traditional part time non-fishery labor of fishermen was payment for product such as forestry work, where men were paid by the amount of wood, cut off company-owned or -leased plots, provided to the pulp and paper companies. This was, to Cat Harbour, the most important source of extrafishery income (though, as noted above, this was regarded as part of the reproduction of the fishery enterprise). In stressing the exploitation and hardship of the fishery (mostly the latter and only very rarely the former), Smallwood promised nonfishery jobs, such as construction, at which outporters were particularly handy, having built their own homes and boats. Conspicuous local development projects were promised both as services and as sources for the hire of outport labor. Of the latter, the most relevant were inevitably attached to the fishery such as community states and thus especially welcome where they were interpreted as antimercantilist. Of course, this also made much more possible the sale of fresh rather than the salted fish necessary to supply the fish plants of industrial and finance capital. Only with resettlement could the promised public infrastructural projects such as sewers, water supplies, town halls, federal buildings and the like really be started. On the strength of the Cat Harbour example, resettlement was also an important feature of the proletarianization necessary for capital in the hydroelectric projects of Labrador and construction elsewhere in Newfoundland and Canada.

Thus, the consciousness of mercantile exploitation was used as the state came (with confederation in 1949) to represent other capital interests. The state, since 1949, was ostensibly no longer simply St. John's Water Street merchants, but U.S. and Canadian industrial and finance capital interests as well. The extent to which these merchant houses continued and were indeed represented in the postconfederation state is, of course, another issue. The political successes were premised on wresting state control to serve another capital. Many merchant houses, of course, became, or were agents of such industrial or finance capital.

Anthropological Studies of Traditional Fishing Communities

One important lesson of this rationalization process in the traditional outport rests in its implications for the social science we practice. For what it has revealed to me, albeit painfully, is the extraordinary inadequate perspective with which my initial research was undertaken, namely, my focus on the local culture [2]. Even though I argued that this could not be understood outside the material conditions and the social history in which it was situated, it generated a view of the outport as an isolated entity. Even recently [4], I published a paper suggesting that we should understand the outport as a type of fishing peasantry. After all, they produced a commodity and did not sell labor power. I am not convinced that this latter analysis is totally wrong, but in no case does it utilize sufficiently (or hardly suggest) the dynamic factor in human history, class struggle, which we view to be critical in capital's rationalization. Antler [6, 12] puts forward a compelling if patricidal argument. It is worth quoting her conclusions here:

> The classification of this fishery as a peasantry is really incorrect. If constitutes a confusion of the conditions of the labor process—the manner in which nature is transformed into specific products—for the mode of production itself.
>
> The same criticism must be made of attempts to analyze the inshore fishery as a specifically maritime mode. Focus on the nature of the raw material, the tools, skills of the workers, or the specifics of the physical environment will not yield salient explanations of social phenomena. I hope that I have demonstrated that the fact that

Newfoundland is on the sea and produces salt fish is among the least interesting aspects of the story.

To produce useful explanations of social phenomena we must employ categories that locate social formations in history and make available for analysis the forces which bring them into being, maintain them and produce new forms. In sum, the proper method of analysis is one that considers the forces of production and the social relations of production.

Our lesson is this: until we adopt a perspective that allows us to examine social formations as dynamic because they are people's movements, rather than, as our fieldwork tradition all too often suggests, isolated pieces articulated in vague ways which require peculiar analysis in each case, social science is not going to make progress, nor indeed to make much of process. But there has been a fluorescence of theoretical work in the past few years. Hindness and Hirst [17], for example, put the case clearly for the focus on class dynamics in causal statements:

> If we are to think of the possibility of transition as the outcome of determinate transformations of definite structures of social relations—as the outcomes, that is to say, of a determinate material causation and not as the theological realization of some inner principle or idea—then it is necessary to consider the specific forms and conditions of class struggle as they appear in determinate social formations dominated by determinate modes of production.

This must be separated from romantic attachment to producers, however, for a sympathetic statement of their ambitions and culture is not adequate for science. They are not the only classes in the struggle. Felt needs may not be an adequate class expression, particularly if the class struggle is not at its most mature point (i.e., with proletarians). Were fishermen's consciousness completely adequate, there would be no need for science at all. But, indeed, the argument here has been that fishermen's consciousness of mercantile exploitation was the avenue by which state political mobilization proceeded, a state participation necessitated because economic rationalization could not have been successful if attempted by the economic agents of the period, the merchants, a dying class in the mid-twentieth century.

My initial Cat Harbour work confused these issues, as indeed has some subsequent material on Cat Harbour's resettlement [3, 4]. I am still uncertain and even frequently confused, but certainly less arrogant. We know the dominant mode of production in most of the world today, and we now understand something of the ways in which various class struggles require it to move if it is to reproduce itself. Our investigations of specific aspects of specific social formations have got to be premised on that understanding. Do not stop field research, do not hesitate to undertake specific community studies. Indeed, increase such studies. But do so informed of the results, methods, standards and insight of a now mature materialism in social science.

REFERENCES

[1] Faris, J. "Cat Harbour: A Newfoundland Fishing Settlement," Newfoundland Social and Economic Studies No. 3, Institute of Social and Economic Research, Memorial University of Newfoundland, St. John's, Newfoundland (1966).

[2] Faris, J. "Cat Harbour: A Newfoundland Fishing Settlement" (with appendices), Newfoundland Social and Economic Studies No. 3, Institute of Social and Economic Research, Memorial University of Newfoundland, St. John's, Newfoundland (1972).

[3] Antler, E., and J. Faris. "Adaptation to Changes in Technology and Government Policy: A Newfoundland Example," in *North Atlantic Maritime Europeans,* R. Andersen, Ed. (Chicago, IL: Aldine, 1979).

[4] Faris, J. "Primitive Accumulation in Small-Scale Fishing Committees," in *Those Who Live from the Sea,* M. E. Smith, Ed., American Ethnological Society Monograph No. 62 (San Francisco, CA: West Publishing Company, 1977).

[5] Poushinsky, J., and N. Poushinsky. "The Canadian Atlantic Fisheries and the State," paper presented at the Annual Meeting of the Northeastern Anthropological Association, Providence, RI, March 1977.

[6] Antler, E. "Maritime Mode of Production, Domestic Mode of Production, or Labour Process: An Examination of the Newfoundland Inshore Fishery," paper presented at the Annual Meeting of the Northeastern Anthropological Association, Providence, RI, March 1977.

[7] Sider, G. "Mumming and the New Year in Newfoundland," *Past Present* No. 71 (1976).

[8] Robb, A., and R. Robb. "A Cost-Benefit Analysis of the Newfoundland Resettlement Program," unpublished (1969).

[9] Alexander, D., et. al. "Report of the Committee on Federal Licensing Policy and Its Implications for the Newfoundland Fishery," Memorial University of Newfoundland, St. John's, Newfoundland (1974).

[10] Mugabane, B., and J. O'Brien. "The Political Economy of Migrant Labor: A Critique of Conventional Wisdom," *Crit. Anthropol.* 11(2) (1972).

[11] Nemec, R. "I Fish with My Brother," in *North Atlantic Fishermen*, R. Andersen and C. Wadel, Eds., Newfoundland Social and Economic Papers No. 5 (St. John's, Newfoundland: Institute of Social and Economic Research, Memorial University of Newfoundland, 1972).

[12] Antler, E. "Women's Work in Newfoundland Fishery Families," *Atlantis* II(2) (1977).

[13] Copes, P. "Resettlement of Fishing Communities in Newfoundland," Canadian Council on Rural Development, Ottawa, Ontario (1972).

[14] Brox, O. "Newfoundland Fishermen in the Age of Industry," Newfoundland Social and Economic Studies No. 9, Institute of Social and Economic Research, Memorial University of Newfoundland, St. John's Newfoundland (1972).

[15] Wadel, C. "Now, Whose Fault Is That?" Newfoundland Social and Economic Studies No. 11, Institute of Social and Economic Research, Memorial University of Newfoundland, St. John's, Newfoundland (1973).

[16] Matthews, R. *There's No Better Place Than Here: Social Change in Three Newfoundland Communities* (Toronto, Ontario: Martin, 1976).

[17] Hindess, B., and P. Hirst. *Pre-capitalist Modes of Production* (London, England: Routledge, Kegan Paul, 1975).

CHAPTER 8
INFRASTRUCTURE INVESTMENTS IN COASTAL COMMUNITIES: A NEGLECTED ISSUE IN STUDIES OF MARITIME ADAPTATIONS

John Maiolo
Paul Tschetter
Department of Sociology and Anthropology
East Carolina University

INTRODUCTION AND RATIONALE

A unifying theme in the rich and varied literature on maritime cultures and industries is *adaptation,* seen as a processual model. The scenario is usually the following: (1) a change occurs in fishing technology; (2) change in social organizational/occupational properties of fishing follows; and (3) adjustments may be required at the institutional/community/cultural levels. (See Stiles [21], Norr and Norr [15] [16], Hepburn [9] [10], Tunstall [24], Bertrand [2], Casteel and Quimby [4], Anderson and Wadel [1], Smith [19], and Summers and Lang [23] for empirical studies on these themes).

Nason [14], in describing the effects of socio-political changes on marine technologies, offers empirical evidence that the present conceptualization of adaptation as a unidimensional model is theoretically deficient. Our view is that the existing model, even as modified vis-a-vis Nason, does not properly represent adaptation as a set of processes which might not only have multiple origins, but which proceed along multiple pathways affecting—and affected by—many different factors. For example, the model does not account for the consequences of major technological changes (of the artifact type, Smith [19]) that are purposely implemented within or near a community and which may or may not be designed with the local fishing industry in view but which affect those industries. We are referring to what are often labeled *infrastructure investments,* defined as the construction of public

203

facilities such as highways, seaports, bridges, airports, sewerage treatment facilities, and the like (Council on Environmental Quality [6]). Norr and Norr [16] allude to the importance of infrastructure investments in a discussion of the possible effects of environment and technology on opportunities for work in maritime settings:

> These alternative opportunities result from the interaction of such factors as the technological development and diversity of the community and society, the relationship between the population size and available resources, as well as a host of economic, communication and transportation factors.

Norr and Norr also refer to "realistic work opportunities outside the community" which facilitate *choices* for work. Our study will incorporate data which deal with this issue as well.

It is fairly clear that the deficiencies in the present model are a consequence, at least in part, of the research foci which are reported in the maritime social science literature. Maritime anthropology field research strategies, for example, have been restricted to empirical referents that are small, relatively homogeneous, primitive or peasant settings, and/or where the maritime activities began and remain grounded in the exploitable ocean biomass. In some of these cases, modern infrastructure technology was not present. However, some of these settings have moved rapidly beyond the stages described in the ethnographies. Infrastructure technology may have been an important factor in these movements, but followup research is often not performed or reported (as, for example, Breton [3], Christensen [5]). In other cases, it is obvious that community infrastructure investments were present but their importance in the change process is virtually ignored or, at best, noted in passing (see Tunstall [24], Goodlad [8]).

The net result of the limited research foci we have described is that we know next to nothing about extremely pluralistic maritime contexts manifesting increasingly high levels of interdependence among formerly isolated communities (economically and socially) in terms of: (1) how they arrived at their current status; (2) the dimensions of integration (economic, social, political or all three); (3) the impact of the first two on what the future holds. We do know that coastal communities in already modernized societies are rapidly becoming (or have become) kaleidoscopes of economic and social activities. They are centers for commercial *and* sportfishing, recreation, retirement, international export, and other multi-dimensional activities.

We view maritime social organization in a way which includes the social structure of commercial and sportfishing, the social structure of fisheries processing and marketing, and the technology of fisheries and boat building. Figure 1 displays the range of occupations which may be affected by infrastructure investments. Infrastructure investments may operate by altering the external or extralocal environments of the maritime industry, e.g., the creation of new external markets. Alternatively, infrastructure investments may change the internal or local environment of the maritime industry. By changing the structure (size and composition) and integration (social, economic, and political) of local communities, infrastructure investments indirectly affect the occupational structure and maritime social organization.

Some might argue that our efforts appear to be oriented toward confirming the obvious; that what we are attempting to demonstrate is so clear as to render research time and literature space unwarranted. After all, anyone who has ever visited a modernizing maritime setting can easily discern the connection between, say, highway improvements and community development. In response to this, we would point out that similar research in other contexts has produced surprising results in our attempts to understand community structure and change (Council on Environmental Quality [6], Maiolo [13]). Second, to *assume* that infrastructure technology plays a role in the change process is not enough. To understand and to demonstrate empirically *how* it does so is crucial to our body of knowledge. Finally, specifically in regard to maritime communities, the link between community infrastructure and fishing technology needs to be established if we are to develop inclusive models of maritime adaptations and appropriate social policies.

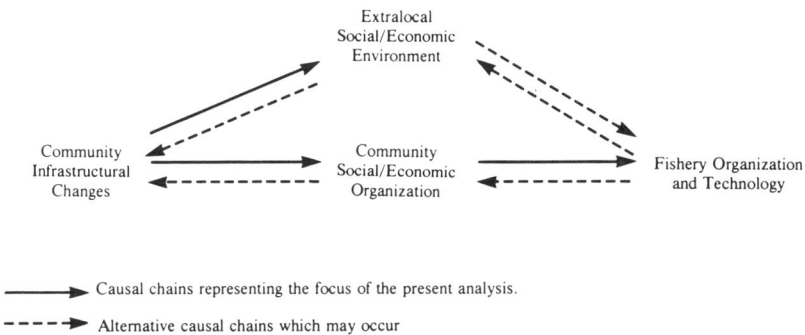

Causal chains representing the focus of the present analysis.

Alternative causal chains which may occur

Figure 1. Conceptual Model of Adaptation in Maritime Social Organization

RESEARCH CONTEXT

In our effort to trace out the effects of infrastructure investments through different segments of neighboring coastal communities, we examined several periods and dimensions of growth in portions of Carteret County, North Carolina. North Carolina is characterized by 335 miles of coastline, 23 navigable inlets and a rich maritime history. An important feature of the coastline is the stretch of barrier islands from Virginia to South Carolina which fence out the Atlantic Ocean. The northernmost section of the islands is labeled the Outer Banks (consisting of Bodie, Hatteras and Ocracoke Islands, and Core Banks). Some island points extend as many as 30 miles from the mainland. From Cape Lookout the islands sweep westerly for about 40 miles, and then take a mostly southerly course to the South Carolina border. None of the islands from Cape Lookout to South Carolina is more than a few miles from the mainland. The differences in distances from the mainland between the northern and southern sections of the islands have played an important role in the development of the coast, but have become increasingly less important as access to the remote northern islands has been facilitated by the construction of bridges and the development of ferry services; i.e., infrastructure investments.

The barrier islands are separated from the mainland by nearly one and one half million acres of estuarine waters rich in a wide variety of fin and shellfish, the exploitation of which helped form the basis for much of the coastal economy and, indeed, the state economy as well. Additionally, ocean fishing, mainly inshore, combined with some offshore fishing is an important part of North Carolina's maritime history. A wide variety of commercial fishing techniques have been and continue to be used. Sportfishing, from casting to billfishing, is a major industry estimated to have contributed over 34 million dollars to the state economy as early as the 1950's (Winslow [25]).

A sprawling area of 573 square miles and nearly 80 miles long, Carteret County is situated slightly south of the center of the state where the barrier islands swing inward to the mainland. We chose the site for our research because the local communities varied in size, complexity and history. Further, fishing villages exist near exploding resort settlements; the county has a relatively recent center of commerce, Morehead City, with a port small by today's standards, alongside the previous center (Beaufort); retirement communities, farming; manufacturing; a nearby military base; and a newly created national seashore. The port's growth has been seriously curtailed by a narrow inlet, a small turning basin, and constant shoaling. The new, large containerized cargo ships can hardly negotiate the inlet and narrow channel (depth of 40 feet, width of 450 feet) which requires dredging about 30% of the time. At the time of the present research, only nine berths are available for ocean going vessels, five of which are preferentially assigned, along with ten storage sheds and warehouses. Combined export and import tonnage was about 2,025,957 in 1980. These are data indicating volume *prior* to the steam coal operations which have been recently set up. We will discuss this question separately below. It is a heterogeneous, interdependent economic and sociocultural milieu. Our analysis traces the development of the social and economic diversity of Carteret County, followed by a projection of impending changes which we believe will continue historical trends.

EARLY SETTLEMENTS

Though portions of the Outer Banks were settled as early as 1584 (Stick [20]), shipwrecked sailors inhabited the islands prior to these settlements, and colonists did not find their way to Carteret County

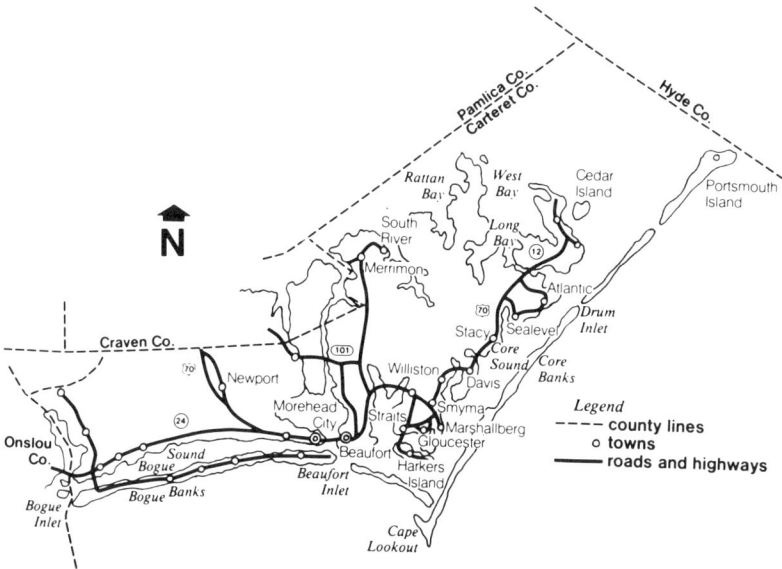

Figure 2. Map of Carteret County, North Carolina

until 1707. Carteret County was attractive in that it offered access through Beaufort Inlet and other waterways; a long growing season for crops (269 days); forests, which provided lumber for ships and boat construction; pine for turpentine, tar, pitch and other naval stores; and an abundance of wildlife for food and furs (Hill [11], Salter [12]). The early development that did occur in the county outside of the Beaufort area was in a northeasterly direction (toward Cedar Island; See Figure 2).

From the very beginning of the colonial settlements in the eighteenth century, the area began to take on a diversified economic appearance. Although reliable estimates as to proportions of the population in different occupations do not exist, it seems most were engaged in agriculture and raising livestock; some effort for cash, some for subsistence. Mill, smith, tavern, legal, and other services soon became available. The production of naval stores for the budding export business, mainly to the West Indies, was present. Commercial fishing appears to have been one of the first business ventures. Except for whaling (from about 1725 to 1875), the commercial fishery declined after an early start and was not of much economic consequence until after the Civil War. Still ([22]:7) has a different interpretation, noting that fishing was a principle occupation throughout the county's early history. We agree insofar as subsistence fishing is concerned, but not commercial fishing. Existing data do not support a contention that commercial fishing was the principal occupation. Whaling, however, was important enough to create the need for settlements to support the industry on Shackleford and Core Banks.

The mainland town of Beaufort, the first port settlement, became an export center establishing the town as the hub of economic, social, and political activity that was to last up to the outbreak of the Civil War.

While some diversification characterized the county in the colonial period, one cannot think of the area as an *interdependent* economy at that time. To be sure, the export business had a unifying effect on easily accessible areas near Beaufort because of the exchanges associated with products and services supplied by local entrepreneurs. With the exception of the whaling settlements near Cape Lookout, the economic net thrown from Beaufort did not reach far. The residents of outlying settlements east of Beaufort seemed to adapt to their immediate economies, isolated by waterways and symbolically unified only by others' conception of them and they of themselves as *downeasters* or *hoi toidahs* (high tiders). Most of these people fished and farmed for their substance. Some boat and shipbuilding began during this period which created a narrow linkage to the area-wide economy. This latter occupation has remained in the county to the present.

Many of the consequences of this isolation and its resulting sub-culture persisted through time, and strain to survive today. Nevertheless, in spite of initial social, cultural and economic isolation of the straits villages east of Beaufort, a backdrop for a substantially inter-dependent economy was forged during the colonial period the catalysts of which were changing demands for goods and services, and the execution of which would be facilitated by the powerful intrusion of infrastructure developments beginning in mid-nineteenth century.

SOCIAL AND ECONOMIC TRANSFORMATION

In an 1887 publication, Earll ([7]:447) took note of North Carolina's "outer bars" describing them as "bald ridges of drifting sand, almost destitute of vegetation. Owing to this fact they have few inhabitants...." He refers to the mainland as "low and swampy, with few settlements of any size along the shore," with the exception of Wilmington, New Bern, and the Carteret County communities of Beaufort and Morehead City.

In 1900 Carteret County had a population of 11,811 with over 19 percent of the population living in Morehead Township. The rest of the population lived in Beaufort Township and the small communities east of Beaufort. As the major population centers, Beaufort and Morehead Township achieved parity by 1910 and remained relatively equal in population until the 1940's when Morehead Township began to grow rapidly. By 1970 Morehead Township, with a population of 12,000, was twice as large as Beaufort. The population of Beaufort grew slowly, if at all, during this period.

By 1976, Carteret County had a permanent population of 36,400. It is estimated that at least 300,000 people visit the county during the tourist season. Although a majority of these tourists visit the area west of Beaufort, it is estimated the number of visitors to the eastern area of the county is growing rapidly with the development of a National Seashore on Core Banks.

Tourism is but one of many industries now flourishing in diversified Carteret County, but it has had a unifying effect on the county. This growing interdependence, however, has not been uniform. Even though the development of early settlements occurred in a northeasterly direction, and the emergence of the fisheries was based (mostly) *downeast,* primarily in the region, it is the settlement pattern to the west of Beaufort which began in the mid-nineteenth century and continues today that ignited further economic pluralism and generally gave Carteret County much of its present social and economic character. At first, the lack of certain infrastructure technologies were responsible for the historical development of eastern and western Carteret County. But, from the mid-nineteenth century on, it was *because* of specific infrastructure developments that the county economy at first partially bifurcated and then later began to come together. The following sections are intended to support this contention.

Major Infrastructure Investments

A major infrastructure investment affecting the development of the local commercial fisheries came in 1858 with the opening of the Atlantic and North Carolina Railway which connected the community now known as Morehead City to the rest of the state and beyond. The impact on the fisheries can be vividly illustrated by reference to the railroad's nickname, the "Mullet Line." Fish could be moved to the interior of the state quickly. With the use of ice in shipping, beginning in 1870, fresh fish and oysters were moved by rail to New Bern (in nearby Craven County, to the west) where large dealerships were created for distribution throughout the region and neighboring states. Also, four firms in Beaufort and five in Morehead were established to handle the increased trade. Earll estimated that the saltfish trade alone in Carteret County became more extensive than any other area on the southern coast ([7]:486). Still notes that "Forest and agricultural products as well as seafood were shipped out to interior points by way of the railroad" ([22]:3). Thus, the traditional economy was boosted by the railroad's presence. But, soon after the installation of the railroad and the Civil War period, another industry began to emerge—tourism. While the Carteret area had always been looked upon as a popular vacation spot, access was difficult. The railroad had the effect of attracting vacationers from the Piedmont section of the state, as well as from Eastern North Carolina.

This period was the beginning of steady population growth to the west of Beaufort. As mentioned, Morehead City's population equalled Beaufort's by 1910. Despite the fact that from town line to town line Beaufort and Morehead are only two miles apart separated by two waterways with an island in between, it was more than a 24 mile trip by roadway between the two municipalities until 1928 when bridges were constructed to connect them. This separation had the effect of creating a great deal more development around the railroad in the western section of the county and facilitated a momentum that has existed until only recently. A trip to Morehead City was easier to negotiate than to Beaufort despite the fact that paved roads did not connect with the former until 1921. Also, Morehead provided easier access to Bogue Banks, whose miles of beaches were attractive.

When the roadways came in 1921, Beaufort was included but, as noted, for all intents and purposes it was a 24 mile road trip from Morehead City (until 1928). After the depression, hotels were constructed in Morehead City along with restaurants and rental cottages. With the construction of a bridge between Morehead and the banks about 1930, the growth of Morehead Township was further enhanced.

Three other major developments, two of the infrastructure variety, affected the economy during the second quarter of the twentieth century. Until the early 1930's Beaufort was at the end of the Intracoastal Waterway. This promoted trade and some tourism. But, when the waterway was extended, its route passed Morehead and docking facilities were built there to attract the North-South travelers. Second, early efforts (1850's) to have a deep water port facility built in Morehead City had failed. Later efforts resulted in a modest facility, in operation during the 1930's, and then deep water port terminals in 1945 (improved again in 1953). Wilmington's facilities were improved also at that time (Still, [22]:20). In addition to promoting the import and export of commodities (cotton, military cargo, tobacco), it provided another tourist attraction and, as an unexpected consequence, a deep hole habitat for sportfish.

The creation of Cherry Point Marine Air Station in nearby Craven County (17 miles from Morehead) in 1941 resulted in the detachment of 20,000 military personnel (Still, [22]:12), providing support to the Morehead City and Bogue Banks tourist industry.

In a report of an important study of the North Carolina seafood industry in 1956, Winslow made note of the traditionalism (in terms of resistance to the adoption of new fishing technology) and occupational pluralism (fishing, farming lumbering) of the state's fishermen. He argued that "paved roads and television" more than "rational considerations" were changing the style of fishing (Winslow, [25]:vi). He then pointed to "new sources of income far larger than that ever derived from the traditional fisheries" (vii). With fish as a commercial food item aside, he argued that a new view had developed whereby "fish are part of a natural environment having many attractions to people willing to pay for relaxation and escape from urban living" (vii).

The miles of accessible beaches are noted as an attraction as well as "the small finfish, which hold little promise as commercial food fish," but which with tourism take on a new importance, and are sought by people fishing from piers, bridges and boats (viii).

As noted above, Winslow then estimated that North Carolina's financial benefits for saltwater sportfishing in the Southeast would be over thirty million dollars per year as compared to slightly under six million dollars per year in the North Carolina commercial fisheries during the same period. Today, it is estimated that tourism pumps nearly thirty million dollars annually into Carteret County's economy alone. Commercial fishing has grown to nearly 70 million dollars annually, a little less than a third of which is accounted for by Carteret County.

During the period following the Civil War to the 1950's, a relatively brief span of about 70 years, the county's economy bifurcated with a great deal of development in the western portion. Tourism had become one of its leading industries. The poor quality of one type of infrastructure facilities (ground transportation) set the stage for the bifurcation while later improvements enhanced diversity in and around Morehead to the exclusion of the eastern portion of the country. The cumulative impact of these infrastructure investments is seen in the population growth rates between 1940 and 1970. While the county's population grew by 72 percent between 1940 and 1970, Morehead Township grew by 146 percent and Beaufort Township grew by 28 percent.

Further, Table 1 is presented to show the diversification in the local community from infrastructure investments using census data on employment in selected industry groups between 1930 and 1970. While fisheries employment has declined in both absolute and proportional terms, employment has most notably expanded in manufacturing, retail trade, services, and government employment. Although the census categories do not permit direct identification of tourism related employment, the figures for retail trade and services reflect the growth of tourism while the growth in government employment reflects the influence of the Cherry Point Air Station.

We now turn to an examination of the fisheries, and how the maritime social organization has responded to the infrastructure investments we have described.

Table 1. Occupational Data for Carteret County: 1930—1970*

	1930		1940		1950		1960		1970	
	#	%	#	%	#	%	#	%	#	%
Agricultural, Forestry										
Fisheries	2,634	49.8	2,097	34.2	2,000	27.7	943	11.7	731	6.5
Forestry and Fisheries	1,429	27.0	1,160	18.9	1,113	15.4	542	6.7	409†	3.6
Fisheries Estimate**	1,415	26.8	1,148	18.7	1,102	15.3	537	6.6	404	3.59
Construction	83	1.6	259	4.2	658	9.1	720	8.9	773	6.9
Manufacturing	368	7.0	423	6.9	791	11.0	828	10.3	1,615	14.4
Retail Trade	452‡	8.5	505	8.2	958	13.3	1,574	19.5	2,122	18.9
Finance, Insurance,										
Real Estate	46	.9	46	.8	84	1.2	195	2.4	171	1.5
Entertainment, Recreation	18	.3	85	1.4	85	1.2	54	.6	65	.6
Public Administration	156	2.9	207	3.4	868	12.0	1,378	17.1	2,068	18.4
Other	1,532	29.0	1,118	18.3	1,764	24.5	2,376	29.4	3,680	33.8
Total	5,289	100.0	6,126	100.0	7,208	100.0	8,068	NA	11,225	NA

*Source: US Census of Population
**Data for fishing only are estimated.
†Data for forestry and fishing are estimated.
‡Includes wholesale, except automobiles.

Fisheries: Types, Labor Force, Social and Technical Organization

Important changes in the social organization and technology of fishing occurred after the Civil War. We will describe a few of them in this section. It is our contention that those changes followed the demands imposed by the diversification and expansion of the area economy. Further, the diversification and expansion were tied to new market possibilities which were opened up vis-a-vis the infrastructure investments in transportation and which must be considered in under-standing the maritime adaptations of the area. Some impacts were more direct than others, but we hope to demonstrate that the temporal sequence of developments in the fisheries provides sufficient evidence to support our contention.

Small crews characterized the social organization of fishing until after the Civil War. Family ties did not seem to be as important as locality in determining the composition of the crews. Following the conclusion of the war, the sizes of the crews in the mullet fishery were enlarged, sometimes to as many as thirty men or more. The large catches were moved to Morehead City or Beaufort for processing, and then shipped by the newly constructed railway although a large share of the catches continued to be shipped by water. The use of ice had the impact of changing a great deal of processing from salting to packing fresh fillets or whole fish.

Surf seining was the most widely used technique up to about 1880. In the 1870's pound nets were introduced for use in the sounds but the practice did not meet with success. In the 1880's, small drag-nets were introduced to be used in the sounds to meet the increased market opportunities (Stick [20]:217).

Fish that were ordinarily avoided for commercial sale (on a large scale) became exploitable with rail transportation and improved road-ways (e.g., trout, bluefish, croaker, pigfish). As a result, limited sea-sonal fishing gave way to what appears to be a rotation system and many smaller crews worked virtually the whole year. Previously members of these crews might have opted for other income-producing or subsistence activities at certain times of the year. This also had the effect of creating the need for different sizes and shapes of nets. With the introduction of diesel and gasoline power at the turn of the century, long hauling was adopted and the boat building industry responded with appropriate modifications in size and style. Interestingly, in some respects (sharing the catch, authority lines, etc.) no significant changes seem to have occurred in the structure of the fishing crews.

With the diversification of the economy other changes can be dis-cerned. The period of the most rapid growth in the shellfish industry, with the exception of the oyster fishery, seems to be at about the same time that tourism emerged as a significant part of the county's econ-omy, just a few years after the improvement of the highway system and the construction of the bridge to Bogue Banks. Shrimp became so important to the newly developed economy that Stick ([20]: 228) was compelled to write, "practically everybody who owned a boat large enough to to pull a trawl dropped whatever else he was doing, rigged up for shrimp, and converged on the shrimping grounds." Eventually overcapitalization affected the economy of the fishery, but the overall fishing industry and the people who worked in it have become diversified enough to better withstand the cyclical nature of shrimping.

Sportfishing became an important activity which accompanied the rapidly growing tourism trade. More than a few commercial fishermen developed a style of converting over to sportfishing throughout the year. This requires, in addition to the gear used for commercial pur-poses, investments in the tackle appropriate for groundfishing and trol-ling.

THE DOWNEAST CONNECTION

We now turn to an examination of the downeast economy and how it has become increasingly tied into the larger economic context. The discussion will include an analysis of the impact of infrastructure investments in the eastern portion of the county which are slowly, but surely, breaking down cultural and economic differences. It is asserted that the era of the nucleated villages is past.

Carteret County has always led the state in the number of fishermen and the proportion of the county workforce in fishing occupations. A large proportion of the people involved in the fisheries has remained located in settlements east of Beaufort. There are several ways in which the downeast settlements were affected by the economic development in Morehead City and its surrounding areas; increased demand for fish, boat building, occupational choices, and the pollution of the estuaries. Further, the linkages which were established with the downeast villages created the conditions for the investment in certain infrastructures in the downeast area itself. We have already touched on the demands for fish, so this discussion will focus on the remaining issues.

Boat Building

Still [22] notes that ships and boats of various sizes were being built in or near Carteret County in the 1700's. The types of vessels included both those for transport and fishing and, after 1820, steamboat construction was developed. He notes that "By the beginning of the twentieth century most of the vessels...were built for the fishing industry." A large share of the boat building for fishing took place in Beaufort, Marshallberg, and nearby Harker's Island. The latter two areas became noted for the *Sharpie* and the *Core Sounder,* two shallow draft vessels perfectly suited to the waters in the area. The former was introduced in the 1870's as a sail powered vessel for the shoaling sounds. The latter, introduced in the 1920's, was diesel powered for outside fishing. Vessels from 12 to 50 feet were built and variations on the *Core Sounder,* skiffs, and pleasure boats are still built in the area today. The booming fisheries that developed after the Civil War seem to have had a great deal to do with the development of the boat building industry in the area. Beaufort boat building was mainly oriented toward the larger vessels and that industry was also influenced by the fisheries development in the 1870's.

The development of the recreational fisheries, mainly in Morehead City, had a significant impact on boat building in Beaufort and farther downeast. Charter and headboat businesses whose growth was interrupted during World War II had begun in the late 20's and 30's thanks to easier access to the county, with the boat builders adapted to the new demands. Other boats were built for non-commercial use. Smaller ones have been and still are used for recreation in the sounds, and for inshore bottom fishing and trolling for gamefish. Yachts, up to seventy feet, were built for affluent professionals and businessmen, including some Europeans. Also, some boats were built as research vessels for the University of North Carolina and Duke University, which developed research stations in Morehead City and Beaufort.

Boat building continues, although with the mass production of fiberglass boats the industry has suffered. One Florida fiberglass boat manufacturer has copied the lines of the smaller skiffs built downeast and has made a sizeable dent in the Carteret market among commercial and sport fishermen. Two local builders have adapted to the changing competition by building fiberglass boats with lines similar to the Core Sounder, and they have successful businesses at present. At the time of the current study, there were about 60 people building boats in the area, some on a part time basis, building 12 to 15 larger boats and 25 to 30 smaller ones per year.

Occupational Choices

Carteret County experienced a dramatic increase in the number and proportion of commercial fishermen during the final 30 years of the nineteenth century. Further, up to about 1940 a significant proportion of the labor force retained fishing as the primary occupational activity. Published statistics tend to understate the number of people with fishing income.

Most of the fishermen until 1900 were from the downeast area. Just as was the case with boat building, it is our contention that the occupational structure downeast changed in response to the changing area economy which had shifted its center to Morehead City. Commercial fishing became a viable income producing alternative and the transition from a local subsistence orientation occurred fairly rapidly.

Today, not too many downeasters can make a living from full time fishing or boatbuilding. For one thing, catch statistics indicate a decline in fish stocks, though demand has remained high. Prices, however, have not kept up. Indeed, exvessel clam and oyster prices, to give examples, are only up about 60% from 40 years ago while the Consumer Price Index has risen nearly 250% just in the past 24 years. Add to this the fact that fuel costs alone have increased by a factor of five during the past eight years, and it becomes clear that the commercial fishermen are caught in their own version of the "cost/price squeeze."

Shrimping has become the major fishing activity but the fishery is subject to severe stock fluctuations, mainly due to weather conditions. In regard to boat building, the mass production of fiberglass vessels has undercut the local market for the smaller fishing and recreational crafts. Most young people who live in the villages either work outside of their immediate area (e.g., Morehead, Cherry Point) or have become involved with tourism which has recently begun to blossom within the downeast region itself. Many fish on a part time basis and supplement their incomes by as much as $11,900 (Maiolo [12]). It should be noted, however, that virtually all of the families in the villages have a boat and enter and leave commercial fishing on a part time basis depending upon "what's runnin'" and the fish prices, particularly shrimp prices.

College and vocational training are seen by many of the young people as vehicles out of the local traditional occupations into technical quasiprofessional positions. Carteret Technical Institute (in Morehead) and East Carolina University (about 90 miles to the Northwest) are the popular institutions for the high school graduates.

Pollution

The decline in fish stocks and the failure of prices to keep up with the cost of fishing are two factors involved with the decline of the number of fishermen. A third is pollution. Clamming and oystering have been impaired by the closing of 12,000 acres stocked with those shellfish. While that number is only about 3% of the total county acreage, it is *prime* acreage. And while a portion of the closed acreage may be unrelated to the fallout of the economic development that has occurred throughout the county, most of it is, in one way or another, related to such development, particularly tourism. As we shall see, plans are now underway to correct the problem but the question of net benefits remains open.

Downeast Infrastructure Investments

Development in the western portion of the county created some economic linkages downeast from the early settlements. These were expanded with the development of the fisheries (late 19th century) and tourism/recreation in the 1920's and 30's. The post-World War II boom in recreational fishing further enhanced the recreational trade. Downeast adaptations were pretty much restricted, however, to the fishing and boat building industries. The social structures remained isolated and essentially intact until fairly recently. Except for Beaufort, where in 1928 bridges were built to connect the town to Morehead, road improvements up to 1939 did not impact heavily for those other than the locals who could get to and from their villages and Beaufort more quickly than by water. Sportfishing and tourism to nearby Cape Lookout required boat transportation most of which was based in Morehead. An important change occurred after 1939, the year a new bridge was constructed to cross the channel from the village of Straits to Harker's Island, an area with an intriguing reputation for being quaint and unspoiled. Even with the subsequent building of two motels, however, the area was mainly an attraction for sportfishermen. It became a staging area for Core Banks surfcasting and Cape Lookout boat fishing.

During this period, the village of Atlantic (farther downeast) also became a popular staging area for fishing the northernmost section of Core Banks. A great deal of shack development (squatting) occurred during this period, mostly on Core Banks, by working class sport fishermen who would simply stake out a patch, put a structure on it, and post a *no trespassing* sign on the door. Enterprising business people in the area responded with the opening of marinas, tackle shops, and food supply stores (typically, all three were combined). Interaction between hosts and tourists was and still is limited to brief business transactions. There is more than a little contempt shown for the visitors, but a style of presentation especially for the tourists has been developed. It is a distant, but friendly, style which imparts enough information about weather, hot fishing spots, and local history to satisfy the visitors.

Three infrastructure investments during the past seventeen years have produced a steady stream of consequences for the area, the most recent of which promises to be the most significant. First, in 1964, a ferry landing was constructed at Cedar Island to facilitate the transport of tourists to Ocracoke (a two and one half hour trip across Pamlico Sound). Roadways were improved to accommodate the increased traffic. Business development responded with more shops and restaurants on Cedar Island. Many of the tourists stop at the villages along the roadway as they travel from Morehead, through Beaufort, and on to Cedar Island. This often includes an out of the way crossover to Harker's Island.

Second, a new bridge was constructed to Harker's Island in the early seventies to replace the older wooden one. The new bridge was almost constructed to link an area near Beaufort to the island which would have shortened the distance from about 22 miles to four! The full set of reasons for the failure of this alternative are unknown, but one of them was the strong resistance of the islanders for fear of an onslought of outsiders. In any case, the new bridge not only responded to but facilitated an increase of tourists, and these were no longer just fishermen. Many were families who sought the attraction of Cape Lookout as a beach area. Several locally-owned ferry businesses developed in response to this changed demand for services. Also, a family campground opened on the island.

A third development was the designation of Core Banks as a National Seashore, coupled with the condemnation of a portion of Harker's Island to facilitate construction of a public campground, ferry service, and marina. This has met with resistance but many local residents feel there is little that can be done to prevent the development.

Cottage development in the typical sense (rather than the shacks), which until recently occurred only to the west, has begun downeast mostly on or near Harker's Island. Property values on Harker's Island have soared, doubling between 1978 and 1981. One informant pointed to a tract of land for which he paid a few hundred dollars just fifteen years ago, then to a piece of property less than half its size nearby that recently sold for between fifteen and twenty thousand dollars! Young adults, who are already prevented from making a living at fishing as their parents and grandparents did, can't even afford to purchase property there, which creates another out-migration incentive for them. Tract development has taken the form of trailer parks, much to the dismay of the locals. They point to them with contempt, and vandalism is not uncommon. The islanders at first viewed the tourist industry as a mixed blessing, but no longer. They feel they have lost control of their island. The influx of needed tourist dollars, once viewed as a benefit, is now looked upon as regrettable.

Fallout from the rapid changes on and near Harker's Island promises to impact the remaining villages downeast. Land prices are already increasing and the signs of more business development are present.

In addition to those discussed, another impact on the lives of the locals is the change in their leisure patterns. In the past visits to the banks, often to shacks they had built, were important leisure activities. But the presence of tourists on the banks and the federal government's removal of the squatters' shacks have combined to undermine that alternative (on one July 4th holiday, the first author counted more than three hundred boats of all sizes at Cape Lookout Bight). Many locals now travel out of the area for vacations, often visiting sons and daughters who have moved away.

IMPENDING ECONOMIC STIMULATION

The present trends in population growth and economic development have made pollution an issue of major concern in Carteret County. Presently, ground absorption sewerage systems used on Bogue Banks and downeast and the treatment plants in Beaufort and Morehead City are taxed to their limits. Effluent runoff discharges into creeks from treatment plants have resulted in the closure of shellfishing areas, and home and cottage construction along with commercial and industrial development have been seriously curtailed. As a result, Carteret County has become a candidate for improved sewerage facilities and an ocean outfall (the discharge of treated effluent into the ocean through a diffuser). Given recent federal government pressure and subsidy incentives to improve sewerage treatment, resort areas like Bogue Banks probably will have outfall systems very soon. Further, we believe that the infrastructure investment will not stop there, but will extend to areas such as downeast Carteret County.

Such an infrastructure investment will create a new round of economic growth and trends towards interdependence. By allowing development of previously undevelopable land, and by reducing the minimum land required for each housing and motel unit by two-thirds, the peak population holding capacity will be increased. This increased pace of population growth under an ocean outfall system will lead to an increase in demands for education, welfare, police and fire, and medical services (Duke University recently located health clinics on Harker's Island and in Atlantic in response to increased demands for health care).

Also, qualitative changes in the types of services desired by tourists and residents can be expected since migration will be the primary source of population growth. Examples of current and projected qualitative adaptations to "new" residents abound. As noted, Harker's Islanders have developed a special style of presentation for tourists. Changing health needs reflect a developing retirement community. Desires for upgrading all levels of education, especially post-secondary education, reflect the desires of new residents. Businessmen want to upgrade the port facilities for containerized cargo and the transport of liquid petroleum gas. Military personnel are putting increased demands on county beaches, including a present demand for a beach on Bogue Banks for military people only.

A most important signal of change and growth in the Morehead City-Beaufort area of Carteret County is the possible construction of support bases for outer continental shelf (OCS) oil and gas exploration and the proposed development of coal export terminals at the State Ports Authority and nearby Radio Island. An OCS lease sale is scheduled for early Fall, 1981, and exploration is expected to begin in 1984. Alla-Ohio Valley Coal Company has begun to export 1.75 million tons annually (mta) of steam coal per year through Morehead City, and they have plans to expand their exports to 10-12 mta by 1984. Gulf Interstate Company has announced plans to export 12 to 15 mta of steam coal from a facility to be built on Radio Island, between Morehead City and Beaufort. The new coal exporting activity could reach 27 mta by 1984, which would mean over 500 ships a year moving through the county's port facilities!

IMPLICATIONS

Although it is difficult to develop a neat causal sequence in which precise weights are attached to the independent and dependent variables, a temporal sequence is discernible. Infrastructure developments produce, through a set of complex, interwoven processes, changes in the social and economic character of maritime communities. The effects of the infrastructure investments can be traced through changes in fisheries' occupations and technology. Throughout this process, the socio-economic context tends to diversify as new demands for goods and services emerge and the labor force adapts. Isolated communities are brought within the ambience of the emerging economy, in a limited way at first, but eventually in a more extended way that is tradition-shattering to the communities. The newly developed economy itself creates pressure for further infrastructure development, implying a never ending process.

At the theoretical level, an inclusive model of maritime adaptations must account for the possibility that change can be initiated from different points. With one exception, we have found that extant literature dwells on a undimensional analytical model. We have chosen here to focus on the effects of infrastructure investments. Other starting points, e.g., cultural contact or resource discoveries, should be addressed as well. To be useful for policy development or evaluation, any analytical model must be truly multidimensional.

There are important marine policy implications that can be drawn from our study. First, industrial and tourist development facilitated by infrastructure investments are mixed blessings. New economic opportunities provided for the residents are counterbalanced by the brokers of development who often ignore the potential damaging effects to natural resources. Opportunities such as commercial fishing may be curtailed. Community traditions may be crushed under the weight of social and economic progress. The most general policy question is one of weighing the rights of new participants who wish to be able to use and enjoy what are essentially common property resources—like beaches, waterways, and fish—against the rights of those whose families' livelihoods have depended upon those resources for centuries. With a multidimensional approach such as we have suggested here, a total perspective may be available within which to rationally address such questions.

ACKNOWLEDGEMENTS

This research was funded by the Department of Marine Affairs, State of North Carolina, with funds obtained from the Coastal Plains Regional Commission, administered by the Center for Marine Affairs and Coastal Studies, North Carolina State University. We are grateful to Marcus Hepburn, James Sabella, and William Still for helpful suggestions, and to Gail Spencer, Bob Davis, Reba Lewis, Rebecca Faison and Matt Albright for research assistance.

REFERENCES

[1] Anderson, R. and C. Wadel, Eds. *North Atlantic Fishermen.* (Toronto: University of Toronto Press, 1972).

[2] Bertrand, A. "Rural Social Organization: Implications of Technology and Industry," in Thomas Fod, *Rural U.S.A.: Persistence and Changes.* (Ames, Iowa: Iowa State University Press, 1978).

[3] Breton, Y. D. "The influence of Modernization on the Modes of Production in Coastal Fishing: An Example from Venezuela." in M. Estelle Smith, Ed., *Those Who Live From the Sea.* (St. Paul: West Publishing Company, 1977).

[4] Casteel, R. W. and G. Quimby, Ed. *Maritime Adaptations of the Pacific.* (The Hague: Mouton Publishers, 1975).

[5] Christensen, J. B. "Motor Power and Woman Power: Technological and

Economic Change Among the Fanti Fisherman of Ghana," in M. Estelle Smith, Ed. *Those Who Live From the Sea.* (St. Paul: West Publishing Company, 1977.

[6] Council on Environmental Quality. *The Growth Shapers: The Land Use Impacts of Infrastructure Investments.* Washington, DC: U.S. Government Printing Office. (1975).

[7] Earll, R. E. "North Carolina and Its Fisheries," in G.B. Goode, Ed., *The Fisheries and Fishery Industry of the United States.* Washington, DC: U.S. Government Printing Office. (1887) pp. 427-497.

[8] Goodlad, C. A. "Old and Trusted, New and Unknown: Technological Confrontation in the Shetland Herring Industry," in R. Anderson and C. Wadel, Eds. *North Atlantic Fisherman.* (Canada: University of Toronto Press, 1972).

[9] Hepburn, M. J. "Technology, Ecology, and Social Change: The Fission and Fusion of Agnatic Fishing Groups as an Adaptive Strategy," Paper read at 76th Annual Meetings of the American Anthropological Association (1977).

[10] Hepburn, M. J. "The Effects of the Crab Trap Innovation in a Small Gulf Coastal Fishing Community," Paper presented at Annual Meetings of the American Society for Ethnohistory (1975).

[11] Hill, Mrs. Fred *Historic Carteret County, North Carolina,* Carteret,North Carolina (1975).

[12] Maiolo, J. *Sociocultural Context and Occupational and Marketing Structures of the North Carolina Shrimp Fishery.* Greenville, North Carolina, Department of Sociology and Anthropology, East Carolina University, Volume III, *Surveys of Fishermen* (1981).

[13] Maiolo, J. R., Ed. *Highways and Communities.* (University Park, Pennsylvania: The Pennsylvania State University Press, 1966)

[14] Nason, J. D. "The Effects of Social Change on Marine Technology in a Pacific Atoll Community," in R.N. Casteel and G.I. Quimby, Eds. *Maritime Adaptations of the Pacific.* (The Hague: Mouton Publishers, 1975).

[15] Norr, J. L. and K. L. Norr "Work Organization in Modern Fishing," *Human Organization.* (1978), pp. 163-171.

[16] Norr, K. L. and J. L. Norr "Environmental and Technical Factors Influencing Power in Work Organizations," *Sociology of Work and Occupations,* 1:2 (1974), p. 219-257.

[17] Salter, B. "Carteret's Commerce and Economy, 1760-1789," in Jean Kell, Ed., *North Carolina's Coastal Carteret County During the*

American Revolution, (Greenville, North Carolina: Era Press, 1975), pp. 97-112.

[18] Smith, M. E. "Fisheries Management: Intended Results and Unintended Consequences," Paper presented at *Symposium on Modernization in Fishing Industries and Communities.* (Greenville, North Carolina: East Carolina University, 1978).

[19] Smith, M. E., *Those Who Live From the Sea.* (St. Paul: West Publishing Company, 1977).

[20] Stick, D. *Chapel Hill, North Carolina:* (University of North Carolina Press, 1958).

[21] Stiles, R. G. "Fishermen, Wives, and Radios: Aspects of Communication in a Newfoundland Fishing Community," in R. Anderson and C. Wadel, Eds. *North Atlantic Fishermen,* (Toronto: University of Toronto Press, 1972).

[22] Still, W. "Preliminary Report on the Croatan Forest," Greenville, North Carolina: Institute for Coastal and Marine Resources, East Carolina University (1978).

[23] Summers, G. and J. Lang "Bringing Jobs to People: Does it Pay," in R. Rodeteld, J. Flora, D. Voth, I. Fujimoto and J. Converse, Eds. *Change in Rural America: Causes, Consequences and Alternatives* (St. Louis: C.V. Mosby and Company, 1978).

[24] Tunstall, J. *The Fishermen.* (London: McGibbon and Kee, 1976).

[25] Winslow, R.S. "Foreward," in G.M. Woodward, *Commercial Fisheries of North Carolina: An Economic Analysis.* Chapel Hill, North Carolina: Bureau of Business Services and Research, School of Business Administration, University of North Carolina (1956).

CHAPTER 9
SOCIOCULTURAL ASPECTS OF TECHNOLOGICAL AND INSTITUTIONAL CHANGE AMONG SMALL-SCALE FISHERMEN

Richard B. Pollnac
Department of Sociology and Anthropology
University of Rhode Island

INTRODUCTION

Although much has been written concerning psychological, social and cultural responses to technoeconomic change in agrarian and industrial sectors of society, little systematic effort of comparable magnitude has been directed at small-scale fisheries. In comparison with agriculture and industry, small-scale fisheries have extremely small impacts on most national economies. Nevertheless, when viewed on a worldwide basis, the number of individuals involved in small scale fisheries is quite impressive. The United Nations (UN) Food and Agricultural Organization (FAO) has recently estimated that there are 9.2 million small-scale fishermen in developing countries [1]. This figure does not include the approximately 4 million employed in associated activities such as fish processing, selling and equipment manufacture.

As producers of high-quality protein in a world suffering from food shortages, the importance of this occupational subculture should not be underestimated. Ongoing and future attempts to improve the technology and production of small-scale fishermen will meet and hopefully overcome many of the same social, cultural and psychological dislocations that occurred and are occurring as a result of change in the agrarian and industrial sectors of society. The purpose of this chapter is to examine briefly the interrelationship between technological and institutional change and several important aspects of man's social adaptation to the occupation of small-scale fishing. The relationship between certain social and technoeconomic aspects of small-scale fisheries will be examined, and a model of these relationships will be

225

developed. Examples of how technological and institutional changes affect social relationships will be provided from actual small- scale fishery development programs, and suggestions will be provided concerning the utility of the model for development programs.

SOCIAL ADAPTATION TO TECHNOECONOMIC ASPECTS OF SMALL-SCALE FISHERIES

Several aspects of small-scale fishery technology result in social relationships that differ somewhat from those found in agrarian social groups [2]. This section examines the relationship between small-scale fishing technology and aspects of workgroup and nonworkgroup structure, the ownership of productive equipment, and degree of social stratification.

Turning first to workgroups, we find that fishing technology is related to workgroup composition and structure. In a comparison of Thai fishermen and farmers, Foster [3] notes that in contrast to farming groups, the size of fishing groups is rigidly determined by technology. This is obviously related to the limited space on a vessel. Further, Norr and Norr [4] note that ocean fishing demands much more reliance on reciprocal interdependence and coordination of crewmen than agriculture. Pulling a net, launching a boat through a heavy surf and responding to the ever-changing nature of the sea requires a high degree of skillful coordination among a compatible workgroup. Thus, technological constraints limit the size of the workgroup, and environmental and technological constraints select for worker efficiency. It appears, therefore, that crew composition should be flexible and not based on prescribed social criteria. Nevertheless, we find that social groups play an important role in workgroup composition among small-scale fishermen.

Kinship plays an important and varied role in the structure of the occupation of fishing in many parts of the world. The importance of kinship in fishermen's workgroups has been extensively cited in the literature from regions as widely separated as Ghana [5], Peru [6], Micronesia [7], Canada [8], the Faroe Islands [9], Ulithi [10], Panama [11], and the West Indies [12]. The need for harmony on a vessel is essential for success at sea, and kinship ties may enhance cooperativeness within the workgroup. Other factors may also increase the tendency toward kin based crews. For example, Gladwin [13] notes that among the Mfante of Ghana, boat crews with family cores are more stable than nonkin-linked crews. On Moala, kinship ties are related to the sharing and loaning of capital equipment such as boats [14] while on Tikopia, canoes are nominally owned by heads of kin groups, but actually by the kin group as a whole [15]. Sabella [6] suggests that the use of kin in the crew among small-scale fishermen from Peru is often related to keeping boat production within the family. Finally, Bartlett [16] notes that having kinsmen as crewmembers in Gloucester, Massachusetts, makes economic sense; that is, kinsmen are less likely to sue, thus reducing the need for expensive liability insurance.

Among some fishing people, however, we find that kinship plays little or no role in crew composition. Glacken [17] notes that family members fish from different vessels on Okinawa. This is done to minimize loss to individual families if a fatal accident occurs.

McGoodwin [18] also reports that kinship does not play a significant role in crew structure among shark fishermen in Northwest Mexico. He suggests that this situation results from the fact that closely related kin are not likely to take orders without complaint, and that they would probably resent their retention through debt peonage, a common technique used to keep crew members among these fishermen.

Further, neither Taiwanese [19] nor Maylay [15] fishing crews are primarily based on kin ties. Norr [20] reports a similar situation in south India, and suggests that the skilled nature of the occupation of fishing results in worker recruitment on the basis of skill and interpersonal ability rather than social ties.

It is important to note, however, that some researchers have found that the role of kinship in crew structure varies consistently within a single society. For example, Pollnac and Ruiz-Stout [21] report variability in the role of kinship in crew structure among Panamanian small scale fishermen. They indicate that overall only 39% of the fishermen interviewed fish with family members. This figure, however, obscures the fact that in the rural areas of their sample 52% of the fishermen fish with kin, in contrast to only 12% in the urban area. This difference is statistically significant $X^2=23.08$, p=0.001). More recent research in the Gulf of Nicoya on the Pacific Coast of Costa Rica suggests a similar pattern. A total of 75 small-scale fishermen were interviewed in Puntarenas, the major Pacific port of Costa Rica, and 50 were interviewed at Costa de Pajaros, a concentration of fishermen in a rural region on the Gulf of Nicoya. For the total sample, we find that a slight majority (52%) of the fishermen do not fish with kin. Of those interviewed, 34% fish with at least 1 relative, 10% with 2, while only 4% fish with 3 or more kinsmen.

As can be seen in Table 1, however, the rural and urban areas differ significantly with regard to the role that kinship plays in crew membership.

Of the rural fishermen 66% fish with relatives, whereas only 36% of urban fishermen do so. This difference is statistically significant ($X^2=10.817$, p=0.01).

Table 2 indicates kin types that fish with respondents in both the rural and urban area. Tabular entries refer to number of respondents reporting designated relatives as a crew member.

The rural column in Table 2 sums to more than 50 because some rural fishermen fish with more than one kin type. Overall, the greatest difference between the rural and urban area with respect to crew membership is the higher proportion of brothers who fish together in the rural area. In the rural area, we find that 38% of the fishermen fish with a sibling, in contrast to only 8% in the urban area ($X2=16.875$, p=0.001).

There is thus a great deal of variability in the role that social groups play in small-scale fishermen's workgroups. It has been indicated, however, that in many societies kinship plays an important role in boat crew composition.

Turning to the structure of relationships within small-scale fishermen's workgroups, Norr and Norr [4] have suggested that the need for coordination within fishing crews and the physical risks associated with the marine environment increase both the need for interdependence and the importance of each worker. This, in combination with the rapid depreciation of equipment and the possibility of

Table 1. Number of Relatives in Crew

Number	Urban	Rural
4	1	3
3	0	1
2	6	7
1	20	22
0	48	17
Total	75	50

Table 2. Relationships between Respondents and Crewmembers

	Frequency	
	Urban	Rural
Relationship		
Father	6	5
Brother	6	19
Son	5	4
Father's Brother	2	3
Mother's Brother	0	1
Nephew	2	1
Spouse	2	0
Cousin	2	5
Wife's Brother	2	2
Non-relative	48	17

equipment loss, decreases the social and economic distance between owners and laborers. They argue that work relationships in fishing crews should be more egalitarian than among farmers, and their data and the ethnographic literature support this proposition. For example, Norr [20] reports that few distinctions are made within workgroups among fishermen of south India; that the owner does not direct work. He participates as an equal. Burrows and Spiro [22] comment on the egalitarian nature of fishing workgroups in Ifaluk society. On Taiwan, Diamond [19] notes that friendship characterizes the relationships between crew members. Gladwin [23] reports that although the navigator is in command of the vessel on Puluwat, he is not aloof. He comments on the egalitarian nature of fishing workgroups in Ifaluk, and contrasts this with the general rank consciousness of the Ifaluk society. Of Arembepe, Brazil, Kottak [24] writes that the captain works like all other crew members. When the fishing begins he is the same as the crew. Knudson [7] stresses the fact that the exploitation of terrestrial resources is an individual act in Micronesia, while marine resources are exploited by cooperative groups.

The same general relationship holds in Nicaragua among Miskito turtle fishermen. There, land hunting partnerships are loose in contrast to the close cooperation demanded between turtle fishermen. Turtle men must have partners they can rely on. Thus, partnerships form around each individual's skill, reliability, and temperament [25]. The need for cooperation in trap fishing among the Matupit of New Britain is given structural expression in groups known as *motoni,* which are associated with particular areas of beach used for fishing-related activities [26]. On St. Kitts in the Caribbean, Aronoff [12] notes that fishing crews are integrated and cooperative, with little stratification, in contrast to cane cutter groups. He notes that fishermen are likely to view their captain as helpful and nurturant, in contrast to cane cutters, who view the head cutter in a negative manner, suggesting that he takes advantage of the men. Firth [15] reports that among Malay fishermen, the crew leader shows a readiness to consult the crew on matters of policy. Mfantese fishermen of Ghana believe that harmony in the boat is essential to safety at sea [5]. Sabella [6] writes that cooperation is so necessary among the fishermen of Caleta San Pablo, Peru, that arguments stop short on the beach. He further notes that crews are very egalitarian. Even the captain performs the same work as the crew. Brandt [27] comments on the egalitarian nature of interaction aboard fishing vessels in Korea, and, finally, Faris [28] suggests that overall there is an ethos of egalitarianism among peasant fishermen.

The egalitarian nature of artisanal fishermen workgroups was commented on in detail because of the important role that workgroup organization plays as an element of social organization. Workgroup organization is so important that when fishing people form part of a society that has a strong system of social stratification, ocean fishing is sometimes organized as the occupation of a low status, caste-like group (e.g. as in Japan and India). Norr and Norr [4] suggest that this caste-like separation of fishermen functions to insulate the larger society from these potentially threatening egalitarian relationships.

Additionally, workgroup organization is often related to shoreside social organization. In many societies crew leaders (e.g. navigators in Polynesia, captains, etc.) also enjoy a leadership role ashore [23, 29]. Further, the friendships which often develop between crew members sometimes form the basis for nonfishing groups. Fraser [30] reports that among Malay fishermen of south Thailand, boat groups are very durable, and frequently serve as the foundation for other social and economic groups.

Turning next to the relationship between small-scale fishing technology, the ownership of productive equipment and social stratification, we find that several scholars have made important observations concerning differences between ownership of the means of production in farming and fishing communities. Firth [15] notes that land ownership has a permanency not associated with fishing equipment. The constant motion and fluidity of the marine environment in combination with sudden, violent storms at sea make fishing equipment especially liable to sudden damage and loss. Norr and Norr [4] argue that the rapid depreciation of fishing equipment in combination with occasional losses result in higher rates of occupational mobility in fishing than in farming. They suggest that this, in turn, results in smaller social and economic distance between owners and laborers in fishing.

Kottak [24] provides a good discussion of how the relatively simple technology of the small-scale fishermen of Arembepe, Brazil, provides relatively equal opportunities for all fishermen to own capital equipment, which results in a relatively eqalitarian community. He notes that the cost of the technology is approximately equal to the average annual earnings of fishermen in the community. Thus the opportunity to buy a boat is theoretically open to all fishermen. He points out, however, that other mechanisms operate to prevent the development of social stratification resulting from income variance between successful and unsuccessful fishermen. These mechanisms include reciprocal exchange networks as well as annual festivals that demand more resources from the more wealthy, thus leveling out the distribution of wealth. He also notes that the relatively short lifespan of wooden plank boats inhibits transgeneration transfer of ownership differentials through inheritance.

Although the ownership pattern that Kottak [24] described for Arembepe is quite common among small scale fishermen, the literature indicates a wide range of possibilities. Ownership patterns include both individual fishermen owners [15, 24] and nonfishermen owners [31]. In some cases several members of a crew will cooperatively own a large boat [31]. In other cases large, sea-going canoes are owned by kinship lineage heads [32] or lineage members in common [10]. In general, the larger and more complex the technology, the more likely it will be owned by nonfishing entrepreneurs (e.g. middlemen or local elites [31] or groups of individuals (e.g. kin groups) [33]. Further, as the price of technology increases, there is a greater likelihood that individuals will emerge who will function as financiers [15, 34, 35]. It is often the middleman (discussed below) who fulfills this function. When the ownership pattern of relatively complex and expensive equipment is individual entrepreneurship rather than cooperative kinship or workgroups, there is great potential for increasing social stratification and inequality. This has led many development organizations to suggest that the best means of introducing complex, expensive equipment is through cooperative organizations.

Another important aspect of small-scale fishing is that as technology becomes more efficient, enabling production in excess of the subsistence level, a need for distribution system develops. Fish is a highly perishable product that is not easily stored without complex techniques such as drying or freezing technologies. Firth [15] notes that a fisherman's catch, in contrast with a farmer's products, needs more outlay in equipment and labor if it is to be stored. This, he suggests, results in a tendency for a greater development of middlemen among fishermen. Further, a fisherman's many hours at sea are physically exhausting, and when he arrives at shore he usually does not have the time or energy to process or distribute his highly perishable product. Thus, the distribution of surplus catch is usually performed by a specialist who is often referred to in the literature as a middleman or fish dealer.

In many fishing communities, females take over the function of buying and selling fish. Female fish buyers are found throughout the world in regions as widely spread as the Caribbean [12], El Salvador, Brazil [31], Ghana [13], India [20], Thailand [36], and Okinawa, [17]. Sometimes this division of labor functions to keep at least some of the profits within the family since the men fish and their female relatives sell the product [13, 31].

Nevertheless, the middleman is not always a kinsman. In many regions the middleman is an unrelated entrepreneur whose sole motive is to make a profit by buying and selling fish. Further, it is often claimed that middlemen exploit the small scale fishermen [37-39]. Often, however, even in regions where outsiders and the government view the middleman as exploiting the fishermen, the middleman is doing an excellent job at performing a vital function and making very little profit. For example, Firth [15], noting that it is a common accusation that middlemen reap the benefits of the fishery, reports that among the Malay in his sample the middlemen make very little profit for the time and energy they expend. Our preliminary observations in Costa Rica have led to the same conclusion. Further, the fishermen themselves often recognize the multifunctional nature of the middleman, and are content with the existing system despite their continuous complaints about prices (a common complaint of primary producers around the world). For example, in Malaysia the small-scale fishermen reportedly appreciate the role that the middleman plays as a financier for capital equipment [35]. Blake [40] notes that among the Madras fishing population in India, the middleman functions as both business contact for fishermen and a dependable source of cash when production drops off and when large expenditures are necessary (e.g. for weddings, funerals and holidays).

In an attempt to gain a more complete understanding of the middleman in Costa Rica, we interviewed 80 small scale fishermen in Gulf of Nicoya. Of these fishermen, 50 were from an urban area (Puntarenas) and 30 from a rural community (Costa de Pajaros). The middleman, or fish buyer, is an important individual in the structure of the small scale fishing industry in the Gulf of Nicoya. On the short strip of the coastline where interviews were conducted in Puntarenas, there were seven active middlemen. At Costa de Pajaros, five were active. Other middlemen existed in both areas, but they were either outside the area sampled or not active during the research period. Ostensibly, the middleman performs the important function of purchasing fish from the fisherman for resale to other middlemen or retailers. He does, however, provide other services for the fishermen. The number of active middlemen in the region and statements made by fishermen suggest that competition exists between the various buyers. Hence, fishermen were asked why they sell to one middleman rather than another. The percent distribution of the first three responses to this open-ended question can be found in Table 3.

The most frequent rationale for selecting one buyer over another is the prices paid for fish. The second most frequent rationale is that a fisherman would rather deal with a buyer who helps him in some way, such as providing loans or picking up parts. Fishermen also select buyers on the basis of what they perceive as fair treatment. This category includes the attributes of honesty, immediate payment for

Table 3. Distribution of Rationale for Selection of Middlemen

Rationale	Percent*
Better prices	48
Provides help (loans, etc.)	45
Fair treatment	31
In debt to middleman	9
Friendship	8
Always buys fish	6
Closer to residence	4
Other	10

N=80

*Total exceeds 100% because entries reflect categorization of the first three responses to an open-ended question.

product, not discarding marginally spoiled fish and so on. Of the fishermen interviewed, 9% report that they sell to a specific buyer because they are in debt to him, while 8% claim they make their decision on the basis of friendship. A small proportion of the fishermen choose middlemen who never refuse their product. Some middlemen refuse to buy when the market is glutted, and the fishermen are forced to let their product rot. Several fishermen noted that they deal with a specific buyer because he is located close to their home. The "other" category includes idiosyncratic responses such as "character of buyer," "landing facilities" and "more responsible."

The first, and therefore most salient, high-frequency responses were cross-tabulated with area of residence. The expectation that urban fishermen would be more likely than rural to select buyers on the basis of price was supported by the data (44 vs 23 percent respectively; $X^2=3.47$, $p<0.05$; one-tailed test). As argued in an earlier paper [41], urban fishermen are more involved in the cash economy. Thus, we would expect that prices paid by middlemen would be their most salient attribute in the urban area. In contrast, the rural fishermen are more interested in the help that the middleman provides in the form of loans, picking up parts for equipment, etc. (37 vs 14% respectively; $X^2=5.52$, $p<0.02$). Finally, there is at best a weak relationship between area of residence and the "fair treatment" category ($X^2=0.02$, $p>.10$). Overall, these findings in combination with our brief review of the literature above suggest that there is a complex relationship between middlemen and social and technological aspects of the small scale fishery. The assumption of middleman as solely an exploiter, however, has led to many attempts to replace him before fully understanding the multidimensionality of his role in the fishing community.

Figure 1 sums up the discussion of the relationship between small-scale fishing technology and aspects of workgroup and nonworkgroup composition and structure, aspects of the ownership and productive equipment, degree of social stratification, and distribution systems. First, it was noted that vessel size and complexity affect both crew size and recruitment of crew on the basis of skill. It should be noted here, however, that more efficient equipment which reduces necessary crew size may result in unemployment and increased social stratification. We have also found that crews are often selected on the basis of social criteria such as kin group membership. Small-scale fishermen workgroups, however, tend to be egalitarian in structure due to the fact that many shipboard tasks require close cooperation between fishermen. These close interdependent ties between crewmembers often result in the formation of groups ashore based on the maritime workgroup.

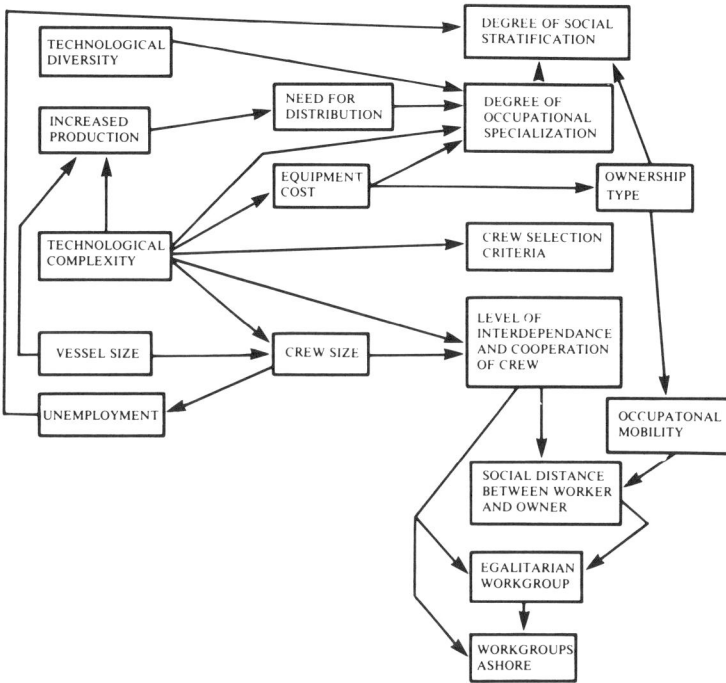

Figure 1. Relationship between technology and social organization

Further, it was noted that the generally low cost of small-scale fishing technology, the impermanent nature of the equipment, and the close cooperation required usually result in little social distinction between owner and laborer within small-scale fishing groups. Nevertheless, as equipment costs increase due to increased size or complexity, the likeli-hood of individual fisherman ownership decreases, thus promoting the development of social stratification and inequality. Additionally, increased costs of capital equipment often lead to the development of financing specialists. Finally, we have seen that as surplus production increases there is an increasing need for distribution and processing specialists. The multidimensional nature of the role of these specialists in the social structure of the small-scale fishing community was briefly discussed.

SOCIOCULTURAL ASPECTS OF TECHNOLOGICAL AND INSTITUTIONAL CHANGE

In this section examples will be provided which will demonstrate the interrelationships between technological and institutional changes and aspects of social organization contained within the model developed in the previous section. A study conducted by Fraser [36] among Malay fishermen of South Thailand provides a good example of the impact that technological change can have on workgroups and other aspects of a sociocultural system.

Traditionally, the Malay fishermen of Rusembilian relied on oars and sail to take them to their fishing grounds. In 1956, groups of boat owners and steerers (traditionally a high-status position in the boat crew) dominated deliberations concerning the best way to motorize the fleet. They decided to introduce tow boats to take fishing vessels to fishing areas and bring them back. Groups of boats would form tow groups associated with a particular tow boat. This new technology immediately placed considerable strain on the traditional social system.

First, membership in tow groups meant that individual boat crews and steerers lost their previous independence with regard to locating fish and timing their return to market. Second, after a period of poor fishing, wives of members of the more skillful boat crews realized that they were subsidizing less successful crews since shares were based on the tow group's total catch. Fraser [36] notes that this situation had broad repercussions in other areas of community life. It resulted in overt hostility between women, and relations between men became strained. The coffee shops, which were the focus for community decision-making groups and which were individually associated with boat crews, manifested a marked drop in attendance, reflecting the social strains. Attendance at coffee shops never fully recovered. Further, traditional village authority figures, the *orang baik* (morally good men), were involved in ownership of tows and their operation. Thus the chief source of authority and means of maintaining village control were undermined. Finally, because the religious leaders of the village remained aloof from the changes, their status increased.

Before long, the strains became too great and the tow boats were eliminated. The reindividualization of fishing did much to restore good relations, but the degree of community organization which was originally based on boat crew membership and the traditional authority of the *orang baik* (whose traditional status depended on boat group affiliation) was never regained. Further, the introduction of nylon nets and individualized motorized vessels reduced the need for a large crew.

Nevertheless, the crews were kept larger than necessary in keeping with traditional crew structure. Fraser [36] argues that this featherbedding plus decreasing catches undermined the sense of pride that traditionally characterized crews. This reduction of group solidarity negatively affected the relatively high status of the steerer and, hence, his status in the community at large.

Thus, a change in technology that was ill-adapted to the traditional social structure of work was rejected, and the negative changes that occurred in the traditional social organization dictated a crew size that resulted in inefficient application of other technological innovations. A similar reluctance to changed workgroup structure was recently reported for small-scale fishermen in Malaysia. Sabri [35] notes that although winches were installed, thus reducing the number of fishermen needed on a vessel, traditional crew size was maintained to provide employment for members of the extended family. In another area of Malaysia, however, Yap [42] reports that improved technology resulted in crew reduction and significant unemployment among fishermen with no alternative occupations. This impoverished class of unemployed fishermen, of course, increased the degree of social stratification within the fishing community, as our model indicates.

The model also indicates that there is a relationship between technological change, equipment cost, equipment ownership patterns and social stratification. Epple [43] provides a good example of how mechanization, because of increased price of capital equipment, altered patterns of fishing boat ownership on Grenada. Before mechanization, 90% of the fishermen owned their own boats. After mechanization this figure dropped to 25%. Sabella [6] also noted that as Peruvian small-scale fishermen began to depend on expensive, highly specialized equipment, their formerly egalitarian communities began to manifest signs of social stratification. Finally, among Malay fishermen, increased costs of productive equipment associated with modernization have resulted in a class of equipment owners. Firth [15] has noted that although equipment modernization has resulted in greater overall returns, increasing capital costs have led to a marked drop in the percentage of earnings going to the labor force. Despite the fact that the fisherman has become, in effect, an employed laborer in the new system, he is treated as a participant in a common enterprise and thus not put on a regular wage basis. His income is still based on a share of the catch. Firth [15] notes that among the Malay fishermen costs are removed from the catch before shares are calculated. Thus, given the periodic nature of production in the marine environment, fishermen often receive next to nothing. He reports that in 1963 the fishermen were in a less advantageous position than when he first studied them in 1939-1940, and that the entrepreneurs were much more economically powerful than their predecessors of a generation earlier.

Even when governments are aware of the potential effect of new technologies on social stratification problems occur and increased disparities in wealth can result. For example, Alexander [44] reports that in Sri Lanka the government was aware of financing problems associated with costly new fishing technology, so they introduced a hire/purchase scheme. Individuals who take part were selected by ballot from qualified applicants. The individual fisherman had to provide a deposit and received a government loan, repayable over five years, to purchase a hull boat with an engine. Unforseen problems developed, however. First, the deposit in combination with the fact that the loan covered vessel and engine, but not gear, meant that the fisherman had to go to private moneylenders. Second, the new equipment deteriorated faster than the old, and there was no provision of maintenance funds. Third, loan repayment was not related to the value of the catch, since it was a fixed monthly payment. During off-periods the payment could exceed income. Nevertheless, production increased, so the government viewed the project as a success and invested more funds in it. The total income to the fishing village increased, but other, less visible problems also increased. Since the number of fishermen increased little over the years since the innovation was first introduced, and the population increased, there was increased unemployment. New boats were introduced, but they rightfully went only to experienced deep-sea fishermen. Important to our discussion, however, is the fact that inexperienced recruits were only drawn from relatives. Therefore, few opportunities existed for those not related to the boat-owning elite to acquire the experience necessary for allocation of a boat. The elite in the community is larger than it was in the past, but the large group of middle class free peasants are finding life much more difficult. There is now a substantial elite, with the bulk of the population being reduced to the poverty level. Alexander [44] suggests that since the elite have political power, and control recruitment to the most favorable occupations, the degree of social stratification will become even more marked in the future. Increases in social stratification have been attributed to similar factors in other communities where costly innovations were introduced [20].

Ironically, in some communities attempts by change agencies to introduce costly fishing technology in a manner that would possibly reduce the potential for increased social stratification, but going around traditional equipment owners and money lenders, have failed because

SOCIOCULTURE OF CHANGE 239

the fishermen viewed the traditional patron-client relationship as legitimate, and the government's planned intervention as illegitimate. For example, Emmerson [34] describes a development program in Indonesia where a more complex, expensive technology was to be introduced to indigenous fishermen using a plan wherein crewmen would collectively own the equipment. Traditionally, crewmen were bound to a boat by an interest free permanent "loan" provided by the boat owner. The boat owner was bound to a moneylender by a similar arrangement. According to Emmerson, the participants did not perceive the relationship as exploitive. It was one of reciprocal obligations, freely engaged in, and viewed as being fair. When this traditional system was threatened by the introduction of the new equipment, the fishermen destroyed the equipment and assaulted a project administrator.

Related attempts to inhibit development of social stratification involve the establishment of fishermen's cooperatives. It was mentioned in the previous section that the introduction of a new institution, the fishermen's cooperative, is often viewed as the ideal means for improving small-scale fisheries while reducing the potential for increased social stratification. In some cases, marked success has been reported [45] and in others failure [46]. The successes have led many governmental and international aid organizations to make release of development funds contingent on formation of fishermen's cooperatives for management purposes. It is thus important to examine sociocultural aspects of success and failure of fishermen's cooperatives among small-scale fishermen.

Proposed fishermen's cooperatives often take the form of a marketing cooperative in an attempt to do away with the much-maligned middleman. The middlemen, however, often resist these moves because they would lose their livelihood if marketing were taken out of their hands. Further, if they form part of the fishermen's kinship network, which is sometimes the case as was noted above, fishermen would be sympathetic with their resistance and continue the old marketing patterns. Fishermen are also frequently reluctant to switch to selling through the cooperative because they are often indebted to middlemen for supplies of capital in times of need [15]. Thus the role of the middleman in the social organization of fishing communities cannot be underestimated in attempts to replace him with a marketing cooperative. The periodic nature of marine resource availability often places him in a role of benefactor to fishermen when the catches are light, and his ability and willingness to give loans when the sea destroys or damages productive equipment reinforce this role. If fishermen's cooperative organizations are to succeed, they must manifest the same type of flexibility to match the periodic nature of the marine resource. For example, Blair [40] suggests that Madras fishermen in India were reluctant to use cooperative marketing schemes because the marketing cooperatives, unlike the traditional middlemen, did not make loans for weddings, funerals, holidays and expenses incurred during unproductive periods.

Fishermen's cooperatives have also been introduced with part of their function being elimination of traditional village money lenders (often, but not always, the middlemen). Alexander [44] provides a good example of the problems associated with one such cooperative. He notes that in Sri Lanka new fishing gear was introduced, sometimes through cooperative organizations, which was of relatively high cost and subject to relatively rapid deterioration in contrast to the traditional gear, which could be replaced out of current earnings and small loans. The new gear thus required provision for replacement. Nevertheless, no provisions for replacement were made, even in cooperative organizations. The form of the fishermen's cooperative organizations were transferred directly from farming where the major resource, land, appreciates through time. Thus, failure to take into account the basic technoeconomic differences between farming and fishing resulted in difficulties.

Another feature of the marine environment also has an adverse effect on cooperative operations. The short-term periodicity of marine resources results in variance in catch and, subsequently, in income through time. Loans made by the government to Sri Lanka fishermen failed to take this fact into account. The required payments were inflexible, appearing monthly irrespective of catch size [44]. Middlemen in most fishing communities have had a long relationship with fishermen and their adaptation to the sea. Thus, they understand these environmental constraints and usually act accordingly, adapting to variability of catch by permitting more flexibility in repayment of loans. Thus, wholesale transfer of cooperative organizational forms from other fields of production to fishermen's organizations, without accounting for the sociocultural and environmental constraints exerted by the marine environment, can result in serious problems.

A proper understanding of the idea of a fishermen's cooperative on the part of potential or actual members is also an essential element in cooperative success. Davenport [29] notes that a Jamaican fishermen's cooperative that failed consisted of individuals who really did not understand the idea of a cooperative. The idea behind such an organization had not properly been communicated to them, and

Davenport suggests that since the captains had the most to lose from the successful operation of the cooperative, they might have been motivated to keep such information from the fishermen. Davenport also notes that cooperative meetings, in the community where the organization failed, conveyed the moral tone of a church meeting and thus inhibited members from initiating interesting activities, such as gambling, around which a stable group could be organized. The problem of communicating the idea of a fishermen's cooperative has been emphasized by Pollnac and Ruiz-Stout [41], who found a great deal of variability in knowledge concerning the role of fishermen's cooperatives among fishermen in Panama. They suggest that such variability can lead to problems in instituting and maintaining this form of organization due to varying expectations on the part of participants. They thus argue for the development of effective techniques to communicate the total meaning of a cooperative in areas where they are planned or in operation.

Fishermen not only need to understand the goals, operations and structure of proposed fishermen's cooperative organization. They must also be provided with a realistic picture of what to expect and when to expect it. Numerous times I have heard the complaint that "A year or two ago someone else was out here asking questions and telling us we would get new boats, but nothing ever happened." Small-scale, rural fishermen are not aware of the bureaucratic labyrinths that often delay development projects, and many change agents do not take the time to inform them of these problems. Thus, rising expectations are frustrated and change agents often fail to obtain cooperation in future projects. For example, Sabella [6] notes that a fishermen's cooperative in Peru failed when government red tape slowed down delivery of motors, and the facts concerning the delay were never properly communicated to the members. In Panama, a FAO/BID artisanal fisheries development project stimulated fishermen to begin forming cooperatives in 1974, and the formation of these cooperatives was well underway in 1975 [11]. By early 1978, however, the cooperative members were becoming disillusioned, because the money for equipment and facilities had not yet been released. Nevertheless, fishermen were still being told that it would happen any day.

Sometimes the funds provided for fishermen's cooperative organizations are insufficient or improperly utilized. Norr [20] writes that a fishermen's cooperative in southern India acquired a small amount of money for loans, but problems soon arose concerning who would obtain the money. Thus, it was equally divided among all members. The resultant shares were not enough for equipment and were spent on food and drink. Another example is provided by Firth [15], who notes that Malay fishermen rejected government cooperatives because the government refused requests for equipment and loans. It turned out that the government was refusing because in one area many fishermen had defaulted on loans. These defaults, however, were the result of failure to adequately check the abilities of applicants. It appeared that some defaulters became cooperative members solely to obtain loans.

This problem is not unique to Malay fishermen. It appears that the commonly accepted procedure of releasing development funds through cooperatives had led to abuse in other regions as well. In some regions where the author has worked, the idea of fishermen's cooperatives was readily accepted by the fishermen. Nevertheless, when delays in funding and early managerial problems began to develop, the better fishermen began to drop out of the organization. In one region (to remain unnamed) the fishermen's cooperative and its members had a poor reputation among better fishermen. Very few active fishermen were observed landing fish at the cooperative dock. In a recent return visit to the area, however, the author was surprised to be told that the cooperative had some 200 members. On further questioning it was determined that most of the members were "inactive," i.e., not fishing, without equipment, etc. The members are thus among the most inefficient fishermen in the area. Nevertheless a great deal of funds will soon be released to buy equipment (boats, motors and nets) for these fishermen to use. Release of these funds was contingent on formation of a cooperative organization, and the credentials of the members did not seem to matter. Thus, a situation similar to that reported by Firth [15], and summarized above, is likely to occur.

A further problem with respect to the continued success of fishermen's cooperatives after their formation lies in the area of management. Too often, change agents idealistically believe that the skills required for running a cooperative can be found among the fishermen themselves. Perhaps they can in some instances, but a cooperative is a complex business and needs to be run by a competent manager. For example, Spoehr [48] writes that a cooperative venture by Carolinian fishermen failed because the operation required managerial skills beyond their traditional cooperative patterns. In addition, Pollnac [41] discusses several cooperatives which failed due to managerial problems. Nevertheless, salaries offered for the position of cooperative manager are often not sufficient to attract qualified applicants.

Traditional workgroup structure and other aspects of community organization can also be factors related to the relative success or failure of fishermen's cooperatives. For example, Davenport [29] in a study of two Jamaican fishing communities, notes that the successful cooperative duplicated the basic social organization of the community, in that natural interacting groups filled the roles in the cooperative. Existing social structures such as kinship groups also seem to be important elements in cooperative success. The UN Research Institute for Social Development [46] reports that cooperatives using existing kinship structures and local leadership obtain more positive results than others. We have commented on the role of kinship in fishermen's workgroups above, but it should be noted that the most independent and successful fishermen's cooperative in the Republic of Panama is one formed around a kinship core. Further, in Chile, where there has been little success instituting effective small-scale fishermen's cooperatives, those organized around kinship cores appears to be succeeding. It seems, therefore, that effective use of existing social organization may facilitate formation of fishermen's cooperatives.

It thus appears that the fishermen's cooperative, an organization which is held by many to be the ideal vehicle for introducing planned change into fishing communities while in the process avoiding increased social stratification, is thus susceptible to many obstacles which may inhibit its success. It is apparent, however, that a knowledge of small-scale fishing societies and cultures can help overcome some of these obstacles and aid in insuring the success of this important institution.

CONCLUSION

A model illustrating the relationship between small scale fisheries institutions and technology and aspects of social organization was developed and examined in relationship to problems associated with fisheries development programs. Although most of the examples examined had negative effects, this is not to be interpreted as meaning that given certain social facts, fisheries development cannot occur. In fact, an understanding of the social organization associated with the small-scale fishermen within a region targeted for development can aid in developing realistic programs that will enhance the probability of sustained development. It is only by understanding the existing social organization and working within it that changes can effectively take place—changes not only in technology, but in aspects of social organization that inhibit change. Additionally, an understanding of local social organization facilitates involvement of fishermen in the early stages of the development program, thus further increasing the potential for project success [49].

In conclusion, it must be noted that social organization is not necessarily the key variable associated with technological change among small-scale fishermen [2], but it can affect project success just as severely as other factors (e.g. funding, natural resources or infrastructure investments) associated with technological change.

REFERENCES

[1] "Artisanal Small Scale Fisheries in Developing Countries," United Nations Food and Agricultural Organization, Committee on Fisheries, Ninth Session, Rome (1974).

[2] Pollnac, R. B. "Continuity and Change in Marine Fishing Communities," paper prepared for the USAID (1976).

[3] Foster, B. L. "Labor Groups in Thai Rice and Fishing Villages, *Human Organization* 34:381-389 (1975).

[4] Norr, K., and J. L. Norr. "Environmental and Technical Factors Influencing Power in Work Organizations: Ocean Fishing in Peasant Societies," *Sociol. Work Occupat.* 1:219-251 (1974).

[5] Quinn, N. R. "Mfantese Fishing Crew Composition: A Decision Making Analysis," PhD Thesis, Stanford University (1971).

[6] Sabella, J. D. "The Fishermen of Caleta San Pablo," PhD Dissertation, Cornell University (1974).

[7] Knudson, K. E. "Resource Fluctuation, Productivity, and Social Organization on Micronesian Coral Islands," PhD Dissertation, University of Oregon (1970).

[8] Breton, Y. "A Comparative Study of Workgroups in an Eastern Canadian Peasant Fishing Community: Bilateral Kinship and Adaptive Processes," *Ethnology* 12:393-418 (1973).

[9] Blehr, O. "Action Groups in a Society with Bilateral Kinship: A Case Study from the Faroe Islands," *Ethnology* 1:269-275 (1963).

[10] Lessa, W. A. *Ulithi: A Micronesian Design for Living* (New York: Holt, Rinehart and Winston, 1966).

[11] Pollnac, R. B., Ed. *Panamanian Small-Scale Fishermen: Society, Culture, and Change* (Kingston, RI: International Center for Marine Resource Development, University of Rhode Island, 1977).

[12] Aronoff, J. *Psychological Needs and Cultural Systems* (Princeton, NJ: D. Van Nostrand Co., Inc., 1967).

[13] Gladwin, H. "Decision Making in the Cape Coast (Mfante) Fishing and Fish Marketing System," PhD Dissertation, Stanford University (1970).

[14] Sahlins, M. D. *Moala: Culture and Nature on a Fijian Island* (Ann

Arbor, MI: University of Michigan Press, 1962).

[15] Firth, R. *Malay Fishermen,* 2nd ed. (Hamden, CT: Archon Books, 1977).

[16] Bartlett, K. *The Finest Kind* (New York: W. W. Norton & Company, 1977).

[17] Glacken, C. J. *The Great Loochoo* (Berkeley, CA: University of California Press, 1955).

[18] McGoodwin, J. R. "Society, Economy, and Shark Fishing Crews in Rural Northwest Mexico," *Ethnology* 15:377-391 (1976).

[19] Diamond, N. K'un Shen: A Taiwan Village (New York: Holt, Rinehart, and Winston, 1969).

[20] Norr, K. "A South Indian Fishing Village in Comparative Perspective," PhD Dissertation, University of Michigan (1972).

[21] Pollnac, R. B., and R. Ruiz-Stout. "Kinship Links among Small-Scale Fishermen in the Republic of Panama," in *Panamanian Small-Scale Fishermen: Society, Culture, and Change* (Kingston, RI: International Center for Marine Resource Development, University of Rhode Island, 1977).

[22] Burrows, E. G., and M. E. Spiro. "An Atoll Culture: Ethnography of Ifaluk in the Central Carolines," Human Relations Area Files, Yale University, New Haven, CT (1953).

[23] Gladwin, T. *East Is a Big Bird* (Cambridge, MA: Harvard University Press, 1979).

[24] Kottak, C. P. "The Structure of Equality in a Brazilian Fishing Community," PhD Dissertation, Columbia University (1966).

[25] Nietschmann, B. *Between Land and Water* (New York: Seminar Press, 1973).

[26] Epstein, A. L. *Matupit* (Berkeley, CA: University of California Press, 1969).

[27] Brandt, V. *A Korean Village* (Cambridge, MA: Harvard University Press, 1971).

[28] Faris, J. C. "Primitive Accumulation in Smale Scale Fishing Communities," in *Those Who Live from the Sea,* M. E. Smith, Ed. (Minneapolis, MN: West Publishing Co., 1977).

[29] Davenport, W. H. "A Comparative Study of Two Jamaican Fishing Communities," PhD Dissertation, Yale University (1956).

[30] Fraser, T. M. *Rusembilan* (Ithaca, NY: Cornell University Press, 1960).

[31] Forman, S. *The Raft Fishermen* (Bloomington, IN: Indiana University Press, 1970).

[32] Firth, R. *Primitive Polynesian Economy* (London, England: Routledge and K. Paul, 1965).

[33] Nason, J. "The Effects of Social Change on Marine Technology in a Pacific Atoll Community," in *Maritime Adaptations of the Pacific,* R. Casteel and G. Quimby, Eds. (The Hague: Mouton Publishers, 1975).

[34] Emmerson, D. K. "Orders of Meaning: Understanding Change in a Fishing Community in Indonesia," paper presented at the Annual Meeting of the American Political Science Association, San Francisco, CA, 1975.

[35] Sabri, J. "Small-Scale Fisheries Development in Peninsular Malaysia—Problems and Prospects," in *Small-Scale Fisheries Development: Social Science Contribution,* B. Lockwood and R. Ruddle, Eds. (Honolulu, HI: East-West Center, 1977).

[36] Fraser, T. M. *Fishermen of South Thailand* (New York: Holt, Rinehart and Winston, Inc., 1966).

[37] Alexander, P. "Sea Tenure in Southern Sri Lanka," *Ethnology* 16:231-251 (1977).

[38] Jimenes-Castro, B. "The Organization of the Artisan Fishermen in the Province of Puntarenas, Costa Rica," in *Proceedings of the Seminar-Workshop on Artisan Fisheries Development and Aquaculture in Central America and Panama,* T. Estes, Ed. (Kingston, RI: International Center for Marine Resource Development, University of Rhode Island, 1976).

[39] Withan, P., et al. "Las Communidades Pesquesras Artesanales: Problemas de su Desarrollo," paper presented at the Seminario-Taller Desarrollo y Investigacion de los Recursos Marinos de la VIII Region, Universidad de Concepcion, Chile, January 9-13, (1978.)

[40] Blake, B. A. "Cultural Adaptation and Technological Change among Madras Fishing Populations," in *Those Who Live from the Sea,* M. E. Smith, Ed. (Minneapolis, MN: West Publishing Co., 1977).

[41] Pollnac, R. B. "Income Periodicity and Economic Gratification Orientations among Small-Scale Fishermen in the Gulf of Nicoya, Costa Rica," paper presented at the Annual Meeting of the Society for Applied Anthropology, San Diego, CA, (1977).

[42] Yap, C. L. "Trawling: Its Impact on Employment and Resources Use on the West Coast of Peninsular Malaysia," in *Small-Scale Fisheries Development: Social Science Contribution,* B. Lockwood and K. Ruddle, Eds. (Honolulu, HI: East-West Center, 1977).

[43] Epple, G. M. "Technological Change in a Genada, W.I. Fishry, 1950-1970," in *Those Who Live from the Sea,* M. E. Smith, Ed. (Minneapolis, MN: West Publishing Co., 1977).

[44] Alexander, P. "Innovation in a Cultural Vacuum: The Mechanization of Sri Lanka Fisheries," *Human Organization* 34:333-334 (1975).

[45] "Manual on Fishermen's Cooperatives," United Nations Food and Agricultural Organization, Rome (1971). [46] "Rural Cooperatives as Agents of Change: A Research Report and a Debate," United Nations Research Institute for Social Development, Geneva, Switzerland.

[47] Pollnac, R. B., and Ruiz-Stout. "Perceptions of Fishermen's Cooperatives by Small-Scale Fishermen in the Republic of Panama," in *Panamanian Small-Scale Fishermen,* R. Pollnac, Ed. (Kingston, RI: International Center for Marine Resource Development, 1977).

[48] Spoehr, A. *Saipan: The Ethnology of a War Devastated Island,* (Chicago, IL: Chicago Natural History Museum, 1954).

[49] Moras, E. R., et al. *Strategies for Small Farmer Development, Vols. 1 and 2* (Boulder, CO: Westview Press, 1976).

·

CHAPTER 10
PROBLEMS RESULTING FROM TECHNOLOGICAL CHANGE: THE CASE OF THE FANTI FISHERMEN IN GHANA

James B. Christensen
Department of Anthropology
Wayne State University

Maritime anthropology may be viewed as one facet of economic anthropology, which in turn is expected to focus more on producers than on production. Neoclassical economists do not, as a rule, concern themselves with the cultural setting when they make an analysis of a particular type of production in a developing country. However, any program that may change traditional patterns has an improved chance of success if there is an awareness of the culture or cultures involved. Any major agricultural program affecting a number of ethnic groups, for example, should take into account the land tenure and inheritance patterns of these groups.

This need for knowledge of indigenous procedures and problems certainly applies to the Fanti fishing industry. In one Fanti case, an attempt by the government to aid rural fishermen through low-interest loans failed because the repayment schedule did not take into account the seasonal differences in income. In another case, a Western economist was shocked by the fact that a Fanti fisherman would be required to pay a 50% rate of interest to a local moneylender on a loan to buy an outboard motor. However, this rate of interest is deeply imbedded and strongly linked with other aspects of the indigenous culture, and predates European contact.

This chapter attempts to consider the contemporary Fanti canoe fishing industry in its historical and cultural perspective. It will describe the nature of the fishing community, fishing techniques, methods of financing and distribution, and the numerous problems facing the industry. The interdependence of sex roles will be considered, for this mode of production could not exist without the contribution of the women.

Certain economic pursuits in West Africa are related to particular ethnic groups, sometimes extending far beyond the confines of their original country. Thus one finds the ubiquitous Hausa trader in the larger markets of the countries bordering on the Guinea Coast, just as the Ewe can be found operating dragnets on the beaches from Benin to Liberia. Historically, Fanti fishermen have been present in coastal towns from Nigeria to Senegal, and they still dominate canoe fishing in Ghana, Ivory Coast and Liberia. Before development of harbors, they manned the surf boats for handling cargo in Ghana and contiguous countries. Today, a large firm in Liberia recruits Fanti crews for their fishing fleet, for they are generally recognized as skilled fishers and seamen.

THE FISHING COMMUNITY

An analysis of the literature dealing with fishermen forces the conclusion that almost universally they are conservative, at least in regard to the nonmaterial aspects of culture. While they may utilize the latest fishing technology they can afford or manage, in matters relating to family, government or religion their attitudes remain more conservative than those of the other segments of the society. This is certainly true for the Fanti of Ghana.

The Fanti are located along the coast of Ghana for a distance of approximately 60 miles in the center of the country and extend inland approximately 20 miles. They are part of the larger, matrilineal Akan grouping of Ghana, and they have a complex indigenous culture. The coastal towns and villages usually contain farmers as well as fishermen, and today a number of these towns have small industry in the vicinity, or offer jobs in government or government sponsored work. The Fanti as a ethnic group have been one of the most progressive in Ghana, or at least one of the most receptive to change. This was the area where the first missionary work began early in the nineteenth century, and the major Fanti town of Cape Coast has long been viewed as the educational center of Ghana.

The orientation of the fishing community remains strongly toward that which might be termed African or "traditional" in most aspects of culture. The attitude toward the government runs from disinterest to antipathy, if not outright hostility. This was the case when the writer first worked with the Fanti in 1950 during the colonial period, and has remained the pattern since independence in 1957. An example of the lack of cooperation of the fishermen with the government occurred in 1973, when many of them ignored the one-cedi tax levied on all adult males by the federal government. In some towns along the coast it required the army, using physical force, to collect the tax. The fishermen remain active and strong in their support of traditional chiefs, and in some localities they wield considerable power through this particular brand of politics.

To understand the basis of political power in the traditional sphere for a group who are largely illiterate and lower class, it is necessary to refer briefly to the autochthonous political structure. Before the pax Britannia, the Fanti area consisted of a number of small states each headed by a paramount chief, or *omanhen*. Each state had a number of military companies or *asafo* (literally "war people") which were patrilineal, while chieftancy, kinship and inheritance were matrilineal. Customary law requires the support of the asafo before a man chosen by the royal clan can be installed as the paramount chief, and the asafo also have the ability to remove him from his position. Since the fishermen remain the most active of all Fanti in the asafo companies, they remain powerful in traditional politics in those native states located on the coast.

In the area of religion, the fishing communities remain the strongest supporters of traditional beliefs and practices. Patronage of the traditional priesthood *(okomfo)* and herbalists is by no means limited to the fishing community, as their clients include members of the established churches and educated elite. However, those in the fishing community are more likely to patronize the traditional priest or priestess than are the literate segment of the Fanti. In the coastal towns, the public dancing of the traditional priesthood is likely to be associated with those asafo companies whose membership is drawn predominantly from the fishing community, as are the drummers and chorus providing the music. Those fishingfolk who do profess to be Christian are more likely to participate in one of the "spiritualist" churches, which are gaining in popularity. These are churches manifesting a high degree of syncretism between Christianity and traditional beliefs and practices.

A long list of religious practices and beliefs associated with fishing could be listed, but two practices in particular are followed by both those who are African and those who are Christian in their religious orientation. One is abstaining from fishing on Tuesday, which is the day sacred to Bosompo, the sea god. The other is that, with few exceptions, every Fanti canoe has an amulet or charm *(suman)* obtained from a priest or herbalist. This is believed to protect the canoe and crew from evil magic, witchcraft and misfortune at sea as well as aiding in obtaining a good catch. A particular member of the crew is designated to care for the suman, installing and removing it daily when fishing. The maker of the suman indicates a number of taboos and practices abhorrent to the suman, and abstinence is required if it is to be efficacious. Most of these refer to taboos associated with sex and certain foods.

In regard to housing, the fishing folk tend to cluster in the older and poorer housing near the beach, due primarily to low income and the location. Their housing is usually lacking in amenities, such as piped water and electricity, now available along the coast. Poor government planning has not helped these conditions as in Cape Coast, where a large housing project was built. The intent was to relocate some of the fishing community, getting them out of their densely populated and deteriorating area. Water, showers, toilets and electricity were installed, rents were low and there were easy credit terms for purchase. Very few fishermen took advantage of the possibility, however. While the project was near the beach it was not near the particular location where they landed their catch.

Fishermen as a group do not have high status among the Fanti. They are generally viewed as somewhat improvident, if not lazy, and irresponsible regarding money. In 1972 a memorandum regarding the problems of the fishing industry from the office of the Regional Commissioner, Central Region, pointed out that the Fanti fished effectively only three months a year and "thereafter remained idle until the next season, drinking most of the time." Osafo-Gyimah and Afful, two economists from the University of Cape Coast, make the following comment: "Fishermen, like drivers, are not the best of savers. In good times, they get a lot of money and spend a lot of money. When the going becomes hard, as it is wont to be sooner or later they do borrow and the first person they turn to is the vessel owner." [1]

These comments are not without basis. They do not save money for the inevitable slack seasons. Like most Ghanaian males, they do drink and smoke. Where formerly their drink was palm wine and their tobacco was a cheap form imported in bulk for a pipe, they now prefer the more expensive bottled beer and manufactured cigarettes. In an area where education is highly prized, they remain largely disinterested in formal schooling, preferring to have their sons follow after their fathers and viewing education for girls as a waste. Those boys who do obtain schooling, often at the instigation of their mothers, rarely follow fishing as a career. It is viewed as a low-status activity, even lower than farming. Criticism leveled at fishermen and others at the lower end of the social scale, so common in the Western world, is also evident in developing countries such as Ghana.

Many of the actions of the fishermen are, however, understandable. They are frequently beached because of motor breakdown, a problem discussed below. When the catch is poor, they sensibly remain ashore as the cost of gasoline is likely to exceed the income from the catch, and alternative types of fishing that were formerly practiced are not an option with current equipment.

If the Fanti fishermen can be characterized as being somewhat improvident and lacking in commitment to work and saving for the future, the Fanti women tend to be hard-working, self-reliant, independent and somewhat penurious. Trading is traditionally in the hands of women in southern Ghana, and economic acumen is often acquired by the female as a child. This training occurs under the tutelage of the mother, and a child from four to eight years of age may be seen selling fish, cigarettes, produce and prepared foods on the street or in the market. After this early enculturation, many women continue to trade throughout their lives. Some become entrepreneurs and wealthy by local standards. They serve as middlewomen in the fishing industry and in the trade in farm produce and imported items, as well as being retailers for most of what is sold in the markets.

The average Fanti wife has a need for some independent income. For one thing, her husband does not always provide her with funds to meet her obligations to her clan. At times, she may be the primary provider for the family, as is the case in the fishing community during slack seasons. The independence of the Fanti female is supported by a number of factors in customary law. In this matrilineal society, she can call on her brothers for support of herself and her children, and the clan is expected to provide her with some type of housing should her marriage dissolve. Divorce in the fishing community is common. It can be initiated by the wife for a number of reasons, with nonsupport being a common one. Since women can support themselves by trading and/or farming when they also have assistance from their kinsmen, there is little inclination to continue an unsatisfactory union. Income from trading or farming her own plot belongs to the female, and it is not uncommon for the wife to be financially more responsible than her fisherman spouse. [2]

TECHNOLOGY AND CHANGE

To delineate change one must first establish a baseline for measuring it. In an earlier paper, I described the fishing economy in Ghana in 1950 as "traditional." However, I ascribe to the principle that, since change is constant, it is difficult to point to a period in time where culture and technology are untainted by borrowing. Some of the equipment of 1950 could hardly be termed traditional, as there were significant changes from that of the nineteenth century. Nets made from pineapple fiber, hand-rolled on the thigh, were first replaced by nets that were handmade from imported cotton twine, and later by imported nets. A sail of canvas had replaced one made from bark cloth or woven matting. With the adoption of more efficient nets, the canoes had increased somewhat in size. Cork had replaced the calabash as a float and lead had replaced stones as weights. Imported dye for tanning nets had replaced its predecessor made from local bark.

This chapter will deal with what could be termed the "rural" fishing industry of Ghana [1] in that it is concerned with fishing along the coast between the urban centers of Accra and Takoradi. While canoe fishing still goes on contiguous to these urban areas, these two port towns have cold storage facilities to handle the catch of large refrigerated vessels, many of them foreign. There are three types of vessels engaged in fishing in the Fanti area. One is the small canoe powered by paddle and sail. While this type was common in 1950 and is still very much in evidence, it is not significant in the production of fish for the market. Another type, recently introduced, is a small trawler with an inboard motor. In the Fanti area only one town, Elmina, can accommodate these motor vessels, because it has harbor facilities in the mouth of a river. Because of the cost, few Fanti fishermen own these vessels, which come in from other parts of Ghana. In time they may replace the canoe. This chapter will deal with the third type, the motorized canoe, which is still responsible for a majority of the fish landed in the rural areas.

The hulls of Fanti canoes have always been made by artisans in the interior, where the tropical rain forest provides the large softwood logs *(Triplochiton scleroxylon)*. Formerly the hulls were floated to the coast on the Pra River. Later they were carried by rail, and today they are hauled by truck. The fishermen contract with a local Fanti carpenter to finish the crude hull. This involves hewing the hull with an adze to the desired thickness (about three inches), charring it and, in the traditional dugout, lashing a number of staves athwart the canoe to provide seats and reinforcement. The carpenter would also nail a plank with a rectangular opening just aft of the prow for inserting the mast, with a step to hold the bottom of the mast nailed to the hull below the plank. The canoe would be finished by carving a design, which includes traditional symbols and a name or proverb in Fanti or English, around the top of the canoe. The design would be painted, the primary function of this being identification.

The traditional canoe of 1950 varied in length from 25 to 30 feet, with a beam of 4 to 5 feet, and a depth of 2.5 to 3 feet. The craft was admirably suited for use on the coast, which lacks natural harbors. The crew would use paddles to get through the surf, and once at sea they would hoist a sail of approximately 250 square feet. The mast would be stepped to windward, with one top corner of the square sail tied to the mast and the other top corner to a diagonal spar. The head of the sail was tied with a line and one corner of the bottom made fast to the prow. A sheet from the other corner led to the stern. They would sometimes use a leeboard, but they could not sail more than 90 degrees to the wind. This problem was offset by going to sea during the early morning hours when there was an offshore wind, and returning after 10 AM, when there was an onshore breeze.

The canoe (*hemba* in Fanti) came in varying sizes and configurations. In 1950, the smaller canoes would be used for inshore fishing with small nets or handlines, while the larger ones would go farther to sea with larger nets. A variety of nets were utilized in 1950 (17 were recorded) including casting nets, bottom nets and gill nets, the major one being a large-surface net *(Ali or Akii)*. A crew of five or eight (including one or two youth as apprentices) was used for the Ali net, with smaller crews involved with other types of fishing.

Beginning about 1960, the Fanti began adapting outboard motors to the dugout canoes and a number of changes resulted. Canoes became larger, and there was a trend toward a massive dugout measuring 35 to 40 feet in length with a beam of up to 6 feet and a depth of more than 4 feet. While the basic hull was still made from a single log, the greater size was achieved by building up the sides by nailing three-inch strips of timber to the hull. The motor was mounted on a triangular bracket of wood, reinforced with steel, and bolted a few feet forward of the stern on the starboard. This side-mounting of the motor was not particularly efficient, as it propelled the canoe through the water at a slight angle. Initially the motors were 15-to 20-horsepower, but the fishermen have moved up to 25-horsepower units on the larger canoes. However, for a vessel of this size, which may carry a crew of as many as 14, they remain underpowered, contributing to a need for frequent motor repair. Some of the large canoes still carry a mast and sail when fishing. The sail may be utilized to conserve gasoline and for emergencies, but actually is little used as an adjunct source of power.

Along with the increase in the size of the canoe has been an increase in the size of the nets, with some being 300 to 400 yards in length. They are now made of nylon, which negates the need for dyeing and also requires less drying. A major adoption in gear is a purse seine with small mesh (0.75 inch), which can be used for catching a number of species of fishes but is used especially for herring. This net along with the Ali (which is a deeper net with larger mesh) are the two major nets used by the motorized canoes. Carrying the Ali net from the beach to the drying racks was formerly a job for women, as five could carry one net coiled on wooden trays on their heads. Today this is a heavy task for ten men. In the 1950s the smaller canoes could be beached and moved above the high tide line by a crew of six. Today, the larger canoes use large steel pipes as rollers and require twice that number of men to store them. The size of the crew has doubled, now ranging from 10 to 14, with 12 the average. Normally 2 or 3 of a crew of 12 would be teenagers serving as apprentices.

Fanti crews tend to be comprised of kinsmen (agnatic as well as matrilineal) along with friends, as the size of the crew makes one comprised entirely of kinsmen impossible. While there is often a central core that stays together over a long period, some turnover in crew membership is common. One of the key men in the crew is the "bosun" or "bosum," who functions as the captain. He is usually appointed by the owner of the equipment or is an owner himself. Other key personnel are the steerman, the "driver" (he handles the motor), and the net caster. The decisionmaking process, at least in regard to such matters as when to fish, where to fish, and when to return to shore is democratic and involves the entire crew [4].

DIVISION OF THE CATCH

One aspect of the fishing industry that is almost universal is that the crew is remunerated, totally or in part, by a share of the catch or a share of the income from the catch. This pattern has decided advantages as far as the Fanti are concerned, and it is doubtful if canoe fishing could function otherwise. To pay wages for those seasons when the catch is small would bankrupt the owner of the equipment. Since operating costs, such as gasoline, are deducted before income is shared, the crew is concerned about fuel consumation and other expenses. Given the difficult conditions they face, the crew probably would be less inclined to work if they were paid wages rather than shares.

In 1950 the most common pattern was for the canoe and net to be owned by one or two of the crew. Ownership of the catching gear by the entire crew was (and is) rare in Ghana. Division of the catch was according to a set formula, with two shares going to the owner(s) of the net, one share to the owner(s) of the canoe, one share to each adult, and a fractional share (one-half or one-fourth) going to an apprentice. When the catch was landed the crew would first remove any large fish (mackerel, sole, etc.) for separate sale and distribution, and also set aside some "eating fish" for the evening meal of each of the crew and their families. They would then divide the catch into wicker baskets equal to the number of shares, with 110 fish being placed in each basket in turn [5]. The landing area of the beach always collected a large crowd of women, who would carefully watch the count and engage in much yelling and shoving. They were in competition for the opportunity to carry the nets back to the drying racks or the baskets of fish back to the village, as they were paid in fish for such work.

The purpose given by the Fanti for beginning with 110 fish during the division of the catch was to enable the woman who smoked the fish to have at least 100 fish for sale. Porterage was paid in fish to the woman who carried the basket to the oven, and the number of prime fish for sale was further reduced by mutilation when being removed from the net or during the smoking process. The woman who purchased the smoked fish in wholesale lots expected to receive a few extra fish (usually 5) for each 100 purchased. This is also consistent with the pattern of trade in southern Ghana where the seller is expected to give an equivalent of our "baker's dozen", at least when selling small fish or produce such as oranges or bananas when the amount sold exceeds 10 or 15 in number.

The price for fish on a given day was determined by bargaining between the women and the fishermen. Each village or town on the coast had a head fishmonger, elected by the others, and known as the *konkohen* (from konko, meaning trade or retail, and hen meaning chief or head). The konkohen and/or her assistants would meet the first canoes to reach the beach with a catch and discuss the price of the fish for that day with the bosum and crew of the canoes. The price would be determined by such factors as the size of the catch, size and species of fishes, and also the catch for the previous days, as the market might be glutted by several days of large catches. Each fisherman would turn over his share of the catch to his wife or a sister, and from that point on the disposal of the catch became the responsibility of the females.

The role of women in the sale of the catch is essentially the same as a quarter of a century ago. One difference at that time was that the women were less likely to travel to inland markets with smoked fish, for two reasons. Since they handled the share of one or possibly two men, they were not likely to accumulate enough smoked fish to make the journey profitable, and also the lines for travel and communications were less adequate than at present. There were female entrepreneurs who would travel along the coast in trucks buying fish from the women for transportation to inland markets and urban centers.

A woman was expected to turn over to the fisherman the agreed price for each day's catch, and an accounting would be held weekly or perhaps only every month or two. She was permitted to keep 10% of the value of the fish for her labor in smoking and selling, as well as any profit she may have realized. If she had suffered a loss she could appeal for a reduction in the amount owed, and this was likely to be granted by the fisherman if he felt there was merit to the claim. While many fishermen turned their catch over to their wives, most claimed it was better to deal with a sibling, as a sister was more likely to give an honest accounting than was a spouse. The tie between a man and his sister was and is a close one, for as noted above, it is to the brother a woman turns in the event of divorce or widowhood.

The increase in the size of the catching gear, and the adoption of the outboard motor, permitted crews to go farther out to sea and obtain a larger catch per canoe, particularly during the herring season. Moreover, since they were no longer dependent on the prevailing winds, a crew might make two or even three trips a day when the catch was good. The traditional method of counting out the catch, 110 fish per share, was too slow for these conditions.

While the catch, or more correctly, the income from the catch, is still divided according to shares, the number of shares allocated to the catching gear has increased due to the increase in cost. Each member of the crew, including the captain, still gets one share, with an apprentice receiving the fractional share. While there is variation concerning the shares allocated to equipment, the most common pattern in 1973 was to award two shares to the canoe, three to the net, and four to the motor. Some crews would allocate as much as six shares to the motor, to have a reserve for repairs and replacement. A majority of the crews interviewed also allocated one share to the equipment owner for his or her function as manager. This was in addition to the regular equipment shares. Only in approximately 20% of the sample were the owner or owners of the equipment also members of the crew. Thus, in the Fanti area around Cape Coast, for a canoe with a crew of 12 the income from the catch after operating expenses would be shared approximately as follows: motor, 4; net, 3; canoe, 2; owner, 1, crew, 11 (figuring two apprentices at a half-share each).

The allocation of the shares of the equipment appears to be determined as much by tradition as by cost and estimated years of use. In 1974 a canoe (including paddles, sail, etc.) was estimated to cost 1300 cedis (1.15 cedis per U.S. dollar) and could be expected to last ten years, barring serious accident. The two major nets required by one canoe were estimated to cost a total of 4700 cedis, with a life expectancy of approximately eight years [1]. Since the cost of the nets is more than three times the cost of the canoe and since nets require constant mending after about three years, the allocation seems hardly equitable. A motor cost approximately 800 cedis in 1974, but repairs could increase the cost considerably; the motor had an expected usage of three years at most.

For a large catch, such as those obtained during the herring season, it is no longer practical to divide the catch by counting. Large fish are still set aside for sale individually, but smaller species are sold by the pan. The standard unit of measure is an enameled or aluminum basin of 1.17 cubic feet, and each pan will hold 250-500 herring. In some localities, the fisherman may turn his share of the catch over to his wife or a woman of his choice, but the most common practice is that followed in the larger towns of Cape Coast and Elmina. Here it is the pattern to turn the entire catch over to one middlewoman. She is often the wife of the bosun or owner, or may be an equipment owner herself. This practice of selling the catch through a middlewoman means that the crew members now divide money instead of fish and that the fisherman and his wife are no longer the economic unit they were under the traditional system. The crew member now settles accounts periodically (usually weekly) with the owner or bosun rather than with the crew member's wife or sister. Under the present system, the wife who wishes to sell fish must purchase it from some middle-woman.

An owner always has some representative, usually a relative, at the beach to check on the catch and the price for each day. Sometimes the representative may be the middlewoman or it might be a member of the crew. This representative may also be present when a crew moves to another locality along the coast for a period of time.

The determination of the price of fish for a given day follows the same pattern as that described for 1950. The konkohen for the town or village meets the first of the canoes to return with a catch and a lively exchange follows between the women waiting to buy fish and the crew. An agreed price is reached between the konkohen and bosun, which becomes the base price for that day, but this is subject to fluctuation. Again, the factors determining prices are the size and species of the catch. Small herring do not command the same price per pan as large herring, and of even less value are what are sometimes termed "junk fish," or small fish of several species caught in the purse seine net. They are too small for smoking and must be sold fresh, dried and salted. The size of the catch in previous days is also a factor, as the market may be glutted. The price per pan usually decreases later in the day, as there is less time available for retailing fresh fish, and smoking must begin later. Price fluctuations will also occur when subsequent landings indicate a much larger or smaller catch than initially antici-pated. Most price fluctuations during the day would be less than 50% in either direction. Extreme fluctuations do occur. Kuranchie records a drop from an initial price of 8 cedis per pan to 20 pesewas (0.02 cedis) per pan during the herring season of 1972 [5]. During the same season in the town of Biriwa, at the end of one particular day, it was impossi-ble to give away the catches of the last canoes to land. They were dumped on the beach and left to rot.

If a crew does not wish to sell at the going price in their own town or village, they may sometimes cruise to another town along the coast, hoping for a better price. Unless they have advance information on the price being paid elsewhere, this is a gamble that may result in a serious loss. Not only do they have the added cost of gasoline, as well as a fee for selling in the new town, but the buyers recognize them as outsiders and drive hard bargains.

INCOME

Estimating the income of Fanti fishermen is almost an impossible task. If one could be present at the weekly or periodic accountings held by crews over a period of years, and the sample were large enough, one could derive an approximation. If one relied on the reports of the fishermen as to the size of their catch and price per pan the results are questionable. Another problem is that breakdowns are common, and many fishermen do not fish the entire year. The income of those who own equipment is affected by the method of financing and the rate of interest, which might be very low if money were obtained from a bank or kinsman, or up to 50% if obtained from a moneylender. Total income from the catch is not reflected in the sale at the beach, as each fisherman gets fish for his family. When a motor is in need of repair and the crew cannot fish as a unit, some fishermen will go out in the smaller canoes. While this may not result in a surplus of fish for sale, it does provide food for family and relatives.

While most would claim to be involved in fishing on a full-time basis, this is not the case for a significant percentage of fishermen. Some drop out to help prepare a farm for planting and a few occasionally work as laborers for short periods. Others do little or nothing during those times of the year when the catch is poor. The intermittant nature of fishing is indicated by Quinn [6] in a study made at Biriwa in a 17-month period during 1967-1968. In her sample of 233 crew members, none was recorded as fishing the entire period. Of the 13 "seasons" (a season varies from 1 to 2 months, with 9 seasons in a year) covered in her report, 101 crew members fished only 2 seasons and only 3 fished a maximum of 7 seasons. Income during this time was reported at L0-20 for 78 men in the sample with a maximum of L151-200 for only eight of the fishermen. [4].

The conservative tendency of the fishing community is also illustrated by their reluctance to quote prices in cedis and pesewas (100 pesewas per cedi) rather than in pounds. When the cedi was introduced in 1966 to replace the pound, the official value was set by the government as being equal to the U.S. dollar, and at the same time the British pound was equal to $2.40. Today many in the fishing community still quote prices in pounds and shillings. It is understood that one pound equals two cedis, and the ten-pesewa coin is referred to as a shilling.

A short-term sample taken by the writer at Elmina and Cape Coast in January 1973 covered a period of 12 fishing days. Gross income per canoe per catch for a single day varied from a low of eight to a high of 272 cedis. After deductions for gasoline, this would give each adult member of the crew a daily income varying from a low of 0.23 to a high of 12.5 cedis. Average daily income for all landings during the period was 2.3 cedis per share after deductions for petrol. Other evaluations indicate comparable incomes. An analysis of archival materials for the town of Biriwa during the main herring seasons of July to September 1972, indicates that the average daily income per share was approximately three cedis. However, it should be noted that this was the income for those who actually fished, and not for all fishermen, as those who did not fish due to bad weather, a bad motor, or some other reason were not figured in the averages [3].

The picture for the owners of equipment involved in canoe fishing is equally dismal. In their analysis of canoe fishing, Osafo-Gyimah and Afful [1] made estimates for the calendar year from August 1973 to July 1974. Their computations included such factors as cost of equipment, depreciation, operating costs, interest on loans, estimates on motor repair and other incidentals. They estimated that cost exceeded earnings by 30% for motorized canoes during the period covered. The picture for the owners of motor vessels was brighter, as their estimated income exceeded cost by 6% [1].

FINANCING EQUIPMENT

At the time of the initial research in 1950, the value of a canoe was approximately L50 (then L1 equaled $2.80), with the main net, the Ali, valued at twice the cost of the canoe. The equipment was owned by one or two of the crew, or sometimes by a fisherman who had retired. Investment in catching gear by nonfishermen was rare, and financing was usually by loans from kinsmen.

Fishermen will discuss sources of capital, rates of interest and method of repayment as it applies to the industry in general. It is exceedingly difficult, however, to obtain reliable data about ownership or source of loans for the equipment of a specific crew. They are reluctant to discuss financial matters with anyone outside of their immediate kin group, and fishermen are not likely to know the affairs of another crew unless they have fished with them.

In 1974 the catching gear was owned or financed in a majority of the cases by non-fishermen. In a sample of 80 canoes from 5 fishing communities, the bosun was asked who owned the equipment. Only in 21% of the sample was the equipment reported as being owned by one or more members of the crew. In 44% of the cases, ownership was accorded to nonfishing males, and in 35%, to females. In no case in Ghana was there reported collective ownership by the entire crew. It is not maintained that these data are reliable, as it is known that males are reluctant to indicate their dependence on females, and the ownership by females may be higher than reported. One is inclined to distrust a response that the owner is "a rich man in Elmina" when that town was too distant to permit the daily contact required to check on the size and price of the catch. A response that a loan was obtained from some man may be given in good faith, but still not be factual, as the man handling the loan may be a middleman for his wife or sister. The data on ownership cited above is suspect for another reason, as none of the bosuns reported split ownership of the catching gear; that is, the canoe and nets being owned by one individual and the motor by another. It is known that split ownership was not uncommon.

While there appears to be a trend toward absentee (i.e., nonfishing) ownership of catching gear, this does not mean that ownership is moving outside of the fishing community. In some cases the owner may be a retired fisherman. The market women who invest in equipment are usually connected with selling and smoking fish.

It is difficult for the fisherman to finance equipment through banks or government agencies. At one time the Agriculture Development Bank made loans available to fishermen to buy outboard motors, since the government viewed the mechanization of the rural fishing industry as a way to decrease the country's dependence on imported food. However, the initial program did not succeed. Repayment of the loan, at a low rate of interest, was due quarterly, and frequently the fishermen were unable to meet their obligations. It was also reported that some of them had no intentions of doing so. Attempts at repossession were sometimes hampered by the inability of government agents to locate the borrower or the motor, as members of the fishing community were not inclined to cooperate. When the government was finally able to repossess a motor after default on payment, the equipment was usually worth only a fraction of the unpaid balance.

The banks do not regard the canoe fishermen as good credit risks, since they have the stereotype of being improvident and careless with money. The insurance required by a bank is viewed by the fishermen as an unnecessary expense and is a procedure not thoroughly understood by them. The rates are high for canoes, as one can be damaged beyond repair should it hit one of the submerged rocks that are a common hazzard all along the coast. Another problem that has developed in recent years is the theft of sections of nets that are usually left unattended near the beach.

The first place a fisherman will turn for financial assistance is to his matrilineal clan and to friends. One advantage of aid from these sources is that repossession is unlikely should be default in his payments. Traditionally these loans have been interest-free, but at the time of the research some kinsmen requested a small rate of interest or a share of the catch. It is no longer possible to state that such loans are free of some form of interest or financial obligation, although this may be only an agreement to sell the catch to the female relative who advanced the money.

The increase in both the cost of equipment and the operating has reduced the ability of the clan to finance a fisherman. With bank loans difficult to obtain, fishermen often have to turn to moneylenders. Being a moneylender can be profitable, as the 50% rate of interest is both common and traditional. There is general agreement that the major source of this type of loan is market women, most often those involved in trading in fish. Not all market women are moneylenders, but a small percentage are affluent. An obvious question is that if the banks view a fisherman as a bad credit risk, why would a moneylender take a risk? The answer is that she is very likely to get her money, eventually. The loan may be formalized by a promissory note, but the transaction is always witnessed, as are repayments. The obligation to repay the loan then falls on the kinsmen of the recipient of the loan should he die or default, and since the good name of the clan is at stake, this is more of a guarantee of repayment than any court action.

The government in Ghana recognized (unofficially at least) the moral responsibility of the clan for the financial obligations of a member. Some businessmen who defaulted on government loans were imprisoned, and it was announced in the press that they would there remain until their relatives paid the debt.

The financial agreement between a moneylender and a fisherman may vary considerably. It may be a simple agreement where a loan, for example, of 1000 cedis requires the repayment of 1500 cedis in a specified period of time (the Fanti traditionally did not compound interest on loans). It could be an agreement where the interest is compounded annually, in which case a bad year could put a borrower deeply in debt. Where the moneylender is a market woman engaged in trading in fish, the arrangement often involves more than a loan repaid with the stipulated interest, for it usually gives the woman the right to purchase the catch of the canoe. To illustrate the possibilities, let us take an example where a market woman loans 800 cedis for the purchase of a motor. If the loan is badly needed she could receive the 50% interest plus the motor's share of the catch until the loan was repaid. In other cases, she may be entitled to only the interest, with the option to buy the catch. Not all moneylenders charge the 50% interest, lower rates being assessed where the borrower was a friend or relative.

Once a working agreement has been negotiated between a woman and a crew, it usually involves more than buying the fish. She is the one the crew will turn to when they need various kinds of financial aid, as they frequently do when the weather is bad or the catch is poor. One common reason for an "advance" is to buy gasoline and oil for the motor. Another is "chop money," an advance of cash of up to one cedi per day per crewmember when the catch is poor or nonexistent and the men need money for food. Motor repair is another common reason for aid requests. Such loans do not normally require interest, and the amount is repaid in fish. This expectation of loan for operating and living expenses extends to the women who buys the fish, even though she may not have loaned the money for equipment. The total picture is one of the crew being frequently in debt to the woman who buys their fish.

ROLE OF WOMEN IN DISTRIBUTION

It must be emphasized that without the contribution of the women, the rural fishing industry could not exist in its present form. There are cold storage facilities available only in the Accra-Tema area and at Takoradi, the two port facilities where the larger fishing boats with refrigeration facilities can land their catch. Even these rely to some extent on market women to buy the frozen fish and sell them in the market. The motorized canoes and small trawlers must rely totally on women to handle their catch.

As indicated above, most crews dispose of their catch to one woman, with whom they have a working agreement, and with whom they have a weekly accounting. In the past it has been possible for the women to appeal for less than the agreed price for a given day, claiming that market conditions had been such that they could not break even. There appears to be an increased reluctance on the part of the fishermen to grant these requests, due to their need for the income and some doubt as to the accuracy of the claims. Some crews are now requiring daily cash sales on the beach, particularly when they sell to other than a middlewoman.

The middlewomen who receive the entire catch of a crew are usually involved directly or indirectly in retailing of fish. Those who are well established often have a number of options open to them for disposal of the catch, but these options vary with the seasons and the species of the catch. They can (1) retail all or part of the catch as fresh fish in the local markets; (2) smoke all or part for future sale; or (3) sell to other women who want fish for retailing fresh and/or smoking. It should be noted that the middlewoman does not have the option of declining to buy the catch when the market is glutted. She is expected to dispose of it as best she can.

While most middlewomen are involved to some extent in smoking fish, not all women who smoke fish are middlewomen. Women who specialize in smoking fish buy fish at the beach, usually paying cash at the time of purchase. A woman in this category has one advantage in that she need not purchase fish when the market is glutted except to the extent that she might be expected to buy from some middlewoman with whom she regularly trades. On the negative side, when fish are scarce such women may not be able to obtain fish. It was a common sight to see a small bus full of women with pans going from Cape Coast to Elmina to buy fish, as the latter town had a large number of canoes as well as trawlers in operation.

The major period for smoking fish is the herring season from July to September, although smoking can occur at any time if the fish are of the appropriate size. The advantages of smoking fish are that they bring a higher price than fresh fish, they can be transported to inland markets, and they can be resmoked in anticipation of a more favorable price at a later date. The disadvantage of resmoking fish is that they eventually become "hard-smoked" fish, which command a lower price in the market.

Once smoked, fish can be sold locally, transported by the owner to a more favorable market area, or sent to a friend or relative at some inland market for retailing, with the retailer keeping a commission from the sales. This latter procedure requires considerable trust on the part of the wholesaler in both the driver of the bus or lorry who delivers her fish and in the retailer. Kuranchie [5] reports that women in Elmina who sold fish in this manner believed their retailers were underdeclaring the selling price at the inland market. The problems facing the Fanti women who smoke fish and how they decide when to sell have been discussed extensively [4,7-9].

Regarding the income of market women from selling and smoking fish, there is the usual problem of obtaining reliable data. Sometimes their margin of profit is considerable, for I have seen women who paid 0.5 cedis for mackerel, cut the fish into five pieces and sell each one for 0.2 cedis, a 100% markup. Similarly, smoked herring would sell for twice the price of fresh herring. At the other end of the scale are the women who claim they do not break even on their smoked fish. In their study of the economics of canoe fishing Osafo-Gyimah and Afful [1] based the value of the catch on the price received by the middlewomen. Of this, their estimate was that the crew received 54% of the net profit, the equipment owners receive 23%, and the middlewomen 23%. They pointed out the inequity of these percentages, since the one middlewomen made almost half as much for selling the fish as did the 12 crew members who caught them [1]. There is some question concerning this estimate of the percentage of profit for the middlewomen on a regular basis. They may be able to obtain this percentage when fish are scarce, but it is doubtful they could do so during the herring season, when the market is glutted. However, there is little doubt that some of these middlewomen make a high percentage of profit during some seasons, particularly when they are engaged in smoking fish. When one recognizes that some of them own all or part of the fishing equipment (thus getting the owner's share), that they may sell to other women at a price higher than they pay the crew, and that they normally make a profit when they smoke fish, it is clear that some of them are making good money. They are certainly making more than the fisherman who works only for his one share of the catch.

Whatever their income, the crucial contribution of the middlewomen and those who smoke fish is that they make it possible for the crew to dispose of their catch without becoming involved in the retailing of the fish. Without the complementary role of the women in the preservation of fish, the system would not work in the absence of facilities to freeze or process fish.

PROBLEMS AND NEEDS

Motorized canoe fishing can only be described as a depressed industry. This is unfortunate for the estimated 70,000 fishers in the central region involved in the industry, and also for the nation, which must spend scarce foreign exchange for imported food. The government and the fishermen claim that there has been a decrease in the fish biomass, and that it has been moving farther out from the coast. The fishermen blame the inboard trawlers and foreign fishing vessels for the scarcity of fish. It may be that a temperature change has caused a reduction of the plankton and a resultant drop in the fish biomass. Whatever the cause, there have been several lean years for the fishermen in the recent past.

In an effort to ameliorate the problem of financing equipment, the government has attempted to introduce cooperatives in each of the fishing villages and towns in the central region. Each cooperative is headed by an executive committee of local fishermen, usually illiterate, with a literate secretary. In 1973 a majority of these existed only on paper and only one cooperative (Elmina) was functioning to any extent. Most of the crews interviewed were not members, and opinion was divided as to the desirability of cooperatives. Some viewed them with favor if they could provide low-interest loans, while others had the usual suspicion for anything connected with the government. The cooperative organization is relatively simple. Membership fees are small, but each member is expected to deposit at least 20 cedis as a working fund for making small loans. If a member wants a large loan, and is viewed as qualified by the membership and executive board, the cooperative guarantees repayment to the bank. One definite advantage of this procedure is that repayment is likely to occur, for the borrower is obligated to his neighbors rather than to an impersonal institution, and the traditional social sanctions regarding loans are operative.

In their report on cooperatives, Osafo-Gyimah and Afful [1] summarize a number of problems that have plagued the movement among the fishermen. Among these are the common ones of mishandling of funds by the local secretaries and weak management by the executive committees. Another problem is that loans have gone to the people least in need of assistance. The cooperatives include women in their membership, and some women have been accused of using low-interest loans to purchase catching gear and then selling it to the fishermen at twice the controlled price set by the government [1]. However, effective cooperatives could ameliorate the problem of financing.

A major problem for the canoe fishing industry is outboard motor breakdown. One frequent cause of this is use of an improper gasoline/oil ratio. For a vast majority of the fishermen, the outboard motor is their first experience in operating a machine, or at least one as complex as an internal combustion engine. Their indigenous culture has not required that they be precise in measurements. The problem is exacerbated by the fact that the canoes are underpowered, contributing to excessive wear. There is a shortage of spare parts, due in large part to the scarcity of foreign exchange, and a crew may be out of action for weeks or even months while they wait for parts and repairs. A frequent complaint is the scarcity of skilled repairmen and overcharging for both parts and labor.

The old fishing patterns are no longer a possibility. Prior to the adoption of the larger canoes and the reliance on the large nets, the fishermen could use a variety of nets with the smaller dugouts. This is not feasible with the current equipment, for without a motor the larger canoes are too ungainly for inshore fishing by use of sail and paddle. In fact they are so large that it is difficult for a fisherman to reach the water with a paddle in an empty canoe because of the high freeboard. Another reason for the abandonment of the old fishing techniques is the apparent movement of the fish biomass farther to sea and out of convenient range of the smaller canoes with sail. In addition, most of the supplementary nets formerly used are no longer available, as they were handmade by the fishermen who claim they can no longer obtain the necessary twine.

THE LIBERIAN PATTERN

When one looks at the problems, financial and otherwise, that beset the Fanti fishermen in Ghana, it is interesting to compare them with those Fanti who have migrated to other West African countries to fish. Migration has long been a pattern for the Fanti, although it has often been to other towns along the coast of Ghana to take advantage of a better catch or better markets. Such fishermen may be gone from home for weeks or even months. During the summer of 1975 the writer was able to do a study of immigrant Fanti fishermen residing in Liberia. Their pattern of work and financing suggest changes that might be implemented among canoe fishermen in Ghana. It is believed that the account given below regarding Liberia also applies to those who migrate to spend several years in other West African countries.

Part of the success that Fanti fishermen have in Liberia is due to the lack of competition from the autochthonous fishermen, most of whom are Kru. The Fanti have been in Liberia since the nineteenth century, first with smaller canoes with sails and nets, and today with larger motorized units described above for Ghana. However, the Kru have never adopted the gear and techniques of the Fanti, although they continually witness their superiority. The Kru still go out in small two-man dugout canoes fishing with hook and line.

A Fanti "company" that is organized to fish in Liberia is always formed in Ghana, just as the members must return there when the company is disbanded. The average company consists of about 20 adult males, each having one share in the company. Also included are four to six male apprentices in their late teens, and eight to ten wives of adult males. The wives and the apprentices each have a one-third share in the company. The company may include some Fanti fishermen who have been born and raised in Liberia, but they also travel to Ghana when the company is formed and disbanded.

The catching gear of a single company normally consists of two canoes, always made in Ghana, and at least three varieties of large nets, for in addition to the Ali and purse seine nets they also use a gill net with large mesh. The equipment may be shipped from Ghana by sea, or it may already be in Liberia when the company is organized, as they may buy the gear of a recently disbanded company that has returned home. Outboard motors are usually obtained in Liberia or from Sierra Leone, as they commonly use one with a larger horsepower rating than is available in Ghana, with 45 horsepower being common.

Each member of the company is responsible for his or her share of the equipment and travel costs, and financing is by loans from kinsmen and/or moneylenders. The latter require the traditional 50% interest. Relatives may charge no interest, but in some cases they require a share of the profits. Financing is sometimes obtained from Fanti residents in Liberia. Two men were reported to have funded some 38 companies that were operating in 1975. The head of the Fanti market women in Monrovia loaned $8000 to start one company.

Each adult male must have a surety in Ghana who will guarantee repayment of his share of the debt should he die or be expelled from the group. Rules and regulations are written and discussed. More binding than the written contract is the force of customary law to conform and pay the debt. Those in Ghana who act as sureties for the loan also choose the head of the company.

A company expects to make sufficient profit in approximately two years to pay off their initial debt for equipment and transportation. In 1975 this debt could vary from $8000 to $15,000, depending on the interest rate and whether the equipment was new or used. The company will remain together for an additional three to four years, continuing the same pattern of saving before returning to Ghana.

There are some significant differences between the procedures followed in Liberia and those followed in Ghana. The catch is usually sold for cash at the beach, including sales to female members of the company as well as to any Liberians who wish to buy. There is no middlewoman as in Ghana. During the herring season the entire catch is turned over to the female members and an accounting is held at the end of the season. Price determination follows the same pattern as in Ghana: the konkohen representing the Fanti women discusses the price with the first canoes. That the women should be arguing the price with their own spouses is not as strange as it may seem, since they must sell the fish and are permitted to keep any profit. All transactions at the beach are carefully observed. One man is designated to handle sales and to do the bargaining for small sales to Liberians. He is always accompanied by the female member (who may not be his spouse), and the money is turned over to her. It is also common to have this couple observed by another couple, who also keep track of total sales.

Accounts are recorded and settled weekly on Sunday, and a literate Fanti is always used as an accountant, one being hired if necessary. Weekly expenses for the company come out of gross profits. This includes gas and oil for the outboards, any repairs, food for the crews while at sea, rent or purchase of housing for members, and also money for expenses incurred by any member who was ill or unusual expenses such as court costs or fines for any member who got into trouble. In the latter case this may be deducted from the individual's share of the profits when they settle accounts back in Ghana. A small allowance is made to each member for food for the week.

The accumulated profits are turned over to various members of the company, including the women. This is regarded as the safest procedure, as it decreases the potential loss due to theft or misappropriation of funds. Banks are not utilized, and usually the money is secretely buried. Unlike the pattern of fishermen in Ghana, where they go through periods of feast or famine, finances are rigidly controlled in Liberia. The whole orientation is toward saving for their return home, and building a house in Ghana is the goal of many. While the living allowance for company members in Liberia is adequate, it does not permit luxuries. Some have income from sources other than fishing, such as women's profits from smoking and retailing fish. Some men use the company funds entrusted to them to make short term loans at a high rate of interest, or to finance their wives in trading.

The bosun, or head of the company, usually goes to sea as the captain of the larger of the two canoes. Second in command is the "second bosun" whose assignment is primarily on the beach. He plans the fishing schedule, decides which nets shall be used, and assigns the men of the company to tasks ashore such as net mending or to sea duty. He also represents the group in any problems involving the company and the community when the bosun is not available. Another major function of the second bosun is dealing with the female members of the company. This may involve adjudicating disputes within the group or between the company and the community. While the bosun has considerable authority, the company is run by consensus. The group can be harsh with a member who they feel has brought discredit or unwarranted financial obligations upon them.

One of the striking differences between those Fanti fishing in

Ghana and those in Liberia is the greater commitment to work on the part of the latter. As indicated above, absenteeism in Ghana may be high, and many fishermen do not work the entire year. Another problem in Ghana is that family and kinship obligations, such as funerals, may be demanding of time and money. In Liberia, each man undertakes his assigned task six days a week, weather and health permitting. There are several reasons for this difference. One is that in Ghana the average fisherman has no indebtedness for the catching gear; in Liberia each member of the company has a share in the equipment debt or in the income the equipment produces. Perhaps more persuasive is the social pressure to conform. The threat that the laggard will be sent home in debt and disgrace is a major factor in ensuring the continued cooperation of company members.

The contribution of the female members of the company exhibits both similarities to and differences from their role in Ghana. Since there is no middlewoman for a canoe, the women are expected to smoke the fish that cannot be sold at the beach and sell them later. When fish are scarce they compete to buy the fish at the beach. They have an advantage in Liberia in that they are virtually the only ethnic group extensively involved in smoking fish and, just as in Ghana, some will travel to inland markets where smoked fish commands a better price than on the coast. The Fanti women in Liberia who are members of a company have one advantage over the market women in Ghana, for in addition to the profit they may make from the sale of fish they have a one-third share in company profits.

Thus, there are members of the same ethnic group, born in or deriving from the same area, behaving quite differently in different locations. At home in Ghana, they have a reputation for being improvident and careless with money: in Liberia, they are seen as hard working and careful with money, if not penurious. The question is, could the Liberian pattern be copied in Ghana? The answer is that some aspects could and others could not. For one thing, the Fanti have less competition in Liberia. Another advantage of fishing away from home is that one avoids many of the kinship obligations that require both time and money at home. While the Liberian Fanti have obligations to their fellow clansmen in Liberia, these are minor compared to those they would experience at home. However, if by some means the crew in Ghana could become an economic unit similar to those in Liberia, and obtain financing at a reasonable rate, it might improve their situation. If the Ghana-based company could adopt something of the same pattern of enforced saving and minimize absenteeism, the lot of the fishermen would be considerably improved.

TREND TOWARD TRAWLERS

While I have observed trawlers in operation in Elmina in the Fanti area, I have not carried out any research involving this particular type of motor vessel. The following summary is based on the report of Osafo-Gyimah and Afful [1]. It is included here to provide a contrast with the problems facing the canoe fishing industry.

The inboard trawlers working out of Elmina, which has a natural harbor, include vessels of 27, 30 and 35 feet in length; their motors vary from 33 to 36 horsepower on the smaller vessels, with 50 to 100 horsepower on the 35-foot boats. Estimated initial costs vary from 11,000 to 22,000 cedis (circa 1973), with an additional cost of 750 to 1000 cedis for nets and other gear. The majority (over 90%) of the owners are non-Fanti from other parts of Ghana, and it is assumed that the vessels are financed through bank loans. These trawlers have two advantages over the motorized canoes. Their capacity is greater and they can go much farther out, and thus could expect a larger catch.

The trawlers carry an average crew of 12, the same as the canoes. They also dispose of their catch through middlewomen. The estimate on the shared income is approximately the same as for canoes, with the crew getting 55%, the middlewomen 22% and the owner 24%. What is strikingly different is the labor efficiency of the motor vessel over the canoes. It is estimated that the 43 trawlers in the sample landed a total of 2500 tons for the year with a total crew of 500 men. This is to be compared with an estimated tonnage of 1500 for 250 canoes, with a crew total of 3000 men. It is assumed that the future trend will be decidedly toward trawlers [1].

The trend may well be toward the trawlers, but this will be at considerable expense to the economy of the coastal towns. Elmina is the only place other than Accra-Tema and Takoradi that provides a harbor, and any more trawlers than they have at present would overtax the facilities. Even now, the trawlers can put to sea and return only at high tide at Elmina. More facilities could be constructed, but this could concentrate fishing boats in a few locations, and would necessitate a move from their home towns by large numbers of fishermen. At present, it is estimated that 70,000 men are involved in the canoe fishing industry in the central region, most of them living in the towns and villages where they were born and raised. Centralization would be equally disruptive for the women involved in the smoking and sale of fish. Conversion to the more efficient trawlers would have to be accompanied by more and better harbors, associated with cold storage or processing plants. Given the cost of this conversion in terms of government expenditure, unemployment, and demographic and market disruption, it is likely that canoe fishing will persist for some time to come.

IMPACT OF INFLATION

As indicated, the portions of this chapter dealing with motorized canoe fishing in Ghana are based on research carried out during a two-year period from 1972 to 1974. However, changes that have occurred in Ghana since 1974, and indeed since this paper was first drafted, have had a strong impact on fishing and the entire economy in Ghana.

The government of Dr. Busia that had been elected by a general referendum was overthrown by a military coup in January 1972. One of the major factors in the coup was Busia's proposal to devalue the currency by 40%. The economic climate of Ghana continued to deteriorate under the military government. The situation was exacerbated by the increase in the price of petroleum, and from 1974 through 1978 the rate of inflation in Ghana has been estimated at 100% per year, a primary cause being a shortage of foreign exchange. In July, 1978 there was a change in the military junta ruling Ghana. There has been a promise to return Ghana to civilian rule and party politics in the near future. However, the government has warned that economic conditions will continue to worsen before they can improve.

One of the more drastic actions taken by the new government in August of 1978 was devaluation of the currency. The official rate in Ghana, which long had stood at 1.15 cedis per U.S. dollar, was changed to 2.75 per dollar, a devaluation of over 100%. Even this action, draconian as it may appear to Ghanaians, is unlikely to significantly alter the negative balance of trade. Insofar as the black market rate for the cedi is indicative of the value of a currency, there has been a steady climb in the rate since the military took over the country in 1972. At that time the black market rate for the dollar was from 1.65 to 2 cedis. By late in 1978 this had risen to 10 to 12 cedis for the dollar [10].

Foreign exchange income from major exports such as cocoa and timber has fallen far below imports. While problems are caused in part by economic factors external to Ghana, the situation has been worsened by what has occurred in the country. Causal factors have been poor planning, poor to corrupt administration, smuggling, favoritism in the allocation and use of scarce foreign exchange, and, reportedly, graft in the government. Even though it is primarily an agricultural country, Ghana has been forced to import large amounts of food.

I have been able to visit Ghana annually since 1974, and while each stay has been too brief to permit any organized research, I have observed the continued increase in both shortages and prices. In 1978 there was a virtual absence of imported food for sale in the stores. Attempts by the government to control prices have been unsuccessful and scarce items end up being sold on the black market. For example, cigarettes manufactured in Ghana have a controlled price of 3 cedis. Spare parts for cars and motors, when they can be obtained on the black market, sell for ten times the controlled price [11]. In regard to purchasing power, a check of prices in the native market early in 1978 indicated that it would cost more than a day's wages for an unskilled worker to buy one large yam, and two days wages to purchase a chicken.

What does this mean for the fishermen? On the positive side it means high prices for the catch at the beach as well as for the women who retail fish. With a shortage of imported food, and the difficulty in controlling the price for locally produced foodstuffs, the price for fish has increased along with everything else. In 1978 smoked herring was selling in a coastal fishing town at prices approximately 500% higher than in 1974. This means that the fishermen could pay off old debts with inflated money, but the cost of new equipment, if it can be obtained at all, is exorbitant. Particularly critical is the absence of spare parts to keep outboard motors in operation. The shortage of foreign exchange means that maintenance and repair of fishing gear is going to be of increasing importance. It is possible that the demand for fish, and the shortage of operating motors, may result in greater utilization of the smaller canoes with sail. However, the rural fishing industry involving motorized canoes will suffer from the economic malaise of the country in general.

SUMMARY

This chapter attempted to describe the impact of the outboard motor on a traditional fishing economy. It has focused on producers rather than on production. It is another example of the principle that any planning by government agencies or aid programs in developing countries should consider the indigenous culture if the aid is to be effective. Programs based on Western economic systems are often dysfunctional. For example, in the Fanti case, aid in the form of low-interest loans from a bank was not successful while loans at high interest, contracted in the traditional manner, functioned well.

The Fanti fishingfolk are essentially conservative, suspicious of government, and have not yet participated in the process of change to the same extent as the rest of the Fanti, particularly with respect to education. Those from the fishing community who do become literate do not become fishermen. The introduction of the outboard motor resulted in significant economic changes in canoe fishing. The dugouts became larger, as did the nets, and inflation in the cost of catching gear made inadequate the traditional pattern of financing through loans from kinsmen.

At present, canoe fishing among the Fanti can only be described as a depressed industry. Inflation, resulting from causal factors external to Ghana, is little understood by the fishermen. The increased cost of catching gear has not been matched by a proportionate increase in the size of the catch for the motorized canoes. The diversified fishing that was carried on with the smaller canoes is not feasible with the larger catching gear. Ecological factors, such as a seeming decrease in the fish biomass, and its movement farther from the coast, have created additional problems. The end result has been a concentration of effort during the main herring season by the motorized canoes, with a decrease in fishing activity during other seasons because of minimal profit.

Financing looms large as one of the major problems. Fishermen are not viewed as good credit risks by the banks or by the government. Their reputation for improvidence has contributed to this, as had the disinclination of some fishermen to work the entire year. This stereotype has caused them to turn to moneylenders for financing, and to the middlewoman for short-term loans for operating and living expenses.

Some of the problems that plague the fishermen are of their own making. One of these is the improper care of their motors, and the resultant frequent breakdowns. The shortage of spare parts is beyond the control of the fishermen, as is the scarcity of qualified repair technicians. This situation might improve were the government to limit the import of motors to one or two standardized brands.

The interdependence of sex roles is an important aspect of the Fanti fishing industry. The fact that the women market the fish, and equally important, cure the surplus fish for later sale, makes it possible to dispose of a large catch that could not be absorbed in the local markets as fresh fish. The economic acumen of some of these market women has moved them into roles as entrepreneurs. Not only do they and/or their associates share the catch of one or more canoes, but they also own or finance a significant percentage of the catching gear. Without these women, the system would not work.

In terms of direct cost per production unit, the recently introduced inboard trawlers are more efficient than the motorized canoes. Lack of harbor space along the coast is a problem, and financing these vessels is currently beyond the ability of virtually all Fanti fishermen. Increased adoption of this type of vessel would require a large investment in port facilities as well as in cold storage facilities or processing plants. The fishermen are ill-equipped, either by training or inclination, to engage in occupations other than fishing. The example of the "companies" that go to fish in Liberia, where the entire crew is collectively responsible for the catching gear, suggest possible ways to make the canoe fishing industry viable in the towns and villages of coastal Ghana.

REFERENCES

[1] Osafo-Gyimah, K., and K. N. Afful "Economic Organization of the Rural Fishing Industry: A Case Study of the Elmina, Bantama and Moree Areas," Economics Department, University of Cape Coast (1976).

[2] Christensen, J. B. "Double Descent among the Fanti," Human Relations Area Files, Yale University, New Haven, CT (1954).

[3] Christensen, J. B. "Motor Power and Woman Power: Technological and Economic Change among the Fanti Fishermen n Ghana," in *Those Who Live from the Sea,* M. E. Smith, Ed. (Minneapolis, MN: West Publishing Company, 1977), pp. 71-95.

[4] Quinn, N. "Mfantse Fishing Crew Composition: A Decision-Making Analysis," PhD Dissertation, Stanford University (1971)

[5] Kuranchie, P. A. "Cost and Returns to Fish Smoking at Elmina: A Reconnaissance Study," Food Research Institute, Ghana (1973).

[6] Quinn, N. "Do Mfantse Fish Sellers Estimate Probabilities in Their Heads?" *Am. Ethnologist* 5(2):206-226 (1978).

[7] Gladwin, C. "A Model of the Supply of Smoked Fish from Cape Coast to Kumai," in *Formal Methods in Economic Anthropology,* S. Plattner, Ed., Spec. Publ. 4 (Washington, DC: American Anthropological Association, 1975), pp. 77-127.

[8] Gladwin, H. "Decision Making in the Cape Coast (Fanti) Fishing and Fish Marketing Systems," PhD Dissertation, Stanford University (1971).

[9] Gladwin, H., and C. Gladwin. "Estimating Market Conditions and Profit Expectations of Fish Sellers at Cape Coast, Ghana," in *Studies in Economic Anthropology,* G. Dalton, Ed., Anthropology Studies 4 (Washington, DC: American Anthropological Association, 1971), pp. 122-142.

[10] *West Africa* (3203):2464 (1978).

[11] *West Africa* (3202):2327 (1978).

CHAPTER 11
METAL TRAPS: A KEY INNOVATION IN THE MAINE LOBSTER INDUSTRY

James M. Acheson
Department of Anthropology
University of Maine

One of the theses that runs through the literature on fishing communities concerns the conservative nature of fishermen, their unwillingness to change, and their inability to accept new ideas. Certainly this stereotypical view of fishermen as traditional rustics who do not quite live in the twentieth century is a highly inaccurate caricature. In the past 70 years, the entire fishing industry has undergone tremendous modernization and mechanization. In Maine, the fishing industry has gone literally from sailboats powered by nothing but wind and the muscle of men to a highly mechanized fleet where advanced electronic gear is in everyday use. This is not to suggest that fishermen do not resist change, and have not rejected innovations many times. But it does underline the fact that we know very little about the process of modernization and the factors affecting social, cultural, and economic change even in modern fishing communities. The object of this chapter is to isolate the social, economic and cultural factors affecting acceptance of one key innovation in the lobster industry in Maine, the single most important fishery in the state. By extension, a discussion of the factors affecting acceptance of this one innovation will hopefully shed light on the process of modernization and change in fishing communities in New England, and perhaps even further afield.

Over the course of the past few decades, many technical changes have occurred in the lobster industry. Diesel engines have begun to be used in large numbers, and the hydraulic trap hauler has become almost universal, along with electronic depthfinders and recorders and radios. Boats have become larger and hull designs have undergone great changes. The adoption of synthetic rope, twine and buoys has greatly changed the type of gear in use. However, these changes have already occurred, and studying them affords limited chances for the type of research required.

One great change is currently taking place; the switch from wooden to metal lobster traps. The change is taking place very rapidly, involves a large number of fishermen and a great deal of money, and affords an unusual opportunity to study the factors promoting and inhibiting change in a major U.S. fishing industry while the change is in progress.

We first began to look seriously at the phenomenon of metal traps in the spring of 1977. Three facts quickly became apparent. First, the diffusion of metal traps was very spotty along the Maine coast. There were many in use in the Portland area, in the towns of Muscongus Bay and in the Stonington area. In many other harbors along the Maine coast, traps were still limited to the traditional wood construction. However, there were enough metal traps in use, and the process had gone on long enough, that we were certain this change indicated a major innovation rather than a small scale experiment that soon would be dropped. Second, the acceptance of metal traps was highly differential, with some men in any particular harbor accepting them relatively rapidly; some men lagging behind; others not accepting them at all. Third, even in communities where metal traps were in the process of being accepted, there was a good deal of debate on their effectiveness and the wisdom of purchasing them. Some very experienced fishermen stated flatly that they were a good thing and said they planned to buy a lot of them. Other equally experienced fishermen stated flatly that metal traps fished no better than wooden traps and would do a good deal of damage to the lobster resource. They doubted the sanity of anyone who believed otherwise.

In studying the diffusion of this innovation, we had two specific research objectives. First, we gathered a good deal of quantitative information on lobster catches, trap types and other factors, to discover objectively which type of trap fished best. This information was obtained from fishermen in the Muscongus Bay region of Maine. We thought that if we could discover which type of trap really caught more lobsters for any given unit of fishing effort, this knowledge would aid us in uncovering many of the critical factors involved in the acceptance or rejection of metal traps. This was based on the naive assumption that one set of lobstermen really knew a great deal more than the other set about the efficiency of metal vs wooden traps. Second, we gathered a good deal of information on social and cultural variables from a large sample of lobster fishermen in four harbors. Before we discuss the type of data we sought, and the kinds of controls required to demonstrate our hypotheses, some general information is needed about the Muscongus Bay region as a whole, and the lobster fishing industry in that area.

GENERAL FEATURES OF LOBSTER FISHING IN THE MUSCONGUS BAY REGION: 1978

The Study Area

This study was conducted in several small fishing communities on or near the Pemaquid peninsula in Lincoln County, Maine. The peninsula lies some 15 miles west of Penobscot Bay, and about 45 miles east of Portland in what is known as the midcoast region of Maine. The entire region is very rural. The closest cities are about 35 miles away. Most of the male population is employed either in the fishing industry, in service industries (stores, gas stations, etc.), or in business connected with tourism, which is the single largest industry in the region. Very few farms have survived to the present. The permanent population of the townships numbers between 600 and 3000, and each contains two or more hamlets. In July and August, the entire population more than doubles as hundreds of "out-or-staters" move into cottages along the ocean for the summer season. Bristol, for example, a relatively large town, has 1721 permanent residents who live in some six major hamlets in 46.7 square miles of land area. In the summer the population exceeds 5000.

The data for this study were collected in the hamlets of Pemaquid Harbor (town of Bristol), which has 39 boats; New Harbor (town of Bristol) with 50 boats; Bremen (town of Bremen)which has 42 boats; and Friendship (town of Friendship) with some 120 boats. Virtually all of the boats in Pemaquid, Bremen and Friendship are lobster boats. New Harbor has both lobster boats and fin fishing boats.

Technology

The American lobster *(Homarus americanus)* is found in the waters off the Atlantic coast of North America from Newfoundland to Virginia. Maine consistently produces far more lobsters than any other state.

The technology employed by lobstermen along the entire length of the Maine coast is relatively uniform. Until recently lobsters were caught in traps, or pots, about three or four feet long, made of oak frames covered with hardwood lathes. Lathes are spaced far enough apart to allow circulation of seawater while still retaining the larger legal-sized lobsters. The open end of the trap is fitted with a funnel-shaped nylon net, or "head," which lets lobsters climb in easily but makes it difficult for them to get out. Inside the trap are one or two other heads, so that the trap is divided into two or three sections, called parlors. The traps are attached to a small styrofoam buoy via a "warp" (polyethylene or hemp rope). The buoys belonging to each lobsterman are marked with distinctive sets of colors, registered with the state. These traps are baited with fish remnants obtained from nearby processing plants. The most important types of bait used in the study area are redfish frames or herring remnants. The traps are usually placed in the water "in strings," or long rows, so that a man can see from one buoy to another in the fog.

Most lobstermen in the Pemaquid area fish alone from gasoline or diesel powered boats 28-34 feet long, equipped with a depth sounder, hydraulic pot hauler, ship-to-shore radio, and compass. The boats of full time lobstermen are designed specifically for lobstering. They have high bows, making them seaworthy when headed into the wind, and low sterns and sides in back of the cabin area to facilitate the handling of lobster traps and to minimize wind action when the wind is on the beam. In 1977 it cost between $17,000-25,000 to have such a boat constructed. In addition, such a fisherman may have from $8,000-15,000 invested in traps and fishing equipment, a pickup truck, dock and some kind of workshop. Replacement values for all capital equipment often run over $50,000.

There is a great deal of variation in the size and scale of fishing operations in the Pemaquid area, and in Maine as a whole. A few local men go lobster fishing from boats as large as 42 feet and run over 900 lobster traps. In every harbor there are a number of part-time fishermen, usually older men or boys, who go fishing only in the warm months of the year with an outboard powered skiff and a few dozen traps.

Seasonal Round

A lobster fisherman's activities vary greatly from season to season. The midwinter months are unquestionably the slowest time of year. During January, February, and March, when men fish 3-10 miles offshore, lobstering is generally more dangerous and unprofitable. Catches are very small, and bad weather and high winds increase trap losses and make the work more difficult. Some men stay ashore during this period to build lobster traps, while others use their boats for scalloping. Those who persist in lobstering during the winter may pull their traps no more than six or seven times a month. Spring (April 15 to June 15) and fall (August 15 to November 15) are unquestionably the busiest months of the year, when men have a maximum number of traps in the water and pull them every chance they get. During the three or four week molting season (June 15 to August 15, depending on the area) traps are typically placed very close to shore – literally a few feet away from breaking surf. During this period, catches are so small that men bring many of their traps ashore and do maintenance work on their boats. In the fall, lobstermen begin to move their equipment into deeper water again. In October and November, usually the most profitable months of the year, traps are placed between 10-35 fathoms. Since the weather can be very rough at this time of year, this fall fishery is the domain of well-equipped, full-time fishermen with large inboard powered boats.

Throughout the year, lobstermen pull and rebait their traps when the sea is calm. When the sea is rough, they have difficulty finding their buoys and operating their hydraulic trap haulers. Moreover, the chances for serious accidents are vastly increased.

Skill

Skill plays a large role in the success of fishermen. There can be great variation in the catches and incomes of fishermen from the same harbor, fishing with the same gear and putting in approximately the same effort. Experienced fishermen say that the most important skill is knowing exactly where to place traps given the bottom conditions and the time of year. The amateur looking at the ocean sees nothing but waves, birds and weather. The highly skilled fisherman sees bottoms of incredible variety. He is thinking of mud, rocks, holes, humps, ridges, edges (where mud meets rocks), channels, the 12-fathom lines and other features. When an experienced man places a trap, he is taking into account not only all of these factors affecting one habitat of lobsters but also wind, tide, location of other men's gear, depth and type of bait used. Increasingly, he is also concerned with the type of trap he uses. The importance of skill is discussed more fully elsewhere [1].

Marketing

Any sizable harbor has at least one dealer or cooperative which buys from local lobstermen and sells to tourists or to one of the three or four large wholesale firms distributing lobsters in Maine and the nation. Typically, a lobster fisherman maintains a long-standing relationship with only one dealer or cooperative, and sells his catch exclusively to that outfit. The dealer or coop provides the lobsterman with dock space, and sells him fuel, bait, paint, gloves and other supplies at low rates of profit. Marketing arrangements differ radically throughout the area. In Bremen, Friendship and Round Pond, fishermen sell their lobster to private dealers. In New Harbor and Pemaquid, virtually all of the fishermen sell to cooperatives in those harbors.

Territoriality

Legally, anyone who has a license can go lobster fishing anywhere. In reality, far more than a license is required. To go lobster fishing at all, one needs to be accepted by the men fishing out of a particular harbor. Once one has gained admission to a "harbor gang," one is ordinarily allowed to go fishing only in the traditional territory of that harbor. Interlopers are strongly sanctioned, sometimes verbally, but more often by the destruction of their lobstering gear. This territorial system is entirely the result of political competition between groups of lobstermen. It contains no legal elements [1].

Violation of territorial boundaries meets with no set response. An older, well-established man from a large family might infringe on the territorial rights of others almost indefinitely, whereas a new man or a "part timer" would quickly lose a lot of fishing gear. Ordinarily, trap cutting involves only one or two men from competing areas. But perhaps once a decade, a series of small incidents will escalate into a full-fledged lobster war involving dozens of men and resulting in widespread destruction of lobstering gear. However, all conflicts are kept very quiet. Trap cutting is illegal, and silence reduces the chances for a victim to retaliate. As a result, the public knows very little about the territorial system or the political mechanisms that maintain it.

In the area around Pemaquid and Muscongus Bay, lobster fishing territories are nucleated [2]. Fishermen maintain exclusive fishing rights to the area within a mile or two from the mouth of a harbor. This sense of ownership grows progressively weaker the further away from the harbor one goes, and more "mixed fishing" is allowed. This middle of Muscongus Bay, for example, is exploited by men from New

Harbor, Round Pond, Bremen, Friendship, Port Clyde and Pleasant Point. When men are fishing ten miles from shore, there is no sense of territorial ownership at all.

While the territorial system is relatively weak in the study area, it is important to note that fishermen cannot set traps in every area where they know fishing is good. In the winter, when the Bremen fishermen are exploiting deep waters between Pemaquid Point, Monhegan and the Georges Islands, they cannot come within two miles of New Harbor. Conversely, in the summer the headwaters of the Medomak River are the exclusive preserve of the Bremen fishermen. Men from New Harbor and other locations are not allowed to fish there.

Harbor Gangs

The men who fish out of one harbor have far more in common than ownership of a common fishing territory. They are informal groups of great importance. Fishermen themselves recognize the importance of such groupings and have a variety of terms for them. They speak of vague entities such as "the Monhegan boys" or the "Pemaquid Harbor bunch" or "New Harbor gang." Some of these groups have rather unique names. The men from South Bristol are referred to as "cunners" (a type of fish). We refer to these groupings as "harbor gangs," although this term is rarely used by the fishermen themselves.

Harbor gang membership strongly influences many aspects of a person's professional career. Friendships are formed on the basis of harbor gang membership. The men who fish from one harbor talk to each other on the radio and swap information with each other. It is the men from one harbor gang that a man can count on in time of emergency. Members of a gang will often get together to perform certain tasks such as building traps or painting boats. Moreover, they generally share a common set of norms and attitudes that mark them off as slightly different from the men of the other harbors.

Perhaps most important, harbor gangs are reference groups. They provide a yardstick for a man to use in measuring his success and skill. They are the primary people a lobster fisherman competes with; they are the people that count in the game of lobstering. Such gangs look inward on themselves. They are the most important unit in a lobsterman's life beyond his family.

The rules defining success within a harbor gang are not always consistent [1]. On one hand, a great deal of prestige accrues to "highliners," good fishermen who catch a lot of fish and earn high incomes.

The most prestige goes to the men who let it be known in quiet ways that they earn a high income by skillfully working a small or moderate number of traps. Such a man is often elected to town office. His advice is sought by other fishermen, and he is very apt to serve as spokesman for the harbor gang in dealing with outsiders of all kinds. The prestige accorded such a man will increase as he gets older, but even a young man who is a good fisherman will be greatly admired and respected in a coastal town.

On the other hand, the prestige accorded a "highliner" many not completely negate the feeling that his success is at someone else's expense. Men who fish huge "gangs" of traps or who fish when the weather is bad are often considered to be taking advantage of others; indeed, to be "taking the food out of someone else's mouth." Such "pigs" or "hogs" can stir up a good deal of antagonism. Feeling against such a man may run particularly high if he is a braggart and his high income is due more to effort and capital equipment than skill.

Most fishermen attempt to escape from this double bind by being secretive about the number of traps they have, their catches and their income. Other men can see where a man has traps, but they have no way of knowing how much he is catching from them. This is information that fishermen rarely talk about.

The strong cleavages between members of harbor gangs have a significant influence on the transmission of information. Fishermen rarely know very much about harbors 15 or 20 miles away. In New Harbor, for example, it is rare for a lobsterman to be able to name more than ten men who fish from Bremen, which is only nine miles away. Highline fishermen are the exception to this rule. The highline fishermen from New Harbor or Bremen know the names of the four or five most successful fishermen of most harbors within about a 20 mile radius. They are, in turn, known by the other highline fishermen within roughly the same radius. At times such men will exchange information, and even form friendship ties. The highline fisherman is in a highly influential position in a harbor gang because of his position of prestige and because of his relatively greater knowledge of the activities of other groups of fishermen. When new techniques and innovations are transmitted between harbor gangs, usually the network ties between "highline fishermen" are usually involved.

METAL vs WOODEN TRAPS

Trap and Catch Data

To obtain the data necessary to test hypotheses concerning the relative efficiency of metal vs wooden traps, members of the research team rode lobster boats owned by some 18 fishermen from four Muscongus Bay towns and recorded a great deal of data on catches, trap style and other factors on some 10,000 lobster traps pulled in while team members were on board.

A large number of factors affect the catch a lobster fisherman obtains. His catch varies dramatically with the season. Even within any season, catches vary with the number of traps in use, the length of time he leaves his traps in the water, the way the traps are made, the specific fishing territory being exploited, and most important of all, the skill of the lobsterman. An intimate knowledge of the bottom and the ability to pinpoint placement of traps in areas where lobsters can be caught has a strong effect on income. According to the fishermen, one of the most critical factors influencing catches and income was the material of which the traps were made (i.e., metal vs wood).

We had to gather data on all these factors in such a way that we could control for certain crucial variables. We did this in the following way:

1. To control for skill, we gathered data only from men who were known as "highliners." The men we chose had been in the lobster business full-time for at least five years.

2. We chose only fishermen who were using both metal and wooden traps. This allowed us to compare catches from metal vs. wooden traps taken by the same man in the same day.

3. Some fishermen stated with great vehemence that there would be a strong variation in the performance of wooden and metal traps with the season. Such a hypothesis was generally phrased in terms of predicting that either wood or metal traps would fish better at different times of year. In order to obtain information on such factors, we gathered data at three times of year: just after shedding in July and August; in the middle of the productive fall fishery (November and December); and again during the spring fishing (May 1978).

4. There is a good deal of evidence to suggest that lobstermen from some harbors generally do better than men from other harbors due to differences in concentrations of lobsters, variation in fishing effort along the coast, and other ecological factors [1]. As a result, we limited our investigation only to fishermen from towns in Muscongus Bay, (New Harbor, Bremen, Friendship and Pemaquid Harbor). Even this attempt at control proved inadequate. For reasons that are not well

understood, the Bremen lobstermen have been doing very well the last few summers when they are fishing the headwaters of Muscongus Bay and the Medomak River, while highline lobstermen from Round Pond and New Harbor further down the Bay were catching far fewer lobsters during the summer season. For this reason it is impossible to compare data on catches during the summer without controlling for the territory where the fisherman placed his traps. That is, we cannot compare catches of wooden traps from New Harbor with catches from metal traps from Bremen. No fishermen experience any locational advantage in the fall and winter since they are all fishing together in deep water, in the middle of Muscongus Bay or Johns Bay.

5. Lobstermen believe that the type and style of trap used strongly influence catch. The vast majority build their own traps and rig them out. They are constantly making minor changes in design. Thus, it is not only that traps used by one man can differ in certain respects from those used by another, but a single fisherman might have several different types of traps which differ, at least in his mind, in important respects. At Davidson's trap factory in Round Point, Maine, lobstermen can choose between some 40 different models.

Controlling for type of trap is not as difficult as it might at first seem, since virtually all of the fishermen in the area under study use traps which are very similar in essential respects -- three- or four-foot traps, with either three or four heads. All of the wooden traps are of the round type, while all the metal traps are rectangular in shape. All heads are knitted of nylon or other synthetic twine. In the study area, only two styles of head are in use, the so called "hake mouth head" (made completely from twine, which have a very narrow opening for lobsters to pass through) and the "hog ring heads" (heads with round metal rings about 5 inches in diameter). To control for type of trap, we selected lobstermen who used either three- or four-foot traps, and used only "hake mouth heads" and/or "hog ring heads". If men were using very different kinds of traps, we excluded them from the sample.

6. Two kinds of metal traps are used in the study area; traps made of aluminized wire, a large percentage of which are produced by a factory in the southern part of the state of Maine, and traps made of vinyl-covered wire. Some of these vinyl-coated wire traps are made in a small factory in Lincoln County, but the vast majority are made by fishermen in their own home workshops. We studied the effectiveness of both types.

7. Since fishermen are presently paid for the number of pounds of lobster they catch within the legal size range, it is critical to assess the

effectiveness of traps in terms of the pounds of legal lobsters they catch. There is a very simple formula to convert length of lobsters measured in millimeters to weight measured in grams. While we were on the boats we recorded the length of lobsters measured on the carapace by using a standard scientific caliper. We made no attempt to weigh any of the lobsters.

The weight of the lobsters alone gives no sure assessment of the effectiveness of a trap. One must also take into account the working time of the bait. Two traps which produce 1.5 lb of lobsters each on a given morning are not equally effective if one has been in the water one day and the other five. To assess the productivity of a trap one must combine data on the weight of lobsters caught with data on the length of time since the trap was previously pulled. For this reason, we will use the number of grams/trap/layover day throughout this chapter in comparing the productivity of various kinds of traps.

8. During periods when we were doing our trap sample we would normally wait until the evening news to get the weather. We would then call fishermen to ask permission to accompany them in the morning. My assistants and I would get up between 3:00 and 6:00 AM, depending on season, and meet the lobstermen at some designated place, normally the dock of the dealer where the fisherman sells his lobsters. We would then spend the day recording data on every trap that was pulled that day.

Lobster traps are generally laid in clusters or strings. One set of data was recorded for every string pulled; the name of the lobsterman, the date, the string position, the type of bottom, the depth of the string, the harbor, the type of bait being used, the number of layover days and the relation of that string to those of other fishermen. For each trap in that string we measured the lobsters and recorded the length of lobsters, whether it was a metal or wooden trap, the number of notched-tailed lobsters,* if any, and the specific details about the trap (type of heads, length, etc.). All of this information was recorded for every trap pulled during the day. Ordinarily there was ample time to record the data, since fishermen would pull 150 - 350 traps maximum in a day (one perhaps every one to three minutes on the average). Normally we would finish between 2:00 and 3:00 PM and be home by 3:00 to 4:00 PM. On certain highline boats, however, one might leave the dock at 5:00 AM on a cold December morning, with a 30 mile an hour wind

---

* (Maine law specifies that whenever a female lobster with eggs is caught, a v-shaped notch must be cut out of one of her tail flippers. Such "notched lobsters" cannot be legally taken by anyone again since they are proven breeding stock.)

and a temperature at 28 or 30 all day and return to dock at 5:30 PM, well after dark.

Analysis of Trap Data

Let us take a look at the data gathered during the summer of 1977 first. From tables 1 and 2, summarizing all the data on catch per trap layover day for wooden and metal traps obtained during the summer of 1977, we would have to conclude that wooden traps and vinyl-covered wire traps do far worse than traps covered by aluminized wire. We obtained data on 2975 traps pulled late in July and early in August 1977. The aluminized traps took an average of 405.3 grams/trap/layover day, while the vinyl and wooden traps caught 166.7 and 167 grams/trap/layover day, respectively. The difference in the means are highly statistically significant. Unfortunately, these figures are highly misleading for several reasons. A large proportion of the aluminized fishing gear is used by the Bremen fishermen in our sample, and summer catches have been very high (probably due to ecological factors) in the Bremen area. Given the figures in Table 1, there is no

Table 1. Grams/Trap/L. O. D. for Metal & Wooden Traps,
July-August 1977

	Grams/trap/lay-over day	
Aluminized Traps	405.3	(n=680)
Vinyl	166.7	(n=369)
Wood	167.0	(n=1882)
Total Traps		2975

Table 2. Grams/Trap/L. O. D. for Metal & Wooden Traps,
by Harbor July-August 1977

	Bremen	New Harbor	Friendship	Pemaquid Harbor
Wood	146.3 (n=400)	179.7 (n=900)	90.1 (n=172)	229.2 (n=210)
Vinyl	135.0 (n=124)	123.1 (n=288)	68.9 (n=23)	219.4 (n=204)
Aluminum	415.4 (n=502)	236.6 (n=154)	236.6 (n=24)	
Mean all traps	305.5 (n=743)	176.0 (n=195)	87.6 (n=195)	224.6 (n=254)

way of separating out exactly how much of the apparent success of aluminized traps is due to territoriality and how much to the innate characteristics of the trap itself.

A far better picture can be obtained by looking at Table 2, which breaks down the summer 1977 data on grams/trap/layover day by both type of trap and fishing area. Several factors should be noted about this information.

New Harbor fishermen did not fare as well, based on the figures on catches produced by various kinds of traps in these two fishing areas. Aluminized traps in Bremen waters in August produced 415.4 grams/trap/layover day. The difference between what a particular type of trap in Bremen produced in comparison with the output of a similar trap from New Harbor are again very significant statistically. For example, when the mean output of aluminized traps pulled in Bremen waters was compared with those pulled in New Harbor, the value of the t was 5.6 (p<0.01). These figures verify the fishermen's claim that fishing in Bremen waters during the summer is better than farther down the Bay.

More important, if we compare the catch figures on various types of traps, we have automatically controlled for ecological differences. That is, if we compare the output of various types of traps for any given area (say Bremen or New Harbor), we are comparing figures from traps placed in the same area and operating under the same conditions. Such comparisons demonstrate with great clarity that aluminized metal traps undoubtedly catch more lobsters than either vinyl or wood. Wooden traps in Bremen produced an average of 146.3 grams/trap/ layover day, while aluminized traps pulled during this same period by the same men from this town yielded 415.4 grams/trap/layover day. The difference in means is highly significant. The value of the t is 24.7, so the results are significant in excess of the 0.01 level. By way of contrast, vinyl traps in Bremen produced 135.0 grams/trap/layover day. The difference between this mean figure and that for aluminized traps pulled in the same area is also statistically significant ($t = 41.2$, p<0.01).

There is also a significant difference between the mean catches produced by various kinds of traps in New Harbor during the summer of 1977. In July and August 1977 wooden traps in New Harbor produced 179.7 grams/trap/layover day, while aluminized traps pulled by the same men produced 236.6 grams/trap/layover day ($t = 21.9$, p = 0.01). The same kind of significant difference can be seen in a comparison of mean catches of aluminized vs vinyl traps in New Harbor during these months. Vinyl traps produced 123 grams/trap/layover day, while aluminized traps produced 236.6 grams/trap/layover day. In this case, the value of the t produced by a standard t test was 25.9 ($p<0.01$).

These figures taken from the data gathered during the summer of 1977 show the general superiority of the aluminized traps. There is, however, a great deal of variation in trap catches over the course of the year, so that the total picture is quite complicated. The data from the winter and spring show that most men continue to do well with aluminized traps, but some men with vinyl or wooden traps outfish those with aluminized gear. All of our data from the summer, spring and fall were analyzed with a multiple stepwise regression program. The results strongly reinforce the conclusion that over the course of the entire year aluminized traps are generally superior to vinyl traps, and that both vinyl and aluminized traps are superior to wood. The data from the regression analysis on the variables connected to trap construction material are summarize in Table 3. In this regression equation, the dependent variable was pounds per trap. There were 110 independent variables, including variables on season, bait used, trap length, number of heads, position, depth and the skill of the man involved. Only the data directly relating to trap construction material has been included, since a complete description of all of the results of these regression results is irrelevant for our purposes.

As we can see from the data in this table, wooden traps and aluminized traps are being compared to vinyl traps, which served as the baseline variable. The B figures (regression coefficient) indicate that wooden traps catch 0.27 lb/trap haul less than vinyl traps, while the aluminized traps get 0.154 lb/trap haul more. Even though these difference in poundage caught are quite small, the difference in catches are significant over the 0.05 level so that we can be reasonably certain

Table 3. Regression Analysis Results
on Trap Construction Material

Variable	B	BETA	Standard Error of B	f	Level of Significance
Vinyl Traps	Baseline	Variable			
Wooden Traps	-0.2767	-0.09448	0.07508	13.584	.001
Aluminized Traps	0.1546	0.04821	0.07886	3.848	.05

that these results did not occur by chance.

The signs of the B and Beta figures are very significant. The fact that the sign for the figures on wooden traps is negative indicates that as the number of wooden traps in the mix increases, the pounds per trap decreases. The opposite is true with aluminized traps. An increase in these traps brings about an increase in catch.

Our analysis also demonstrated that other factors were far more important in influencing lobster catches than the trap construction material. This can be done by comparing Beta figures. First in importance were factors connected with season (Beta 0.295); next was length of trap (Beta .190); third was skill of the fisherman (Beta 0.10), and then came bait used (Betas ranging from 0.138 to 0.880). Near the bottom of the list was trap construction material. As we can see from Table 3, the Beta figure for aluminized traps was only 0.048, while that for wooden traps was -0.094 [3].

Given all of these results, there can be no question that aluminized traps produce significantly more lobsters per unit of effort than either vinyl or wooden traps.

We did not expect these results, although certain fishermen did tell us that aluminized traps did better. In summer 1977 two very good fishermen said that it really did not make any difference what kind of material was on the outside of a trap. What counted was the bait and where the trap was placed (i.e., the skill of the fisherman). For months we were prepared to believe this hypothesis, which seemed sensible in every respect. These data demonstrate beyond all doubt, however, that what is on the outside of a trap does make a substantial difference. (See Acheson [3] for a complete analysis of all of these data.)

Why should aluminized traps fish so much better than traps with wooden lathes or traps covered with vinyl-coated wire? There is no certain answer at this point. Two hypotheses have been advanced by certain fishermen. Many say metal traps, since they have no tendency to float, stay on the bottom better while wooden traps, even when weighted, have a tendency to float and thus move somewhat due to wave action, wind, tide, etc. (During storms, the pressure of wind and tide is so strong on trap, warp and buoy, that they can be dragged for miles.) Lobsters, so the story goes, prefer to crawl into traps which are more stationary. One fisherman explained this tendency of lobsters in the following words. "Of course they don't like it if the trap moves. Would you like to go into a house that was jumping all over the lot? It's the same thing." Maybe so. Second, some fishermen believe that lobsters are repelled by the smell emanating from the vinyl-covered wires. At least one scientist believes that they are correct [4].

Economic Issues

From the point of view of the fisherman, the critical question concerns whether or not it is advisable to invest in metal or wooden traps. Unfortunately, there is no way this question can be answered by looking at the figures on relative physical productivity for a month or two. Several factors complicate the issue. First, metal traps are far more expensive than wooden traps, and do not last as long. The 4-foot aluminized traps, for example, cost $27.50 during the summer of 1977 so that a pair of these traps, equipped with warp line, toggles and buoy ran about $65.00. A single 3-foot oak trap could be bought for $12.00, and a pair of them fully rigged cost about $35.00. Moreover, a wooden trap, it is estimated, lasts about 5 to 7 years, while an aluminized trap lasts about 3 to 4. Most important, investment in lobster traps lasts over a period of years, so that the discount rate or the time value of money must be taken into account.

The idea of a discount rate is a standard concept in economics and accounting. Basically the idea is that money received at present can be invested and made to earn interest. The value of the money to be received in the future must be discounted in ways to take into account the interest rate and the length of time involved. If the interest rate is 5% annually, the $1000 to be received in a year is worth $950 today. It is not worth $1000 since its value must be discounted to take into account the interest lost.

More specifically, metal and wooden traps produce different income streams over different numbers of years. Last, the physical output of a trap varies dramatically over the course of a year, along with the price the fisherman receives for lobsters (Supply and price usually vary inversely.) There is no way the physical output, or the net revenue a fisherman receives from a trap, can be estimated from the figures on physical productivity gathered during short, discrete periods.

Businessmen and bankers are faced with making decisions involving all of these variables, and they have developed a set of accounting techniques to handle such problems. The most widely used techniques by accountants and businessmen for evaluating investment options is to compare the Net Present Values (NPV) of the investment in question. The formula for the Net Present Value of an investment is as follows:

$$NPV = \sum_{T=1}^{N} \frac{NCF_t}{(1+i)^t} - C$$

where NCF = net cashflow
   i = interest rate or marginal cost of capital
   C = initial cast of the project
   N = expected life of the project

To obtain information on the NPV of an investment in wooden vs aluminized traps, detailed information on costs, interest rates, catches and revenues for 10 metal and 10 wooden traps from June 15, 1977, to April 1, 1978, was obtained from one local fisherman. The following is assumed:

1. that the interest rate is 8.75% (This was the interest rate he was actually charged in the summer of 1977 on a secured loan to buy traps.)

2. that an aluminized trap cost $32.50 and a wooden trap cost $17.50 (fully rigged). These are the actual costs he paid during the spring of 1977.

3. that a metal trap will last 4 years and a wooden trap will last 6 years. After 4 years a metal trap will be completely depreciated, while a wooden trap will have a salvage value of $5.00.

4. that the net cash flows will remain constant over the course of the investment.

5. that the project will terminate in 4 years. This short time horizon will be used to minimize the effect of inflation, changes in costs of material, changes in prices for lobsters, and so on.

6. that a fisherman already has a boat, dock, pickup truck and workshop. The only decision he is currently making concerns the traps themselves.

In order to obtain net present value figures for investments in wooden vs aluminized traps, we need to have data on net cash flows, i.e., the gross revenue minus cash costs associated with each type of trap. To obtain this information, information on prices paid for lobster was obtained from the New Harbor Co-op from June 1977 to the present, along with data on pounds of lobsters caught by a local fisherman in ten of his wooden traps and ten aluminized traps. The results are summarized in Table 4.

Table 4. Revenue from a Sample of
Aluminized and Wooden Traps

			Wooden Traps		Aluminized Traps	
Year	Month	Price Received* ($/lb)	Lobsters Caught (lb)	Total Revenue ($)	Lobsters Caught (lb)	Total Revenue ($)
1977	Jun	1.90	26	49.40	40	76.00
	Jul	1.30/2.30†	6	9.33	37	61.10
	Aug	1.40/2.00†	55	86.40	86	155.00
	Sep	1.40	83	116.20	129	180.60
	Oct	1.50	96	144.00	155	232.50
	Nov	1.80	104	187.20	171	307.80
	Dec	2.40	62	148.80	85	204.00
1978	Jan	2.75	28	77.00	33	90.75
	Feb	3.00	19	57.00	30	90.00
	Mar	3.00	24	72.00	33	99.00
	Apr	3.60	?	?	?	?
Totals			502	947.13	799	1479.75

*On the 15th of the month.
†Price received, soft/hard.

There are, of course, enormous costs involved in the lobster business. This particular fisherman (see Table 4) pays about $5200 for bait during the year, another $3200 for gas, and it cost him another $500 cash (to say nothing of his time) to maintain the traps he already has. Since he has 500 traps, and his variable costs are $8900, his cost per trap is $17.80.

If ten wooden traps yield $947.13, the gross revenue for one trap per year is about $94.71. Since ten aluminized traps yield $1476.00, one trap produces a gross revenue of $147.60. If variable costs per trap are $17.60, then the net cash flow for a wooden trap is $76.90 per year and the net cash flow for an aluminized trap is $129 per year.

If the net cash flow for a year per aluminized trap is $129, with an interest rate of 8.75 percent, the project lasting for four years, and the initial cost of the investment being $32.50, then the NPV is as follows.

$$NPV = \sum_{T=1}^{N} \frac{NCF_t}{(1+i)^t} - C$$

$$= \frac{129}{(1+8.75)^1} + \frac{129}{(1+8.75)^2} + \frac{129}{(1+8.75)^3} + \frac{129}{(1+8.75)^4} - 32.50$$

= present value of $129 recieved for 4 years minus $32.50
= $420.22 − $32.50
= $387.72

Calculating the NPV of a wooden trap is slightly more complicated, since the trap lasts for six years and the project will be over in four. After four years the traps will not be completely depreciated and may be sold for "salvage value." Let us assume that this salvage value is $5.00 per trap.

If the net cash flow for a wooden trap is $76.90 per year, with an interest rate of 8.75%, the project lasting four years, an initial cost of $17.50, and a salvage value of $5.00:

$$NPV = \frac{76.9}{(1+8.75)^1} + \frac{76.9}{(1+i)^2} + \frac{76.9}{(1+i)^3} + \frac{76.9}{(1+i)^4}$$

−present value of $5.00 in 4 years−$17.50 initial cost
= $250.00 + 3.57 − 17.50
= $236.25

One can go through all of the calculations to obtain the answer or else treat the $129 received for four years as an annuity, and use the present value interest formula for an annuity.

The figures on the net present value of aluminized vs wooden traps again demonstrate the superiority of the aluminized lobster traps. The NPV for these aluminized traps is $387.72, while the NPV of wooden traps is only $236.25. This comparison takes into account the differences in physical productivity, the life of the traps and the initial costs.

Certainly the NPV for wooden and aluminized traps in Maine as a whole are not this high. The lobsterman who volunteered these figures is one of the very best I have ever seen. It is not only that he is highly skilled; he works hard. This man pulls traps about 160 days a year, so that each trap is pulled about 80 times over the course of the annual cycle. The average lobster fisherman works perhaps 110 to 130 days per year. However, it should be noted that this man's catch per trap is not especially high. From the wooden trap, he is obtaining only 0.625 lb. every time the trap is pulled (50.2 lb. per trap per 80 hauls). This man earns a very high income, but his success is due not only to skill but also to an enormous amount of effort.

ADOPTION AND REJECTION OF METAL TRAPS: SOCIAL FACTORS

General Observations

Given the obvious advantage of aluminized lobster traps, why is there such confusion and debate concerning the relative efficiency of such traps? Certainly many of the lobstermen who continue to favor wooden traps are bright and enterprising people who are very competitive and interested in raising their income.

The answer is that most fishermen do not have the information necessary to accurately judge trap efficiency. When they finally obtain accurate information, a large number of them quickly begin to invest in large numbers of metal traps.

There are two factors which make it difficult, if not impossible for most fishermen to estimate the efficiency of wooden and various kinds of metal traps. First, there are so many variables involved that even if an individual acquires a few traps to test, and keeps records on them, he will not be able to conclusively determine if the investment is justifiable. As we have seen, one has to take into account not only all of the factors influencing physical output of the different types of traps (bottom, season, depth, heads, number of lobsters caught, trap type, location, proximity of gear, bait, type of bottom, etc.), but also the factors influencing revenues and cost over the long run (i.e. cost of traps, maintenance costs, discount rates, exvessel prices for lobsters, etc.). It is difficult to handle and sort out such a welter of information without statistical training.

Second, it is very difficult to obtain information from other lobstermen. One cannot observe what others are doing. One might be able to see some of the catches they bring in and observe where some of their traps are, but it is impossible to tell with any accuracy what they are catching.

The competitive nature of lobstering and the importance of knowledge in determining success also hinder access to information. Men from adjacent harbor gangs are thought of as enemies, and are often treated with open hostility. They are, after all, men who can and have intruded on one's fighting territory and have destroyed fishing gear of men in your harbor gang, if not your own traps. This basic distrust manifests itself in derogatory stereotypes of men from other harbors, and an unwillingness to share accurate information with them. Fellow members of a harbor gang are conceptually not enemies, but they are competitors. Providing fellow harbor gang members with information which would help them compete for a finite supply of lobsters is not to the individual's advantage.

Fishermen will often volunteer general information with close friends or relatives, but even in these cases the flow of information is clearly restricted. Evasion is the rule, and deliberate lies are common. The stories about the ways lobster fishermen misinform each other are legion. Some men have used "decoy traps" (buoys attached to rocks or concrete blocks) to suggest that lobsters are in certain unproductive areas. Others stretch the truth about the advantages or disadvantages of certain kinds of lobster gear. Many men, when they find a "sweet spot," will hide its existence from competitors by avoiding the area except when they can pull those traps without being observed.

With regard to metal traps, a variety of misleading stories are being told. In 1977 one heard that there was no difference in catches. The only reason that people ostensibly adopted them was to avoid the worm problem (marine worms can destroy wooden traps), and to ease the work load, since they are lighter and easier to handle out of water. These are both perfectly valid reasons for accepting aluminized traps, but these obvious advantages have been used to mask the fact that many of the owners of aluminized traps suspect they fish better. In fall 1978 those in the know persisted in talking about the advantages of metal traps. The sociolinguistics is interesting. They pretend that there is no difference between aluminized and vinyl traps (which are both called metal). Some of the perpetrators of the metal trap myth know better or strongly suspect the truth.

Given the confusion and misinformation, the critical question is how do fishermen decide to accept or reject aluminized (and/or vinyl) traps? Two preliminary observations were made that had an enormous influence on the way we went about answering this question.

First, it was noted that the response to metal traps came far later in some harbors than in others. In Bremen, for example, metal traps gained rapid and widespread adoption between 1974 and 1975. In New Harbor, such traps were just gaining wide acceptance by winter 1978. In Round Pond and Pemaquid, only a very small number of men have begun to experiment with metal traps of any kind. This set of observations suggested that responsiveness to this innovation was linked somehow with harbor gangs, with all this in turn indicates about competition, restricted flow of information, and so on.

Second, it quickly became apparent that within a harbor gang the response to metal traps is highly differential, with some men accepting such traps very early, others lagging behind and others not adopting them at all. Thus, a good deal of emphasis was placed on attempting to define the characteristics of early, middle and late adopters of metal lobstering gear.

To sort out factors affecting the differential responsiveness between and within groups of fishermen, we obtained data on virtually every lobster fisherman in New Harbor, Round Pond and Pemaquid Harbor in November and December 1977, and a large sample from Bremen. In addition to collecting information on age, education, work experience, fishing experience and other basic personal data, during the survey each fisherman was asked about his source of information on metal traps, his opinion of them, the number of metal traps he owned, his plans for the future vis-a-vis investment in traps and his attitudes toward fishing. This information was heavily supplemented by extensive open-ended interviews, and participant observation which took place over the course of several months. Though the open-ended interviews are not amenable to statistical analysis, they provided a good deal of insight into patterns of response, and resulted in many insights that are impossible to obtain via quantitative methods.

Quantitative Differences Between Early and Late Adopters

Our survey turned up five critical sets of factors which are related to the rate of adoption of metal lobster traps.

First, there is a substantial difference in the age distribution of early adopters, as opposed to middle and late adopters of metal traps. As can be seen in Table 5, all of the men who adopted metal traps early are clustered in what lobstermen think of as their "prime fishing

Table 5. Age by Adopter Category*

	Under 25	25-40	40-55	55-70	Over 70	Totals
Early†	00.0	10.0	02.0	03.0	00.0	15.0
Late	11.0	13.0	14.0	15.0	03.0	56.0
f_E	00.0	10.0	02.0	03.0	00.0	
F_E	03.0	03.0	03.0	03.0	03.0	

*The results of a chi square test on age distribution for early adopters of metal traps appears below. The observed frequencies are obtained from Table 5; since there are 15, the theoretical distribution in each cell is 3.

† Early adopters were defined for purposes of this analysis as men who had at least 25 metal traps before June 1977. Middle range adopters had at least this number of traps by January January 1, 1978. Late adopters had no metal traps by January 1978.

$$ X = \frac{\sum_{i=1}^{K} (f_1 - F)^2}{F_1} $$

$$ = \frac{3^2}{3} + \frac{7^2}{3} + \frac{1^2}{3} + \frac{0^2}{3} + \frac{3^2}{3} $$

$$ = 3 + 16.3 + .333 + 0 + 3 $$

$$ = 22.633 \quad DF = 4 $$

$$ P < .001 $$

Therefore, reject the hypothesis that there is no difference in the observed and expected frequencies.

years." No early adopters were under 25 years old, and none was over 70. Most important, 11 of the 15 men (or 66%) in this early adopter category were between 25 and 40. A chi square test was run on the age distribution of early adopters. We can safely reject the null hypothesis since the chi square statistic is significant beyond the 0.001 level. This means that there is under 1 chance in 1000 that this clustering in ages in the early adopter category could have occurred by chance.

The age distribution of late adopters is far more evenly distributed. Of the late adopters, 11 (or 20%) were under 25; 18 (or 32%) were over the age of 55; 3 were over 70. In short, a very high percentage of the late adopters were either very young or relatively old. Only

13 (or 23%) of these late adopters were between 25 and 40.

Second, the early adopters of metal lobster gear have a great deal more invested in their business than the late adopters. This is indicated in any number of ways which are amenable to statistical analysis (Table 6).

1. Late adopters have smaller boats, which are naturally less expensive. Late adopters have boats averaging 28.8 feet, while early adopters have boats with a mean length of 31.6. (This difference in means is statistically significant according to our test (t is 1.82, p = 0.07).

2. Late adopters have far fewer traps than the early adopters. The early adopters reported an average of 389.3 lobster traps, while the late adopters have a reported average of 305.4 traps each. This difference in means is highly significant statistically. (A standard t test produced a t value of 29.07, an unbelievably high figure (p < 0.001). This means that there is less than a 1 in a 1000 chance of these results occurring by chance.)

3. The lobster boats used by late adopters are, on the average, older than those used by early adopters. The boats of the later adopters are 11.5 years old on the average, while those used by the early adopters are 9.9 years old. The difference in these two means is highly significant statistically as well $t = 2.05$; p < 0.05).

Table 6. Some Social and Economic Characteristics of Early, Middle and Late Adopters of Metal Lobster Traps: July—August 1977

	$\bar{x}$		
	Early Adopters*	Middle Adopters†	Late Adopters‡
Age (years)	41.30	52.20	43.20
Education (years)	12.37	12.50	11.01
Number of Traps	389.30	307.00	305.00
Age of Boat (yrs)	9.90	11.75	11.50
Length of Boat (ft)	31.68	28.80	28.80

*N = 16
†N = 4
‡N = 56

The difference between the amounts invested by early adopters and late adopters is greater than one might think by looking at these figures alone. A boat that is a few feet bigger and a few years newer costs several thousand dollars more than a smaller, older boat. Traps are very expensive; and metal traps are much more expensive than wooden ones. Although we have no solid, systematically gathered evidence to buttress the assertion, there is no question that the amount of ancillary gear owned by early adopters is greater than that of later adopters. All these factors mean that early adopters may have two or three times the amounts invested as later adopters.

We were able to tabulate total investment for a few individuals with great accuracy. One well-established, highline fisherman had over $85,000 invested in his boat, mooring, traps (half metal), dock, pickup truck and workshop. A young man with only two years experience had only $9500 invested in his boat and wooden traps. He had no truck, dock or workshop. While these two individuals are at the ends of the continuum, such differences in investment are by no means rare.

Third, as can be seen in Table 6, there is no statistically significant difference between early adopters of metal traps and late adopters with regard to educational level attained. As is indicated by Table 6, late adopters had a mean educational level of 11.0 years, while the early adopters went to school for an average of 12.3 years. The difference in means is not significant ($t = 0.685$; $p < 0.40$). These findings tend to contradict studies which indicate that people with a higher educational level are more apt to take on new innovations as opposed to people with lower educational levels (e.g. Rogers and Shoemaker [5]).

Most fishermen would not be particularly surprised by these results. They have long maintained that it is years of experience in the industry, and not years of formal education that make a "good fisherman" with all this term indicates about the ability to identify successful innovations. However, there is no solid evidence that years of formal education do not translate into lobstering skills. The hypothesis is untestable, given the small sample at hand. Most lobster fishermen, at present, enter the occupation after high school and a few might complete one or two years of technical school in programs designed to prepare them for a career other than fishing. Thus, most fishermen entering the occupation have between 10 and 13 years of education. Most men who have college degrees or graduate education leave the area, and certainly do not enter fishing. There are, however, a few men with bachelor's degrees who have become fishermen. Generally they do very well, along with men with one or more years of technical training.

Many of these men have been among the earliest adopters of metal lobstering gear. Their numbers, however, are too small to make any definite statements.

Fourth, and perhaps most important, a very high proportion of early adopters are identified as highline fishermen. Correspondingly, a very high proportion of those who adopted metal traps late were rated low, or not very successful in fishing. As can be seen in Table 7, 9 out of 22 highline fishermen (41%) adopted metal traps early. Only four of the low-success (13%) adopted metal traps early.

A log likelihood ratio for this contingency table was run. The results (Table 7) demonstrate that there is a low probability that these differences could have occurred by chance. In other words, there is strong evidence linking fishing success with speed of adoption of this innovation. Conversely, low success in fishing is associated with a late rate of adoption.

Fifth, there is some evidence that the early adopters of metal traps are more strongly committed to the fishing industry than late

Table 7. Rate of Adoption of Metal Traps and Fishing Success*

Speed of Adoption	Fishing Success			
	Highliner	Middle	Low	Totals
Early & Middle	9.0	9.0	4.0	22.0
Late	13.0	16.0	25.0	54.0
Totals	22.0	25.0	29.0	76.0

*Log-Likelihood Ratio for contingency table on fishing success and rate of adoption of metal traps.

$$G = 4.60517 \left(\sum \sum f_{ij} - \sum \log f_{ij} - \sum R_i \log R_i - \sum C_j \log C_j + \log n \right)$$

$G = 4.60517$ (9 log 9 + 9 log 9 + 4 log 4 + 13 log 13 + 16 log 16 + 25 log 25 log 25 − 22 log 22 − 54 log 54 − 22 log 22 − 25 log 25 − 29 log 29 + 76 log 76)

$= (4.60517)(1.239)$

$= 5.705 \quad DF = 2$

$P < .06$

adopters. Commitment, like all attitudes and values, is very difficult to measure objectively. We had two open-ended questions in our interview schedule designed to assess the interest and commitment to lobster fishing. These questions were:

a. "Would you advise a young man to go into fishing at the present?" and "If the fishing industry in Maine went completely broke, where would you go and what would you do?"

The results of these two questions by adopter category are summarized in Table 8.

As can be seen from Table 8, 10 out of 15 (66%) of the early adopters said they would advise a young man to go fishing whereas only 12 of 37 (32%) of the late adopters answered this question positively. The results of the chi square analysis indicate that this difference in response between early and late adopters is statistically significant. We would like to argue that this set of responses is indicative of a greater level of interest and commitment on the part of the early adopters. During the interviewing process, we received the very strong impression that the men who were experimenting and adopting

Table 8. Adopter Category by Commitment Indicators

Question	Response to Question	Early Adopters	Late Adopters	Totals
Would you advise a young man to go fishing now?*	Yes	10	12	22
	No	5	25	30
	Totals	15	37	52
If the fishing industry in Maine went completely broke, where would you go, and what would you do?†	Stay in fishing but move to other area	2	4	6
	Get other job or retire in area	11	30	41
	Totals	13	34	47

*Results of analysis of question: chi square = 3.81; degrees of freedom = 1; $p < 0.05$
  Therefore: Do not reject H_o
†Results of analysis of question: chi square = 3.818; degrees of freedom = 1; $p < 0.05$
  Therefore: Do not reject H_o

metal traps were more enthusiastic about fishing. They talked about it more, and spent hours analyzing fishing trends. They have done well in fishing. They enjoy it. And they would have few reservations about enjoining someone else to try the same thing -- providing that young man did not go fishing in the same area and thus compete with them.

All of these figures suggest a great deal about the characteristics of men who adopted metal lobster traps. On the whole, the early adopters are at the height of their lobstering careers. Most are between 25 and 40, an age bracket fishermen think of as their prime years. Lobstering for them is an all encompassing occupation, not a hobby. They are not young enough to think of getting into some other occupation, nor are they old enough to think of retiring. They are serious fishermen. They are in an occupation in which they have a good deal of interest and have had a good deal of success. Virtually all of the men in the early adopter category h: been in the business long enough to build up a substantial number of traps, and have earned enough to have a large, well-equipped boat. The late adopters of metal traps are spread relatively evenly in every age category; they have far less invested; very few of them are highline fishermen; and there is substantial reason to think that they have less interest in fishing. All of these factors interrelate with each other in a variety of ways which influence the decision to purchase or not purchase metal lobster traps. In general, they can be classified as: (1) economic factors, and (2) factors related to the structure of harbor gangs.

Economic Factors

A great deal of the willingness to invest in metal traps can be explained simply in terms of the ability to invest. Many of the late adopters are either very young men or very old. Neither is apt to have a lot of money to invest in expensive new fishing gear. The old fishermen, like old people everywhere, are apt to be hard pressed. Fishing is a young man's game, and older fishermen are apt to be well past the years when they can afford a few thousand dollars to invest in experimental gear. Many are in process of retracting their fishing operations, and are looking forward to retirement. They want to depreciate the gear they have, and get out of the business. Other men are already retired, and do a little lobstering to supplement their social security. Since they cannot earn too much at lobstering without jeopardizing their social security payments, they clearly have minimal interest in investing heavily in gear which promises to raise both costs and income. In addition, all of these older fishermen, in the back of their minds, appear to be thinking in terms of investing only in those things which will result in an immediate cashflow from which they would benefit. One 76 year old fisherman put it very well when he said:

> I ain't going to invest in no metal traps. I'll be damned if I'll put a lot of money in gear that is going to outlast me. Besides, it would be a form of welfare. If I bought a gang of metal traps, chances are that (his nephew) would inherit them to use. He already gets enough welfare off the state without any help from me.

The very young men are hard pressed for still other reasons. They typically have had to spend every dime they saved and could borrow to get a used boat and enough gear to begin fishing on the most minimal level. Moreover, most of these men are generally interested in buying standard wooden traps, which they consider less risky. Some are having trouble enough making a living with what they consider proven fishing gear. In addition, the price of the wooden traps makes them very attractive. A man who is new to the business wants to build up the number of traps he has as quickly as possible, and he can get far more wooden traps for his money. Many of them are not interested in metal traps for still another reason – they are not completely certain they will be able to survive in the competitive game of lobstering. Some of them will undoubtedly fail. A good many of the younger men are clearly wondering if they would not be better off in some other occupation. Some of them are just lobstering temporarily. More than a few are thinking of leaving lobstering permanently. As one nineteen year old fisherman phrased it: "Maybe I'll stay in fishing, but maybe I'll go to college. In the meantime, I'm not going to put a lot of money into fishing. I don't really know if that is what I'm going to stick with."

However, many of the late adopters are neither young nor old. In fact, 27 (or 48%) are between 25 and 55. Many of these men, even though they are in what are considered their prime earning years, also have great difficulty raising funds for new investment. As one man phrased it, "This business is just like any other. If you haven't got any savings, you can't buy anything big on your own, and the dealers and banks don't want to lend it to you either. The only time you can get a lot of money for new fishing gear is when you don't need it."

By way of contrast, Table 7 demonstrates that a very high percentage of the early adopters of metal traps were also highline fishermen. Many of these men either had the money to purchase metal traps, or had the collateral and history of success so that it was relatively easy to obtain loans from dealers, banks, or other sources of capital.

Harbor Gang Structure

In many respects, the highline fisherman from any harbor and his less successful competitors inhabit the same social field. They are, after all, members of the same harbor gang, the primary unit of identification for fishermen, and the single most important reference group. However, there are some important differences among men within harbor gangs which are linked in important ways to the adoption of metal traps.

First, staying ahead of the competition is the primary goal for highline fishermen. Fishing, for these men, is not only a way to make a living. It is also a team sport in which one strives to beat other men and avoid being beaten by them. A great deal of the competition for lobsters stems not only from a desire to increase income, but from a knowledge that having greater catches means greater influence and higher social standing as well. Men playing the highline game put in the most hours. They are the ones who leave before dawn on most days, and return after dark. They are the men who have the largest boats and the most fishing equipment. In this competition, they are constantly making changes to ensure that they have the best equipment available. If you do not compete in equipment or techniques, your competition will outfish you. And with the competition hot on their heels, these men are constantly looking for and experimenting with new techniques and types of gear.

Some of the less successful fishermen are clearly not as competitive. Some scarcely seem to be fully able to understand their more successful colleagues. As one man put it: "If one of them goes out at 5:00 AM, someone else will start at 4:30 and let him [the first man] know it. If they think another kind of trap will help them better, they'll go buy a whole gang of them, and give the others away. They are just crazy." This misses the point completely. The behavior of these highliners is highly normative, given the success orientation they share with most other middle-class Americans. To be sure, some highline fishermen take competition to an extreme, but what is equally puzzling is the lack of drive and ambition which one can observe in some of the less successful fishermen, particularly the less successful fishermen in their prime years.

Second, there is a distinct difference in the way highline fishermen and average fishermen obtain information about new techniques and equipment. The highline fisherman -- and most early adopters are highliners -- are linked into some wide-ranging networks. They are vitally interested in the industry, and make an effort to reach out to other men who are doing things of significance in their world. They know more people in other harbors, and are better known by them than the average fisherman. These ties play a great role in the diffusion of innovations. For example, virtually all of the early adopters in New Harbor, Round Pond and Pemaquid Harbor obtained the information on metal traps via direct links with men in Friendship or Bremen.

Perhaps more important, these highline fishermen (i.e., early adopters) are constantly experimenting on their own. Every year they change the type of heads they use; try out new kinds of bait; experiment with new fishing areas. Experimentation and routine innovation is a way of life with these men and it is a constant source of entertainment and conversation. In this respect, they are living up to the standards of a highly technical, utilitarian culture, one in which machinery is appreciated, and inventiveness is highly valued. They also watch each other like hawks. It is not surprising that they would be the ones to try metal traps when they first appeared, and to appreciate their merits. Given the competition within and between harbor gangs, it is not surprising that they are very quiet about what they have observed.

The average fisherman obtains information via a very different set of processes. He may do some experimentation, but on the whole the information he has comes directly from watching other fishermen in his harbor gang. He emulates the kind of behavior that appears to bring success. He certainly does not have the wide ranging ties highliners have. When we asked fishermen from Bristol (New Harbor, Pemaquid and Round Pond) where they heard about metal traps and what convinced them to buy them, the late adopters answered that they had heard about them from other men in the hamlet in which they lived. They were far less specific than the early adopters about the virtues and problems of converting to metal traps.

In summary, the reasons that early adopters and late adopters take on metal lobster gear differ dramatically. The early adopters, by and large, have both the motivation and means to accept new fishing gear. Most of the early adopters are highliners in their prime years who will take on any new type of gear, including new types of traps, which promises to increase their fishing effectiveness and their incomes, and help them maintain their position as highliners. They take on innovations to stay ahead of other fishermen. Moreover, they are able to obtain such traps in that they have access to money that can be used for investment. They are also better able to assess the effectiveness of such new gear because their ties to other highline fishermen gives them access to a large pool of knowledge concerning new techniques. This picture does not apply to middle and late adopters.

Most of the middle and late adopters say they would prefer to stay with wooden traps. They are beginning to switch to metal traps out of a sense of self-preservation. They are not making the changes in an attempt to become highline fishermen or to beat others. Rather, they are coming to recognize that wooden traps cannot compete with metal traps. They are beginning to see that when the two types of traps appear in the same small area, the metal traps will take the most lobsters. They are not happy about making the changes to more expensive, less sturdy fishing gear, but many are starting to feel they have no choice as long as many fishermen who exploit the same waters are switching to such traps in large numbers. In the future, when the adoption of metal traps has become a thing of the past, I think it will be possible to see the spread of metal traps not in terms of a market pull argument, but in terms of factor push. These arguments do not appear to hold true for the early adopters, but factor push arguments certainly appear to explain much of the behavior of middle and late adopters.

LONG-TERM EFFECTS

As the general effectiveness of metal lobster traps becomes more widely known, more fishermen will undoubtedly adopt them. There is a possibility that they might become standard equipment throughout the lobster fishing industry. If this occurs, the effects on the lobster industry might be very marked. Their adoption may, in part, lead to the same kinds of problems that can now be observed in other fishing industries.

It is generally conceded that most of the major fisheries in the U.S. have been greatly overexploited for too long by too many fishermen. The result is depletion of fish stocks, underutilization of capital resources, destruction of fish breeding stocks, and, where opportunity costs are low, the acceptance of low incomes [2,6].

While a good many Maine fishermen believe that the lobster fishery of Maine is essentially sound, the consensus among the most experienced state and federal biologists is that the lobster fishery is poised on the brink of disaster [7-9]. They argue that fishing effort and the number of traps in the water have increased to the extent that only 6% of the lobsters which molt into the legal size range ever survive to extrude eggs even once [2,10,11]. In their opinion, there are not enough eggs in the water to maintain the stock. They believe the small size of the breeding population, in combination with a general cooling of water temperatures, will bring about ecological disaster. They predict that the

1980s will see declining catches, decreasing incomes for fishermen and perhaps widespread unemployment. The widespread adoption of metal traps may exacerbate this situation. Since metal traps are more efficient, their adoption may result in more lobsters being caught each year, which would reduce further the numbers that survive to breed, and hasten oncoming disaster.

Even if the increased use of metal traps should not further harm the breeding stock, it will certainly lower the efficiency of the fishermen. Metal traps are more expensive than wood, and since the industry as a whole will probably not be able to take more lobsters in the long run that it is currently harvesting, the return to investment will probably be lowered. Some lobstermen see this situation very clearly. One New Harbor fisherman expressed it well when he said:

> Everyone ought to stay with wooden traps. We'd be a lot better off if they did. The men who are now going to metal traps are better off. But they won't be for long. Soon everybody will have the damn things. When that occurs, we'll all be catching the same amount of lobsters. It will just cost us a lot more for gear.

A similar kind of trap escalation occurred in the Casco Bay region in the early 1960s. Some men bought very large boats, hired one or two helpers and greatly increased the numbers of traps fished. They were better off until other people also began to expand the number of traps they owned. There are only a finite number of lobsters that can be caught. Many men are presently catching the same number of pounds they were previously, and many are catching less. The only difference is that now they must maintain, bait, and pull 1800 to 2400 traps where they formerly had to tend only 400 to 600. Most men in Casco Bay favor a trap limit which would force everyone at the same time to drastically lower the number of traps they fish. If the experiences of the Casco Bay fishermen are any guide, the fishermen who are now adopting metal traps in the Muscongus Bay region of Maine may wish that they had retained the less expensive wooden traps.

On the other hand, a general move to metal lobster traps might ease fishing pressure, particularly if fishermen move to adopt the aluminized traps. These traps are expensive now, and they are made by only one firm in the nation. If many men moved to adopt them, the price might well increase drastically. If aluminized traps became standard, with their increased price, the entry costs into the industry would undoubtedly increase greatly. Since it is already very difficult for a young man to obtain the $20,000 or so needed to start lobstering on a scale that promises success, a drastic increase in the cost of entry might greatly lower the number of men who enter the lobster fishery.

This, in turn, could operate to lower the number of traps in the water and generally decrease fishing effort. Given the state of the lobster stock, that might be a desirable state of affairs.

Exactly what will occur in the future is, of course, impossible to predict with any certainty. There probably will be vastly more metal lobster traps in use. There are those who fear that their general adoption may prove to be a situation where technological advance may help speed biological disaster.

REFERENCES

|1| Acheson, J. M. "Technical Skills and Fishing Success in the Maine Lobster Industry," in *Material Culture: Styles, Organization and Dynamics of Technology*, H. Lechtman and R. Merrill, Eds. (St. Paul, MN; West Publishing Company, 1977).

|2| Acheson, J. M. "The Lobster Fiefs: Economic and Ecological Effects of Territoriality in the Maine Lobster Industry," *Human Ecol.* 3:183-207 (1975.

[3] Acheson, J. M. *Production Possibilities of Aluminized, Vinyl and Wooden Lobster Traps,* (Orono, ME: University of Maine Sea Grant Publications, in press).

[4] Bowles, F. Personal communication (1977).

[5] Rogers, E. M., and F. Shoemaker. *Communication of Innovations* (New York: Free Press, 1971).

[6] Crutchfield, J. "The Marine Fisheries: A Problem in International Cooperation," *Am. Econ. Rev. Proc.* 54:207-218 (1964).

[7] Anthony, V. Address given at the Fisherman's Forum, Rockland, ME, March 18, 1978.

[8] Morrissey, T. Personal communication (1978).

[9] Thomas, J. Personal communication (1978).

[10] Krouse, J. S. "Maturity, Sex Ratio, and Size Composition of the Natural Population of American Lobster, *Homarus americanus,* along the Maine Coast," *Fish. Bull.* 71:165-173 (1973).

[11] Thomas, J. "An Analysis of the Commercial Lobster *(Homarus americanus)* Fishery along the Coast of Maine, (August 1966 through December 1970), National Marine Fisheries Service Technical Report, National Oceanographic and Atmospheric Administration, Washington, DC (1973).

INDEX

313